The Reluctant Imperialists

The Reluctant Imperialists

BRITISH FOREIGN POLICY 1878-1902

C. J. Lowe

The Macmillan Company

Library of Congress Catalog Card Number: 69–10896

FIRST AMERICAN EDITION 1969

Originally published in Great Britain in 1967 by Routledge & Kegan Paul Ltd., London

The Macmillan Company

Printed in the United States of America

To Nicholas, George

and Claire

Contents

MAPS

Preface

In the course of the last thirty years the progressive opening of government and private collections of papers has permitted the production of a large amount of scholarly work on various aspects of British Foreign Policy between the treaties of Berlin and Versailles. The working of what was until recently the 50-year rule has meant that this is rather less true after 1907, but in general now that the archives are open into the 1930s the history of foreign policy can now be written from the original sources.

But so far nobody has attempted to utilize these specialist studies to produce a book of manageable length for students on the pattern of Seton-Watson's classic interpretation of foreign policy in the nineteenth century, the later parts of which were written before the basic work could be done. This lack this book attempts to remedy. Although there is a certain amount of original work in it, it is essentially an attempt to interpret the spadework of others—as is apparent from the text. A list of acknowledgments here would be tedious and pretentious since sources are indicated in the footnotes, but where extensive quotation has been made in the accompanying short collection of documents illustrating policy full acknowledgment has been made.

References in the text to numbered documents (e.g. Doc. 72) refer to this collection.

The purpose of the documents is less to define what policy was than to give students some idea of the dialogue that lay behind it. For this purpose most official despatches—not all—are inadequate since, as Renouvin points out, they do not explain the 'arrières pensées'. They did not need to: they were simply instructions to foreign service officials and, since they were liable to be published in a Blue Book, a good deal of caution was necessary. To get at the reasons behind policy it is necessary to read the private correspondence and, where possible, the memoranda prepared for the Cabinet. The latter are particularly useful in that they explain not only the alternative courses from which the choice has to be made but also the strategic factors which influenced the decisions. In a class of their own are the letters of the Prime Minister to the Sovereign. Sometimes, particularly in the case of Disraeli and Rosebery, they are fairly explicit in revealing the differences within the Cabinet or the real consideration behind policy. But it should be borne in mind that Queen Victoria was no disinterested spectator and often held strong views of her own: it is obvious that in many cases the letters were aimed as much at convincing her as at explaining Cabinet decisions. In this respect the view that she held of Gladstone—that he regarded her as another Department of State—seems fully justified by his letters. They say very little beyond the bare bones of Cabinet decisions, though wrapping this up in such an involved style as to make it seem a lot.

It was also decided that the criterion for selection should be significance rather than novelty. Accordingly, although the majority of these documents are published here for the first time, a large number are selected from what is already in print. Since the sources for these are widely scattered and often out of print it was thought that this would perform a useful service. No doubt much of significance has been omitted either through lack of space or through ignorance on the part of the selector.

I am indebted to the Keeper of the Public Records for permission to reproduce the Cabinet Memoranda in the Cabinet 37 series. The letters to the Sovereign (Cab/41) are from photographic copies in the Public Record Office of original letters preserved in the Royal Archives and made available by the Gracious Permission of Her Majesty the Queen. Those of Lord Salisbury and Sir Michael Hicks Beach are printed by kind permission of the present Marquess and Earl St. Aldwyn. Acknowledgements are also due to the publishers of the following works from which quotations have been taken at length: Lady Gwendolyn Cecil, *Life of Robert Marquis of Salisbury*, 4 vols. 1921–32 (Hodder and Stoughton); A. G. Gardiner, *Life of Sir William Harcourt*, 2 vols. 1923 (Constable); A. Ramm, *The political correspondence of Mr. Gladstone and Lord Granville 1876–86*, 2 vols. 1962 (O.U.P.).

The work is being published in two parts with a dividing line at 1902 and it is anticipated that the second part will follow shortly.

C. J. LOWE

Abbreviations

Archives, etc.

A.M.E.	Archivio Ministero dell'estero, Rome
A.S.C.	Archivio di Stato Centrale, Rome
B.D.	British Documents on the Origin of the War
B.M. Add. Mss.	British Museum Additional Manuscripts
Cab.	Cabinet Papers
D.D.F.	Documents diplomatiques français. First series
F.O.	Foreign Office Correspondence
G.P.	Die grosse Politik der europäischen Kabinette
K.P.	Kimberley Papers
Q.V.L.	Queen Victoria's Letters
S.A.W.	Haus, Hof und Staatsarchiv, Wien
S.P.	Salisbury Papers

Journals

B.I.H.R.	*Bulletin of the Institute of Historical Research*
Econ. H.R.	*Economic History Review*
E.H.R.	*English Historical Review*
H.J.	*Historical Journal* (formerly *Cambridge Historical Journal*)
H.Z.	*Historische Zeitschrift*
J.A.H.	*Journal of African History*
J.M.H.	*Journal of Modern History*
R.H.	*Revue historique*
R.S.R.	*Rassegna Storica del Risorgimento*
S.R.	*Slavonic Review*
T.R.H.S.	*Transactions of the Royal Historical Society*, 4th series.

The commonest error in politics is sticking to the carcasses of dead policies.

Salisbury, 1877

I

The Anatomy

Two hours were taken up in a windy and wearisome discussion. . . . No practical result was arrived at.

Rosebery, 1894

In a perceptive inaugural lecture delivered some ten years ago a
distinguished Professor of Politics developed David Hume's
suggestion that taste in philosophy is much the same as taste in
poetry or music and applied this to his own field. 'What is there',
he asked 'behind any political judgment but the merest preference of taste?'[1] What is true of politics in general is equally
true of one branch of politics in particular, foreign policy. To
put this at its simplest in terms of the late Victorian age, obviously
there was a moral, Christian, urge behind Gladstone's support of
'peoples struggling to be free', but equally there was always a strong
missionary element in British imperialism: it is an unprofitable
exercise to try to analyse which of the two outlooks was most
prone to humbug or to disguising its true motivation, since both
possessed these characteristics to a marked degree. Nor, needless
to say, can the controversies of British foreign policy in this period
be explained in terms of the class background or childhood
deprivations of its exponents: the supporters and opponents of
imperialism came from much the same social classes and had all
been brought up by nannies. What divided them was their ideas
and on this score there was a good deal in W. S. Gilbert's doggerel
on the origin of political parties, making allowance for the fact
that some later changed their minds.

Accepting their division into two broad patterns of thought—
which have been termed the 'Consolidationist' and the 'Forward'
—what tastes distinguished these? Firstly it should be stressed

[1] W. H. Morris-Jones, *Taste and Principle in Political Theory* (Durham, 1957) p. 7.

that these two schools by no means coincided with the terms Liberal and Conservative initially: there were elements of both in either party and if the Conservatives became increasingly identified with the Imperialist cause by the time of the South African war, the Liberals were by no means Little Englanders and 'pro-Boers'. Within the party, after the retirement of Gladstone, Harcourt and Lloyd George fought a losing battle against the Liberal Imperialism of Rosebery and Grey, a factor that was responsible for the much vaunted continuity of foreign policy.[2]

The real division was between Gladstone and his opponents. Until Gladstone took up the Bulgarian cause in 1876 party differences on foreign policy were minimal. There were differences of approach on various questions—for example on Italian unification and the defence of India—but these were not on a party basis. Indeed, given the kaleidoscopic nature of British politics until the seventies, it is difficult to see how they could have been. But Gladstone's sudden conversion to the liberation of the Bulgarians and assumption that he was the 'chosen vessel of the Almighty' in this respect changed things considerably. There had always been a marked religious vein in Gladstone who, after all, until 1876, was probably more interested in Homeric and biblical controversy than in politics.[3] But his discovery in that year of a new affinity with the political masses on the basis of a crusade for righteousness in foreign policy, the liberation—or at least the non-oppression—of subject peoples, whether in Bulgaria, Afghanistan, the Transvaal, Egypt or Ireland, gave full scope to his messianic urges. Once this was elevated into a political principle by the electoral confirmation of his belief after the Midlothian campaign in 1880, this inevitably made him, as Salisbury jibed, 'the apostle of absolute negation in foreign affairs'. These Gladstone increasingly regarded as irritating distractions from the real task imposed upon him by Providence, the liberation of Ireland.

The success of Gladstone's adoption of the decrees of Providence as a political programme reflected the religious earnestness of the age. To many of the electorate, the largely non-conformist

[2] But there was a general consensus amongst foreign diplomats that Conservatives were less prone to isolationism than Liberals. E.g. Deym to Kálnoky 4 December 1888, S.A.W. VIII.105/46D.

[3] R. T. Shannon, *Gladstone and the Bulgarian Agitation* (London, 1963) pp. 3, 267, 271.

lower-middle class, it was self evident that the object of political life was to further good moral causes, as Dilke found out to his cost. But by no means all were convinced that Gladstone had a monopoly of communication with the Almighty. Gordon, after all, was just as good a Christian as the man who let him die. Hence the somewhat curious paradox that whilst Gladstone derived the precepts of his Midlothian campaign from ethical and moral considerations, this was equally true of those who advocated a policy of expansion. The missionary societies clamoured for annexations of territory in order to abolish slavery and bring Christianity to the heathen: they fiercely opposed Gladstone's withdrawal from the Sudan, opposed any concessions to Germany in East Africa in 1890 and were Rosebery's best allies in the struggle for Uganda. That they were an important element in the growth of the empire was assumed without question by the *Saturday Review in* 1897: 'the flag has followed the Bible and trade has followed the flag'.[4] Nor was this sense of the divine purpose in imperialism confined to the missionaries: it would be surprising if it were in an age which could happily assume that it was by the decree of the Almighty that Britannia ruled the waves. There was a general assumption that British imperialism served some great moral purpose and few saw anything incongruous in 'philanthropy and 5 per cent'. (The exception, not surprisingly, was Dilke.) Those who had tender consciences on this score were reassured by the thought that the active promotion of Christianity should 'sanctify the spirit of Imperialism'. How general this was may be inferred from Baden-Powell, who was quite blunt about it. The taxpayer, he thought, expected two results from imperialism: to see both Christianity extended and 'some compensating development of industry and trade'.[5]

Gladstone in the eighties denied this: he believed that the acquisition of further overseas territories would be of very little commercial value to England; that trade should best be developed by means of what has since been labelled 'informal empire'; that reliance should be placed simply on free trade, which also possessed the advantage that it had an improving moral effect upon relations between states. Nor is it easy to refute his argument.

[4] Quoted in R. Hoffman, *Great Britain and the German Trade Rivalry* (New York, 1964 ed.) p. 281.
[5] J. Hobson, *Imperialism* (London, 1938 ed.) p. 201.

The actual increase in British overseas trade derived from the vast territories annexed after 1880 was negligible: by 1901 it only amounted to 2½ per cent of the total, 75 per cent of which was still with foreign countries; a fact which made the imperialist argument based on commercial opportunities look ridiculous.[6] But this did not prevent trade from being an important consideration in foreign policy. Firstly, despite the small overall percentage of trade involved, there were inevitably pressure groups to whom it represented a considerable proportion of their turnover and who, in consequence, clamoured for annexation when faced with the threat of French, German, or Russian exclusive régimes. It is this sort of pressure which frequently explains the transition in the formula 'trade with informal control if possible: trade with rule when necessary',[7] as Gladstone's West African policy in the eighties illustrated. Secondly, the real impact of commercial considerations upon foreign policy was in terms of threats to overseas markets in areas such as South America, Turkey and China. For a variety of reasons, these could never follow the formula, despite the activities of pressure groups such as the China Association, because international rivalry was too intense.

It was this sort of preoccupation which almost entirely governed Lansdowne's reaction to the growth of Russian influence in Manchuria, since it was Britain's commercial interests that were mainly affected: 'we are the Power,' he acknowledged, 'which has a largely preponderant interest in the trade of Northern China.'[8] Nor was this without effect upon relations with Germany. Though the *Saturday Review*'s picture of a world in which 'the German bagman is struggling with the English pedlar' was a little fanciful, this was a fair reflection of the British trade press, who were concerned that in areas where British trade had once been predominant it was being squeezed out by that of Germany. Without suggesting for one moment that trade determined the conflict in 1914, there is probably some truth in the suggestion that 'it may rightly be viewed as a basic cause for the anti-German orientation of British world policy'.[9] Essentially the problem by 1900 was that with the decline in comparative industrial efficiency, the British share of world markets, though still enormous, was shrinking: hence both

[6] *ibid.* p. 35.
[7] J. Gallagher and R. Robinson, 'The Imperialism of Free Trade', *Econ. H.R.* 1953 p. 13.   [8] Lansdowne Memorandum 16 April 1901, Cab/37/56/23.
[9] Hoffman pp. 279, 281.

a determination to hold on to those still possessed and the imperialist idea of developing new, closed, markets for the future. Chamberlain in 1896, dazzled by visions of farming his new-found estates, even told his constituents that this was what the Foreign Office was for: to get more territory for the Colonial Office to develop. Nor can this be dismissed as merely the Birmingham view of foreign policy. Salisbury might shudder at this suggestion but Hicks Beach, his Chancellor of the Exchequer, thought the protection of British trading interests in China quite sufficient motive to go to war. Palmerston, after all, had often taken this view in the past.

If the protection of trade was a major formative influence behind policy, the means by which this could be carried out were equally important. This meant that the whole pattern of British strategical thinking—what there was of it—was bound up with the problems of seaborne commerce and a far-flung empire dependent upon the sea for communications and defence, a complete contrast to the Continental states. Apart from momentary scares in 1888–9 inspired by Boulanger, the danger of a French invasion was not taken seriously: the Admiralty in particular scoffed at it and based all their planning on the 'blue water' theory, defending commerce and the various colonial harbours from Esquimault to Freetown. These were legion because, with the replacement of sail by steam, coaling stations and strategic bases had to be secure all over the world, but especially on the one really vital route, that to India.

Since Trafalgar it had been an unquestioned assumption in England that she should hold control of the seas: 'Its Credit and its Navy', Selborne told the Cabinet in 1901, 'seem to me to be the two main pillars on which the strength of this country rests and each is essential to the other'. The reasoning behind this argument was simple. Britain's wealth depended on her seaborne trade which, averaging some £710 million a year in the period 1880–1900, was three times that of France and ten times that of Russia. This gave her an enormous vested interest in naval supremacy since British financial strength was correspondingly vulnerable to naval attack: defeat in a maritime war, thought Selborne, would mean 'a disaster of almost unparalleled magnitude in history'.[10] Given this interdependence of a strong financial

[10] Selborne Memorandum 16 November 1901, Cab/37/59/118.

5

position and a powerful navy, it is not surprising that all British governments, whatever their political complexion, pursued a big navy policy, epitomized after 1889 in the Two Power Standard. There was very little deviation from this. Gladstone in 1893 stood out against what he called 'militarism' and the destruction of his life's work, but nobody else supported him: Harcourt and Morley, moved to apoplexy by the annexation of Uganda, said nothing about the Spencer Programme. The conclusion is inescapable that naval pre-eminence was taken for granted by politicians and public alike much more quickly than other tenets of the imperialist faith. This is not altogether surprising as naval supremacy had been an unquestioned assumption since 1815: the naval race was simply due to the discovery that other powers, initially France and Russia, were challenging it.

Since British influence in Europe always depended upon whether or not seapower could be brought to bear, this often made the facts of naval strength the determining element in policy. Hence, for example, the collapse of Rosebery's Armenian projects in 1895 when it was discovered that not only was the Mediterranean fleet unable to sail up Mt. Ararat but that it could not even pass the Straits. This was a powerful argument for changing policy. To a large extent it was the Admiralty's consciousness of naval deficiencies vis-à-vis France and Russia that lay behind the diffidence of British policy in the Mediterranean throughout the late eighties and nineties. In retrospect their worries were unnecessary and their margin of safety—29 capital ships to 28 French and Russian—sufficient, as the Fashoda and Boer War crises proved. But they could never be sure about this and, as they pointed out, 'our stakes are out of all proportion greater than those of any other Power'. Unfortunately this was a never ending problem. As soon as supremacy against France and Russia had been achieved new naval powers arrived on the scene: by 1901, apart from Japan, both the United States and Germany were building battle fleets, which made the old Two Power standard in its strict sense an impossible dream. Already the position had been reached by 1901 that annual expenditure, which in the first year of the Naval Defence Act in 1889 had stood at £4 million looked like rising to £43 million by 1907 if the current rate of increase were not checked.[11] This made a strong case for

[11] *ibid.*

6

abandoning 'Splendid Isolation' and seeking the alliance of another, friendly, naval power.

Military power and planning exercised only a negative influence upon British foreign policy, in the sense that lack of power automatically ruled out certain courses. Salisbury for example in 1895, in drawing up the problems to be put to his newly created Defence Committee, ruled out any participation 'in a Continental war at a distance away from our ships' on purely utilitarian grounds. It was not in our interest to do so because the military forces available for use were so much smaller than those of our potential allies that

> when peace came to be made our influence in framing the stipulations agreed upon would probably be in exact proportion to our military contribution to the campaign.[12]

There was some force in the argument. With a total strength of 280,000, of whom 30,000 were in scattered colonial garrisons and 70,000 in India, this left precious little for a continental campaign until the date—'I hope a distant one'—when conscription was adopted. At the time this was regarded as politically unthinkable, and all Roberts' efforts later to persuade people that it was a good democratic cause failed to impress. It followed from this that British influence in Europe was strictly limited. As Salisbury told Courcel in 1896, the fleet could not sail up the Seine; in calculations governed by the employment of standing armies of half a million upwards British potential could be ignored; it was only in issues where seapower was thought decisive, such as the Mediterranean, that Britain counted for anything.

In the second place, this presented severe problems in the one region where Britain had a land frontier to defend, India. Though there were vast differences of opinion as to how this should be done—what Salisbury called the Quettites and the anti-Quettites —there was some general consensus that the only effective means was by action elsewhere. Hence the vast British interest in the Ottoman Empire and in finding allies to defend it. Apart from the concept of prestige, 'which those who govern Oriental nations cannot afford to overlook', the independence and goodwill of the Sultan were vital if Russia had to be counter-attacked in the Black Sea. In 1885, for example, the only way the War Office could see

---

[12] Salisbury, Proposals for a Committee of Defence October 1895, Cab/37/40/64.

to defend India at the time of the Pendjeh crisis was by means of an expedition to Batoum. Moreover until the late eighties there lingered the idea of recruiting the Turks, who had an army of 300,000, to fight some sort of diversionary campaign and this was only abandoned as it became clear from the attitude of the Sultan that this was chimerical. As the basic Anglo-Turkish rift over Egypt and sympathy with the persecuted Christian minorities progressively widened, it had the effect of removing one of the main reasons for the British interest in the maintenance of an independent Sultan, as Salisbury recognized in 1896. Instead, in its place, there was growing recognition that India could not be defended at all, that the only possible course in practice was to reach an agreement with Russia, an argument that drew added strength from the simultaneous problem in China.

It might seem from this that Britain had little interest in Europe in this period, and in general this was true: seapower bred a sense of isolation from Continental problems. But the increasing over-extension of British commitments as against her resources—the reason Salisbury gave for opposing any further annexations in China—produced a considerable interest in European politics. If Britain were isolated in Europe her empire became a standing invitation to attack and consequently, if for no other reason, there was a considerable incentive to assist in maintaining a balance of power. This had been a concept traditional since 1815 and it was all the more applicable in an era when naval predominance could no longer be taken for granted. Hence there was a basic British interest in opposing the hegemony of any one power, which remained throughout this period: the reason why this is not obvious at first sight is that it was concealed by other considerations. In Salisbury's eyes, even in the seventies, Germany was the only real potential menace to Britain because France and Russia were comparatively weak and, although his suspicions of Bismarck's intentions lessened after 1878, he never entirely abandoned this basic assumption, which came back into full flower in the late nineties. As France and Russia were the weaker powers, it was a British interest to avert any further deterioration of their position, a consideration which lay behind Salisbury's constant efforts to avoid a Balkan war in the seventies and eighties since this would give Germany a free hand in the West.

But other interests led in an entirely opposite direction. The conflict with Russia over Constantinople, Central Asia and later over China, meant a certain identity of interest with the Central Powers; as did the increasing strain upon relations with France caused by Egypt. This, more than anything else, brought a direct involvement in European politics since, as Baring recognized by 1885, 'Berlin and not Cairo is the real centre of Egyptian affairs'. Hence the tightrope act of British diplomacy in the eighties and nineties; getting sufficiently close to Berlin to ward off any danger from the 'hungry powers', yet not so close as to become a dependent, like Austria. As long as France feared Germany and Russia was blocked by Austria-Hungary the British position was relatively safe, since this wrecked the *Dreikaiserbund*, the real nightmare of British Foreign Secretaries. Hence, paradoxically, the welcoming of the Franco-Russian alliance, although it heightened British difficulties, because in the long run it both removed all danger of a revival of their bad dreams and provided a basic check to Germany. As long as Bismarck's Germany was eminently satisfied with the existing order of world affairs there was no real antipathy in London: it was only as the restless spirits came to power in Berlin, intent themselves on a new *Weltpolitik*, that priorities began to change in England.

In their personal attitude towards Europe and its problems there was a considerable difference between the two men principally concerned. Gladstone was not in theory an isolationist and frequently spoke of England as a 'member of the European family of nations' who should 'play her part in its public life'. But Gladstone had a very curious interpretation of what this should mean in practice: far from its leading to greater participation in European affairs it led to greater aloofness, simply because it was wrong to work with one power against others. It was this concert mania, for example, which wrecked the best chance of settling the Egyptian question by straightforward Anglo-French action. In the insistent pursuit of his mission, the 'common accord of Europe' under the 'fostering care of England', Gladstone and Granville rapidly became divorced from the realities of European politics. Nor was it surprising that other statesmen could not recognize anything but the naked pursuit of British interests accompanied by pure humbug, since Gladstone, in his preoccupation with the 'higher good', tended to regard everyone else's interests as base pursuits. Consequently, this aversion from the 'sordid and demoralizing consequences of trade' made him isolated, if not isolationist: as Salisbury commented, with some exasperation, the only achievement of Gladstone's Concert of Europe was to concert the Continent together against England.

Salisbury, who rarely talked about Europe, had a totally different approach and was much more European minded. Although he would never make a binding alliance if he could help it—he did eventually accept that with Japan in 1902—he was always ready for bilateral collaboration in limited agreements. His point of view was quite simple: the fate of the Danes in 1864 who went to war in reliance upon Palmerston's promises had made a deep impression upon him as a young man and cured him of any desire to make promises he could not guarantee to fulfil. Nor had he any great faith in treaties: in theory the Turkish position was cast iron after the triple guarantee of 1856, but the changed circumstances of Austria and France made this a dead letter by 1877, a fact he often harped on. Moreover, in contrast to Gladstone, who was never happier than when in tune with the people, Salisbury thought public feeling was obviously fickle: there was 'no means whatever of knowing what may be the humour of our people'. Thus the concept of a Midlothian type of campaign, drawing up great principles to which the populace were invited to adhere as the basis of foreign policy, was unthinkable to Salisbury: his idea was much more that the people were a nuisance. (For example, the only real reason he could see for hanging on to Constantinople in 1877 was that popular feeling expected it.) For this reason, if no other, Britain could not make military alliances on the continental pattern.

But this did not mean a policy of no commitments: this would reduce him to the absolute negation in foreign affairs that he so criticized in Gladstone. Salisbury was fully conscious that the idea of treating each question on its intrinsic merits was an impossible ideal. Diplomacy to him was a market place in which you bought and sold and he was quite willing to offer to perform what he knew he could reasonably expect to carry out, in return for solid benefits. Hence the Mediterranean Agreements. In this respect there never was any change in his outlook, as he explained to Berlin in 1896. But what did alter was the nature of British interests in various parts of the world and the attitude of the 'great oracle' towards them. By 1898 public hostility made it impossible to envisage continuing to support the Ottoman Empire whilst British interests were now much more engaged in the fate of China. It was this more than any basic change of attitude which produced 'Splendid Isolation', in the sense of isolation from European commitments, since no other European power shared Britain's interests.

But though public opinion was clearly of considerable importance as a factor governing British foreign policy in this period, any exact measurement of this is an extremely difficult task. To take but one example, the Press. It is clear that various newspapers had strong opinions on foreign affairs, but whether these represented anything more than the owner's or editor's personal views is debatable.[13] What is more probable is that if their connections were good enough a paper might be representative of official policy, but it is a gross assumption that it always was. In the case of *The Times*, for instance, it cannot even be said that its correspondents' reports represented editorial policy: the editors gave considerable liberty in this respect. As the *History of 'The Times'* points out, any sort of judgment of this nature can only be made 'when one has in each case examined and weighed the various influences on the production of the paper'. Since *The Times* is the only newspaper to have been the subject of an objective study of this kind, this puts serious limitations upon the use of the press as an historical source. As a guide to public opinion in the pre-Gallup era it is rather nebulous, particularly since most people are not interested in foreign policy, and it is only when it speaks with something like unanimity—as for example on the Armenian massacres—that it can be assumed to be representative of public opinion in general.[14] That popular feeling upon foreign policy existed is obvious—witness the agitation against the Bulgarian and Armenian horrors—but an exact assessment of its importance is not possible, if only because of its confusion. As Salisbury remarked at the height of this in 1895, 'when the great

[13] 'Lord Salisbury told me that the general belief that public opinion in England was influenced by the Press was mistaken since the great majority of the people do not read newspapers.' Deym to Kálnoky, *supra*.

[14] Salisbury doubted even this—to Currie 23 November 1896, S.P. He thought the press a nuisance: 'Our newspapers do us an infinite harm especially with Germany and Russia.' To the Queen 19 December 1895, Cab/41/23/41.

oracle speaks, we are never quite certain what the great oracle said'.

Thus although there was an explicit assumption that public opinion was the deciding factor in British foreign policy, it was more of a negative that a positive force. There were certain actions which current feeling made it impossible for a government to perform—such as supporting the Turks in 1877 and 1896, or making a public alliance with Germany in 1901—but rarely, if ever, was public opinion recognized as strong enough to determine a positive course of action.

This is equally true of its manifestation in the House of Commons. Members did occasionally have strong feeling about foreign questions—this was to play havoc with Gladstone's Sudan policy—but usually the administration could outwit them. It is evident, for example, that Granville had no greater inclination to keep them properly informed on the real issues than Salisbury had, and by variations on the theme that it was premature to publish before negotiations were completed, the House could always be prevented from exercising any real influence. Provided that an administration kept in reasonable touch with the climate of opinion, anything needing ratification could get through on the basis of party loyalty and discipline. This is abundantly clear in the Blue Book policy of successive administrations. These were not actually falsified—though Disraeli and Chamberlain got very near to this—but as a guide to the important issues of foreign policy in this period they are very limited, since anything in the nature of a confidential discussion with foreign powers was eliminated. The one exception to this was Gladstone's publication of important papers during his second administration when he tried to prove that in action over Tunis and Egypt his hands had been bound by the follies of his predecessor, but after this there was a general conspiracy of silence.

There were obvious reasons for this. In Palmerston's time, the heyday of the Blue Book, the only force of opinion that mattered was the House of Commons whose members, lacking party discipline, could be effectively influenced by a deluge of Blue Books. By the mid-eighties this was no longer true: with something approaching a mass electorate and a party machine the ordinary member lost his independence. Now the political leaders could work directly with the people and the last thing the new masters wanted to read were Blue Books on such abstruse matters as foreign policy. Paradoxically, it has been pointed out, 'as Parliament became more democratic its control over foreign policy declined'.[15] All that really remained in this respect was the ultimate sanction that Parliament had to approve an alliance or a declaration of war. This was of great importance but, considering the unexpected ease of the passage of Lansdowne's Japanese alliance—which Salisbury said would never get through—and the war fever of August 1914, it was probably overrated.

One of the most pronounced characteristics of the conduct of foreign policy was its essential amateurishness. One or two individual members of the Foreign Office's professional staff had some influence on the construction of policy in the region they were responsible for, notably Anderson in Africa and Bertie in the Far East, but in general the Office had very little effect on policy until after the retirement of Salisbury.[16] Even the Permanent Under-Secretary, although he occasionally received ambassadors, was mainly preoccupied with routine work until 1900. Currie, for example, who held this office from 1889 to 1893, regarded it as a great innovation to write minutes himself: Pauncefote, he claimed, had never done so. His long association with Salisbury since 1878 as Private Secretary obviously gave the latter confidence in his judgment—in 1895 he proposed giving him *carte blanche* at Constantinople—but even in his case it seems doubtful if he had any appreciable influence.

Part of the reason for the lack of influence of the Office lay in the system of private correspondence. This, given the Blue Book habit, was the means of ensuring secrecy even in the event of a change of administration, since it contained anything really confidential or in the nature of an explanation of the actual purpose of policy and was removed by the outgoing Minister. Crowe's complaints of lack of information about Chamberlain's negotiations with Germany reflected office feeling in the new era after 1900: there was a similar lack in the earlier period but nobody thought it particularly remarkable. All Salisbury's important

---

[15] H. Temperley and L. Penson, *A century of Diplomatic Blue Books* (Cambridge, 1938) p. ix. One important purpose behind them was as a means of moral pressure on foreign powers, particularly Turkey.

[16] 'After 1906, men who had been clerks began acting as true advisers.' Z. S. Steiner, 'The last years of the Old Foreign Office', *H.J.* 1963 p. 59.

negotiations with Bismarck were kept from the official correspondence. Representatives abroad were probably more influential than the Office since the impression that men like Odo Russell or Malet formed of Germany, or Lyons of France, could influence policy considerably: for example the war scare of 1888 was partly founded on Lytton's reporting of the Boulangist crisis. But ambassadors were by no means always listened to: the *Leitmotiv* of Morier's letters from St. Petersburg in the eighties was the necessity of an understanding with Russia, but Salisbury took precious little notice of this at the time. Cromer's influence on Egyptian policy was considerable: almost certainly it was he who converted Salisbury to the tacit abandonment of evacuation in 1888, but his views were not always accepted: Rosebery, in 1895, rejected his advice to collaborate with Italy in the Sudan whilst Salisbury, in 1897, overrode him in ordering the advance to Khartoum.

The ignoring of expert advice was one of the characteristics of the amateurishness of the age. Salisbury in particular made a fetish of it, constantly ridiculing the pretensions of generals and admirals to omniscience. This in itself was probably a healthy attitude but when it extended to the failure to create a General Staff or any effective political planning of Imperial Defence it went too far. Admittedly the Duke of Cambridge and most of the Sea Lords were fatal obstacles to this but the Cabinet showed little recognition of their responsibility. Beresford in 1886 commented strongly on 'the disadvantage England rests under, through posesssing no outline even of a plan of campaign';[17] which was still true in Fisher's time. Salisbury's complaint of 1877 that the 'system of never making a plan beyond the next move is bearing its natural fruits' was equally applicable in the Boer War. 'The Government', Wolseley noted with weary resignation in 1899, 'are acting without complete knowledge of what the military can do, while the military authorities on their side are equally without full knowledge of what the Government expects them to do'.[18] Salisbury, it is true, set up a Defence Committee of the Cabinet in 1895 to try to remedy this state of affairs. What he wanted it to do in particular was to decide 'what is the work for which the Army and Navy have to be fitted, and how are they to

[17] Cab/37/18/45.
[18] Wolseley 5 September 1899, Cab/37/50/69.

be fitted for it?' But this, part of his battle with Goschen to determine whether the Foreign Office or the Admiralty were to control foreign policy, ran into the sands of departmental obstructionism and Cabinet reluctance to have outside experts present at the deliberations of their committee. Devonshire, its president, could only urge in its favour in November 1900 when making a progress report, that it 'has not, I think, been altogether useless': Hicks Beach, who all along had thought Salisbury's idea the wildest optimism, thought it a great achievement that it settled momentous issues like the docks at Bermuda.[19] It took the disasters of the Boer War and the emergence of Hankey to make an impression on this state of lethargy.

The fact that the Foreign Secretary took the decisions in foreign policy might lead to the expectation that he knew something about it. But although most had some experience in office in a related field—usually the India Office or the Colonies—in general apart from this their knowledge on first taking office was slight. It was impossible to contemplate the system prevalent under the autocratic Continental monarchies[20] of appointing a professional diplomat to the post, for the simple reason that the minister was responsible to Parliament, not to the Crown. His title might be 'Her Majesty's Principal Secretary of State, etc.' but this was a polite fiction by the seventies, on a par with the Queen's Speech. Certainly the Queen had influence on foreign affairs, particularly through her aversion to particular policies and politicians, but the fact that Salisbury and Rosebery were the royal favourites for the post was not the decisive reason for their appointment. They were, and had to be, front-rank politicians in their own right. The fact that they, as most Foreign Secretaries in the nineteenth century, were peers was incidental. Avoiding the hurly-burly of the Commons helped to diminish the burden of the office and it was of some advantage for the man who dealt with foreign powers to be a nobleman: but the main reason was simply that in an age when great territorial influence was still a useful parliamentary asset, a majority of leading Whig and Tory politicians were peers and it is not surprising that they monopolized the second great office of state. But although this was inevitable, given the British political system, it did possess the disadvantage of its

[19] Cab/37/40/64; 53/71.
[20] Also sometimes in France and Italy.

15

being largely accidental whether a new minister knew anything of foreign affairs on his appointment: Iddesleigh, in 1886, confessed to Malet that he did not 'pretend to fathom the secrets or understand the abstruse diplomacy of the day',[21] a serious disadvantage when dealing with Bismarck. That, nevertheless, Britain produced some great Foreign Secretaries was due to the forced concentration of the work, the daily reading of reports, discussions with foreign diplomats, the necessity of writing instructions, and above all to sheer length of time in office. Whereas other ministers played musical chairs at frequent intervals, tenure of the Foreign Office was only abandoned for the premiership or for enforced retirement. The law of Buggins' turn was not applied to this department of state.[22]

One of the major hazards—along with the swings in public opinion and the party system—was the fact that if the responsible minister quickly acquired expertise his colleagues did not. Information was circulated after 1880 especially to the more important members and any really crucial despatch was discussed in Cabinet, but most members, preoccupied with their own departments, lacked either the inclination or the information to take a responsible interest in what was going on. This presented considerable difficulties because foreign policy, like any other governmental activity, was a collective responsibility and however much the Foreign Secretary might think that the course he wished to pursue best suited British interests, this was of no avail if he could not convince his colleagues. Obviously the day-to-day conduct of affairs could not be referred to them without complete paralysis and even Gladstone fully subscribed to the traditional view that for this it was sufficient for the Foreign Secretary to consult the Prime Minister. But there was a complete divergence in outlook between Gladstone and Salisbury by the eighties. Gladstone held that everything should be discussed *ad nauseam* in Cabinet, a process which even his colleagues found wearisome and which perhaps partly accounts for the feebleness of Granville's performance. Salisbury, who had found this practice welcome enough in 1877 when his main object had been to prevent Disraeli from doing anything, changed his mind by 1886. When positive action

[21] Iddesleigh to Malet 12 September 1886, F.O. 343/2.

[22] Salisbury 13 years, Granville 9 years, Grey 9 years. See T. Gosses, *The Management of British Foreign Policy before 1914* (Leyden, 1948).

was required, 'the necessity of adapting our foreign policy to the views of a Cabinet of fourteen or sixteen men, usually ignorant of it and seldom united in their view', was in his opinion the major disadvantage under which Britain laboured in competition with Russia! Rosebery, when being groomed for office by the Queen and Salisbury in 1886, was told bluntly not to bring too much before it, for 'nothing was ever settled satisfactorily in the Cabinet', a lesson which he took to heart.[23]

Certainly Gladstone later fumed at Rosebery's utter independence, his 'total and gross misconception of the relative position of the two offices we respectively hold, and his really outrageous assumption of power, apart from both the Prime Minister and the Cabinet'.[24] Nor was Rosebery alone in this respect. For the last six months of 1886 Salisbury had his wings clipped by the ebullient Churchill's conduct of his own personal foreign policy but, once he was removed and Salisbury became both Prime Minister and Foreign Secretary, there was very little reference to the Cabinet unless some positive commitment was to be undertaken. For example, although the Mediterranean and Heligoland Agreements were put before the Cabinet, this procedure was not followed where any of the private correspondence between Salisbury and Bismarck in 1887 and 1889 on the subject of an alliance was concerned or with the various assurances of support conveyed to the Italians between 1888 and 1892. Rosebery of course took this much further: apart from his assurances to Hatzfeldt which were diametrically opposed to general Cabinet feeling, extensive negotiations with the Austrians were conducted in the Spring of '94 without any reference to his colleagues whatsoever.

But the amount of freedom this provided should not be exaggerated, for it was only enjoyable as long as no binding commitment was required. Once this arose Cabinet control was complete. No positive decision was taken in these years without their collective responsibility, for behind them loomed the Parliament and the electorate. Inevitably, this created a built-in tendency towards inertia, as Disraeli discovered in 1877, Salisbury in 1895 and Chamberlain from 1898 to 1901. Those who wanted to change policy always found it uphill work, and Salisbury's dictum of 1877 that 'purposeless vacillation . . . is what suits the nation best' was

---

[23] Q.V.L. 3rd series I, 45, 195.
[24] Gladstone, Memorandum on Appointments of 1892. B.M. Add. Mss. 44711.

still fundamentally true in 1902. Though it led to somewhat unexpected results, Lansdowne's Japanese alliance of this year was essentially a distraction from the real decision at which the Cabinet baulked—that of making a military alliance with a Continental power.

II

The Eastern Question, 1878-82

The Porte, it is abundantly proved, is not strong enough
to stand alone. It must be held up. We offer ourselves as
supporters on the East, Austria on the West.

Salisbury, 1878

The significance of 1878 in the history of British foreign policy is
precisely that it was in this year that the British position as a
European Power was re-established. Although from 1815 to 1860
there had been almost continuous participation in European politics, in Palmerston's later years and Gladstone's first ministry
there developed a conscious sense of isolation from the Continent which seemed equally reciprocated. So much so that in 1876
the three Northern Courts showed every sign of solving the
Eastern Question by themselves without any reference to England.
Nor, despite Disraeli's quick reaction to this, was it easy to re-
integrate England into European politics until it had been decided
just what British interests were. The perils of participation without
any clear decisions of this nature were amply illustrated by Salisbury's flounderings at the Constantinople Conference in 1876-7,
which equalled any of Gladstone's later efforts. With the Cabinet
hopelessly divided until March 1878—Disraeli observed that there
were twelve members and seven policies—any consistency was
impossible: 'English policy is to float lazily downstream, occasionally putting out a diplomatic boat-hook to avoid collisions.'[1]

But from March 1878 onwards, with the appointment of Salisbury to the Foreign Office, there was considerable, if far from
complete, harmony between the two principal members of the
Cabinet, and British foreign policy began to acquire some consistency of purpose. It had a number of false starts; ideas which,

[1] Salisbury to Lytton 9 March 1877, in Lady Gwendolyn Cecil, *Life of Robert,
Marquis of Salisbury* (London, 1921) II, 130.

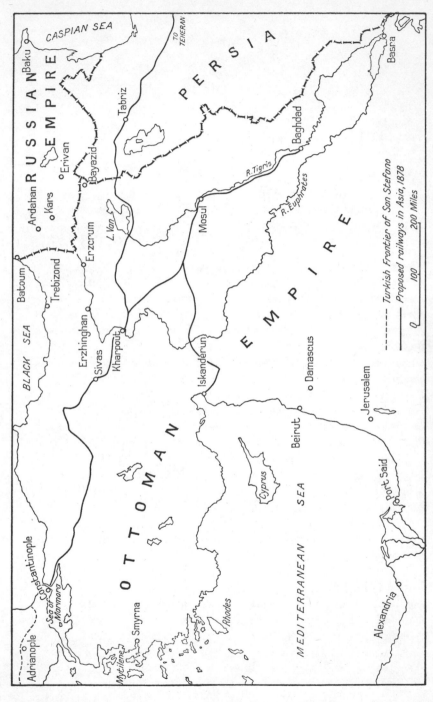

British policy in the Near East, 1878

though attractive enough at first sight, proved impossible to execute in practice; the result, as Salisbury acknowledged, of trying to do in three months what should have been built up gradually over the previous three years; but in general the concepts of 1878–82 remained the basis of policy in Europe for the next twenty-five years.[2] Nor was there any great difference when Gladstone took over the reins in 1880. Gladstone's personal theory of foreign policy as expounded during the Midlothian campaign was a complete contrast to that of Disraeli and Salisbury but, partly due to Whig restraint, the difference in practice was barely noticeable. It is a basic error to take Gladstone's Midlothian pronouncements as Liberal foreign policy: this, after all, was an election campaign when he had to develop a line antagonistic to that of Disraeli, and his actions, once in office, were very different. Gladstone himself in September 1880 recognized 'the expediency of maintaining as far as might be a continuity in Foreign Policy'[3] and certainly he made no attempt to abandon participation for isolation. If anything, he did the reverse, for his conception of the Concert of Europe involved England taking the lead just as much as Disraeli's programme of 1878. Although he disliked alliances and talked rather in terms of 'bringing about the "common accord" of Europe'[4] it was not Gladstone's Utopianism that accounted for the failure of his policy but the rival attractions of Bismarck. That the Disraeli-Salisbury conception of foreign policy based on close collaboration or alliance with Austria, Turkey and France had worn thin by 1885 was less the result of Gladstone's actions, as Salisbury liked to pretend, than of Bismarck's determination to build a rival system and make Berlin the pivot of European diplomacy. Until a government in London was prepared to develop England's potential to become a great military power—unthinkable until forced upon them in 1915—the voice of Berlin was louder than that of London and all Foreign Secretaries had to work with the restrictions that this imposed.

[2] See L. M. Penson, *Foreign Affairs under the Third Marquis of Salisbury* (London, 1962) pp. 2–3.

[3] Gladstone Memorandum of conversation with Granville, 23 September 1880 in A. Ramm, *Political Correspondence of Mr Gladstone and Lord Granville, 1876–1886* (Oxford, 1962) I, 181.

[4] Quoted in W. N. Medlicott, *Bismarck, Gladstone and the Concert of Europe* (London, 1956) p.1. As he points out, the difference between the parties, as opposed to personalities, on foreign policy was slight, pp. 24–5, 319.

It was significant that it was the Eastern Question that brought England back into Europe. The policy of abstention and isolation pursued from 1864 to 1876, if deplorable, is at least understandable in view of the problems then in dispute. From the British viewpoint there was little to choose between victor and vanquished in 1866 or 1870 and even if there had been, given the almost complete lack of military power on the Continental scale, it would have been difficult to have intervened effectively in any case.[5] But the threatened disintegration of the Ottoman Empire was totally different. Though there were considerable internal differences of opinion as to what policy to adopt, there was no doubt that British interests were involved, or that, with her preponderance of naval power, she possessed the means of influencing events. The principal difficulty lay not in identifying the problem but in arriving at any decision to resolve it in view of the violent internal dissension that the project of supporting the Turks aroused. This distaste was not confined to Gladstone or the nonconformist conscience, but was equally marked within the Conservative Cabinet. Hence the importance of the final decision to do something, to go to war, if necessary, since the determination to confine the Russian destruction of Turkey to within certain well-defined limits necessitated a search for allies and brought England back into the mainstream of European affairs. As Disraeli emphasized in 1879 his idea of foreign policy was 'not to be neutral and non-interfering but to act and act with allies'.[6]

British concern with the impending collapse of the Ottoman Empire had three main aspects, Bulgaria, Asia Minor and Egypt, and although all three were closely connected, it is convenient to consider them separately.

Defending Turkey in Europe: Bulgaria and the Austrian alliance

It was assumed without question that the Big Bulgaria of San Stefano would be simply an extension of Russia and would bring her much too close to Constantinople. This was to be resisted since it would, by reducing Turkey to dependence upon Russia,

[5] H. Temperley and L. M. Penson, *Foundations of British Foreign Policy* (Cambridge, 1938) pp. 305–18. For a recent analysis see R. Millman, *British Foreign Policy and the Coming of the Franco-Prussian War* (Oxford, 1965).

[6] Disraeli to Salisbury 14 October 1879, quoted in W. N. Medlicott , *The Congress of Berlin and After* (London, 1938) p. 386.

'threaten the free passage of the Straits, and also menace English interests in other places where the exercise of Turkish authority affects them'.[7] The problem was how to resist. Though Layard and Salisbury initially had some idea of using the Greeks for this purpose, building them up as a barrier against Slavdom, it was soon obvious that they were not yet strong enough to be effective. The Sultan, not unnaturally, was completely unwilling to accept them as allies on the basis of first strengthening them with some of his best provinces.[8] Consequently Salisbury had to fall back on the expedient of dividing Bulgaria in two, leaving the southern half, Eastern Roumelia, under Turkish suzerainty. The object of this was simply to enable the Turks to garrison the line of the Balkan mountains, which, it was thought, would provide a viable defence system. But although this was provided for by the Treaty of Berlin, actually obtaining it proved a long drawn out battle.

Although the Berlin Congress was a considerable victory for Disraeli's and Salisbury's concept of British interests in the Balkans, so much so that the latter announced that 'we have done with the Eastern Question in English politics',[9] this was not in fact the end of the crisis. On paper all looked well, but how much of this was put into effect depended almost entirely on how long the attitudes and relationships of the powers were to remain what they had been in 1878. Above all, the enforcement of the terms of the treaty in Bulgaria, providing for the separation of the two provinces, their evacuation by Russian troops by 3 May 1879 and the establishment of Turkish garrisons on the Balkans, depended on the continuation of Austro-British co-operation, the isolation of Russia and the Sultan's willingness to further British interests as distinct from his own.

Initially it was far from clear in London whether the Tsar would actually accept the Congress decisions. Russian actions in Eastern Roumelia and the stiff fight they put up in the boundary commissions over every single point gave a distinct impression of delaying tactics. Dondukov-Korsakov, the head of the Russian administration in Bulgaria, was actively engaged in raising a local militia in Eastern Roumelia to oppose the Turks if they reoccupied the province; whilst Todleben, the military commander, openly

---

[7] Salisbury to Disraeli 21 March 1878 in Cecil II, 213. Doc. 1.
[8] Medlicott, *Congress* p. 34.
[9] *ibid.* p. 138.

announced that he had instructions not to withdraw. Salisbury, on balance, was inclined to think that the Tsar would abide by the treaty and that these actions were simply 'the usual duality' of Russian policy,[10] but for a long time this was far from clear. One expression of this doubt was a firm guarantee to the Sultan on 26 October 1878 of British support to execute the treaty if evacuation had not taken place by the following May and, although this was slightly qualified on 24 November by the addition that this would need parliamentary approval, it was never withdrawn.

Another was the determination to work with Austria. Andrássy, the Austro-Hungarian Foreign Minister, had wavered at first under Russo-German pressure but the British stand in support of the Turks against attempts to exert collective pressure upon them to carry out their obligations before Russia had performed hers, convinced him that more could be obtained from collaboration with London. In October 1878 he rejected Bismarck's attempts to resurrect the *Dreikaiserbund* and embarked on a programme of checking Russian influence in Bulgaria by a rigorous enforcement of the treaty against her, an attitude which made him a natural British ally. So much so that Salisbury intervened in his favour at Constantinople, warned the Sultan against any encouragement of the local opposition to the Austrian occupation of Bosnia and Herzegovina, and tried to promote an Austro-Turkish alliance. In Bulgaria the British representative, Palgrave, was instructed to work with the Austrians at all times: 'we attach a very high value to the alliance'. This attitude was taken so far that when Palgrave failed to follow the Austrian lead and struck out on his own in support of the Liberal and supposedly Pan-Slav groups in Bulgarian politics, he was exiled to Bangkok. Collaboration with Austria continued throughout 1879 and achieved a major success in July with the complete Russian evacuation of Bulgaria which, Shuvalov virtually admitted, was the product of Russian isolation in Europe.[11] Nor did the Anglo-Austrian achievement of their major objective lessen their determination to work together since general suspicion of Russian intentions in the Balkans, mostly without any foundation, continued to dominate British and Austrian policies. In May Salisbury suggested to Vienna that they

[10] To Loftus 16 October 1878 in Cecil II, 344.
[11] Medlicott, *Congress* pp. 154–62, 172, 177–84, 375–6; C. E. Black, *The Establishment of Constitutional Government in Bulgaria* (Princeton, 1943) pp. 74, 151, 154.

agree on a policy of future co-operation thoughout the peninsular: Haymerlé, who succeeded Andrássy in October, still
thought it self-evident in February 1880 that while their interests
were still 'so closely parallel to those of the English we should be
unwise to abandon England'.[12]

Yet despite this identity of interest and common accord no
formal alliance ever materialized: instead, by 18 June 1881,
Austria had re-entered the *Dreikaiserbund* and made her peace with
Russia in the Balkans, with corresponding ill-effects upon the
British position in Europe. The explanation for this lies partly
with Bismarckian diplomacy, partly in British internal politics.
The most serious result of the Berlin Congress for Bismarck was
the emergence of Austro-Russian hostility and Anglo-Austrian
collaboration in the Balkans. Although a certain amount of
Austro-Russian tension was a good thing in his eyes, if it went too
far and produced an Anglo-Austrian-French (Crimean) coalition,
he was in danger of losing his freedom of manoeuvre.[13] Hence in
order to recover control of European politics, his intention even
as early as October 1878 was to revive the *Dreikaiserbund*, an
attitude which precluded any idea of encouraging an Anglo-
Austrian alliance and from which he now set out to wean Vienna.
In this way Bismarck's offer of a German alliance to Andrássy in
October 1879 was not so much that Bismarck was choosing between Austria and Russia as that he was forcing Andrássy to
choose between England and Germany; and, once the question
was posed in this manner, there could be little doubt of the
response.[14]

Bismarck's support of Austria may have been far less than that
provided by England during the preceding twelve months but a
German guarantee against a Russian attack was more than England could provide, assuming that Bismarck kept his word. The
fact that a Russian attack was unlikely was all part of the game:
the point was to get control of Austrian policy. Nor did the
Austrians at first realize they were being forced to abandon their

---

[12] Haymerlé to Kálnoky 13 February 1880 in Medlicott, *Bismarck, Gladstone* p. 52.
[13] E.g. his remarks to Odo Russell in January 1876: 'Germany could not well
afford to let Austria and Russia become too intimate behind her back—nor could she
let them quarrel with safety to herself.' Quoted in W. N. Medlicott, 'Bismarck and
Beaconsfield' in *Studies in Diplomatic History . . . in Honour of G. P. Gooch*, edited by
A. O. Sarkissian (London, 1961) p. 229.
[14] *ibid.* p.246.

natural British alliance for a somewhat problematic deal with Bismarck. The Austro-German alliance was welcomed in London and assured of British support. To judge from the response of Disraeli and Salisbury to Bismarck's approach through Munster on 26 September 1879, they personally favoured a firm alliance with Austria and Germany. Disraeli made no bones about it: he told Munster that he would 'willingly enter into an alliance with Germany' and that in return for support in the East 'we will in that case keep France quiet'. Salisbury, though much more suspicious of Bismarck than his chief and doubting strongly if France would 'take any rash action' under her present republican government, made no objection. On 15 October he assured Munster 'that we could prevent any French Government from joining Russia against him' and that he could 'rely on our goodwill and assistance in the contingency of an attack on Austria and Germany'.[15]

Nor were the prospects hopeless, in Disraeli's view, of getting such an alliance through parliament. He was so strongly imbued with a sense of the importance to England of her position as a European power—a view made evident in his Guildhall peroration on *Imperium et Libertas* on 2 July 1878—that he thought it might even prove the election winner so sorely needed by his party by the end of 1879. It was quite probable, he thought, that it would 'be hailed with something like enthusiasm in the country' and, even if it were not, at least the party would acquire the reputation of having 'a strong and intelligent policy'.[16] But the issue was never put to the test. Bismarck, if he had ever intended the approach seriously, dropped the subject completely once the prospect of the *Dreikaiserbund* reopened and dragged the reluctant Haymerlé in his wake. It is not impossible that he was embarrassed by the warmth of the British response. If, as seems apparent, the last thing he wanted was an alliance with England in which Disraeli would probably be the dominant partner,[17] it is logical to infer that the point of the manoeuvre was to get a negative response for Austrian benefit. If so he was disappointed; which would explain his later complaints of a lack of response when this seems the reverse of the truth. Bismarck was always thorough.

The final touches to the process of breaking up Anglo-Austrian

[15] Medlicott, *Congress* pp. 386–8; Cecil II, 367–8. Docs. 6, 7.
[16] *ibid.* p. 366.
[17] Medlicott, *Bismarck and Beaconsfield* p. 249.

collaboration in the Balkans against Russia were provided by the change of government in England in April 1880. Not that Gladstone's Bulgarian policy was noticeably different from Salisbury's: as the Russians complained, it was just as bad. For all the sympathy with freedom expressed during the Midlothian campaign— 'Liberty is what I wish to defend, and I care not who is the assailant'—his main preoccupation in respect to Bulgaria in 1880 was 'to keep the Bulgarian Liberals and Roumelians quiet', sentiments which Salisbury would have echoed.[18] Whereas Salisbury supported the Austrian view that the Bulgarian Liberals were a menace on the grounds of their supposed Pan-Slav feelings, Granville did so because they would upset the cherished Concert. Palgrave's suggestion that they were simply Pan-Bulgar and if anything pro-British, 'wishing to model the country, within reasonable limits, on English institutions', got no more of a hearing from Gladstone than from his predecessor. Bulgarian Liberals who petitioned him to oppose Battenberg's *coup d'état* of 9 May 1881 were told to use the proper channels and, after nearly two months of deliberations, Granville simply urged moderation on both sides. The significant point was that Battenberg's action was approved by both Russia and Austria, and Gladstone preferred to avoid disrupting the Concert.[19]

Nor can Gladstone be blamed for the Turkish failure to garrison the Balkan mountains, an omission which made nonsense of Salisbury's efforts since 1878 to build up 'a wall across the Peninsular of the Balkans and across Armenia which shall give a respite to Turkey for twenty or thirty years'.[20] A good deal of the point of this had been lost with the cession of Varna to Bulgaria, since this enabled the mountains to be by-passed by the coastal route: but the Turks, in any case, had doubts of the wisdom of throwing their army forward with a hostile, armed, population in their rear. Moreover, the moment to have moved the Turkish armies forward was in July 1879 when the Russian armies withdrew, but the Sultan had hesitated then for fear of the effects upon St. Petersburg. In view of his intense resentment against Austria after the occupation of Bosnia and Herzegovina, and his suspicion of British intentions in Asia Minor, this is not surprising. To have

[18] Medlicott, *Bismarck, Gladstone* pp. 29–31, 108, 111.
[19] Black pp. 78, 153–4, 198–9, 202–7.
[20] Salisbury to Layard 25 June 1878, in Cecil II, 304.

done so would have fatally alienated Russia and made him completely dependent upon Austria and England whose protection was a very mixed blessing. Turkish survival depended upon his ability to play off one set of enemies against the other and there were already signs, before the advent of Gladstone in April 1880, that he regarded Russia as the lesser evil.[21] As in Asia Minor, the advent of a Liberal government only accentuated changes which had already begun. If the Sultan had entertained doubts about exclusive reliance on England before, such course of action would have been completely foolhardy now with Gladstone intent on the organization of a European concert against the Turks.

But if Gladstone's policy in Bulgaria showed no marked difference from that of his predecessor, his attitude towards the Montenegrin and Greek questions was in complete contrast to Salisbury's. Salisbury had kept out of these issues because, in his view, they were of no particular British interest and their development would only annoy the Turks unnecessarily.[22] But Gladstone plunged in headlong. Despite his great insistence on the European powers' acting in concert and objections to 'a system under which one of them is to be placed under moral suspicion and espionage', he did not include the Turks. They were, in his eyes, not only non-Christians but 'the one great anti-human specimen of humanity'. Hence his main idea after 1880 was to organize the Concert against them, principally in enforcing the Berlin Treaty in favour of Montenegro and Greece 'without delay'.[23] It was this which finally wrecked all prospects of Anglo-Austrian collaboration in the Balkans since, in the eyes of Vienna, Gladstone became even more of a menace to the *status quo* than the Russians.

This, however, was a gradual process. Despite the alliance with Bismarck in October 1879, Austrian interests were still more in accord with those of England than of Germany, and Haymerlé was in no hurry, despite the German alliance, to drop England. As he acknowledged in February 1880 they still had much in common and for some time he still cherished the idea of making England, not Russia, the third partner. He had no objection to Gladstone, nor Gladstone to him: for, despite his electioneering tirades against

[21] Medlicott, *Congress* pp. 253–4, 361–2.
[22] 'The Montenegrin and Servian question does not interest us in the least . . . Parliament would not vote a shilling for a war in such a cause.' To Elliot 3 June 1878, in Cecil II, 261.
[23] Medlicott, *Bismarck, Gladstone* pp. 26, 30. Doc. 12.

Austria in 1879, Gladstone promptly retracted these once in office and welcomed working with Vienna. It was only as his Montenegrin campaign got under way that Haymerlé became really uneasy, as Gladstone's determination to bombard Dulcigno was completely contrary to the interests of Austria, who abhorred anything which further weakened the Turks. By September disillusionment was complete. Now Haymerlé admitted that 'since England is so actively trying to undermine Turkey, and can no longer be counted on', he had no alternative but to succumb to Bismarck's pressure and accept an understanding with Russia.[24]

The chain of reasoning in St. Petersburg was completely different but led to the same result. The combination of Salisbury's declaration on the Straits[25] in 1878, his military consuls in Armenia, and the constant airing of Layard's ideas in the British press, had made Russia suspect the worst. They were perfectly willing, Gorchakov claimed in January 1880, to accept 'equal influence' in Turkey: the obstacle to Anglo-Russian understanding lay in

> the grandiose plans of Beaconsfield's imperialistic policy by establishing in the Straits, in the Black Sea and in Asia Minor the definite military, political and commercial preponderance of England.[26]

Since Gladstone repudiated these schemes completely—where they had not already been tacitly abandoned by his predecessors —and proceeded to organize the Concert against Turkey, there was now a very different emphasis in St. Petersburg. Though reserving judgment until he saw what Gladstone actually did, Giers now spoke openly of the difference between England and Russia being 'more apparent than real' and welcomed the Concert as contributing to 'the repose and equilibrium of Europe'.[27]

Nor was Russia, in contrast to Austria, alienated by Gladstone's sponsorshop of the Montenegrin cause. Though somewhat indifferent to the Greeks, Montenegro, like Bulgaria, was a good Russian cause and enforcing the Treaty against Turkey rather than against Russia was a project the Russians naturally supported. Their enthusiasm for Gladstone waned somewhat when he turned to the Greek question in 1881 and began to talk of solving this by

[24] *ibid.* pp. 52, 80, 87, 180.
[26] Medlicott, *Congress* p. 396.
[25] See next section.
[27] *Bismarck, Gladstone* p. 57.

naval action, since a British fleet in the Bosphorous was equally obnoxious to them whether commanded by Gladstone or Disraeli. But this was in a minor key. Giers, with rare perception, recognized in May 1880 that British interest in the Straits was mainly a response to fears for their Indian empire: that 'a satisfactory arrangement in Asia would diminish the keenness of our antagonism in the Near East and in consequence the danger of a violation of the Straits'. Since tension in Asia abated after Gladstone withdrew from Kandahar and dropped Salisbury's schemes in Persia, there was no reason to expect antagonism in Europe: in fact some officials in St. Petersburg even advocated an Anglo-Russian *entente* as an alternative to the *Dreikaiserbund*.[28]

Thus if Gladstone's diplomacy finally killed the Austrian alliance by leaving Haymerlé no choice but to enter Bismarck's *Dreikaiserbund*, it opened up the prospect for Britain, at least in theory, of a viable alternative in the form of an understanding with Russia. This, at its height during the settlement of the Montenegrin question from April to October 1880, was nevertheless an illusion. The forces dragging Russia in the direction of Berlin and Vienna were much stronger than those which led to London. There was no real chance of an English alliance, the most that could be achieved was a transitory understanding: and much as Giers wished to take advantage of the opportunities that this offered, there could be no permanence in it. Under the English parliamentary system there could be no security: Gladstone, said Saburov, was but 'a shining meteor—a meteor which will pass'. The real factor in Russian foreign policy was fear of Germany, not fear of England, and—given the impossibility of reliance upon France at this time—this left the alternatives as either isolation or accepting Bismarck's form of a German alliance, the *Dreikaiserbund*.[29]

Once this conclusion had been reached others followed. Since it was necessary to reach an Austro-Russian *détente* the policy of San Stefano had to be finally abandoned and all the emphasis placed on keeping the Balkans quiet, a point made apparent by Austro-Russian approval of Battenberg's counter-revolution in Bulgaria on 9 May 1881. Once the Montenegrin settlement had been reached, Russia, too, as Saburov had forecast in June 1880,

[28] *ibid.* pp. 58–60. See also Chapter IV.
[29] *ibid.* pp. 242–4, 324.

was 'on the side of the Powers that are guardians of Turkey',[30] an attitude that made Gladstone a nuisance, not a welcome ally. Finally, it is logical to assume that security at the Straits and expansion in Asia were connected. Though fear of British action at the Straits played at best a minor role in the decision at St. Petersburg to make a German alliance, one of the incidental benefits of this alliance was the support of the German powers for the Russian view of what closure meant.[31] With this behind them the enthusiasm of ardent Pan-slavs such as Skobelev could be channelled, with Bismarck's encouragement, into Central Asia, which made British isolation in the face of the three Northern courts inevitable. When to this was added the rupture with France brought about by Egypt, Gladstone's Concert of Europe became a Continental League: what Salisbury later called a 'Concert of Europe directed against us'.

Turkey in Asia: the Cyprus Convention

The second part of Salisbury's solution to the Eastern Question lay in turning it into the West Asian Question. His schemes for the defence of Asia Minor were, in his eyes, far more important than the attempts to bolster up Turkey in Europe since, seriously underrating its capacity to survive, he was convinced of the impossibility 'of setting the Turkish Government on its legs again, as a genuine reliable Power'. Instead all the emphasis was now to be placed on building up Turkey in Asia under British auspices, in order to protect the whole complex of Imperial communications with India from Russian encroachment. This idea was closely connected with the current problem in Central Asia, the unreliability of the Afghan Amir, the feebleness of Persia, and Salisbury's conviction that no 'stable arrangement can be arrived at in the East'. If it did nothing else, giving Turkey a new lease of life as an Asiatic power would provide a breathing space during which the defence of India could be constructed around strategic railways in southern Persia.[32]

Hence the importance attached at the Berlin Congress to giving the Turks control of the passes to Erzerum and the Alashkerd

[30] *Bismarck, Gladstone* pp. 107, 250.
[31] i.e. that they were closed and that the Turks could make no exception to this. Article II of the Treaty of 18 June 1881, printed *ibid.* p. 339). See next section.
[32] Cecil II, 213, 375–7. See also Chapter IV.

valley route to northern Persia, since in this way it was hoped that Russia could be kept away from the Euphrates and the Persian Gulf. Layard had much more positive ambitions. If British influence were put behind developing Turkey in Asia, he argued, then strategic railways could be built from Iskanderun via Baghdad to Karachi: this opened up the prospect of creating a British preponderance of influence throughout the Near East with enormous benefit for trade and Imperial communications. The military advantages of the latter scheme were obvious, since it would get around the basic problem poised by the dispersal of the British army between England and India:

> This design would give England with the recent addition of Cyprus the first strategic position in the world enabling her army in India to co-operate with that in England with the rapidity and force of irresistible power, in defence of a country in whose progress and consolidation England is vitally concerned. . . .[33]

Moreover, transforming the Turkish ally into an effective Asian power possessed the solid advantage that it did not conflict with the contradictory demands of British public opinion. The simultaneous popular pressures for resistance to the Russian advance upon British communications with India and for the dismantling of Turkish rule over Christian populations, could not be resolved in Europe and were the basic cause of the government's lack of a foreign policy during 1876–7. But in Asia there was no problem because the vast majority of the Sultan's subjects there were Moslems and, it was assumed, even the Christian minorities in Armenia and the Lebanon could be appeased by the introduction of good government. Hence the basic idea of the Anglo-Turkish convention of 4 June 1878 was the rejuvenation and reform of Turkey in Asia from above, in exchange for a British guarantee to defend the Sultan's Asiatic empire against any further Russian encroachments. 'We want', Salisbury told Layard on 13 August, 'besides our demands as to Cyprus . . . our reforms in Asia, and security for their being carried out.' Here the essential point was the employment of Europeans in a supervisory capacity in the Turkish provincial administration, for the simple reason that 'good Government in Asia means Government by

[33] 'Memorandum, Asia Minor and Euphrates Railway' 17 July 1878, printed in D. E. Lee, *Great Britain and the Cyprus Convention Policy of 1878* (Harvard, 1934) p. 197.

good men'. Without these the grant of a constitution or reform decrees by the Sultan were so much waste paper in Salisbury's eyes as he thought that no Turk could be relied upon: the 'Pasha class' was a term of abuse with him. This was why he concentrated upon getting Europeans appointed to influential positions in the Gendarmerie, the judiciary and the financial inspectorate, out of which, it was hoped, would emerge something bearing a strong resemblance to British India. This was one argument for the acquisition of Cyprus: it would become the showplace for the effects of British rule for Asia Minor which 'would do more to maintain English prestige than half a dozen Campaigns'.[34]

But the main reason for acquiring Cyprus was the problem of defence. Apart from the public agitation over the threat posed to the Suez Canal by the Russian approach to Constantinople, reflected in Derby's 6 May 1877 despatch, there was considerable concern at the prospect of Russian egress at will from the Bosphorous and acquisition of a port on the Aegean. This led to the despatch of Colonel Home in 1876 to survey the possibility of England's seizing the Dardanelles as an effective counter measure in what was assumed to be the forthcoming partition of Turkey. Home, initially, was strongly in favour of this move on the obvious grounds that if 'these Straits be held by England, or a power friendly to England, the Bosphorous is of comparatively little importance'. But increasingly it was apparent that the drawbacks outweighed the advantages. The chief drawback, according to General Simmons at the War Office, was that it would take 50,000 troops to make it effective if Russia held the Bosphorous, which was beyond British strength and would 'prove an element of embarrassment by an inordinate increase of our yearly natural expenditure'. The suggestion that it might even force the adoption of conscription killed it stone dead.[35]

Moreover it was increasingly realized that simply bottling up Russia in the Black Sea did not really satisfy British requirements. Although Derby included the closure of the Straits in his Blue Book despatch of 6 May 1877 as an essential British interest, by 1878 it was an embarrassment. As the whole weight of British concern swung from Europe to Asia under the influence of Layard

---

[34] *ibid.* p. 77; L. M. Penson, 'The Foreign Policy of Lord Salisbury, 1878–80' in *Studies in Anglo-French History*, edited by A. Colville and H. Temperley (Cambridge, 1935) pp. 129, 134–5. Doc. 8.   [35] Lee pp. 38–40, 180–1.

and Salisbury, the main defence requirement became some means of stopping Russian domination of the Armenian plateau, which would give them the ability to march on the Mediterranean or the Persian Gulf at will. For this purpose a base on the Dardanelles was much too limited and Salisbury began to consider a radically different programme, an alliance with the Sultan which would enable him to pass the Straits and make use of British naval supremacy in the Black Sea. Hence the reservations on this point in the Anglo-Russian Agreement 30 May 1878 and the attempt on 16 June to persuade the Sultan not to oppose such a move.[36]

Salisbury thought that the Sultan's right by the 1871 Treaty of London to call up warships was a dead letter, since fear of Russia would always be too great for Turkey to take this step. What Salisbury wanted was to transfer this decision from Constantinople to London so that British interests would be the dominant consideration, not the Sultan's. This he hoped to achieve by a secret agreement with the Turks that they would not oppose a British passage through the Straits, holding out the bait that in return he would support Turkish retention of Batoum. The Grand Vizier was not unfavourable to the project—he thought Turkey's European obligations might be met by firing blanks at the fleet as it went through the Narrows—but it ran into opposition from the Sultan and the British Cabinet. The latter, shrinking from the complete overthrow of past policy, reiterated as recently as May 1877, thought the Cyprus Convention sufficient leverage upon the Turks without any additional agreement and consequently Salisbury had to rest content with his declaration at the Congress on 11 July. British obligations respecting the closure of the Dardanelles and the Bosphorous, he there asserted, were limited to 'an engagement with the Sultan to respect in this manner His Majesty's independent determinations in conformity with the spirit of existing Treaties'. This, however, showed clearly enough the way his mind was moving: if the Treaty of Paris were being abolished why keep the Straits clauses? As he explained later, he intended to repudiate any 'international obligation on our part' to respect the closure of the Straits if he thought the Sultan was being subjected to outside pressure, a doctrine that transferred the key to London.[37]

[36] *ibid.* pp. 62, 68, 77–9, 195. Docs. 2, 3, 9.
[37] Medlicott, *Congress*, pp. 103–4, 121–2; *Bismarck, Gladstone* p. 40. Docs. 4, 5.

Thus by 1878 British strategic interests were no longer covered, as Layard had supposed in June 1877, by keeping 'a very powerful fleet between the Coast of Egypt and the entrance to the Dardanelles'. They were to be defended by the dominance of Asia Minor and for this there were two essential requirements. In the first place Malta was too far away so that a nearer naval base was needed (to which it was hoped the British public would cling 'as tenaciously as it has clung to Gibraltar'); and secondly, the co-operation of the Turks. Hence the acquisition of Cyprus by agreement with the Sultan on 4 June 1878. In return for the protection of his territories in Asia from further Russian encroachment, the Sultan agreed to collaborate in a programme of administrative reform. The clause in the agreement making it dependent upon Russia's retaining any of her conquests in Armenia was mere window dressing, since Salisbury had already agreed with Shuvalov that she should do so.[38]

It was on this latter point, Turkish collaboration, that all Salisbury's schemes foundered. Just as Turkish resentment of Austria helped to wreck the idea of building an Austrian prop to what remained of Turkey in Europe, so in Asia the Sultan's growing awareness and fear of British ambitions made him increasingly distrustful of his alliance with England. Nor was his attitude unreasonable. The importation of Europeans for the supervisory posts in the reformed administration was extremely unpopular with his subjects. They, under the impact of the Afghan war, British encouragement of France to take Tunis, and the Dual Control in Egypt, were inclined to attribute similar intentions to England in respect to Turkey. Nor was it surprising that men like Osman Pasha, the defender of Plevna, resented, resisted and finally stopped the appointment of Baker Pasha to command of the Gendarmerie. Moreover the essence of the British reform schemes was to create some sort of responsible government with power in the hands of ministers, rather than the Chief Eunuch: this was a trend not calculated to appeal to Abdul Hamid II, whose concept of reform was simply an increase of absolutism. The more Layard pressured and threatened him the more he became convinced this was part of some sinister plot and, abandoning the English alliance, returned to the old idea of playing off all the Powers against each other. England may have saved him in 1878 in the

[38] Lee pp. 75, 183; *Foundations* p. 365.

process of saving Turkey, but it was difficult for him to avoid the suspicion, after the cession of Cyprus and the arrival of Salisbury's military consuls in the frontier provinces, that this was barely distinguishable from a partition of his empire in which Asia Minor had become the British share.[39]

The key to the situation lay in finance since, as the Sultan himself announced, a loan was the only way to save Turkey and was 'the most effectual means of promoting British interests and policy in his dominions'. Without a loan reform was impossible since there was no means of paying for the Gendarmerie when the Turkish army had not been paid for twelve months. Even with a loan reform was far from certain: Salisbury consoled himself after his failure with the thought that the Sultan would probably have spent it on 'palaces and ironclads'. But for six brief months in 1878 the desperate financial condition of Turkey led Salisbury to believe that reform and finance could be linked together in a system which would effectively turn the country into a British protectorate.[40]

From August to November he pressed the idea on the Cabinet of a Turkish loan of £8 million guaranteed on British supervision of the revenues of the Asian provinces, but entirely without result. It was, admittedly, a bad time. In November the House of Commons had to vote supplies for the Afghan expedition whilst the ever-present example of the Khedive Ismail was discouraging to the supposition that they would get their money back: but the Cabinet's rejection of the project was politically very short-sighted for a party which had committed itself to the reform of Turkey. Opposition from Gladstone was to be expected, but it was discovered that even the government supporters reacted violently against the idea. This, Salisbury told Layard on 18 December, 'puts an end, I fear to all financial schemes which involved any notable sacrifice . . . on the part of the British Government'.[41] Since a similar fate befell Layard's scheme to promote reform through railway development with the unwillingness of the promoters to move without a government guarantee, which was equally unforthcoming, by 1879 it was plain that no

[39] Medlicott, *Congress* pp. 295, 306, 313–17. On Abdul Hamid II's attitude to reform see B. Lewis, *The Emergence of Modern Turkey* (London, 1961) pp. 174ff. Doc. 13.
[40] *Congress* p. 307; Lee p. 152.
[41] Cecil II, 314.

further progress would be made. Half-hearted attempts were still made to induce some measure of reform, to avert what Salisbury regarded as impending doom, but these were, as expected, completely without effect.[42]

The problem really was whether to conciliate or cajole. Salisbury, with occasional exceptions, inclined towards the former until the end of 1879. By then, he thought, conciliation had gone far enough and, evidently abandoning the prospect as hopeless, wanted only to establish that 'our responsibility for Turkey is at an end'.[43] But this got him no further. Using the fleet to coerce the Sultan into reform, as he did for one brief moment in 1879 in an attempt to force the appointment of Baker Pasha, defeated its own object, since the only effect it had was to weaken British influence at Constantinople. Evidently Layard's grandiose dreams—shared for a while by Salisbury in 1878—had already collapsed before the advent of Gladstone. To become effective they demanded the co-operation of the Sultan, an impossible task when there was no financial inducement that could be offered and when British reforms were likely to make him into another Khedive. This was the last thing Abdul Hamid II would accept: his abolition of the office of Grand Vizier in 1879 and the patent mockery of his Constitutions showed his intention to remain an absolute ruler. With the alternative of Russia to lean on, who positively discouraged reform in Asia, it is not surprising that he discovered where his true interests lay. After all, as Salisbury recognized by 1880, the only effect of British pressure for reform was to make 'virtue so disagreeable while vice is so very pleasant'.[44]

The actual difference in British policy towards Asia Minor brought about by the advent of the Liberals in April 1880 was, therefore, minimal, a fact which has been obscured by the combination of Salisbury's abuse of his successors and Gladstone's denunciations of the Cyprus Convention. The ideas behind policy might differ but, in practice, Gladstone's actions turned out to be much the same. Initially, like Salisbury, he pressed upon the Sultan the absolute necessity for reform if he were to retain British support: much as he disliked the Turks personally Gladstone fully admitted their necessity to British interests and, indeed, those of

[42] Lee pp. 140–1. Doc. 10.
[43] Salisbury to Layard 6 November 1879, in Cecil II, 319.
[44] Penson p. 138.

Europe.[45] But, increasingly, he paled under the prospect of British responsibility for reform in Asia Minor and Granville was quite prepared to abandon this campaign in return for the withdrawal of the British obligation to defend Turkey in Asia. With this concept the Liberals were totally out of sympathy, denying completely the validity of the strategy of defending India in the Near East. The acquisition of Cyprus, they maintained, was 'of no advantage to the Country either in a military or political sense'— which was true enough after they had acquired Egypt.

But in the event there was no great change. Though they abandoned what remained of Salisbury's grand design in Asia and wrecked what little influence Britain still retained at Constantinople by the pressure in favour of Montenegro and Greece— above all by the occupation of Egypt—it is apparent that it was largely played out anyway. Salisbury might complain in 1885 that they had 'thrown it away into the sea without getting anything whatever in exchange' but it was not a very marketable commodity. Nor, in fact, did they abandon Cyprus. Despite all Gladstone's criticism of Disraeli's iniquity in 'filching the island of Cyprus from the Porte' it was decided not to return it. Hartington, whose Indian strategy was much the same as Salisbury's and whose pressure in 1882 to defend the Suez Canal was to be decisive, opposed giving it up. Instead it was decided that 'the fear of letting Russia in (to Asia Minor) outweighed the other considerations': or, as Granville put it after the defeat at Majuba Hill, 'we had to pay some attention to public opinion'.[46]

North Africa—Tunis and Egypt

The third prop of Salisbury's schemes in 1878 for the protection of the Ottoman Empire lay in his ideas for the reform of government in Egypt. British interest in Egypt went back to Nelson's operations against Napoleon in 1798 and certainly, by Palmerston's time, it was fully recognized as a position of great strategic importance across the route to India. But, after the basic check administered to Mehemet Ali in 1840, there had been little attempt to

[45] Ramm I, 448. Doc. 11.
[46] Medlicott, 'The Gladstone Government and the Cyprus Convention', 1880–1885', *J.M.H.* 1940 pp. 186–208.

interfere with the position of financial, cultural and political predominance that the French built up in the fifties and sixties with the Khedive Ismail. Palmerston, it is true, did his best to wreck de Lesseps projects for a Canal; but it was not until well after the completion of this new highway to India in 1869 that a start was made to reverse this trend by Disraeli's purchase of the Khedive's holding of Canal shares in 1875. Even then there was no thought of supplanting the French. Derby made this quite clear to Lyons at the time: it was simply a question of 'preventing an exclusive interest from being established as against us'. There is no reason to suppose that he was simply being ingenuous. Even Disraeli, the foremost exponent of what Derby disgustedly called the 'Occupy, fortify, grab and brag' school of thought, was strongly opposed to taking Egypt in 1876. In his view this was but a minor part of the Eastern Question in which 'Constantinople is the key to India and not Egypt and the Suez Canal'.[47]

Nor was this through any lack of encouragement. Bismarck, Disraeli complained, was constantly 'harping about Egypt': it was quite evidently his purpose from 1876 onwards that England should take it in order to solve the Eastern Question by partition. Nor did the German Chancellor change his mind after the Berlin Congress. At a time when he was urging on France to take Tunis to distract her from the gap in the Vosges, he used equally seductive tactics upon London. It was a German interest, he told Odo Russell, 'that English influence should be greater in Egypt than that of France'.[48] There was even some support for this in the Cabinet. Derby and Disraeli, for opposite reasons, might reject any idea of taking Egypt, but Salisbury at this stage seems to have favoured it. An ardent partitioner in 1876–7, it was only logical that he should suggest some territorial rearrangement 'to provide ourselves with a *pied à terre*, in place of that which we shall infallibly lose at Constantinople'.[49] But the victory of Disraeli's strategy of 're-plastering' Turkey in 1878 meant that any idea that Salisbury had of taking Egypt had to be discarded, for the simple reason that if Turkey was to be protected rather than partitioned then France must not be alienated.

[47] Ramm I, 265; R. Robinson and J. Gallagher, *Africa and the Victorians* (London, 1961) pp. 82–3.

[48] Russell to Salisbury 2 March 1879, in Medlicott, *Bismarck, Gladstone* p. 118. See also *Bismarck and Beaconsfield* pp. 240–1.

[49] To Lytton 9 March 1877 in Cecil II, 130.

As long as this remained the dominant consideration Egypt took second place to the maintenance of the old Crimean alliance since, with Waddington strongly denying any interest in a Russian alliance and assuring Salisbury of French neutrality in the event of a war in the East, it was obviously sensible to do nothing to upset Anglo-French relations. It was true of course that the French problem could have been solved by unleashing Bismarck upon them: and with memories of 1875 there was a lingering suspicion in London that this was the major object of Bismarck's diplomacy in the East: to create a Balkan imbroglio in order to acquire a free hand in the West. But such a solution was completely contrary to British interests. Though Gambetta's hope that the day would dawn when England would be unable to tolerate German predominance in Europe was still but a distant prospect in 1878, it was already a firm conviction that a strong France was a necessary part of the European equilibrium. Salisbury, whose entire sympathies were pro-French and anti-Bismarckian, argued strongly in 1877 that one of the main reasons for keeping Russia from going to war was in order to preserve her as a counterweight upon Germany:

> If it can be done for twelve months more, France's preparations will be sufficiently complete to make a *coup de main* from Berlin impossible. . . .[50]

In many ways this remained the basic difficulty in British policy until 1904: how to live with the fact that France was the major obstacle to British ambitions in Africa yet necessary to prevent complete German hegemony in Europe. It is sufficient comment on the theory that Britain pursued a policy of isolation to state that this was a problem.

It was against this background then, the presuppositions that the strategic interest in Egypt was subordinate to that in Constantinople and that it was essential to maintain Anglo-French understanding, that Salisbury evolved British policy in North Africa from 1878 to 1880. Its main outlines were sketched out in the course of informal conversations with Waddington at Berlin in 1878 and then, to some extent, made explicit in writing afterwards. The basic idea was that England should have Cyprus, France should have Tunis, and that Egypt should be shared

[50] *ibid.* 2 March 1877, p. 129. For his attitude in 1870 see pp. 33–4.

between them. Tunis presented no difficulties: there was no British commercial interest worth mentioning and the strategic importance that Granville dredged up in 1881 in a desperate attempt to stop the French, did not occur to Salisbury. In Tunis, Salisbury told Waddington, 'England was wholly disinterested'. In exchange for recognition of the British 'right to a dominant influence in Western Asia' (by which Salisbury meant the Cyprus Convention), England accepted in Tunis 'the influence which the geographical position of Algeria naturally gave to France'. Though there was no suggestion that France should proceed to annexe Tunis in the confirmatory despatch which Waddington, with great forethought, got out of Salisbury after the Congress, the fact was that Salisbury accepted it. He told Lyons privately at the time that if 'France occupied Tunis tomorrow we should not even remonstrate'; but naturally, in view of Turkish susceptibilities, he was not going to announce this publicly in advance.[51] Even so he gave virtual public recognition to his promises by recalling the British Consul-General, Wood, in 1879 when he became an embarrasment to his relations with Paris. Certainly Waddington had no doubts as to Salisbury's, or Bismarck's, attitude. That he did not proceed to immediate annexation was due to his own internal difficulties, though these were in part caused by the effect that such a move would have upon French relations with Italy.

In Egypt the situation was more complex. The financial default of the Khedive, produced mainly by Ismail's anticipating Keynsian economic policies in a century wedded to the doctrines of Micawber, resulted in the appointment of two European controllers of Egyptian finances in November 1876 to supervise income and expenditure on behalf of a Public Debt Commission. This proving inadequate to satisfy the bondholders, a further enquiry took place; the result of which was a report in August 1878 which utterly condemned the Khedive's personal rule as the source of the Egyptian bankruptcy. Once this was accepted by the British and French governments they turned him into a constitutional monarch and appointed an Englishman and a Frenchman in the key financial positions in his Cabinet. In September 1879, after Ismail had attempted to get rid of foreign control by promulgating a pseudo-democratic constitution of his own devising, he was deposed by Anglo-French pressure on the Sultan.

[51] *ibid.* 332, 333. Docs. 14, 15.

The two financial ministers were now changed into permanent advisers to the new Khedive, Tewfik, with the proviso that they could not be dismissed without the consent of the British and French governments. This represented a fundamental change, since, in effect, provided the Khedive carried out their advice, London and Paris were now ultimately responsible for the government of Egypt, however much they tried to evade the issue. The Control led inexorably to intervention for, as Gladstone later recognized, it

> seemed to put upon us a moral compulsion to *advise* the Khedive in his difficulties. Having thus advised and the advice being taken, we could not abandon him in his difficulties but had to carry him through, *ergo* to make war.[52]

Why did they establish a system which both in London and Paris was afterwards looked upon as a disastrous mistake? Salisbury originally hoped that the French would be satisfied with an English administration as long as it paid the bondholders, but he rapidly abandoned this idea when he discovered his mistake. Though regarding international government as 'worse than Turkish misrule', by July 1878 he was resigned to collaboration with France and told Waddington that he 'disclaimed any intention of establishing an exclusive footing in Egypt' or that he meant to occupy it. But equally he could not permit the French to do so. Since Britain owned 80 per cent of the shipping that went through the Canal, the importance of which as regards India was enhanced by the rapid disintegration of Salisbury's schemes in Asia Minor in 1879, such a move would be far too dangerous. Instead, Ismail's attempts to get rid of Anglo-French influence in 1879 forced them closer together. In September, having collaborated in the appointment of Tewfik, Salisbury and Waddington secretly agreed to exclude any third power from influence in Egypt and warned Tewfik that 'they were prepared to take action to any extent that might be necessary to give effect to their views in this respect'. Though not ready for action in 1879 this was clearly envisaged and once committed to this position it was difficult for either power to break away without sacrificing its Egyptian interests to the other. If the interests of the bondholders were the original motive for Goschen's mission in 1876 from which all this derived,

[52] Ramm I, 473.

by 1879 checking France was the major influence upon British policy.[53]

But in Egypt, in contrast to Tunis, Salisbury was very careful to give no assurances for the future, an attitude which clearly reflected his own feeling that sooner or later British intervention was inevitable. In July 1878 Waddington was told that in the event of the Turkish Empire going entirely to pieces, whilst he could do what he liked with Tunis, 'he must not hold us bound to any promise as to Egypt'. In September, when Waddington again pressed for written assurances, this time in the form of an Anglo-French Convention on Egypt, he was told that this would put the Khedive in an impossible position. The real reason, Salisbury explained to Disraeli, was that whilst parity of influence was necessary at the moment,

> The state of affairs may change and it may suit us at some future period to push ahead; and then any obligatory engagement would be highly inconvenient.

In other words this was a temporary necessity induced by the priority given to propping up the Sultan, and, if, as Salisbury constantly predicted at this time, the Turkish empire were to collapse in the near future, he obviously wanted his hands free to take Egypt. Lacking the troops in 1879—the year of Isandhlwana —to 'act materially against the Khedive', Salisbury was equally unwilling to accept isolated French action: hence his use of the Sultan to depose Ismail.[54] But what evidence there is suggests that this was more a matter of expediency than of principle and that, if faced by Arabi Pasha, Salisbury would have reacted in much the same way as Gladstone and Granville.[55] After 1880 the danger from Russia had largely receded, the Austrian and Turkish alliances were collapsing and the French understanding was no longer so important.

Like his Conservative predecessor Gladstone had every reason to preserve the French *entente*: to him France was important as a Philhellene, an ally in his campaign of harrying the Turks, as well as co-ruler of Egypt. Hence the almost pained surprise with which Granville discovered that the Republican government in Paris had

[53] Cecil II, 323, 330–3; Salisbury to Malet 19 September 1879, copy in B.M. Add. Mss. 44461/43. Doc. 17.
[54] Cecil II, 332–5.
[55] See, for example, Disraeli to the Queen 21 February 1879. Doc. 16.

annexationist ambitions, when this was a trait Gladstone had assumed to be confined to the arch-fiend Disraeli. He was, he told Granville later, 'a little disappointed at not finding in Gambetta any sign that he counts popular principles for anything in the matter'.[56] As Ferry, under pressure from Algerian and French diplomats, who were alarmed at the increasing signs of Italian activity in Tunis, slowly pushed Gambetta towards annexation during 1880–1, in London Granville and Gladstone had to make up their minds what to do. On principle they did not like it. In May 1880 when Freycinet, as a preliminary to annexation, tried to obtain confirmation from London that the Liberals would abide by Salisbury's promises, Granville hedged as far as he decently could. Lacking any appreciation of Salisbury's policy of relieving the barbarians of various parts of the Ottoman Empire, he emphasized heavily that Tunis was not his to give; that he could not answer for Italy; and sent two warships to counter French pressure in a current lawsuit in which a British subject had an interest.[57]

In April 1881, after the French invasion, he wanted to try to bluff them out, though afraid of going to the lengths of collaboration with Italy to do so. He even raised the hare of the dangers of a fortified Bizerta, 'impregnable by ships of war and neutralizing Malta', though in later years the Admiralty argued that Bizerta was of no importance. But Gladstone ruled this out. Unimpressed by the naval argument he was convinced that Disraeli's Cyprus treaty made it impossible to protest on moral grounds, whilst he considered that Salisbury's declaration, 'whatever it may have been, . . . binds us'. In this he showed much sounder sense than Granville who, for all his vague talk of doing something, had no real idea of what he could do and only succeeded in irritating the French unnecessarily. As he told Lyons with unconscious irony when he sent a despatch protesting against the military occupation, 'of course I wish to ruffle her as little as possible . . .'.[58] In that case why ruffle her at all, particularly in view of the increasingly desperate situation in Egypt?

Although, due to Gladstone's firmness, the Tunis affair did not become an Anglo-French dispute, it did bring out a certain degree

[56] Ramm I, 335.
[57] *ibid.* 241. Doc. 18.
[58] *ibid.* 262–4; Temperley and Penson p. 414. Doc. 19.

of suspicion on Granville's part which did not improve the chances of their collaboration in Egypt. Here, by September 1881, the position of the Dual Control was in jeopardy. The military revolt and 'dictatorship of the colonels' led by Arabi Pasha had deprived the Khedive of any real power in the country and ruined his ability to act as tax collector on behalf of the bondholders. If the Control was to mean anything, therefore, there had to be some sort of action to restore the authority of the Khedive, who had got in this mess precisely because he had taken the advice of London and Paris and become, as Freycinet put it, 'un Souverain à la mode anglaise'. But there were two opposing policies. In Paris, Ferry and Gambetta, who emerged from behind the throne to head a government from November 1881 to January 1882, worked steadily towards intervention: a policy culminating in the Gambetta inspired Joint Note of 7 January 1882. This, whatever its defects, had at least the merit of recognizing the logic inherent in the position since 1879 and threatened intervention to support the Khedive. In French eyes this was the more necessary since if Arabi's movement triumphed in Egypt it might produce a wave of Pan-Islamic feeling throughout North Africa, affecting their position in Tunisia and Algeria.[59]

But this was anathema to Gladstone. He had always maintained that Egypt should remain under Turkish rule and was bitterly opposed to any idea of partition, despite his fulminations against Turkish misrule in Europe. If there were to be any departure from the existing order he favoured 'Egypt for the Egyptians', but even this was to be strictly subordinated to the paramount issue of maintaining Turkey, as he explained to Granville in October 1882:

> I am averse to establishing Egyptian Independence on account of the heavy shock it would impart to the general fabric of the Ottoman Empire, about which I have been steadily conservative, I think like you, not from love of it but from dread of the evils of a general scramble for the spoils.[60]

Nor had he, in contrast to Salisbury, Hartington and Northbrook, any concern for the Suez Canal. With the somewhat altruistic idea that the only British concern in India was the well-being of the

[59] Robinson and Gallagher pp. 94–6; E. Malet, *Egypt 1879–1883* (London, 1909) pp. 87, 103, 127, 127–9.
[60] Ramm I, 327, 448.

Indians, he had no sympathy with strategic arguments based on the necessity of shipping out troops quickly in an emergency. Even supposing the Canal were blocked, this did not matter since, he argued, it 'seems to be forgotten by many that there is a route to India round the Cape of Good Hope'.[61]

When to this was added Granville's basic uneasiness and jealousy of French intentions—based partly on intermittent evidence that they were cultivating Arabi—Liberal policy towards Egypt becomes intelligible. Although recognizing, as in the case of Tunis, that their hands were tied by their inheritance from their predecessors of 'the principle of joint action with France in Egyptian affairs', which, to Gladstone, was 'the main matter as far as the affairs of that country are concerned', they did not take this to mean any commitment to intervention. They, like Salisbury, put all the emphasis upon 'moral force' and if anything more than this were needed it should be supplied by the Turks, not by England and France. This Gladstone stated quite clearly in September 1881, when the Egyptian crisis first forced itself upon his attention, and there is nothing to indicate that he ever subsequently changed his mind.[62] Malet, who had the task of interpreting contradictory directives from London, was 'perfectly certain that the Liberal Government did not desire to be obliged to intervene in a military sense in Egypt': to him the reasons why they did so were an enigma, explicable only in terms of 'force of circumstances'.[63] This was precisely the Liberal difficulty. Wedded to the Dual Control through·lack of anything better, all Gladstone's rising doubts against 'England and France mixing so much in the affairs of Egypt'[64] made no difference. Lacking any clear idea of what they did want to do, all they knew was that they did not like the French projects; but out of loyalty to the Dual Control they hesitated to throw them overboard.

Hence they were led from one expedient to another. In October Turkish intervention was dropped because the French disliked it; whilst Granville, heavily prompted by Malet, took the opportunity to write a Blue Book despatch emphasizing the British desire to avoid intervention and to encourage Egypt in the 'full exercise of that liberty which it has obtained under successive Firmans of the

[61] Medlicott, *Bismarck Gladstone* pp. 32–3.　　[62] Ramm I, 290–1. Doc. 20.
[63] Malet pp. 36, 59, 61.
[64] To Granville 4 October 1881, Ramm I, 299.

Sultan'.[65] Nor, as Malet pointed out, had England anything against the Chamber of Notables that Arabi Pasha, influenced by the 'Young Turks', had extracted from the Khedive. On the contrary it was to be encouraged, in the hope that Egypt would be secure 'from the return of arbitrary rule, which wielded by the late Khedive, so nearly brought the country to ruin'.[66] Yet Gladstone's Cabinet agreed to Gambetta's Joint Note of 7 January 1882. This, assuring the Khedive of British and French support 'against all cause of complications, internal or external, which might menace the order of things established in Egypt',[67] meant—if it meant anything—that they would support him against the Notables. Granville apparently did not realize this and took it to mean support only against the Turks, but it quite ruined whatever credit he had acquired in Egypt from the 4 November despatch. He had rushed into it, probably without much thought, because, as he told Gladstone on 15 December, 'we shall be in a scrape, if we are not prepared with any policy'.[68]

This new point of departure was fatal since, all observers agreed, from then onwards Arabi and the Nationalists were convinced that following the French occupation of Tunis they were next on the list: now they determined to overthrow the Dual Control before it overthrew them. Once Arabi came to power on 5 February intervention was really a matter of time unless the Powers were prepared to accept the loss of financial control, and anarchy in Egypt. But as late as 29 May Gladstone assumed that 'we have no alternative but to persevere and urge decisively Turkish action' whilst Freycinet was rebuked 'very sternly' for proposing Anglo-French occupation at this time.[69] The Sultan's offer of a free gift of Egypt to England on 25 June was rejected without even bothering to refer it to the Cabinet. Instead Gladstone now embarked on a new panacea—reference to the Concert —and was not now prepared to do *anything*, either alone or with France, 'apart from any reference to the authority of Europe'. This, he thought, offered the ideal solution since, even if the Sultan declined to act as a European mandatory in one of his own

[65] Granville to Malet 4 November 1881 in Malet p. 198.
[66] Malet to Granville 26 December 1887, *ibid.* p. 211.
[67] *ibid.* p. 218.
[68] Ramm I, 320, 328. For Cabinet opinions see Robinson and Gallagher pp. 96–7. Doc. 21.
[69] Ramm I, 375; Malet pp. 243–63.

provinces and to uphold a constitution he detested, the Concert would 'provide for or sanction a military intervention other than Turkish under their authority'.[70]

This enabled him to procrastinate indefinitely—to the fury of Hartington and Northbrook who wanted action—by insisting on the need for 'reference to Europe', until it finally became obvious, as it had been to Dufferin all along, that the Conference would never decide anything. Left to his own devices, Gladstone would still have done nothing: fully absorbed at home, he resented anything which distracted Parliament from an 'undivided attention to . . . the establishment of peace and order in Ireland'. But, as the power of Arabi and the Nationalists increased, Hartington and Northbrook, to whom the security of the Canal was the paramount consideration, insisted on action to the point of resignation and gradually won over Granville. The bombardment of Alexandria followed swiftly, on 10 July, but the decision to intervene militarily to protect the Canal was not arrived at until the 24th. As late as the 22nd Gladstone thought sole action 'still remote', but Granville by now expected it if joint action fell through. As it became apparent on the 23rd that Freycinet would not co-operate, an invitation was issued to Italy, the assumption still being that England was acting in the name of the Concert. Not until 25 August when sole action was well under way, after the collapse of the French government with Freycinet's defeat in the Chamber on 29 July, did Gladstone perceive the possible advantages to be derived from it, notably the end of the Dual Control which had got him into this mess.[71]

In attempting to understand this sudden abandonment in the month of July 1882 of all that Gladstone and Granville had professed since September 1881, two considerations stand out. In the first place, right up until the last minute Gladstone assumed he was acting in the name of the Concert. Once he had accepted that intervention of some sort was necessary, it was a comparatively easy transition from the refusal of the Turks to accept the mandate of the Constantinople Conference on 6 July, to substituting England and France or Italy. This, to his mind, was different from the Anglo-French intervention envisaged by Gambetta in the name of the Dual Control, which Granville had so deplored in

[70] Ramm I, 380–1; Malet p. 273. Doc. 22.
[71] Ramm I, 386, 401–3, 411. Docs. 23, 24.

February. Nor was it unreasonable of him to suppose that France or Italy would join him. The whole burden of French policy for the previous twelve months had been to urge Anglo-French intervention: Freycinet had temporarily receded from it in February after Gambetta's defeat on this issue but had taken it up again by May. Nor is there much doubt that this was the policy Freycinet advocated in July: even the French Chamber initially accepted intervention to protect the Canal on the 19th and their complete *volte-face* on the 29th was totally unexpected.

The case of Italy was very similar. Since 1879 Rome had been stressing her great interest in Egypt and her desire to turn the dual into a triple control: Mancini had made specific suggestions to this effect in 1881 and Menabrea, the Italian ambassador in London, had offered her assistance as recently as 16 May 1882.[72] Hence Mancini's refusal on 29 July was as unexpected as that of Freycinet and the fact that Gladstone consequently found himself sole occupier of Egypt was an unfortunate accident. It had certainly not been his intention and had come about more by the indirect influence of Bismarck than anything else. For, although Bismarck at no time made his opposition to French or Italian intervention apparent, he certainly managed to convey this impression. From 1876 he had been encouraging London to take Egypt and, viewed against the background of his determination to destroy any English dominated system of alliances or Concert of Europe, his attitude in 1882 made sense. By opposing any European mandate to the Turks and discouraging France and Italy he finally destroyed the Concert and pushed England into an isolated position, which he exploited for years afterwards. This sense of conscious direction of German policy *may* have been due to others' reading into it a consistency which it did not possess, but it seems unlikely. Certainly Robilant, the most penetrating interpreter of the oracle that Italy possessed, had no doubt that this was Bismarck's object and viewed any Italian departure from the safe haven of the Triple Alliance in England's company as potentially disastrous.[73]

The second factor that really determined Gladstone's intervention in Egypt was the Cabinet revolt. Hartington, by June, had become increasingly restive under Granville's technique of

[72] G. Talamo, 'Il mancato intervento in Egitto', *R.S.R.* 1958 pp. 420–1, 431–3.
[73] *ibid.* pp. 434–8.

deluging his colleagues with telegrams but avoiding discussion of Egyptian affairs in Cabinet. He wanted some action; whether Turkish, Anglo-French or British was a matter of indifference to him. The essential, to the mind of the Secretary of State for India, was to protect the Suez Canal from Arabi's potential for destruction and unless this were done, he told Granville on 19 June, he would resign. As leader of the Whigs, Hartington alone was a considerable political force and his position was made impregnable by the support of the Radicals, Dilke and Chamberlain. They, convinced by June that Arabi had ceased to represent the progressive movement in Egypt and had become simply a military dictator, now voted for his suppression in the name of freeing Egypt from his and foreign control.[74] Since the only alternative, which Freycinet in fact suggested at this point, of reaching an understanding with Arabi was ruled out by this move and 'our obligation to respect the just claims of the Khedive', Gladstone had to bow to the Cabinet majority. Hence the instruction on 3 July to Admiral Seymour to destroy the fortifications at Alexandria:[75] this it was hoped would somehow overthrow Arabi, but instead real danger to the Canal from Arabi's forces now rapidly materialized.

After this Gladstone was on the slippery slope. He did not personally believe in any danger to the Canal and kept voicing his objections to sole British intervention; but, gradually deserted even by Granville, he was now 'willing to defer to your decision and judgments'.[76] In all probability, the point which weighed with him was the necessity of keeping the administration in being to enable it to deal with Ireland: if he were to join Bright in resignation then her wrongs would never be righted. Hence much as he had deplored on 5 July anything which would distract Parliament from an undivided attention to matters immediately connected with the establishment of peace and order in Ireland, and denied any British 'separate right' to protect the Canal, expediency demanded that the administration should not break up over Egypt.[77] The Cabinet majority wanted a military expedition and the 'Mahdi of Midlothian' accepted their judgment, much as he kicked himself for it in later years. His only consolation was that,

[74] Robinson and Gallagher pp. 106–7, 110.
[75] Gladstone to the Queen 2, 3, July 1882, Cab 41/16/32, 33. Doc. 23.
[76] Gladstone to Granville 9 July, Ramm I, 388.　　　　　　　[77] *ibid.* 386.

as he told the House of Commons on 24 July, it would bring the 'blessings of civilized life' and the 'reign of law' to this Moslem world:[78] much the same idea as Salisbury had for Asia Minor.

Gladstone's conquest of Egypt with Wolseley's defeat of Arabi Pasha at Tel-el-Kebir in September, closed what still remained of the last gap between Conservative and Liberal foreign policy in the Near East. In his pursuit of the Concert of Europe during the previous two years Gladstone had tried to develop an alternative foreign policy along the lines of permanent diplomacy by conference, an offshoot of his conviction that 'the Almighty has employed me for His purposes' and given him a directive to right the wrongs perpetrated by Disraeli.[79] But, in practice, it had only worked at all because it suited Bismarck and to some extent Giers at the time, not because they shared Gladstone's convictions. It was evident once the Three Emperors' Alliance had been concluded that the Concert was dead and its failure over Egypt was but a final demonstration of this. Afterwards, when the Liberal government 'had discovered that it possessed no heaven-sent prescription for a Concert of Europe',[80] its policy became indistinguishable from that of the Conservatives, except for the degree of incompetence in its direction under Granville. With the appointment of Rosebery as Liberal Foreign Secretary in 1886 even this difference was removed and from then onwards, as Labouchere was wont to complain, Salisbury's foreign policy was carried out whether or not he was in office. This trend was well demonstrated from 1882 to 1885 as, first in Africa then in Central Asia, the Liberals reaped what they had sown.

[78] See the excellent analysis in Robinson and Gallagher pp. 111–21. For contemporary criticism of Gladstone, of which 'Mahdi of Midlothian' was amongst the mildest, see Medlicott, *Bismarck, Gladstone* pp. 316–17.

[79] *ibid.* p. 1.

[80] *ibid.* p. 319.

III

The Egyptian Lever

O for the day when we shall escape from the consequences of the original folly there.

Gladstone, 1885

The Evacuation of Egypt

Nothing is more clearly attested than Gladstone's firm determination to evacuate Egypt at the earliest possible opportunity, a
policy first enunciated two days after the battle of Tel-el-Kebir,
followed a week later by a timetable for the operation, the first
part of which had actually been carried out within a month.[1]
There was no reason to suppose in September 1882 that the Egyptian expedition would be any different from that to Abyssinia in
1867, which had been completed within twelve months. When
Gladstone said 'rescue and retire' he meant it. Yet, in fact, this
punitive expedition turned gradually, accompanied at each stage
by repetition of the intention to withdraw—a French critic
counted sixty-six such declarations in forty years[2]—into permanent occupation; and the Khedivate, which Gladstone purported
to strengthen, became little more than a pale reflection of Sir
Evelyn Baring. Why? Was this just another example of Gladstone's humbug?[3] was it, as the French became convinced,
simply *perfide Albion* betraying the *entente* for the pursuit of her
own strategic interests? or was it simply that Gladstone was sub-
merged by the tide of events?

Strategic considerations were obviously of some importance,
but they were far from being predominant. Certainly the Queen

[1] Ramm I, 421, 429. Doc. 27.

[2] W. L. Langer, *European Alliances and Alignments* (2nd. ed. New York, 1950)
p. 281.

[3] Wolseley referred to him in 1885 as 'that old crocodile'; M. Shibeika, *British
Policy in the Sudan, 1882–1902* (London, 1952) p. 303.

regarded the events of 1882 as a heaven-sent opportunity for 'securing to ourselves such a position in Egypt as to secure our Indian Dominions and to maintain our superiority in the East'.[4] Similarly Hartington (and Northbrook), even in the mounting chaos of 1884, thought the security of the route to India of such paramount importance that they opposed immediate evacuation, despite the dire domestic and foreign consequences.[5] But it is misleading to take this as representative of Cabinet policy. Gladstone himself thought the only British interest the Canal but, paradoxically, to his mind this was an argument for early evacuation. Gladstone's principal idea after Tel-el-Kebir was to squeeze the French out of the Dual Control, not in order to slip into their place but in the name of 'freedom and self-development, as far as may be, for Egypt'. Since the Control in his view had been responsible for the necessity of intervention it was only logical, if evacuation were to be carried out, for the Control to be first demolished, thus averting any compulsion to intervene in the future.[6] This idea was taken further by the Radicals. If Egyptian institutions were built up and the Canal problem solved by reducing French influence in the Company and a new international guarantee of free passage, then, thought Dilke and Chamberlain, the 'moral tutelage' that Britain would gain in Egypt would suffice and troops could speedily be withdrawn. This idea, which may have owed something to Gladstone's Italian experiences, was clearly enunciated in 1882 as 'Egypt for the Egyptians ... the only good solution of the Egyptian question'.[7]

But what the Cabinet overlooked in its determination to eliminate French influence as a preliminary to evacuation was that the very break with France which it light-heartedly promoted turned out to be one of the most serious obstacles to the reconstruction and evacuation of Egypt. At the time it assumed France to be impotent and, as Tissot mournfully reported in November 1882,

L'Angleterre ne marchande pas les conditions d'une entente dont elle croit pouvoir se passer. Elle ne cherche pas une rupture de parti pris, elle la redoute encore moins.[8]

[4] The Queen to Harcourt 18 September 1882, cited in Robinson and Gallagher p. 123.   [5] *ibid.* p. 143.
[6] Ramm I, 327, 441, 473. Docs. 25, 26, 27.
[7] Robinson and Gallagher pp. 123–5.   [8] D.D.F. iv. p. 530, note 4.

This was short-sighted. Lyons at the time warned Granville that it was dangerous to infuriate the French and simultaneously withdraw troops from Egypt: the Whigs, sceptical of the results of Radical ideas of a self-governing Egypt, thought this could only end in French control.[9] They may have been right but Radical ideas were never put to the test since the whole concept of self-government foundered at birth on the twin difficulties of the Sudan and Egyptian finance. Once these forced Gladstone and Granville to seek international agreement to the revision of Egypt's public obligations, the French bargaining position rapidly improved and, as Gladstone regretfully acknowledged, 'I think our position extremely weak, and France, in default of her good-will, far more in a condition to break off, than we are'.[10]

The problem of the Sudan had been brewing for years before it forced itself upon the attention of Gladstone's Cabinet, with the result that when they did at last recognize its extensive implications, it was too late to do anything about it. Essentially Khedive Ismail's conquest of the Sudan over-extended Egypt's resources, especially since it involved him in an expensive war with Abyssinia at the same time. By 1877 the Khedival treasury was on the verge of bankruptcy and his desperate economy measures—stopping the payment of all state employees in the Sudan—allied with the attempted suppression of the slave trade, the only compensation that Egyptian officials could see in Sudanese service, alienated both the rulers and the ruled alike. Since, in addition, the 40,000 troops who held down the Sudan were in scattered garrisons and consisted for the most part of unwilling, conscripted, fellaheen, whose 'first prayer was water, and their second, to be saved from being sent to the Sudan',[11] it may be appreciated that the Egyptian hold was a slender one, needing little to overthrow it. It only needed the religious fanaticism of the outbreak of the Mahdia, at a time when Egyptian attention was absorbed by the Arabist movement and the conflict with the Dual Control, for the authority of the Khedive to collapse completely outside Khartoum, as it did by September 1882.[12]

But, until the news of the massacre of Hicks Pasha's army

[9] Robinson and Gallagher pp. 126-7.
[10] Gladstone to Granville 3 June 1884, Ramm II, 198. Doc. 29.
[11] Cross to Granville 29 December 1883 quoted in Shibeika p. 131.
[12] P. M. Holt, *The Mahdist State in the Sudan, 1881-98* (Oxford, 1958) pp. 29-33.

reached London in November 1883, the implications of this situation for Liberal policy in Egypt were not appreciated. To the extent that the revolution in the Sudan had been an object of consideration since September 1882, it was thought of as 'a private matter to be suppressed by the Khedive'. Repression, in London, was vaguely thought of as beneficial, since it would reopen trading relations with the equatorial provinces and make possible a new drive against the slave trade. But this was in a minor key: the main point was that this was Egypt's affair and that London should not interfere, as long as there was no likelihood of repression affecting Egyptian finances. Hence the stupor produced by the defeat of Hicks: there had been nothing like it, thought one minister, 'since Pharaoh's host perished in the Red Sea'. Now that Egypt's last effective army had gone the Khedive's ministers cast around for British or Turkish assistance, which in turn, Baring pointed out, made it difficult for him to maintain an attitude of strict reserve on the question as he had been instructed.

This state of affairs gradually brought about a complete *volte face* in Liberal policy towards Egypt. Once more Gladstone found himself in a position in which he had to give advice and, having given it, he could not evade responsibility for the consequences. Disliking equally the employment of either British or Turkish troops, except, characteristically, for the defence of Suakin to protect the route to India, the Cabinet came to the conclusion that it would prefer the abandonment of the Sudan. Clearly Egypt could not pay the cost of extensive operations and certainly neither England nor Turkey was going to do so. Hence the decision to 'recommend' the withdrawal of Egyptian troops coupled with a guarantee that England would defend the frontier.[13] Becoming protectors of Egypt, as Northbrook complained, meant of course that the policy of withdrawal had to be at least temporarily abandoned. The Khedive now requested that the British garrison should not be withdrawn from Cairo to Alexandria as had been intended, lest it should encourage a new wave of religious fanaticism similar to that in the Sudan: Baring even recommended sending reinforcements from England to hold Wadi-Halfa. To make matters worse, it seemed probable that no

[13] Granville's appreciation of the situation ran: 'It takes away somewhat of the position of a man if he has to sell his racers and hunters, but if he cannot afford to keep them, the sooner they go to Tattersalls the better.' Quoted in Shibeika p. 130.

Egyptian minister would remain in office to enforce the abandonment of the Sudan, so that direct British rule would have to be imposed, extending the occupation for five to ten years. This, with the prospect that 'bastinadoed fellaheen would be reported to Parliament at the rate of a hundred cases a week' naturally appalled Gladstone; the occupation was unpopular enough with the Radical wing of the Liberal party as it was; direct administration, as Northbrook now advocated, would wreck the party completely.[14]

Although the latter nightmare did not arise since, when Sharif resigned, as Baring had anticipated, Nubar Pasha agreed to take office on the basis of the British recommendations, Gladstone soon had another cross to bear. The decision to send Gordon to the Sudan on 18 January 1884 proved to be the last nail in the Liberal coffin. It was taken largely as the result of press agitation, led by the *Pall Mall Gazette*, in the hope that this action would appease at least the anti-slavery group amongst the government's critics, and to get out of the tangle Granville and Hartington had got into over Gordon's employment by Leopold in the Congo; sending him to the Sudan killed two birds with one stone.[15] But the object of this mission, ostensibly a fact-finding tour to 'collect information and report on the situation in the Sudan',[16] was ambiguous from the start, since Gordon quickly arrogated to himself the position of adviser to the Cabinet. Hartington noted on 15 January that Gordon might ask the Government to appoint him Governor-General of the Sudan, and Gordon's own views were clear enough from the *Pall Mall Gazette* interview published on 9 January and his letter in *The Times* of 14 January. Despite this the Cabinet proceeded with his appointment, trying however to bind him with strict instructions. But Gordon was unpredictable. As Baring pointed out, 'a man who habitually consults the prophet Isaiah when he is in a difficulty' was unlikely to obey instructions, a suggestion that was well borne out by the amplifications that Gordon began to give his mission as soon as the train steamed out of Charing Cross. This difficulty, at least in part, had been foreseen by Gladstone, who wanted it to be made clear that Gordon was

[14] Ramm II, 145, Robinson and Gallagher pp. 133-5.
[15] See Shibeika pp. 146-54; *History of 'The Times'* III, 24-6 stresses Gordon's enormous popular reputation.
[16] Dilke's record of the Cabinet Committee instructions to Gordon on 18 January, Shibeika p. 156.

'not our agent for the purpose of advising on that point': but this was far from clear to the public.[17]

For, whatever the Cabinet intended, once Gordon reached Khartoum the combination of changed local circumstances and his sense of commitment to the entire Egyptian personnel made evacuation impossible on any other basis than that of sending a large scale relief expedition composed of British troops. To this Gladstone, despite pressure from Hartington, was inexorably opposed, as were Harcourt and the Radicals. Gladstone was convinced that Gordon was quite capable of getting out if he wanted to, that the major danger was 'that they were not about to become the slaves of Gordon's (probably) rebellious ideas'. By September he was convinced that Gordon had gone mad: 'I called him at the outset inspired and mad, but madness is now uppermost.' Chamberlain, who shared Harcourt's views, thought the whole business a deep laid scheme of Hartington's to commit the government to the reconquest of the Sudan and so perpetuate the occupation of Egypt. With Selborne and Hartington threatening to resign on the one hand and Harcourt on the other, Sudan policy threatened to bring down the Government, as Gladstone put it with feeling on 1 August 1884,

at a moment when we have already on our hands a domestic crisis of the first class likely to last for months, and a foreign crisis of the first class, morally certain however to be decided or developed in a few days.[18]

The 'foreign crisis of the first class' which beset the government by the summer of 1884 derived from the perpetual problem of Egyptian finance. By the end of 1883 the finances of Egypt showed a current deficit of £1 million in a total budget of £8 million. There was worse to come. In a memorandum of 2 April 1884 Gladstone set out the problem. The attempts to hold the Sudan and especially the Hicks disaster had cost £2½ million yet, on top of this, Egypt was now called upon to pay £4 million indemnity for the damage to property in Alexandria in 1882. This could only be met by some change in the law of liquidation, or an Egyptian loan guaranteed either by the Powers or by Britain. The first proposition meant braving a European conference, with the

[17] Shibeika pp. 154, 160–3; Ramm II, 149–50. Docs. 38, 39.
[18] Shibeika pp. 276, 280; Robinson and Gallagher, p. 141; Ramm II, 221.

57

French in a strong position, as Gladstone acknowledged on 3 June:

> I think our position extremely weak, and France, in default of her goodwill, far more in a condition to break off than we are; having nothing but her indemnity men to deal with, while we are and shall be pressed by the first and daily necessities of government in Egypt, a very different matter.

This seemed bad enough, but the alternative was even worse. As Baring put it, in a nutshell, 'who is to be sacrificed, the bondholder or the English taxpayer?' The last thing Gladstone could afford to do by the summer of 1884, given his parliamentary position, was to risk a repetition of the Egyptian debates in February and March, in which the government majority slumped disastrously. It was clear from these that opinion in the House of Commons ran strongly against any further involvement in the affairs of Egypt and that any proposal to the House that they should guarantee the Egyptian debt would be an invitation to suicide for the Liberal Administration: better by far to seek a deal with the French, which Gladstone, characteristically, rationalized as 'it is all in the sense of giving back to Europe what had been held exclusively'.[19]

But this Conference, which met in London on 28 June, proved a complete fiasco. Once the Cabinet decision to try a conference was taken on 2 April Granville tried beforehand to reach agreement with Ferry, on the basis of an agreed timetable for the evacuation of Egypt in return for support of the British financial proposals, but this all came to nothing. Ferry at one stage in May offered to neutralize Egypt in exchange for a British guarantee to evacuate within two years, a term which in the haggling that ensued was extended to three and a half, unless 'the powers consider it desirable to prolong the occupation'. It was evident that there would be considerable pressure from the Opposition against these terms and the tendency of the Radicals to join with the Conservatives, on the grounds that Egypt was being handed over to France (what Gladstone called 'Forsterism'), would need watching. But Gladstone himself welcomed Ferry's proposals as 'the most liberal offers ever made' and was evidently prepared to

[19] Ramm II, 175, 186, 198, 204; Robinson and Gallagher pp. 137, 140. Docs. 30, 31.

conclude on this basis, as was a majority of the Cabinet. The difficulty arose when Granville tried to tie up the financial proposals as part of the package deal. French objections to British presidency over the *Caisse*, terms which Gladstone thought the House would insist on, meant that Ferry would not agree to commit himself wholeheartedly to Britain before the opening of the Conference. With overtures from Bismarck for Franco-German collaboration against Britain pouring in every day, Ferry preferred to exploit this new situation and, when the Conference opened, took the lead in attacking the British proposals. Finding himself supported only by Italy, Granville had no choice but to adjourn the Conference on its first day, with the result that a solution to the Egyptian problem was as far off as ever.[20]

Throughout the summer and autumn of 1884 a solution along European lines seemed blocked. Correctly identifying the source of the trouble in Bismarck's determination to wreck the conference and Ferry's negotiations with Berlin, Gladstone and Granville were yet baffled as to the basic *cause* of this. It was obvious that, despite this setback, as Gladstone and Northbrook agreed, 'unless an understanding can be had with France there is little or no chance of any understanding at all'.[21] Equally, with the evidence of Bismarck's displeasure mounting with his outbursts over Angra Pequena, it was evident that something would have to be done to improve Anglo-German relations. But, since Granville could not understand what was wrong with them in the first place, barring Ampthill's guesses, British policy was reduced to writing private letters to Herbert Bismarck and trying to tap somebody in Ferry's Cabinet, in the vague hope that this would provide a solution.[22] For as long as Bismarck was intent on his colonial *entente* with France, an *entente* which seemed to be cemented by their joint stand on the Congo question in the Autumn, a European solution to the Egyptian question was ruled out: it was only when this *entente* broke down after Bismarck's colonial aspirations had been satisfied that the settlement of Egypt began to move again.

[20] Ramm II, 189, 193, 195, 210–12.
[21] *ibid*. 219, 237–8, 240.
[22] 'Ampthill seemed to know little about the matter–but he is probably right as to the row being very much an electioneering matter.' Granville to Gladstone 18 August 1884, Ramm II, 230, 238.

The Egyptian Lever

Gladstone and Bismarck: the Congo Dispute

The origin of the Anglo-German estrangement which ruined Granville's Egyptian Conference during June–August 1884 lay in colonial disputes, primarily over West Africa. Originating in Angra Pequena—soon to become part of German South West Africa—the dispute spread to the Congo and, from the general onslaught on the colonial front which ensued between August and December 1884, Bismarck emerged victorious with not only South West Africa but also the Cameroons, Togoland, New Guinea and German East Africa. The results are clear enough but the reasons for this conflict are much more open to dispute. Briefly there are three main explanations offered for this new departure on Bismarck's part. Firstly, that it was 'pure' diplomacy in the traditional manner, the object being to draw France into the German alliance network;[23] secondly, that it was accidental, the product of Bismarck's pique over Angra Pequena and Granville's misunderstandings;[24] thirdly, that Bismarck launched his colonial policy 'largely for reasons of domestic policy'.[25] Whilst there is some compatibility between the second and third view, the first clearly stands alone. This controversy is of some importance from the point of view of British policy, since the criticism that can be made of Granville's actions varies according to the interpretation that is adopted of Bismarck's intentions. For example, if it is accepted that his object was to use colonial disputes with Britain to promote an understanding with France then most of the criticism of Granville's ineptness is irrelevant: on the other hand, if the second thesis is accepted, then Granville in particular and the Liberal Government in general had only themselves to blame for what followed.

The Angra Pequena dispute blew up on 7 June 1884 when Munster protested to Granville at the action of the Cape government in announcing the annexation of this spot on 29 May, when

[23] 'Bismarck quarrelled with England in order to draw closer to France.' A. J. P. Taylor, *Germany's First Bid for Colonies* (London, 1937) p. 6, a view repeated in *The Struggle for Mastery in Europe* (Oxford, 1954) pp. 292–8.

[24] 'Fundamental misunderstandings arose—whose immediate cause was accidental, but whose deeper origin must be sought in the British Government's ignorance of the real nature of Bismarck's intentions.' S. E. Crowe, *The Berlin West Africa Conference* (London, 1942) p. 39.

[25] W. O. Aydelotte, *Bismarck and British Colonial Policy* (Philadelphia, 1937) p. 18, a view supported by E. Eyck, *Bismarck and the German Empire* (London, 1950) pp. 273–5.

Bismarck had already announced that it was under the protection of the German Empire on 24 April. On Bismarck's instructions, Munster now threatened a complete reversal of the existing German policy of support for Britain in Egypt unless her demands were satisfied, a threat repeated by Herbert Bismarck in an interview with Granville on 14 June. According to Granville this was the first that he had heard of Bismarck's wish to annex Angra Pequena. Despite the fact that there had been a series of German enquiries since February 1883—the last of which he left unanswered for six months—he had assumed it was a matter of no importance and that what Bismarck really wanted was for the Cape to annex it and provide protection for Luderitz, the German trader principally involved. This was why he had left it to Derby and the Colonial Office to settle in a leisurely exchange with Cape Town. Ludicrous as this may seem there were in fact sound reasons for this assumption. All Bismarck's utterances until 24 April 1884 were to this effect and both Ampthill in Berlin and Munster in London still assumed this to be true in June. The famous 5 May dispatch, which in January 1885 Bismarck said had posed a clear alternative of either accepting German colonial demands as the basis of a general Anglo-German understanding or facing hostility in Egypt, was not presented to Granville: and Bismarck could hardly complain if Munster 'bungled the matter completely' when he deliberately kept him in the dark as to what he did want.[26] If it is true, as Crowe suggests, that even Bismarck himself was none too sure of his own intentions, that 'he made up his mind to events as they went along',[27] it is not really surprising that Granville was completely baffled by the whole affair and, even in August, could still think it 'possible that Heligoland is at the bottom of it'.[28]

Nevertheless, despite Granville's own high-mindedness in his conversations with Herbert Bismarck (he 'objected to anything in the nature of a bargain between us. Each question should be discussed on its own merits')[29] the Cabinet's reaction to the discovery of a dispute with Germany which threatened to wreck their hopes of an Egyptian settlement was swift. Harcourt, in his usual

[26] Aydelotte 26–43, 51–71, 90–3.
[27] Crowe p. 39: 'It is impossible to exonerate Bismarck from the charge of a certain duplicity in the whole affair.' Docs. 36. 37.
[28] Ramm II, 230, 249.
[29] Herbert Bismarck, quoted in Aydelotte p. 93.

way, was apoplectic at the news—apparently conveyed to him for the first time by Herbert Bismarck—that Derby had annexed something, whilst the Cabinet, as Dilke drily noted, 'decided that Bismarck, who was greatly irritated with the Government, was to have all he wanted'.[30] But much to Granville's surprise even this failed to appease Bismarck's wrath. In the first place it became apparent that French opposition on the subject of Egypt was now based upon an understanding with Germany and, since no progress could be made, the Conference was finally abandoned on 14 August. Secondly, with the Reichstag elections approaching, Anglo-German relations grew worse as Bismarck, deliberately working up colonial questions for electoral purposes, discovered a new dispute in New Guinea and protested violently against Derby's action in allowing the annexation of as much of the hinterland of Angra Pequena as the Cape Government could lay its hands on. But worse was yet to come when, as the Franco-German understanding at last matured, Bismarck launched his offensive on yet a third front—that of the Congo.[31]

There is no reason to believe that Bismarck had any more real interest in the Congo than in the other colonial questions that he took up in 1884: the point was that this offered an excellent terrain for co-operation with France against Britain. Not that Bismarck wanted to push matters to a complete break with London: on the contrary for all his talk at this time of a 'League of Neutrals' he completely excluded any question of war.[32] It was not Bismarck's purpose to alienate Britain, only, as Herbert gracefully put it, 'to squash Gladstone against the wall, so that he can yap no more'. If Gladstone, Liberalism, and parliamentary government could be so completely discredited by means of this colonial quarrel, then so much the better:

> He (Gladstone) must be driven *ad absurdum* in the general interest, but first he must ride the English deeper into the mire so that his prestige will vanish even among the masses of the stupid English electorate.[33]

Bismarck's gains from this were obvious. In the first place it would

---

[30] Dilke note of Cabinet meeting of 21 June, *ibid.* p. 97.
[31] Aydelotte 114–24, Crowe 60–1.
[32] G.P. iii. nos. 680, 693.
[33] Herbert Bismarck to Holstein 3 September 1884, N. Rich and M. H. Fisher, *The Holstein Papers* (London, 1959–63) III, 131. See also p. 130.

ruin the reputation of Liberalism in Germany and eliminate for ever the danger, real enough for Bismarck at the time, of 'English influence' at Potsdam—colonial policy was essential for this 'because it was popular and conveniently adapted to bring us into conflict with England at any given moment'.[34] But there was more to it than this. Getting rid of Gladstone would admirably serve Germany's European interests. When Bismarck declared Gladstone incompetent he was not feeling sorry for Britain but for Germany: Gladstone's Russophilism was as much a nuisance to Bismarck as his moral approach to European politics was incomprehensible.[35] Courcel sensed something of this from the beginning of the tirades against Gladstone to which the French were constantly treated in 1884:

> Making due allowances for the antipathy which Prince Bismarck has long professed for the leader of the English Liberal Party, one can believe that this sortie was calculated to make me understand that Gladstone's policy would receive no support from Germany and that we had nothing to fear from antagonising England. But what is perhaps true of Gladstone's policy would no doubt be untrue of that of the Conservative or co-alition Cabinet which would succeed him.[36]

Bismarck himself bore this out: according to Eckardstein he frequently made the remark in private that 'the friendship of Lord Salisbury is worth more to me than twenty marshy colonies in Africa'.[37] This seems inherently probable. That he was trying to get rid of Gladstone and to bring back Salisbury has at least the merit that it makes sense of his sudden immense interest in colonial matters in 1884–5 and his comparative, though not entire, neglect of them afterwards.

By September 1884 the Franco-German front on the Congo question had been created and all that remained, Bismarck thought, was to use this to beat Gladstone and Granville to their knees. Since in fact the Berlin West Africa Conference that followed from 15 November to 26 February turned out to be a major success for British policy, it is clear that something went wrong with Bismarck's programme. The question is, what? The answer would

[34] Herbert Bismarck to Schweinitz in March 1890 cited in Eyck p. 275.
[35] Bismarck thought Gladstone the most incompetent English minister since Lord North: Medlicott, *Bismarck, Gladstone* pp. 34, 160.
[36] Courcel to Ferry 25 April 1884; D.D.F. v. no 247: See also no. 227.
[37] No date, cited in Aydelotte p. 21.

seem to be that Bismarck did not understand sufficient of the background to the Congo question.[38] When in June 1884 he had first sought French co-operation in a stand against the Anglo-Portuguese Congo Treaty and announced his refusal to recognize it, he had assumed that France and Germany had a common interest in this question. But, in fact, this was untrue, as emerged clearly enough from his negotiations with Courcel in August. The French had no liking for Bismarck's ideas of 'reciprocal free trade in the territories which either power occupied on the West Coast of Africa', and took the view that they would have to be well paid elsewhere to adopt this suggestion, principally in Egypt.[39] Since in fact Bismarck did not intend to pay their price in Egypt, the alliance was founded upon an equivocation from the start.

The German idea was much more that the French should expose themselves over Egypt with tacit German support in order to drive home to the British where their true interests lay, an intention made quite explicit in the Holstein correspondence: 'we will only gain England's goodwill—albeit a goodwill accompanied by gnashing of teeth—by way of an alliance with France.'[40] Not surprisingly in these circumstances the French were increasingly doubtful of the advantages to be gained from collaboration with Bismarck. Ferry, even in August, had no desire that the Conference should be used as 'a war machine against England' whilst Courcel, by December, had serious doubts as to where this policy was leading them. It was very noticeable that, despite Bismarck's airy talk of a vast Paris Conference on Egypt, nothing had yet materialized:

> Je veux bien qu'il incline pour nous: mais il faudra le payer, et, si nous le marchandons, nous verrons bien vite surgir de difficultés auxquelles nous ne pensions pas.[41]

Against this background of cross purposes and mutual recriminations the *entente* began to crumble as soon as it was exposed to the

[38] This is Crowe's view: 'Bismarck was a great European but not a great Colonial statesman.' Crowe pp. 192–4.
[39] Courcel to Ferry 17 August 1884; D.D.F. v. no. 372.
[40] Wilhelm von Bismarck to Holstein 1 September 1884. *The Holstein Papers* III, 130.
[41] Memo by Ferry 22 August; Courcel to Ferry 3 December 1884; D.D.F. v. nos. 376, 475.

harsh reality of detailed negotiation at the Berlin Conference. As Bismarck gradually discovered that, far from using the French, they were using him, he soon found himself in the position 'where in order to save his policy he had to completely reverse its trend'. It is this which explains Granville's unexpected 'diplomatic triumph'.[42]

The essence of the situation in the Congo—and for that matter generally in West Africa—lay in the fact that the Liberal Cabinet in London did not wish to annex any more territory. This Bismarck never understood: a prisoner of his own propaganda over Angra Pequena, he came to believe that British colonial acquisitiveness was the main enemy to his current programme. (Of course to some extent it *had* to be if Bismarck's object was to be fulfilled.) But in fact this assumption was wide of the mark. Up to December 1882 all projects from colonial governors or ambitious diplomats foundered on the simple objection voiced by Kimberley to further annexations in West Africa: 'The coast is pestilential; the natives are numerous and unmanageable.'[43] For years Morier, at Lisbon, had urged the veiled annexation of the coastline of the Congo by means of the Portuguese, but completely without effect. Partly this was a question of preferring to deal direct with the native chiefs,[44] but largely it was sheer 'Tenterdenism', what Disraeli once called a fixed resolve to do nothing. That Granville, suddenly, on 15 December 1882, embarked upon Morier's plan by recognizing Portuguese claims to the Congo was due to a change of circumstance, the French ratification on 30 November of de Brazza's treaties with the chiefs at Stanley Pool. British policy in the Congo, as in West Africa generally, was to maintain freedom of trade: French policy, on the contrary, was highly protectionist. Hence the erection of Portugal 'as the watchdog of Free trade'.[45]

This object emerged quite clearly in the agreement with Portugal which was finally signed on 26 February 1884 since it provided that in the newly recognized Portuguese territories Britain was to obtain most favoured nation tariff treatment. From the British point of view this was the ideal arrangement since the Portuguese

[42] Crowe p. 194.
[43] Kimberley 6 April 1882, quoted in Robinson and Gallagher p. 165.
[44] e.g. Lister in 1876: 'It is far better to have to deal with the worst savages than the best-intentioned Portuguese.' Quoted in R. Anstey, *Britain and the Congo in the 19th Century*, (Oxford, 1962) p. 54.
[45] *ibid.* pp. 55, 84, 99–102; Robinson and Gallagher p. 170.

incurred all the costs of administration whilst Britain would get the lion's share of the trade. Why then was this treaty so easily overthrown and before the end of the year Portugal replaced by a tripartite division between Portugal, France and Leopold II's International Association? Partly, of course, because the opposition of Bismarck was decisive. His threat to Malet on 29 November that he would oppose British claims on the Niger if they did not accept the International Association certainly brought Granville to heel immediately.[46] But this is by no means the entire explanation. The reason why Granville was so prepared to sacrifice the Congo for the Niger was equally important.

This was partly a question of priorities. Kimberley, for example, had always thought the Niger delta more important than the Congo and certainly great efforts were made from June to November 1884 to back up British claims in this region by despatching Hewitt on treaty-making expeditions in the Delta. But, more, it was simply that British and German interests in the Congo were by no means so opposed as both Bismarck and Granville originally assumed. The only British interest in the Congo was trade and the traders in fact turned out to be as opposed to the Portuguese and as favourable to Leopold as Bismarck was. Once this was evident from the great campaign worked up by Mackinnon and Hutton in the press, Chambers of Commerce and the House of Commons in favour of Leopold, there was no point at all in opposing Bismarck's views: this was clear from the manner in which in October Granville readily accepted that the Conference should legislate for the Congo but strongly objected to its having jurisdiction on the Niger.[47] Hence the somewhat curious result of Bismarck's conference was the discovery that Britain and Germany saw more or less eye to eye on the Congo and were jointly opposed to any extension of the French sphere. Since Bismarck's own interests in the Niger Delta were catered for by the acquisition of Togoland and the Cameroons, he had no reason to support France unduly in this region, and the last reason to practise blackmail disappeared when the Liberal Cabinet surrendered completely to current German claims in New Guinea. Now that Bismarck had enough colonies with which to satisfy the Reichstag the hunt was called

[46] Anstey pp. 106, 177.
[47] Robinson and Gallagher pp. 170, 175. On the British opposition to the Anglo-Portuguese Treaty see Anstey pp. 113–60.

off; as was evident from the fact that Malet obtained the Lower Niger for Britain, and that Granville's Egyptian finance proposals were accepted at Berlin early in the New Year. But, if this Berlin West Africa Conference was a diplomatic triumph for Granville, it was so in the sense that the main objects of British concern were the Niger and Egypt. In the Congo the real victor was Leopold II who had outwitted everyone, including Bismarck and Ferry, by his pre-emption clause and cultivation of Mackinnon. As the latter found to his cost, once Leopold's nebulous International Association was in control, British merchants got very short shrift from the new régime in the Congo Basin.[48] But at the time Granville and Gladstone were pleased enough with their achievement for the main result of this settlement of West Africa was that now the Egyptian question would move again.

The Egyptian Settlement of 1885 and the abandonment of the Sudan

When the Egyptian Conference was finally abandoned in August 1884 the Liberal Government, unable in view of its internal difficulties to simply do nothing, marked time by the classical expedient of sending Northbrook out to Cairo to report on the financial situation, though this was already clear enough. As Gladstone noted on receipt of Northbrook's recommendations in September, 'They cannot I suppose prove more than insolvency and that we knew long ago'. But Northbrook's report in fact proposed the abandonment of the old policy of a negotiated withdrawal and the adoption of the clear alternative of British supremacy, a Treasury backed loan and indefinite occupation, a view in which he was supported by Hartington but which every Commoner in the Cabinet rejected. Gladstone was quite certain that Parliament would never accept it, 'without a change in our policy root and branch: such as we could not make', whilst Harcourt thought it the best argument for immediate evacuation. It was clear that the original idea of withdrawing once Egypt had been set on its feet had become a mirage: first the Sudan, now finance, made it apparent that Egypt would never recover without a British administration maintained at least in part at British expense. Moreover, there were strong political objections to this course since, even if the Cabinet were to adopt these root and branch

[48] *ibid.* p. 209.

changes, there was every prospect that it would founder in the Commons in the face of a Tory, Irish, Radical, coalition. If this were so, Harcourt argued, 'it is far better to be beaten on a policy consonant to our other principles and those of our Party'.[49]

In these circumstances Granville had no alternative but to return to the old idea of an approach to the interested Powers with a view to immediate withdrawal and on 25 November the question was reopened. That he was this time successful where he had failed in June was due to two changes. In the first place Bismarck had lost interest in Egypt: his experiences with Ferry had led to some disenchantment but, more important, his essential objects had been attained. He had fought and won the Reichstag elections on the colonial issue; he had, he thought, forced Gladstone and Granville to disgorge. As he told Munster quite bluntly on 25 January 1885, 'Egypt in itself is quite indifferent to us and is merely a means of overcoming England's objections to our Colonial aspirations'.[50] This by no means meant that he was now ready to support Gladstone, as his overtures to Russia during the Pendjeh crisis and to France in May 1885 over the Canal negotiations demonstrated. But the old drive had gone and if, as now transpired, Ferry were willing to accept Granville's Egyptian proposals, Bismarck had no interest in opposing them. That Ferry accepted the Liberal government's financial proposals in 1885 where he had rejected them the previous June was due to change of circumstance. In the first place London now offered practically everything that Paris wanted. In its desperation to rid itself of 'the Egyptian phantom', which had quite spoilt Gladstone's Christmas, French proposals for an international loan and the control of the *Caisse* over Egyptian finance, linked to a guarantee that negotiations on freedom of navigation of the Canal and evacuation were to follow, were now accepted by the Cabinet and incorporated in the London Convention of 17 March 1885. The only concession to the British idea of 'freeing' Egypt was a minimal reduction in the interest on the coupon. In this case, as in the delays that followed the Suez Canal Conference's recommendations in June 1885, it did not seem worthwhile to Paris to push

---

[49] Ramm II, 266; Harcourt, Cabinet Memorandum 16 November 1884 cited in Robinson and Gallagher pp. 147–9. Docs. 32, 33, 34.
[50] Bismarck to Munster 25 January 1885, Dugdale I, 188. Doc. 35.

things to a breach with London since the only effect of this would be to promote an Anglo-German understanding. Besides, so at least thought Waddington, the March Convention satisfied French requirements; with the international fetters finally riveted on Egyptian finance, evacuation was bound to follow; no ministry in its senses would so limit its freedom of action if it did not intend to retire immediately since, as Baring pointed out, the government of Egypt was now impossible.[51]

The apparent settlement of the Egyptian problem by March 1885 still left that of the Sudan. Although there was the rather unsettling prospect of possible French intervention in Egypt, were British withdrawal to anticipate international recognition of her neutrality, this concern did not extend to the Sudan. The Sudan was not regarded as part of Egypt proper and, when the policy of abandonment was enforced from January 1884 onwards, there was no realization in London that it might have international repercussions. As Gladstone succinctly put it, 'I care more that we keep out of the Sudan than who goes in'. The Gordon relief expedition was no exception to this attitude. When after long drawn out objections Gladstone was finally pushed into permitting preparations for it and despatching Wolseley to Cairo, it was still to be no more than a raid on Khartoum 'to capture and bring him (Gordon) back'. At the same time, in recognition of Gordon's objections to leaving the province in complete anarchy, some attempt was made to organize something to follow him, ranging from Turkish troops to the Mudir of Dongola with two steamboats. It was against this background that there emerged the idea of giving it to Italy. Gladstone thought of this at quite an early stage. On 10 January 1884 he suggested, 'Massowah, give it up (to Italy) to make a friend', a consideration which was not without importance as the year wore on. Certainly the Italians were friendly enough: at this time Nigra told Granville 'that Italy's only wish is to support us, and to do what is agreeable to us in Egypt', a prediction that was amply borne out in June when Italy was the only power to support the British proposals.[52]

But when Northbrook revived this project at the end of September as part of his solution to the Egyptian problem, Granville,

[51] Ramm II, 300, Robinson and Gallagher pp. 150–1. In fact the Suez Canal Convention was not signed until October 1888 and was a pointless exercise since Britain continued to control Egypt. [52] Shibeika pp. 253–87; Ramm II, 146, 221–2.

with Gladstone's agreement, turned it down, much as he appreciated Italian friendliness, on the grounds that,

> on second thoughts it appears to me to be rather early to give the Italians the Queen's shilling—and to hand over on our own authority, any portion of the Ottoman Empire to a European Power. It would be a regular red rag to France.[53]

Clearly, to Granville, whilst there was still some hope of an accommodation with France over Egyptian finance, he would not risk alienating her: it was only as the full extent of Franco-German collaboration became clear in the preparations for the Berlin Conference that he changed his mind. As Gladstone now pointed out, 'Italy has a good claim and it is very important to keep her as breaking what would in some sense be the concert'.[54] Hence on 20 October Granville's overtures to Nigra, 'speaking as a friend and not to the ambassador of Italy', enquiring whether Italy would like Massowah if, as seemed probable, the Turks did not take up their claim. In point of fact Granville never did make a formal offer of Massowah; as he pointed out when pressed by Nigra on 23 December, it was not his to give; but he made it quite clear that Britain would raise no objections and would even commend the project to the Turks, an attitude which Nigra thought 'as favourable as could reasonably be expected'.[55]

Clearly therefore the Italian occupation of Massowah on 5 February 1885 took place with British encouragement, though Granville strenously denied, as Mancini seemed to think, that this was 'a service that Italy was performing for England'. It was, he insisted, simply 'an act of friendship from England to Italy';[56] Mancini may have thought he was keeping out the French but this was the least of Granville's worries.[57] Granville had little or no concern with the Sudan, all that the Liberal government wanted was to be able to wash its hands of it as quickly as possible, an attitude which now gave rise to the most curious episode of all. The search for a replacement for Gordon—when he was brought

[53] Ramm II, 272.
[54] *ibid*. 278–80. Gladstone to Granville 17 October 1884.
[55] Nigra to Mancini 20 October, 23 December 1884. *L'Italia in Africa, Serie Storici* I, 'Etopia—Mar Rosso Documenti 1883–5' (Rome, 1955) nos. 344, 374.
[56] *ibid*. no. 353.
[57] C. Giglio, 'I, negoziati italo-inglesi per Massana', *Il Risorgimento*, October 1952 pp. 160–75.

out—appeared to have settled on the Mudir of Dongola, to whom it was proposed to give a subsidy of £100,000 a year: in return he was to attempt to govern the Sudan.[58] But in January 1885, when the final preparations for the occupation of Massowah were being made, Lumley, the British ambassador at Rome, made the startling proposal that Italy should take this on, sending an army via Suakin to join Wolseley and then when he retired, becoming the rulers of the Sudan. In this way, he urged, '. . . just as the Crimean alliance prepared the political resurgence of Italy, so joint military action in the Sudan . . . would be the prelude to her rise to colonial power'. Whilst it cannot be proved that Granville originated this idea it seems unlikely, as Mancini observed, that Lumley would have aired this in such detail without instructions, but, whilst it fits in well with current Liberal policy of abandoning not only the Sudan but also Egypt, in fact Granville could not be pinned down. By the time Nigra took it up officially on 9 February the situation had changed. Wolseley's expedition had discovered on 28 January that Gordon was dead: news which, when it reached London on 5 February, produced such a popular outcry that overnight, to save themselves, the Cabinet committed the country to a re-conquest of the Sudan. Now it was felt that, 'The desired moral effect would be weakened if, at this present moment we were to appeal for help, however friendly it might be'.[59]

This decision of course made complete nonsense of all previous Liberal policy in the Sudan and no sooner was it made than it was abandoned. In the Commons debate on a vote of censure on 23 February Goschen satirized his own party's policy as 'to go to Khartoum to please the Whigs . . . to retire from Khartoum to please the Radicals'.[60] Surviving by a bare 14 votes in a confused situation in which no clear idea emerged, except perhaps that much as the death of Gordon was deplored, nobody—not even the Conservatives—had any desire for the reconquest of the Sudan, the government quickly lost its enthusiasm for a policy of action. The reason was simple enough since, as Gladstone continually urged upon Granville in April and May, 'if we cannot kill the war in the Sudan it will kill us'. With both Baring and

[58] Ramm II, 281; Shibeika p. 289.
[59] Mancini to Nigra 22 January, Nigra to Mancini 9 February 1885 in C. Zaghi, *P. S. Mancini* (Rome, 1955) pp. 164–5, 169. Possibly the real reason was the effect upon France at a critical point in the Egyptian negotiations.
[60] Quoted in Robinson and Gallagher p. 152.

Wolseley expressing their doubts, Gladstone by April persuaded his colleagues to drop the idea, partly on the grounds—though this was not the real reason—that they could not fight both the Mahdi in the Sudan and Russia in Afghanistan at the same time.[61] Since this decision was confirmed by the Conservative administration when they took office in June, Wolseley's force was withdrawn to Wadi-Halfa and the Sudan abandoned apart from the small garrison at Suakin. This, equally, ruined any chance of Italian participation, as the military authorities in Rome thought even the relief of Kassala an extremely risky business if their flanks were unprotected,[62] so Italy confined herself after all to Massowah and the interior was left to the Mahdi and his successor, the Khalifah Abdulla.

But from March 1885 onwards all consideration of Egypt and the Sudan was dwarfed by the sudden prospect of war with Russia in Central Asia. This had the effect that, despite the March Convention, the evacuation of Egypt had to mark time, though Gladstone still thought this was only a matter of months. In June, partly as the result of their disasters abroad, the Liberal administration disintegrated and the final settlement was left to their successors. This was to be important since there were considerable differences between Gladstone and Salisbury in their attitudes towards the evacuation of Egypt, which had the result that Gladstone's legacy turned into a permanent feature of the landscape of British foreign policy.

[61] Shibeika pp. 304–5, Ramm II, 354, 379, 380. According to Dilke, Gladstone was quite explicit: 'I am not prepared to go upon any terms, Russia or no Russia.' Quoted in Robinson and Gallagher p. 155. Doc. 40.
[62] Italian General Staff Study, 12 February 1885 in Zaghi pp. 175–8.

IV

The Defence of India

> The whole Indian world here is divided into Quettites
> and anti-Quettites—who hate each other with all the
> fervour of Big Endians and Little Endians—and at
> present the Quettites are much in a minority.
>
> *Salisbury,* 1877

Gladstone's use of the Pendjeh incident to abandon the Sudan, as
demonstrated by the ingenious way he linked the two together in
the Cabinet discussions of 12–16 April and the debate on the vote
of credit on 21 April 1885, aptly underlined the connection between British policy in Egypt and India, the Western and Eastern
halves of the same problem. As Kimberley, Secretary of State for
India, said at precisely this time, did anyone really suppose 'that
if we did not possess an Indian Empire we should have interfered
in Egypt?' Moreover, thought Kimberley, there was more than
coincidence behind the timing of the Russian advance in Central
Asia and the British embarrassment in Egypt since, with an army
in Cairo and unable to extricate themselves, it was apparent that
the Cabinet would find difficulty in simultaneously opposing
Russia in Afghanistan. This assumption, given the Liberal record
since 1880, was not altogether surprising: as Gladstone himself
was constrained to remark in December 1884, 'some of the
Foreign Governments have the same notion of me that Nicholas
was supposed to have of Lord Aberdeen'.[1]

The Basic Problem

The Pendjeh crisis, which lasted from the initial Russo-Afghan
clash in February until the signature of the preliminary boundary
agreement on 10 September 1885, was an extremely important

---

[1] Kimberley to Ripon 22 February 1884, to Dufferin 13 March 1885, in R. L.
Greaves, *Persia and the Defence of India* (London, 1959) p. 64; Gladstone to Granville
7 December 1884, 9, 14 April 1885 in Ramm II, 291, 356, 358.

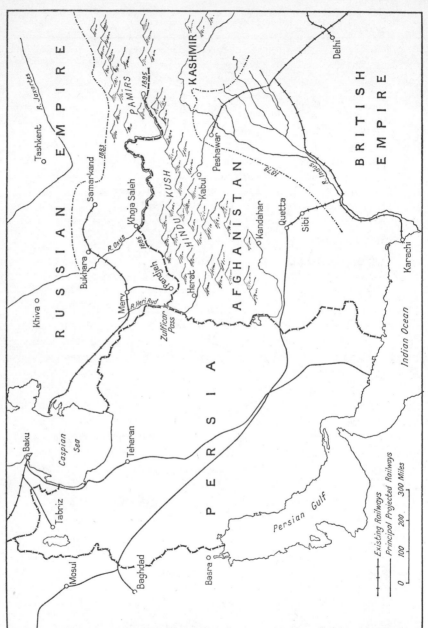

The defence of India

stage in the evolution of British policy in Central Asia. Until Pendjeh it had fluctuated, the subject of almost endless debate both in Simla and in London. The familiar statement that Britain had two foreign policies—that of London and Simla—is a vast over-simplification. There were in fact almost as many policies as there were people concerned in their formulation; they were legion: the Viceroy and his Council, the Bombay and Madras Presidencies, the minister at Teheran, the ambassadors at St. Petersburg and Con-stantinople, the India Office, Foreign Office, War Office, and, last but not least, the Cabinet.[2] It is not even that the debate broke down into a dialogue between London and Simla, since the most diverse views were held in both places. But, broadly speaking, two distinct trends can be discerned which were diametrically opposed, and for which supporters could be found in most, if not all of the policy-making agencies. It was this situation, further complicated by the crystallizing of these two trends into rival party doctrines, which prevented the formulation of any effective British policy in Central Asia until the harsh reality was made apparent by Pendjeh.

The basis of the problem was quite simply the Russian advance across Central Asia after the Crimean War which gradually swallowed up the independent Khanates of Turkestan—Tashkent and Bukhara by 1866, Khiva in 1873, Merv in 1884. This had two consequences. In the first place, whereas in 1863 the Russian frontier was still some 500 miles from the Oxus, the annexation of Bukhara made the Russian and Afghan boundaries conterminous and Afghanistan itself now became the 'buffer state' between the British and Russian Empires in the East. Secondly, the Russian advance from the Caspian, which was accompanied by the con-struction of a railway, brought the Russian railhead to Merv by 1886, a mere 200 miles from Herat, whilst the British railhead was still more than 400 miles away to the south of Quetta. Merv itself by the 1880's was but a shadow of its former glory and consisted of a few mud huts, but its strategic importance was considerable: it had been a fertile oasis and under a civilized power could become so again, thus providing an excellent jumping-off point for the invasion of India. As Lytton put it in 1877, 'to judge of Merv by what it actually is, would be like judging of Sevastopol by what it

[2] 'There were as many Anglo-Indian views on this as there were Anglo-Indians.'
A. P. Thornton, 'British Policy in Persia 1858–1890, *E.H.R.* 1954 p. 563.

was under Turkish dominion . . .'.[3] According to Sir Henry Raw-linson, a senior member of the India Council, this represented a much greater menace to the security of India than the advance to the Oxus, since a turning movement via Merv and Herat had been the traditional route for the conquest of India in the past as it by-passed the formidable barrier of the Hindu Kush.[4]

Hence there were two fairly distinct problems. The first, the old one of relations with Afghanistan, simply made more acute by the closer proximity of the Russians on the Oxus: the second, the relatively new one of the Russian advance from the Caspian towards Herat, which brought up the whole question of Persia. To these two problems were offered two basically distinct solutions, a contrast which probably originated in the difference in outlook of the Bombay and Punjab administrations. Rawlinson, whose experience had been in Bombay and Persia in the days when Bombay virtually conducted its own foreign relations with Persia and had itself driven them out of Herat, was the first advocate of the 'forward' view, in which he was joined by Lytton, Roberts and, later, Lansdowne and Curzon in India, and Salisbury at home. The essence of their view was well summed up by Cross.[5]

> The Russian Empire is looked upon in Central Asia as the growing and spreading power, and that the British Empire is not so regarded. So people worship the rising sun.[6]

In this situation it was not considered safe to wait until the Russians debouched upon the Indian plain, since Roberts up to 1885 certainly regarded the Indian princes as unreliable and was 'doubtful as to the wisdom of encouraging a high state of efficiency amongst the troops of independent States'.[7] Salisbury went even further. The main danger, he urged in 1884 after the Russian acquisition of Merv, was not an actual Russian invasion via the Khyber or Bolan passes, but

> the production of intrigues and rebellions among the Natives of India, the gradual weakening of respect, for the English arms, disaffection towards the English Raj, and the crumbling away of our resources before Russia has struck a blow against our frontier.[8]

[3] Lytton to Cranbrook 2 July 1877 in Greaves p. 63.
[4] *ibid.* p. 57; Thornton p. 560.
[5] Secretary of State for India, 1886–92.
[6] To Salisbury 31 May 1887 in Greaves p. 34.
[7] F. S. Roberts, *Forty One Years in India* (London, 1897) pp. 523–4.
[8] Salisbury in the House of Lords, 10 March 1884 in Greaves p. 67.

Hence, for reasons that were less military than political, the 'forward' school advocated the defence of India beyond her frontiers, in Afghanistan and Persia, the policy which lay behind both the Afghan war of 1878–9 and the Herat conflict of 1885.

By contrast, the 'Punjab' school, which took its doctrine originally from Lawrence and consisted of such figures as Northbrook and Ripon among the Viceroys, Argyll, Hartington and (by implication) Wolseley at home, bitterly contested the forward policy. In their eyes India should be defended on the Indus; no good ever came out of meddling with Afghanistan, as was proved by Auckland's disastrous campaign of 1838–9. This view was taken so far that even when Sher Ali, the Amir, alarmed by the seizure of Khiva, approached Northbrook in 1873 for an alliance, he was turned down. Much as Northbrook liked the idea, and suggested that if the Amir unreservedly accepted British advice in external relations, Britain should help him with money, arms, and troops if necessary to expel unprovoked invasion, Argyll opposed him.[9] Instead, Granville took up Lawrence's idea, expressed in 1869 just prior to his departure from India, of direct negotiations with the Russians to reach an understanding on Central Asia, emphasizing that they 'cannot be permitted to interfere in the affairs of Afghanistan, or in those of any State which lies contiguous to our frontier'.[10] In consequence an understanding of sorts was reached in 1873, vaguely establishing the Oxus as the boundary of Afghanistan—hailed by Shuvalov as settling the Central Asian question for at least twenty-five years—and this was considered enough for Sher Ali: Argyll recommended it to Northbrook as quite sufficient to remove apprehension of danger from without. Similarly, in Persia in 1873 when the Shah, alarmed like the Amir by the fate of Khiva, made approaches to London, he was told simply to 'live in friendship with both England and Russia'. Obviously Argyll and Granville rejected any idea of defending India on the Oxus and, in so far as they ever questioned Shuvalov's optimism, they were inclined to the Lawrentian strategy of simply threatening Russia 'that an advance towards India, beyond a certain point would entail on her war, in all parts of the world, with England'. This certainly was to be Liberal policy in

[9] Thornton pp. 567–8; W. K. Fraser-Tytler, *Afghanistan* (Oxford, 1950) pp. 130–1.
[10] Lawrence, 4 January 1869 in G. J. Alder, *British India's Northern Frontier 1865–1895* (London, 1963) p. 165.

1885 and was still advocated by Wolseley, in opposition to Roberts, as late as 1889.[11]

Thus there were two basically different approaches to the problem of the defence of India. The first, the forward view, advocated the establishment of the Oxus as the primary line of defence and the incorporation of Afghanistan and Persia as British allies. The alternative, the Punjab programme, repudiated this idea, regarding the Indus as the outer bulwark and relying purely upon diplomacy to keep the Russians as far away as possible.

The Afghan War

That this difference of approach became a party matter by 1880, with all the emotional overtones that this involved at the time of the Gladstone-Disraeli struggle, was the outcome of the Afghan war of 1878-9. Salisbury, at the India Office from 1874-7, immediately set about reversing Argyll's policy. Whilst agreeing with Northbrook 'that a Russian advance upon India is a chimera', he thought it more than likely that an attempt might be made 'to throw the Afghans upon us'. Forsyth's reports on his mission to Kashgar in 1873-4 had painted a lurid picture of Russian agents running wild in Afghanistan, 'purchasing the allegiance of the turbulent chiefs', and Salisbury was certainly impressed by the increase of Russian influence at Kabul. Hence the idea of 'listening posts', to be established at Herat, Kandahar and Kashgar, simply in order to obtain trustworthy information as to what was going on in Central Asia. As Salisbury pointed out to Disraeli, all their information came from St. Petersburg, Teheran, or from a local Agent at Kabul 'who writes exactly what the Ameer tells him'. But the difficulty was to get the Amir to accept British Agents. Salisbury did not want to send a mission to Afghanistan against the Amir's wishes, but he did want 'to tell the Government of India to make the Ameer wish it'. It was, he thought, a problem of diplomacy, to which Northbrook demurred: he took the view that opening this question with the Amir would inevitably involve a war, and resigned rather than accept this policy. Salisbury, convinced that, if necessary, England would have to fight to defend Afghanistan against invasion, now pressed Northbrook's 1873 scheme upon Lytton, the new Viceroy, a pressure that lay at the

[11] *ibid.* pp. 172-5; Thornton p. 562; Fraser-Tytler p. 135; Greaves p. 41.

root of the struggle that followed. Whilst it is true that he did not insist on a mission at Kabul and put more emphasis upon getting control of the outlying provinces, particularly Quetta and the Bolan, Salisbury certainly gave Lytton a fairly free hand in persuading Sher Ali whilst he remained at the India Office.[12]

It was this insistence on 'listening posts' which brought war, for Lytton, after temporizing with the Amir's envoy at Peshawar until March 1877, broke off relations and began to think in terms of deposing Sher Ali for someone more pliable, or even breaking up Afghanistan into separate chiefdoms, annexing as much as was necessary and pushing the Indian frontier to the Hindu Kush, with 'an outer line on the Oxus for ultimate boundary'. Clearly the concept of the Granville-Shuvalov agreement of 1873 of Afghanistan as a buffer state had been abandoned. With the news of the arrival of a Russian mission at Kabul on 26 July 1878 Lytton acted, sent an ultimatum to Sher Ali and made preparations for war. When a British mission was refused entry on 19 October he launched a two-pronged attack on 21 November: by May 1879 Sher Ali, abandoned by the Russians, had fled and a treaty had been concluded with his successor, Yakub Khan. This annexed Khyber, Pishin and Sibi, and the Kurram; provided for the establishment of British Agents where required; and established relations along the lines of Northbrook's suggestions of 1873. In September 1879, after the murder of the Agent in Kabul, the capital itself was occupied and the administration, such as it was, taken over by Roberts.[13]

This, the logical conclusion of the 'forward' policy, has been attributed to Disraeli's 'policy of hostility to Russia', in contrast to the Russophile inclinations of the Liberal Party. Argyll constantly after 1876 and Gladstone, particularly during the Midlothian campaign, denounced Conservative policy in Afghanistan as 'dishonouring to England': according to Florence Nightingale, by 1880 India was debated in Parliament with the same vehemence 'as if it were a *home* question'.[14] But this use of Indian policy as a vehicle for party recrimination tended to obscure the truth, which was that Salisbury and Disraeli were as reluctant to enter into any

[12] Fraser-Tytler p. 139; Cecil II, 70–5; Monypenny and Buckle II, 774, 1249–51; Thornton p. 567; Alder pp. 50–7.
[13] Fraser-Tytler pp. 139–45, 148. This was the Treaty of Gandamak.
[14] S. Gopal, *The Viceroyalty of Lord Ripon* (Oxford, 1950) pp. 1, 6.

conflict with Russia over India as the Liberals had been, and sought an understanding just as much as their predecessors. Whilst Salisbury had been at the India Office he had certainly encouraged, with Disraeli's approval, the adoption of the 'forward' policy and a firm line with Sher Ali, but this was not because he viewed war with Russia as imminent. It was simply that he thought the best way to defend India was to obtain reliable information as to what was happening beyond the Indian frontiers.[15] There was nothing particularly Conservative in the idea of offering protection to Sher Ali, since Northbrook had thought him quite agreeable to this in 1873; the mistake was in the timing, since by 1877 the Amir, abandoning hope after the failure of the Northbrook negotiations, had now turned to Russia.[16]

Hence by 1878 there was good reason to regard the Amir as unfriendly; certainly Roberts was quite impressed by the evidence of Russian influence in Kabul that he found there in 1879. But this was not the real reason for the Afghan crisis. This lay in the Near Eastern crisis of 1878. Kaufmann's action in despatching a mission under Colonel Stolietev to Kabul in June 1878 was part of the Russian preparation for war in Europe. As Skobelev put it, 'without a serious demonstration towards India . . . it is impossible to think of a war for the Balkan Peninsular'. But with the peaceful solution to the Balkan crisis at Berlin, Stolietev's treaty with Sher Ali was a liability which was promptly denounced by Gorchakov, and on 22 December the mission was withdrawn, lest it upset Anglo-Russian relations.[17] Hence, there was no question of an advance on Kabul to eject Stolietev: this had been arranged by negotiation between London and St. Petersburg. The real explanation of what followed—just as the contrast between Russian promises in London and performance in Central Asia is in terms of the inability of Gorchakov and Giers to control Kaufmann—was the inability of Disraeli to control Lytton.

Disraeli, and even more Salisbury, sensing that action in Afghanistan might well slow down the Russian evacuation of Bulgaria, were determined by September 1878 to settle this problem by negotiation with Gorchakov, and were more insistent than ever that Lytton should confine himself to the acquisition of

---

[15] Thornton p. 565. See M. Cowling, 'Lytton, the Cabinet and the Russians: August to November 1878', *E.H.R.* 1961 pp. 59–79. [16] Fraser-Tytler pp. 135, 143.
[17] Skobelev, cited in Alder p. 61; Roberts 421–2; Monypenny and Buckle II, 1249.

Kandahar (which had the great merit that it could be kept). But Lytton, flatly against instructions, on 20 September advanced to and was repelled at the Khyber, an action which now involved the prestige of the British Raj. As Disraeli commented bitterly to Cranbrook, Salisbury's successor at the India Office,

> When V-roys and Comms-in-Chief disobey orders, they ought to be sure of success in their mutiny. Lytton, by disobeying orders, has only secured insult and failure. . . . To force the Khyber, and take Cabul is a perilous business.

In the Cabinet discussions that followed, all, bar Cranbrook, were for limiting action at the most to the Kurram valley and it was only his insistence on the gravity of affairs and the necessity of supporting Lytton, plus further independent action on Lytton's part, which precipitated the general advance on 21 November.[18] Thus there is no reason to suppose that the conquest and disintegration of Afghanistan was part of any Conservative plot for the creation of a scientific frontier in North West India. That Lytton thought in these terms by August 1878 is quite clear, but no one else did. It is only in the sense that they appointed him, as Disraeli admitted to Salisbury earlier, that his Cabinet must bear responsibility for what followed.

> Had it been a routine age, we might have made, what might be called, a more prudent selection, but we foresaw what would occur, and indeed saw what was ocurring; and we wanted a man of ambition, imagination, some vanity, and much will—and we have got him.[19]

With the disintegration of Afghanistan after the death of Sher Ali and Roberts' capture of Kabul in October 1879 this new problem had to be faced: as Cranbrook now told Lytton, 'Afghanistan as a whole could no longer exist'.[20] It was this situation which produced Lytton and Salisbury's new alternative, the break up of Afghanistan, with the British annexation of Kandahar and the cession of Herat to Persia, which was now to be built up as the main bastion for the defence of India. This, the Herat Convention, was accepted by the Shah in November 1879 on the basis that in return for Herat he would protect Merv from the Russian advance from the Caspian, with British 'moral support', would permit a

[18] Disraeli to Cranbrook 26 September, to the Queen 26 October 1878, *ibid.* 1254–8; Salisbury to Disraeli 24 September 1878 in Cecil II, 341.
[19] Disraeli to Salisbury 1 April 1877 in Monypenny and Buckle II, 1251.
[20] Cranbrook to Lytton 12 October 1879 cited in Fraser-Tytler pp 148–9. Doc. 41.

railway from Kandahar to Herat, and improvements in communications from the Gulf inland.

But it was rejected by Disraeli's Cabinet. More or less manoeuvred into Lytton's Afghan adventures against their will, the experiment with a client Amir had not been a conspicuous success; and even Disraeli was against this new extension of responsibility. Consequently the Shah's proposals for a defensive alliance were refused on 27 December, with results similar to the rejection of Afghan advances in 1873, and Lytton was back where he started as far as the reorganization of Afghanistan was concerned. That he was saved at this late stage from an impossible position was due to the appearance of what Salisbury had assumed to be impossible, a capable successor to Sher Ali in the person of Abdur Rahman. In March 1880 he crossed the Oxus and by July had accepted the basic provisions of the Treaty of Gandamak as modified by the Liberal Viceroy, Ripon, and, with some British help, now imposed his rule upon the turbulent chiefs.[21]

The net result then of Lytton's 'forward' policy was the control of the Khyber and Kurram passes, the annexation of Sibi and Pishin and the establishment of relations with Kabul upon the basis sought in 1873. Although this came under heavy criticism from Ripon as a 'terrible want of moral sense in political affairs', in fact it was no mean achievement and, whilst it is possible that the lack of trouble in Afghanistan in the eighties was 'a tribute to the efficiency of a pacific approach' as exemplified in Ripon's policy, this is unproven. Abdur Rahman's realism might equally well have been a tribute to Roberts' military abilities or the result of twelve years of living in Russia. Moreover, though much was made of the immorality of Conservative proceedings and Lytton's 'distorted perspective', in fact the arrangements that Ripon made for relations with Afghanistan in June 1880 and the position taken up *vis-à-vis* Russo-Afghan relations by Hartington in the House of Commons on 1 August 1881, were markedly similar to the Treaty of Gandamak. The only real difference was the return of Kandahar province in March 1881, stigmatized by the Queen as 'political and Party expediency'. But although this was of considerable strategical significance, and demonstrated the adherence of the Liberals to the Punjab school, it hardly amounted to the

[21] Thornton pp. 570–1. The principal modification was that Kandhar was returned to the Amir. Doc. 42.

major change in policy towards Afghanistan that both its critics and apologists claimed. Perhaps the real credit for the new phase of Anglo-Afghan relations in the eighties should go, in any case, not to Lytton or Ripon but to Abdur Rahman, the 'right choice for the wrong reasons'.[22]

The Pendjeh Incident

The acceptance of responsibility for the defence of Afghanistan by the agreement with Abdur Rahman in June 1880 solved the problem of Anglo-Afghan relations but created a new one: the definition of Afghanistan in the face of the Russian advance from the Caspian and Tashkent. In the eighties this soon became inseparable from the Persian problem since, at its simplest, if Russia could be kept out of Persian territory—specifically that of the Tekke Turcomans and Merv—then she could be kept away from the 'open' Afghan frontier. The negotiations of 1873 had established that the boundary of Afghanistan lay on the Oxus but, apart from the unsatisfactory results of this in the Pamirs, and the marked Russian reluctance to concede their exclusion from Badakhstan, it left the whole question of the Persian-Afghan boundaries wide open.[23] This mattered little as long as Persian integrity was not in doubt, but by the eighties it was.

At one time Palmerston had envisaged the independence of Persia as 'a great object to us not merely with reference to India, but as connected with the independence of Turkey'; the inference being that infiltration through Teheran was the back door to Constantinople. Probably it was with this in mind that he had removed control of Persian affairs from the India to the Foreign Office. But this situation, in which, as Rawlinson grudgingly recognized, 'we can only throw out hints', was anomalous by the eighties. The back door to Constantinople aspect had largely faded out and, as Salisbury himself acknowledged, 'were it not for our possessing India, we should trouble ourselves but little about Persia'. But although in 1879 he had been in favour of handing back control to India, this was never carried out, with the result that Persian policy in this crucial period was subject to the same conflicting interests that had bedevilled relations with Afghanistan

[22] Fraser-Tytler pp. 155–7; Gopal pp. 8, 25–7, 34. Docs. 43, 44, 45.
[23] Alder pp. 176–85.

earlier: so much so that Salisbury, on one occasion, simply told Nicolson at Teheran to do as he thought fit.[24]

Like Afghanistan, Persia was an 'outlying portion of the defences of India' and the subject of much the same concern. Throughout the seventies Simla urged a variety of schemes to check Russian influence at Teheran, schemes which Tenterden thought amounted to 'an English protectorate over Persia'. Napier, the Commander-in-Chief India, after the fall of Khiva, even advocated the use of British officers to build up a Persian guerrilla force on the model of the Peninsular campaign.[25] But all these schemes were rejected at the time, on the dual grounds that they were unnecessarily alarmist—'the crude excursions of an untutored fancy', as Lytton ironically commented—and because,

> The demerit of such a policy would be its exceeding costliness; and that it would precipitate the conflict between ourselves and Russia. . . .[26]

But although averse to any action in 1874, by the end of 1878 Salisbury had changed his mind. Partly because he had come to the conclusion that force was the only thing that Russia respected in Asia and that 'no other remonstrances will be of any use'; perhaps because of his growing involvement with the establishment of British influence in Turkey-in-Asia; partly because of his growing conviction that 'the Shah will serve us better in Herat than the Amir', he was now prepared to negotiate at Teheran.[27] The upshot of this was the Herat Convention. By this Salisbury hoped, as he explained to Dufferin, 'to provide halting-places where the process of change may rest awhile'—in other words time to build the Herat and Seistan railways—and thus outflank any Russian advance before it started. But the scheme was wrecked by the Cabinet's caution after the disastrous end to the Treaty of Gandamak, and, on 27 December, Salisbury had to give a negative reply to Persian enquiries as to whether they could expect British support if attacked. By March 1880 the Herat Convention was dead,

[24] Palmerston to Durham 27 October 1835 in C. K. Webster, *The Foreign Policy of Palmerston* (London, 1951) II, 741; Salisbury minute, 22 May 1889 in Greaves p. 25; Thornton pp. 554, 573.

[25] Greaves pp. 26, 34.

[26] Salisbury, minute 6 October 1874 *ibid.* p. 49.

[27] Salisbury to Northcote 24 September 1879 in Cecil II, 376. For his attitude towards Asia Minor see Chapter II.

the Shah, not unnaturally, loth to risk war with Russia with no guarantee of support.[28]

The *coup de grace* to any prospect of Persian collaboration in the defence of India was given by the arrival in power of the Liberal government on 28 April 1880. On 18 May Granville promptly announced, in the spirit of Midlothian, that he had no desire to be 'always nagging' St. Petersburg about Persia and that he would much rather act 'in concert with that Power'. Signs of the Liberal understanding of concerted action were not slow in following: on 30 October strategic railway construction was stopped whilst still well short of Quetta and on 15 April 1881 Kandahar was evacuated. It was illogical, to say the least, after this patent withdrawal, for Hartington to threaten war in the event of 'interference by any foreign Power with the external or internal affairs of Afghanistan': the Shah at least drew the obvious conclusion and now simply went over to Russia: as he complained to Nicolson later, all that he ever got from England was 'good advice and honeyed words—and nothing else'.

The corresponding Russian move in this acting 'in concert' was the negotiation with Teheran of the withdrawal of Persian claims over the Tekke Turcomans and the capture of Geok Tepe by Skobelev in January 1881, coupled with renewed promises by Giers in March that Russia would not take Merv and that she would pursue 'a moderate course' in Central Asia. Small wonder that Lobanov was very non-committal when Granville urged that they should extend the concept of the 1873 negotiations now to define the Persian North and North-eastern frontiers: it seemed plain enough that Russia could define them by herself. To Hartington the situation seemed pretty hopeless by August 1882 since, as he told Ripon, the Cabinet had abandoned all expectation of an effective Central Asian policy.[29]

The situation was made worse by the new relationship with Afghanistan. From October 1882 onwards, Abdur Rahman began to press the Government of India for some definition of his frontiers with Russia, a request which had to be turned down. The India Office, having discovered that Afghanistan had considerable

[28] Salisbury to Dufferin 4 February 1880, *ibid.* 377; Greaves p. 51; Thornton p. 571. There is some discrepancy here, Greaves blaming the collapse of the negotiations on Granville, but Thornton's evidence is more convincing.

[29] *ibid.* pp. 572–3; 578; Part II in *E.H.R.* 1955 p. 55; Gopal pp. 33, 38. Docs. 46, 47.

claims beyond the Oxus, had no wish to reopen this delicate question, since negotiations with Russia could only reveal the mistake that had been made in 1873. But putting off Abdur Rahman with a present of twelve lakhs, as was decided in June 1883, was an expedient which would not work indefinitely. In January 1884, after a series of incidents with Russian exploratory missions, the Amir took matters into his own hands, crossed the Oxus and occupied Roshan, which immediately precipitated a collision with Bukhara. This effectively revealed the dangers of the position since, as Ripon had pointed out in 1881 and now repeated, they had become responsible for Abdur Rahman's actions without really being in a position to control him:

> The moment one great nation says to another, 'I will not permit you to interfere with this small state on my border', it becomes responsible to the other nation for restraining the smaller state from injuring its neighbour, and may justly be called upon to exercise that restraint or to allow the other nation to redress its own wrongs.[30]

Thus by 1884 a tense situation already existed on the Upper Oxus when on 13 February, the Russians finally announced the annexation of Merv. Their advance in this direction in 1883–4 had not gone unnoticed in India and Roberts, in December 1883, in particular drew attention to the dangers this presented once the Russian railhead reached Sarakhs, leaving a distance of 202 miles only to Herat. His solution to the difficulty was to recommence the construction of the strategic railways:

> Nothing will tend to secure the safety of the frontier so much as the power of rapidly concentrating troops on any threatened point. . . .

But this, he maintained, came up against disbelief in Russian ambitions against India and the prejudiced assumption that facilities for massing troops 'meant an aggressive policy, and were made with the idea of annexing more territory'.[31] Certainly Ripon refused to consider it in 1882, on the grounds that it would 'check the progress of India',[32] but in April 1884, after the shock of Merv and the Cabinet's desire to make some sort of a stand, Kimberley now ordered its resumption as far as Quetta, on the grounds that

[30] Ripon to Kimberley 29 March 1884 in Alder p. 180. See also pp. 182–7, 196–7. Docs. 48, 53.
[31] Roberts pp. 513–14.
[32] Gopal p. 37.

the occupation of Merv was 'a very grave occurrence, bringing as it does Russia into immediate contact with the Herat territory'.[33] Moreover, renewed and urgent attempts were now made to persuade St. Petersburg to delimitate the Afghan frontier in this region, pressure which resulted in agreement in May 1884 that a joint commission should be sent to survey the boundary. But, although the British party arrived in the autumn of 1884, the Russians simply procrastinated, giving their troops as much time as possible to advance from Merv on Herat. It was from this that the Pendjeh 'incident' sprang.

Although Gladstone professed great indignation at this duplicity, on the grounds that only two weeks before Giers had promised that there would be no further advance before the delimitation commission got to work and that 'it was a very solemn covenant', the clash between Russian and Afghan troops at Pendjeh on 30 March 1885 was the logical result of the tactics that Russian commanders in Asia had pursued for the previous twenty years. Exactly the same promises had been made many times before in relation to Khiva and Merv with no different result. In fact in March 1884 the India Office had drawn up an exhaustive review of Russian promises and actions over this period, running to nearly 150 pages, and concluded that they were not worth the paper they were written on.[34] De Staal in February 1884 had explained the Russian annexation of Merv as due to

> the great difficulty which both Russian and English statesmen had always acknowledged to exist for a civilised Power to stop in the extension of its territory where uncivilised tribes were its immediate neighbours.[35]

But there was little consolation in this: as Rawlinson pointed out, the logic which had 'taken Russia from Ashkabad to Merv, must necessarily take her from Merv to Herat'. It was all very well for Argyll to welcome Russia as a civilizing power but where would this stop? Salisbury put his finger on the real point in a speech at Hackney in May 1885. Granted that Giers was sincere when he made these promises and that his difficulty lay in controlling the military, this didn't make it any better since, 'whether swindler or

[33] Kimberley to Ripon 22 February 1884 in Greaves p. 65.
[34] *ibid.* p. 103.
[35] no date, in Fraser-Tytler p. 160. Doc. 49.

bankrupt you are very careful about trusting him the next time'. Moreover, even making all allowances,

> It was not wise to seek as the main object of our policy to rest the defence of India upon the guarantee of Russia ... we must do it ourselves.[36]

Hence the effect of the Pendjeh incident was to remove the defence of India from the realm of political controversy. In June 1884 proposals from the military members of the Viceroy's Council for a considerable expansion of the military establishment and strategic railways, together with the fortification of Herat, had been dismissed by Ripon as likely to 'do more to shake our real power in this country than the Russian occupation of a dozen Mervs'.[37] At the time Kimberley had supported him, discounting any real danger of a Russian invasion or attack on Herat,[38] but as the year wore on he grew less sure. Certainly he did nothing to oppose Ripon's resignation in December and replacement by Dufferin: by April 1885 he had completely accepted Roberts' views and now advocated that 'India should have a properly armed frontier such as exists between the great Continental States'.[39] Nor was Kimberley alone. There was sufficient support for this attitude in the Cabinet by March 1885 for him to be able to instruct Dufferin with Cabinet approval that 'an attack on Herat will mean war with Russia everywhere'. As he explained with the enthusiasm of the newly converted,

> it is now not a mere question about a few miles more or less of Afghan territory but of our whole relations with Russia in Asia.[40]

Even Gladstone, recognizing that a stand had to be made, promised in the House of Commons on 27 April to see 'right done in the matter' and, although his conception of 'right' was rapidly sacrificed to expediency when he abandoned Pendjeh, he did stick on the Zulficar pass and the approaches to Herat. All this was a far cry from the traditionally Russophile attitude of the Liberals, particularly when Granville and Northbrook began to make serious preparations for a naval war in the Far East and tried to persuade the Sultan to consent to British warships passing the

[36] Salisbury 6 May 1885, Rawlinson no date, in Greaves pp. 66, 105.
[37] Ripon to Kimberley 24 June 1884 in Gopal p. 44.
[38] Greaves p. 4.
[39] Minute by Kimberley 5 April 1885 *ibid.* p. 32.
[40] Kimberley to Dufferin 27 March 1885 *ibid.* p. 76. Doc. 50.

Straits. As both Kimberley and Churchill observed with perfect truth in July, 'there is substantial concurrence of opinion between us'.[41]

Overwhelmed by his own domestic troubles, with his Cabinet disintegrating around him and increasingly preoccupied with Ireland, Gladstone, now convinced that he could present 'an excellent record at home and abroad',[42] finally resigned on 12 June. Apparently in his optimism he had assumed that 'the great Russian question is probably settled', but this was far from being the case as a long drawn out debate continued for another three months as to the precise meaning of what had been agreed.[43]

The position that Salisbury inherited was that Granville had obtained from de Staal on 10 June Russian acceptance of arbitration on the responsibility for the Pendjeh affair, but they still refused to accept the British case for Afghan control of the all-important Zulficar pass,[44] the obtaining of which was critical if the Russian advance on Herat was to be blocked. The point of this was simple: the Russian generals were fully aware of the strategic importance of the position and were not inclined to withdraw; in fact, as Giers told Morier later, in St. Petersburg there was a strong body of opinion 'in favour of a march upon Herat, and of the annexation of that city'.[45] Though Salisbury himself thought war on the whole unlikely, it was plain that the solution, in view of British weakness in Central Asia, depended far more upon the general European situation and the effect that this had upon 'the Emperor of Russia, with whom the decision lies'.[46] Plainly Salisbury did not want a war over this; if for no other reason, it would take another two years to get the railway to Kandahar; the only effective means of retaliation, forcing the Straits, would be difficult in view of British isolation in Europe. As he commented on his inheritance from Gladstone,

> They have at least achieved their desired 'Concert of Europe', they have succeeded in uniting the Continent of Europe—against England.[47]

[41] Kimberley to Dufferin 10 July 1885, *ibid.* p. 79; Churchill to the Queen 11 July 1885, W. S. Churchill, *Life of Lord Randolph Churchill* (London, 1906) I, 485–6. Docs. 51, 52.
[42] Ramm II, 366–7, 372.
[43] *ibid.* On 3 August Currie told Bismarck that the Zulficar issue 'is very likely to lead to war'. Greaves p. 93.
[44] Ramm II, 385. Docs. 51, 52.
[45] Morier to Salisbury 18 April 1888 in Greaves p. 118.
[46] Salisbury to Dufferin 7 August 1885 *ibid.* p. 81.
[47] Cecil III, 136.

In this respect Salisbury had the initial advantage of Bismarck's better disposition towards him, and hence his solution to the problem was to approach Berlin in order 'to restore the good understanding between the two countries which we value of supreme importance'.[48] This approach had two main attractions. In the first place the India Office was pressing for the extension of the guarantee of Afghanistan to Persia, a step which Salisbury dismissed as impracticable. But an Anglo-German guarantee, if it could be obtained, would be a very different proposition:

> Generally, any arrangement under which the integrity of Persia might become an object of material solicitude to Germany so as to lead her to join with England in guaranteeing it could not fail to be of the utmost advantage to Indian interests to which the integrity of Persia . . . is as essential as the integrity of Afghanistan.[49]

Secondly, if it did come to war with Russia, as Salisbury had told Bismarck on 2 July, he would in one way or another force the Straits and it would be much simpler to accomplish with Bismarck's assistance than against his opposition. As a first step Currie was sent to see the Bismarcks to induce them to mediate with Russia on the Zulficar pass issue, the inducement being that 'he would be laying the foundations of a closer and more intimate alliance between the two countries'.[50]

But, unfortunately for Salisbury's hopes, Berlin showed little interest in such an alliance. From the German viewpoint there were two main objections. The first was that although Bismarck had considerable regard for Salisbury personally there was no guarantee that Gladstone would not return to office (as in fact happened in January 1886). Though Salisbury had thought there would be 'continuity of policy in this matter' Bismarck did not, and, to his mind, dealing with Gladstone was an impossibility. Their second objection was yet more formidable. Any such alliance with England would seriously irritate the Russians, a consideration which led Herbert to the conclusion that 'the water is too hot for us to put our finger in'.[51] A similar fate befell Salisbury's scheme for Anglo-German collaboration in the development of

[48] Salisbury to Bismarck 2 July 1885 in Greaves p. 92. Kimberley noted Bismarck's preference for the Conservatives, *ibid*. 91.
[49] Cabinet Minute August 1885 *ibid*. p. 99.
[50] Currie to Bismarck 3 August 1885 *ibid*. p. 93. Docs. 54, 55.
[51] Currie to Salisbury 4 August 1885 *ibid*. p. 96.

Persia: having ignored the suggestion for three months Bismarck finally announced in January 1886 that he was 'unwilling to side for or against England or Russia on points where their interests were opposed'.[52] Plainly enough, with his Three Emperors Alliance recently renewed at Kremsier, an English alliance was merely an embarassment.

This in itself was some advance, considering the manner in which Bismarck had openly egged on St. Petersburg whilst Gladstone was in office, but it effectively threw Salisbury back on his own resources as far as the defence of British interests in Central Asia was concerned. Fortunately the problem was solved for him in St. Petersburg where, suddenly, at the end of August, they accepted the British case over Zulficar and signed an agreement on 10 September giving preliminary definition to the boundary from there to the Oxus. The motives for this *volte face* are not entirely clear. It may have been that St. Petersburg recognized, as de Staal certainly did, that Salisbury was highly unlikely to cede what even Granville had refused; or simply, as Herbert Bismarck noted, that Russia was not yet ready for a conflict in Asia.[53]

But, in all probability, it was a reflection of the changing balance of power in St. Petersburg. There is considerable evidence that Giers had never been a supporter of the Russian advance in Central Asia. In his view, as in that of Skobelev, the Balkans and the Straits were the key issues. It is possible of course, as Thornton rationalized, that pressure in Central Asia was a deliberate distraction, 'to induce us to send as many troops as possible to India and keep them there far away from the real object of their ambition'.[54] But, apart from the inherent improbability of Russian policy's possessing so much coherence, Thornton's view does not altogether square with the facts. If he were correct in this assumption then surely the last thing that should have happened in September 1885 was a settlement in Central Asia just when the Bulgarian question began to move. Logically, pressure on Herat should have doubled in order to increase the distraction from the Balkans. Whilst it seems probable that there was a connection between the 'European and Asiatic poles of the Russian cosmos',[55] the exact

[52] Malet to Salisbury 9 January 1886 *ibid.* p. 100.
[53] Meyendorff, I, 254; *The Holstein Papers* III, 148.
[54] Thornton to Salisbury 29 July 1885 in Greaves p. 82. Thornton was ambassador at St. Petersburg in 1885.
[55] Morier's phrase, *ibid.* p. 108.

nature of this would seem to have been the reverse of that suggested by Thornton. Pressure for advance in Asia came from the military, particularly Kaufmann, not from Giers. In the latter's view this was a hindrance, not a help, to the main objects of Russian ambition, as he explained clearly in a remarkable letter to Saburov in 1880:

> The question of the Straits has an intimate connection with the Asiatic situation. The security of India and the freedom of communication with India form the final objective of all the Eastern policy of England and it is that which gives the Straits their principal importance for her. The prolongation of her fears in Asia can only perpetuate and amplify her hostility towards us in the Near East, and every Eastern crisis can only be aggravated by division in Asia. On the other hand a satisfactory arrangment in Asia would diminish the keeness of our antagonism in the Near East and in consequence the danger of a violation of the Straits.[56]

Hence Granville's activities in April and Salisbury's in July were not without their effects in St. Petersburg in creating alarm for the main objects of Russian concern. True, Granville had been checkmated when Bismarck supported Russia, but there was no guarantee of a repetition of this with Salisbury. Hence, since the Tsar wished to avoid any reopening of the Eastern Question,[57] Giers' policy at last prevailed, and it was in this sense, not Thornton's, that the reopening of the Bulgarian question determined a settlement in Central Asia. As long as this was a running sore in Anglo-Russian relations, Salisbury was likely to retaliate at the Straits; if this were cleared up he would have no incentive to take action.

But although the tension was taken out of Anglo-Russian relations by the agreement of 10 September 1885, it was impossible thereafter to ignore the Russian presence in Central Asia. The details of the boundary took another two years to settle and even after that still brought minor flurries of alarm, of which the great Pamirs question of 1893 was simply an extension. In consequence, the British military establishment in India was steadily increased in the next few years until it stood at 70,000 in 1894—nearly double that of 1884—and Roberts' strategic railways extended, 'for a struggle which . . . I consider to be inevitable in the end'.

[56] Giers to Saburov 18 May 1880 in Medlicott, *Bismarck, Gladstone* p. 59.
[57] Medlicott, 'The Powers and the Unification of the Two Bulgarias in 1885', *E.H.R.* 1939 p. 70.

The Defence of India

Robert, pushing these ideas, increasingly urged the adoption of the principle accepted by Kimberley in 1885 of a fixed frontier:

For India special arrangements must be made, and viewing England and Russia as continental powers in Central Asia . . . is regarded out here as essential to the maintenance of this great Empire.[58]

But this was still not altogether accepted in London. Wolseley particularly scorned it in favour of having 'our hands free all over the world', and preferred to keep the reinforcements under his own control, a preference which was not without an element of the personal rivalry which was so marked between these two leading military figures of the age.[59] But it was not entirely a personal matter. Salisbury, who in turn rejected Wolseley's strategy as meaningless without control of the Turks, pronounced the idea of a fixed frontier impracticable: 'it will be a war not of battles but of devastation . . . and that will imply not a frontier line a frontier region.'[60] What this meant in practice was increasing attention to Persia again as the root of the problem, with the resurrection of the old ideas of raising a British trained Persian force and the Seistan railway. But, compared with the root and branch differences of principle which had made a coherent policy impossible up to to 1885, these were mere tactical divergences. From 1885 onwards it was common ground that India would have to be defended beyond the Indus, leaving precisely where to the circumstances of the moment. It was this situation, fundamentally, which lay at the root of the Liberal adoption of a bi-partisan approach to foreign policy under Rosebery and what it amounted to, really, was simple recognition of the principle enunciated by the Queen in 1880:

She (Russia) is our *real enemy* & Rival—the only one perhaps (& she believes it) we *Have*.[61]

[58] Roberts pp. 520, 524; Roberts Memorandum 22 August 1888 in Greaves p. 3. It was on these grounds that Morier later told Giers that Pendjeh had been a blessing in disguise; Thornton p. 578.
[59] Greaves p. 41.
[60] Minute by Salisbury 19 August 1887 *ibid.* p. 39 Doc. 56.
[61] The Queen to Gladstone 20 June 1880 in Gopal p. 31.

V

The Mediterranean Alliance

The countries with which we are most liable to go to war are France and Russia, and the worst combination we have any reason to dread is an alliance of France and Russia against us.

D.M.I., April 1887

Although this development had been predictable even in 1885, with the combination of the Anglo-French dispute over Egypt and the tension with Russia in Central Asia, it was not until 1887 that final recognition was given to what had been an increasing preoccupation in London during this time. The prime causes of this were the growth of the Bulgarian crisis and the failure of the Anglo-Turkish negotiations on the evacuation of Egypt. The Bulgarian crisis brought the Anglo-Russian clash back to Europe and concenrtated it at the Straits, at the same time as the French opposition to an Anglo-Turkish settlement of Egypt made an Anglo-French clash in the Mediterranean seem inevitable. Salisbury's solution to this problem was to seek allies. Even in August 1885, before the Bulgarian crisis broke out, and at a time when relations with France were relatively friendly, he had suggested an alliance with Germany as the cure to the problem of Russia in Persia, so it is not surprising that he turned in the same direction in the much more serious situation of 1886–7. The difference was that Bismarck was now more receptive than he had been in 1885 since, as Austro-Russian relations deteriorated over Bulgaria, Italy and England became of more importance to him. Hence the development in 1887 of the Mediterranean Agreements, an understanding between Britain, Italy and Austria (with some German backing) for the defence of the *status quo* in this region, an alliance plainly directed against Russia and France, and which remained the dominating factor in British foreign policy for the next ten years.

When Salisbury came into office in June 1885 the Egyptian question was in fact fairly dormant. The explanation is simple. The convention that Granville had signed on 17 March governing the terms of the European loan, plus Gladstone's constant assurances, had convinced Paris of London's sincerity. Moreover, from the end of May onward, Bismarck increasingly indicated that the honeymoon was over, that the persistence of the *revanche* in France made his policy of working together impossible, that what he called the 'Coburg era' was about to dawn. Indeed, Bismarck's own ideas on Egypt—probably deliberately—were now completely unsatisfactory. Whilst he still spoke of secretly undermining the current financial and Canal negotiations he also advocated bringing back the Turks.[1] This, Freycinet thought, was contrary to the trend of French policy over the previous forty years: it was much better to leave the British alone than to accept this since, sooner or later, they would go anyway. Consequently, if Germany were moving towards a British alliance, as Courcel thought, this was not the time for France to compromise herself unduly with England who was, as Freycinet pointed out, her 'natural ally'. Hence his policy of caution at this stage, combining reassurances to Berlin of the pacific intentions of his ministry—despite the bitter Franco-German press war, which bore all the marks of inspiration—with inaction at London, whilst allowing his newspaper, *La Liberté*, to openly advocate a renewal of friendship with England, and leaving the initiative in Egypt entirely to Salisbury.[2]

Salisbury himself was not averse to an understanding with France. He told Waddington in June that he held to the ideas exchanged in 1878, and thanked Freycinet via Lyons for his forbearance over Egypt: as he told Drummond-Wolff on 1 September, with an air of surprise, 'France is not nearly so far from us as we thought'.[3] Hence, that he now embarked on an ambitious attempt to solve the Egyptian question by means of Drummond-Wolff's mission to Constantinople was not due to any pressure from or hostility towards France, or any urgency in the situation

[1] G. P. iii. no. 704.
[2] P. B. Mitchell, *The Bismarckian Policy of Conciliation with France* (London, 1935) pp. 201–3; D.D.F. vi. nos. 32–9; vi. bis. no. 2; G.P. iii. no. 707.
[3] D.D.F. vi. nos. 38, 43; Cecil III, 236.

in Egypt; after his exchange of views with Bismarck in July he was reasonably confident of German support there. But his attempts in August to extend this German support into any sort of general alliance against Russia failed, so that, as far as the future was concerned, Salisbury was thrown back on his own resources. Not that he envisaged war with Russia in Central Asia as at all probable; but, in case of future complications, he wanted to avoid the position in which Granville had found himself in the previous April when a united Continent had blocked any possibility of retaliation upon Russia via the Straits. What he contemplated in fact was a deal with the Sultan whereby, in return for the evacuation of Egypt, the latter would permit the British fleet to pass through the Straits in the event of war with Russia.[4]

There was however a considerable difference between Salisbury's and Gladstone's conceptions of evacuation. Gladstone had regarded it as a matter of simple justice, in the light of his general slogan that England should be 'no less just than strong', and couldn't get out fast enough: he even told Waddington on 11 May 1885 that he hoped to leave Egypt before the expiration of his term of office:[5] Salisbury, by contrast, though he was opposed at this time to any idea of annexation, had no intention of giving away one of the few cards he possessed:

> My great objection to fixing a date for our evacuation of Egypt, is that relief from our hated presence is the one bribe we have to offer, the price we have to pay for any little advantages we may desire to secure.

To his way of thinking diplomacy was a question of bargaining, not moral principle, and if he was prepared to evacuate it would be on his own terms: what he had in mind was set out clearly to Drummond-Wolff on 13 August:

> The end to which I would work is evacuation, but with certain privileges reserved for England. I should like a Treaty right to occupy Alexandria when we pleased . . . and perhaps one or two other things.

Although recognizing that this would be difficult he thought it by no means impossible, particularly if the uncertainties about

---

[4] G.P. iv. nos. 782, 783; Greaves, pp. 240–4; Salisbury to Drummond-Wolff August 1885, P.R.O. 30/6/128. Doc. 57. For the negotiations with Bismarck in August 1885 see Chapter IV.

[5] M. P. Hornik, 'The Mission of Sir Henry Drummond-Wolff to Constantinople, 1885–7', *E.H.R.* 1940 p. 602.

British policy were resolved by a clear Tory win at the forth-coming election. For this reason he preferred to avoid fixing any clear date for evacuation for the present. All he wanted for the moment was some move to appease the Sultan and the best way to do this was to make the Turks co-occupiers until evacuation actually took place.[6]

But the scheme largely misfired. An agreement was reached on 24 October for sending a Turkish Commissioner to Egypt but the larger project fell through. The Sultan had no desire to adopt an attitude of hostility towards Russia which could only compromise him, and no Turkish troops were forthcoming. In fact this was just as well since as soon as the Turkish Commissioner reached Cairo he wanted to reverse the policy of the abandonment of the Sudan, which Salisbury had fully accepted, and embark on the reconquest of Dongola. Consequently, for the following nine months nothing happened. In Egypt Drummond-Wolff and Moukhtar Pasha wrangled indefinitely over the abandonment of the Sudan until Gladstone, in office again from January until June 1886, settled the question by withdrawing half the British garrison. But evacuation was as far off as ever since no progress had been made with the organization of an Egyptian army; so much so that by May Freycinet was reduced to urging the Porte to send Turkish officers and N.C.O's so that this might be accomplished and Britain's major excuse for delay removed.[7]

Nor was French diplomacy any more successful outside Egypt. Until the election of November 1885 Freycinet had abstained from pressure on the Suez Canal settlement at Salisbury's request until the political position in London had been clarified. But attempts in December and January to move Berlin and London brought no results since Bismarck merely referred him to Salisbury: Rosebery, who succeeded as Foreign Secretary in January, took six weeks to reply and was then very discouraging, leading Freycinet to suspect the worst.[8] Overwhelmingly preoccupied with Ireland, in a politi-cal situation in which the Liberal Party was breaking up, it was not to be expected that even Gladstone would show his former zeal where Egypt was concerned; certainly he told Waddington in March that though he personally favoured evacuation, 'this was

[6] Salisbury to Drummond-Wolff 18 August 1885 in Robison and Gallagher p. 258; to Drummond-Wolff 13 August, to Paget 18 August, Cecil III, 235. Doc. 58.

[7] Hornik p. 603; D.D.F. vi. nos. 49, 248. Doc. 59.

[8] *ibid.* nos. 144, 153, 158, 204, 208.

not an opportune moment and the position in Egypt was too complicated'. Rosebery, who did 'not care very much for France' and shared Salisbury's views on Egypt, had no intention of doing anything. As he told Cromer,

> my policy would be to leave things alone for the present, and shield the Egyptians from the intolerable nightmare of new Commissioners, Projects, Reports and Conventions.[9]

In effect, therefore, by July 1886, when Salisbury returned to office, Freycinet had achieved precisely nothing by his twelve months of waiting for the British electoral position to clarify. This was to prove fatal. For, by May 1887, when at last Salisbury's negotiations bore fruit, Freycinet had been replaced by the short-sighted Goblet and Flourens, whose own parliamentary position was in turn too delicate, and the Anglo-French dual over Egypt recommenced.

Apart from British internal difficulties, the main reason why an Egyptian settlement was so long delayed was that from September 1885 onwards it was increasingly pushed off the centre of the European stage by the Bulgarian Question. As long as this remained the main preoccupation of the European powers it was difficult for Freycinet to achieve anything in Egypt since what slight interest France had in Bulgaria—and this was minimal—was more or less identical to that of England. It was too dangerous even for her to simply support Russia with an eye to the possible *quid pro quo* over Egypt, since, if Bulgaria should produce a European war on this basis, the results for France could be catastrophic. Despite Freycinet's eagerness to claim that he initiated the Franco-Russian alliance by co-operation with Russia in this period, all the evidence is to the contrary; he kept out of involvement in Bulgaria as far as humanly possible.[10] In any case, why should he support Russia? Even when he abandoned hope of getting much out of Salisbury in September 1886 he still thought the Egyptian question could be solved by collaboration with Berlin. Hence, it was not French action but the triangular Anglo-Austro-Russian contest in Bulgaria, which created the British alignment with Austria and Italy for the defence of the *status quo* in the Mediterranean. France

[9] *ibid.* no. 210; Zetland, *Lord Cromer* (London, 1932) p. 127; Q.V.L. 3rd. series I, 48, 50.
[10] B. Nolde, *L'alliance Franco-Russe* (Paris, 1936) pp. 351-2.

only became linked with Russia in British eyes *after* this was created, largely owing to her joint action with Russia in opposing Drummond-Wolff's convention.

The Bulgarian crisis of 1885–7 originated in the revolution in Eastern Roumelia on 18 September 1885 and proclamation of the union of the two Bulgarias by Prince Alexander three days later. In St. Petersburg there was no sympathy with the action of the Bulgars in reconstructing the Big Bulgaria of 1878. The rising friction between Prince Alexander and the Tsar since 1883 burst into a violent personal antipathy in 1885; on 22 September Russian officers were withdrawn from Bulgaria and a Bulgarian delegation to the Tsar told that this union was 'completely contrary to the will of Russia'. The reasons for this *volte face* were not hard to seek: according to White, Prince Alexander was the main barrier to Russian influence in Bulgaria and they would do nothing which would assist him to maintain his influence. Since there was no possible gain for Russia in this situation, consequently, the last thing they wanted at this stage was a reopening of the Near Eastern question with all its attendant dangers. Since 1881 Russian policy had been based upon the *Dreikaiserbund* as a means of staving off Austro-German pressure and the Tsar saw no reason to change course now. Similarly, in Vienna and Berlin the main consideration was that Bulgarian affairs should not disturb the even tenor of their relations with Russia. Bismarck's solution was to suggest action by Turkey to suppress the infringement of the Treaty of Berlin, if necessary supported by a conference to 'drown the question in ink'.[11]

In view of British policy in 1878, when Salisbury and Disraeli had been largely responsible for the creation of two Bulgarias, it was logical to anticipate that Salisbury would be as eager to suppress their union as Bismarck. Initially this was so: on 19 September he sent a circular to Berlin, Vienna and Rome advocating the maintenance of the Treaty of Berlin, apparently on the assumption that the events in Philippopolis were the work of Russian agents. As he explained to the Queen on 24 September, if Britain were now to take the lead in tearing up the settlement she had imposed seven years before, 'her position will not be honourable and her

---

[11] W. N. Medlicott, 'The Powers and the Unification of the Two Bulgarias, 1885', *E.H.R.* 1939 pp. 70, 263; C. L. Smith, *The Embassy of Sir William White at Constantinople* (Oxford, 1957) pp. 15–16, 28–9.

influence will be much diminished'. If he had remained of this persuasion there would have been no crisis but, by the time the conference was summoned on 15 October, Salisbury had changed his mind and now supported 'the wish of the people of Bulgaria'. It was this which created a Bulgarian 'question' since, but for this sudden change, the Powers would have settled the question without any difficulty.[12]

The explanation of this change of heart did not lie in any particular sympathy for the Bulgarians: Gladstone might think that Britain's only interest in the Balkans lay in the ejection of the Turk and the 'furthering of the freedom of the Christian nationalities', but not Salisbury. Though he made speeches and wrote Blue Book despatches to this effect, and described the work of the Three Emperors to the French as repeating the repressions of the Congress of Verona, this was simply good public relations. Once he had decided to oppose Russia at the conference it was mere common sense to make as much as possible of the democratic argument in the hopes of attracting French and Italian support: they, like England, were governed by public opinion. This, Waddington thought, lay at the root of Salisbury's curious policy, completely at odds with previous Conservative doctrine: public opinion had veered strongly in favour of the Bulgarians and Salisbury was due to fight an election in November.[13] But this was not the entire explanation. The original object in separating the two Bulgarias had been to enable the Turks to garrison the line of the Balkan mountains as an effective barrier against Russia. But this had never materialized since the Turks had omitted to send troops forward when the Russians withdrew, whilst the cession of Varna to Bulgaria turned the position in any case. Hence if it were true, as White urged and Salisbury increasingly inclined to believe, that the Bulgars themselves and particularly Prince Alexander were the best barrier against Russian expansion in the Balkans, then the object of British policy must be to keep him on the throne. Since any acceptance on his part of a demand from the Powers that he abandon Eastern Roumelia would promptly lead to his overthrow in Bulgaria, Salisbury, from 28 September onwards, insisted that Britain could not be a party to his deposition and put forward 'personal union' as a solution to the problem. Whether at all he

---

[12] Medlicott p. 68; Smith p. 21; Cecil III, 241.
[13] D.D.F. vi. no. 94; Medlicott pp. 74–5, 284; Smith pp. 22–3.

was influenced by the Queen's eagerness to support 'poor Sandro' is difficult to estimate, but the central point is that he shared her assumption that if they allowed Alexander to be upset 'we may find ourselves with a Big Bulgaria under a Russian Prince'.[14]

The main difficulty with 'personal union' however was its repercussions upon Balkan politics. Kálnoky, and even Bismarck, were at first reasonably disposed towards it, but quickly disavowed it when it became plain that the result would only be to encourage Serbia and Greece to stake out their claims to aggrandisement, and probably produce a general onslaught upon the Ottoman Empire. Hence the decision of the *Dreikaiserbund* to insist on the return to the *status quo ante* in Bulgaria, in contrast to Salisbury's plan, which produced a complete deadlock at the Constantinople ambassador's conference by 12 November. There appeared to be a good deal of truth in Giers' bitter comment that, simply for the sake of doing Russia a bad turn,

> the British Cabinet is risking the lighting of a conflagration in the East which could finish off the Ottoman Empire and set fire to Europe.[15]

But in fact this was not so likely as it seemed. Salisbury talked a lot about the wishes of the people but he had no intention of encouraging the crumbling away of the Ottoman Empire, quite the reverse. In the case of Bulgaria what he was aiming at was the construction of a new barrier against Russia with which to prop up the Sultan's control of the remainder of the Balkans, not the liberation of more people from the Turks. This was, after all, precisely the time of his negotiations with the Sultan via Drummond-Wolff, one of whose cardinal objects was a closer understanding with Constantinople. This becomes abundantly clear if his attitude towards the Bulgarian question is taken in conjunction with that towards Greece and Serbia. From the beginning he had been quite prepared to take the initiative in dissuading the Greeks from seeking compensation, if necessary by force: when it became apparent that Kálnoky could no longer hold back the Serbs he was the first to suggest that they should be steered in the direction of Bulgaria rather than Macedonia. Nor, in fact, was there the slightest possibility of war with Russia over this issue: if the Eastern powers were successful in persuading the Turks to intervene in Eastern Roumelia, he had no intention of going beyond verbal

[14] Salisbury to Lyons 16 October 1885, Cecil III, 245; Medlicott p. 69.
[15] Giers to de Staal 5 November 1885 quoted in Medlicott p. 276.

opposition.[16] Essentially he was bluffing, as it turned out, very successfully.

The chief ingredient in this success was the Bulgarian victory over the Serbs at Slivnitza on 19 November and the almost complete destruction of the Serbian armies that followed, since, as Salisbury pointed out to the Queen, this made it 'impossible for Russia to separate the two Bulgarias'. The general wave of popular enthusiasm for them led the Italians to repudiate their support for Turkish military intervention, whilst Freycinet, abandoning his almost complete reserve, now openly adopted Salisbury's views. De Staal, and even Giers, now recognized that Prince Alexander could not be unseated and that the important thing was to close down the Bulgarian episode with the least possible damage to the *Dreikaiserbund* after the strained relations with Austria during the Serb-Bulgar conflict. This made a settlement possible and Salisbury, by the simple tactic of blockading the Greeks whilst pressing the Turks to negotiate with Bulgaria, was in a fair way to achieving this by the time he resigned on 6 February. Since Rosebery, as in Egypt, completely accepted his policy, with which Gladstone agreed, the change of government made no difference and a Turkish-Bulgar agreement based on Salisbury's idea of personal union and recognizing Alexander as ruler of Eastern Roumelia, was signed on 6 April 1886.[17]

What effect did this first phase of the Bulgarian crisis have upon the British position in Europe? First and foremost it reinforced the existing Anglo-Russian rivalry in Asia with a similar hostility in the Near East. The Tsar was now convinced that England, not his German allies, was Russia's real opponent in Europe, whilst Giers characterized Salisbury's action as a 'reversion to the wild Imperialist policy of Lord Beaconsfield'.[18] This sentiment was fully reciprocated in London. The Queen constantly fulminated against Russian 'devilry', whilst Salisbury made no bones about the fact that the object of his Bulgarian policy was that 'an independent national feeling might be got up in Bulgaria that, joined to that already existing in Roumania, might make the Russian passage to Constantinople very difficult'.[19] Moreover the old Russophile

[16] *ibid.* pp. 77, 284; Smith p. 29; Cecil III, 249, 252.
[17] Salisbury to the Queen 20 November, Cecil III, 251; Q.V.L. I, 50, 53, 55; Smith pp. 35–51; Nolde p. 336; D.D.F. vi. nos. 141, 143.
[18] Medlicott p. 283.
[19] Q.V.L. I, 70; Cecil III, 249–50. Doc. 60.

attitude of the Liberals was now completely dead, as was amply demonstrated by the violent reaction of Gladstone and Rosebery to the Russian repudiation of the free port status of Batoum in July 1886, a reaction completely out of proportion to the importance of the issue at stake.[20] In this way Bulgaria completed what Pendjeh had started.

Secondly, it established Salisbury's reputation in Europe. The absolute success of the policy, which he alone of European statesmen urged, if opportunist and due largely to luck—White thought that but for Slivnitza it would have been literally another Pendjeh —owed something to his perserverance, and brought dividends when it became apparent that Russia had placed herself in a hopeless position. Admittedly he made very little impression on the *Dreikaiserbund,* since Radowitz supported Nelidov throughout the crisis and Bismarck managed to avoid any serious strain on Austro-Russian relations. The basic position did not allow him to do otherwise. As he pointed out to Hatzfeldt, in response to gestures of Churchill's, Germany could not possibly abandon Russia unless and until England signed a hard and fast alliance, which she could never do in view of the fact that the government might change overnight and abandon Germany, as Gladstone had abandoned Austria and Turkey.[21] But, nevertheless, after Slivnitza Bismarck was much more inclined to play a double game and certainly took a hand in producing the April agreement: if, as Salisbury suspected, he was simply using England to pull his chestnuts out of the fire, this at least was some advance on the disastrous isolation of April 1885.[22] If it did nothing else, Salisbury had established that England had re-entered the market place in the Near East, a precondition of the advances of 1887 in the renewed Bulgarian crisis. The Queen's view, if biassed, was not totally inaccurate:

> Lord Beaconsfield raised up the position of Great Britain, from '74 to '80, in a marvellous manner. Mr. Gladstone and Lord Granville pulled it down again during the five years of their mischievous and fatal misrule, but already in seven months Lord Salisbury raised our position again.[23]

[20] Q.V.L. I, 152–3; Ramm II, 457.
[21] Bismarck to Hatsfeldt 9 December 1885, G.P. iv. no. 789; Medlicott p. 67.
[22] Cecil III, 253–5; Smith pp. 35–6.
[23] To Salisbury 1 September 1886, Q.V.L. I, 196.

As Rosebery had surmised in March 1886, as long as Prince Alexander and the Tsar remained unreconciled they had not heard the last of the Bulgarian problem. This was demonstrated almost immediately after Salisbury's return to office by the kidnapping of Alexander from Sofia, his enforced abdication, and the long drawn out tension that followed. Opinion in Britain from the Queen to Gladstone was unanimous in condemning what Salisbury termed Russia's 'simply piratical' action, but the difficulties commenced when it came to doing something about it. The Queen, in her indignation at the treatment of poor Sandro by 'these Russian fiends', urged Salisbury to conduct wholesale purges in the diplomatic service as a prelude to much more forceful action at Constantinople: 'let England's voice be heard again'.[24] But to Salisbury's mind this was not so easy. Various factors, among them the strictly limited amount of Secret Service money and the traditions of the service made it difficult to find capable diplomatists; but, even when this was surmounted by the appointment of White in place of the luckless Thornton, basic difficulties still remained. Foremost among these was lack of military power:

> As land forces go in these days, we have no army capable of meeting even a second-class Continental Power; that is, we could never spare force enough at any one point to do so. The result is that, in all places at a distance from the sea, our diplomatists can only exhort, they cannot threaten; and this circumstance often deprives their words of any weight.

Moreover, in dealing with a power like Russia, any British Foreign Secretary suffered from the difficulties inherent in the constitution; the lack of political stability and 'the necessity of adapting our foreign policy to the views of a Cabinet of fourteen or sixteen men, usually ignorant of it and seldom united in their views'.[25]

Hence British opposition had to be limited to what the Cabinet would accept in the way of diplomatic action in collaboration with the powers signatory to the Treaty of Berlin, since there was no possible question of the isolated use of force. Here there was an unexpected difficulty. A Cabinet meeting on 7 September revealed that Churchill, backed by Smith and Hamilton, was unwilling to support the traditional policy of opposition to Russia

[24] *ibid.* 178–88, 190–2, 213.
[25] Salisbury to the Queen 29 August 1886, *ibid.* 194–5.

in the Balkans, taking the view that the possession of Egypt and Cyprus made this superfluous, and urging instead that everything should be concentrated on the struggle in Afghanistan. Although he was outvoted by the 'older and wiser heads', this opposition, in view of the precarious position of Salisbury's administration, made things doubly difficult.[26]

The elections of 1886 had been fought almost entirely on the issue of Home Rule, and Ireland completely dominated the political scene, all but excluding any consideration of foreign affairs. This struck quite forcibly the few people who gave any attention to these abstruse matters, and, as Dilke put it at the time:

> When we are thinking about Ireland, which is very commonly the case, we are apt to forget all else, and both our relations with foreign Powers and those with our dependencies drop into the background.

But to make matters worse neither the Conservatives nor the Liberals had a clear majority. The issue of Home Rule had split the Liberal Party which, otherwise, in alliance with Parnell would have controlled the House of Commons. But the Liberal-Unionists, some 78 in number, led by such contrasts as Hartington and Chamberlain, although opposed to Gladstone's Irish policy would not join the Conservatives and, for the life of this Parliament, continued to sit on the Opposition benches. Hartington, though offered the Leadership of the House, declined: to accept would break up his following and all hopes of an eventual reconstruction of the Liberal party on non-Gladstonian lines. Hence the best Salisbury could obtain in August 1886 was a promise of support from the outside, support which gave him a working majority but which made any positive moves, apart from Ireland, extremely difficult. As he was to remark later, resolute government outside Ireland was impossible.[27]

As a result of this situation therefore, Churchill, despite being in a minority, was in a position to impose his views on foreign policy since Salisbury, however much he disagreed with him, had to concentrate on keeping the government in being. As he explained to Cranbrook, who was equally irritated by Churchill's activities,

> Like you, I am penetrated with a sense of the danger which the

[26] *ibid.* 201-3, 220.
[27] C. J. Lowe, *Salisbury and the Mediterranean* (London, 1965) pp. 3-4.

collapse of our Government would bring about: otherwise I should not have undertaken—or should have quickly abandoned—the task of leading an orchestra in which the first fiddle plays one tune and everybody else, including myself, wishes to play another.

Since he was Leader of the House, Chancellor of the Exchequer, backed by Hamilton, Smith and Beach, and champion of Tory democracy with close links with Chamberlain, Randolph had to be treated with 'the utmost forbearance'. Since, in his view, involvement in European politics was sheer stupidity it was impossible, until he committed the error of resigning, for Salisbury and Iddesleigh to adopt any sort of positive policy either in Bulgaria or anywhere else. As Salisbury had explained to the Queen in August, British diplomats were often condemned to making bricks without straw; but Churchill's determination to make large cuts in military and naval expenditure made things even worse. The latter's view that 'our present huge and increasing armaments are quite unnecessary' if only foreign policy were conducted 'with skill and judgement', could not have been further removed from Salisbury's, whose real worry was that Smith and Hamilton had erred on the cautious side in their departmental estimates. Hence the alacrity with which he accepted Churchill's resignation in December since, despite the danger this presented of the break up of the government, the alternative was by then even worse.[28]

The apparent gravity of the situation was due to the expectation current in London that a Russian invasion of Bulgaria was imminent in order to suppress the widespread hostility to General Kaulbars and his mission. Kaulbars, nominally Russian Minister at Sofia, had in fact assumed the 'protectorship' of Bulgaria after the enforced abdication of Alexander and was currently occupied with persuading the Bulgarian Assembly at Tirnova to elect a Russian candidate for the throne. Since this was meeting with little success, St. Petersburg, wounded in its *amour propre* by this patent ingratitude, adopted the view that the Bulgarian people were being terrorized into this anti-Russian course by 'brigands', from whom they would have to be liberated. It was this prospect of 'liberation' which was so alarming to London, since it would destroy all hope of an independent Bulgaria's acting as a barrier to

[28] Cecil III, 322, 327, 336; W. S. Churchill, *Lord Randolph Churchill* (London, 1906) II, 235. Docs. 61, 62.

the advance of Russia on Constantinople. Hence the British attempt to mobilize the support of the powers signatory to the Treaty of Berlin.

But the difficulty was that, in view of Churchill's attitude, which he did not trouble to conceal, it was extremely difficult to state with any assurance just what British policy was. Iddesleigh and Salisbury, working on the assumption that Austria at least would oppose Russian expansion in the Balkans and that she should be supported,[29] drew up a memorandum defining British policy at the end of September which was intended to bolster up the confidence of Vienna in British intentions. But the effect was not very encouraging. As Iddesleigh admitted, owing to party politics, the nature of the constitution, and the importance of public opinion, it was difficult to predict in advance what British policy would be on hypothetical issues: all he could say was that for a clearly defined object such as the defence of Constantinople, 'England no doubt would fight'. Yet, on the strength of this, Austria and Germany were expected to take a decided stand over Bulgaria. Bismarck was frank, brutally so: he did not intend to lift a finger for Prince Alexander or the Bulgarians. As far as he was concerned Bulgaria and even Constantinople was a Russian sphere of interest in which he would not intervene; he could not recognize as involving the *casus foederis* of the Dual Alliance any war arising from Bulgaria. Kálnoky adopted a similar attitude. He did not think that 'simply to protect the Bulgarian people from the rough usage of General Kaulbars it was worth plunging Europe into war'. Only if Russia showed unmistakeable intention of taking possession of Bulgaria, permanent establishment in the Balkans and arriving at Constantinople would he move.[30]

Thus, despite his own desire to maintain traditional policy at Constantinople and to collaborate with Austria in checking Russian influence in the Balkans, Salisbury, so far, had met with little success. The combination of Bismarck's complete reserve and the impression created abroad by Churchill's attitude had defeated him. All that he could do was play a waiting game, whilst giving his own views official currency by his Guildhall speech on 9 November in which he made it clear that Britain would support

[29] Cecil III, 321. This was a false assumption, as White pointed out to Ponsonby at the time; see Q.V.L. I, 206–7.
[30] Lowe pp. 6–7.

Austria.[31] This policy of wait and see became even more imperative in December and January with the development of Franco-German tension over Boulanger and Bismarck's parliamentary engineering. Now, if Hatzfeldt's remarks were to be taken at face value—and Salisbury's letter to the Queen suggests that he at least did so—there was not the slightest possibility of Germany's supporting Austria in the Balkans, as all their forces were needed for the western front. As British resources, unaided, were insufficient to do more than protect Constantinople itself, it was now all the more essential to keep the Bulgarian question in cold storage; make the British position clear to St. Petersburg, but avoid any controversial move which might spark off sudden action on the part of the Tsar. For the present the Bulgarian regents should be supported but the election of a prince to replace Alexander postponed as long as possible. The last thing Salisbury wanted to do was to promote any sort of a conflict, whether Franco-German or Anglo-Russian. In any case, even if he wanted to push Austria forward, his own parliamentary position did not permit positive action. According to Waddington, who had it from Derby, the Liberal Unionists would not support Salisbury in a war in the East any more than Churchill would; in which respect Goschen was no improvement, as Salisbury discovered. In these circumstances, as he told the Queen, the advice from Swaine, the military attaché in Berlin, to court a war in the Black Sea, was 'of doubtful wisdom in itself; and quite impracticable under a Parliamentary Government'.[32]

Hence it follows that Salisbury was far from being 'the great perturbator of the peace of Europe' that Labouchere denounced on 31 January.[33] This, perhaps a fair judgement on his Bulgarian policy in 1885, was wide of the mark by 1887. That within the next two weeks he made an arrangement with Italy for the defence of the Mediterranean, extended in March to Austria, does not alter this contention, in fact it supports it. For if the character of these negotiations is investigated, it is clear that they were initiated not by Salisbury but by Robilant and Bismarck, and had their origin in Italian Mediterranean aspirations and the problems that

[31] Iddesleigh told de Staal this was meant seriously: Q.V.L. I, 222. It was, perhaps, aimed at Budapest as much as St. Petersburg.
[32] *ibid.* I, 255, 261–3, 265; Smith pp. 72–3; D.D.F. vi. bis. no. 13. Docs. 63. 64.
[33] Q.V.L. I, 267.

these created for the renewal of the Triple Alliance.[34] Moreover, these were strictly defensive arrangements for the preservation of the *status quo* in the Mediterranean and adjacent seas, whose content was so deliberately imprecise that the Cabinet was free to define them almost as it saw fit. If Salisbury welcomed Robilant's advances—as he obviously did—he was no more inclined to adopt a bellicose stance over Bulgaria after the conclusion of the agreements than he had been before. What he wanted, as his letter to Morier of 19 January indicates clearly enough, was something which would help to deter the Tsar from action and provide a second line of defence if this failed: but on no account did he want to provoke any Russia activity. As delicately as possible Morier was to reiterate British support of Austria, 'nor will Austria want for other allies. Italy is very deeply preoccupied . . . and she has made overtures to us very unusual in the earnestness . . . with which they are pressed'. To Salisbury the limited alliance that he proceeded to conclude was a buttress of peace, not a preparation for war: the last thing he wanted was to provoke any Russian activity.[35]

Obviously from the viewpoint of stabilizing the situation in the Balkans, Salisbury welcomed the Italian advances. Italy and Britain had a lot in common, as had been recognized in Italy since 1882. From 1884 onwards successive Italian foreign ministers had been seeking an alliance with London and Robilant had made specific advances during the previous Autumn. But their weakness at that time had been that they were confined to the Egyptian question, at a time when Salisbury's prime interest had been Bulgaria: on Bulgaria Robilant had maintained a strict reserve. Now it seemed that the position had changed. But Robilant's proposals of 26 January contained another aspect which was by no means so welcome, the effect of which was 'to offer an alliance in case of war against France'. This Salisbury rejected out of hand. He had no objection to general collaboration with Italy in the Mediterranean since their interests were 'very similar'; nor did he dispute that 'if circumstances arise for it, Tripoli should be occupied by Italy and not by France'. He thought that if France were to attack Italy then British assistance 'might be very probably looked for': but he made it quite clear to Corti and Hatzfeldt that this would not apply in the case of 'preventive wars', in which case he 'did not hold out any hope of English sympathy and aid'. Moreover, there could be no question of a formal alliance providing for mutual naval assistance, as Robilant wanted, since 'England never promised material assistance in view of an uncertain war'. But providing these limitations were recognized Salisbury thought the suggestions for mutual support in the maintenance of the *status quo* in the Aegean, Adriatic and Black Seas and the African coast 'more acceptable'. Since this attitude was shared by the Cabinet there was no obstacle to the Italian *entente* and, since Robilant was quite willing to be satisfied with a simple exchange of notes that amounted to no more than a declaration of intent, leaving the definition of material co-operation to be decided by the governments if and when the time came for action, by 12 February the arrangements were completed.[36]

By 24 March they had been extended to Austria. The negotiations with Vienna from 23 February onward were along similar lines to those recently conducted with Rome, but they served to bring out even more clearly the nature of the agreement. As in the case of Italy, the pressure to conclude came from Berlin, Kálnoky initially showing little interest. Again he would have preferred an alliance binding 'not only the present but future British governments' but, like Robilant, he had to be satisfied with a more limited agreement. As Salisbury pointed out, Gladstone's views on the subject of Austria were notorious—even Goschen had felt some qualms on working with her—but Károlyi was sufficiently convinced, as Corti had been, of Salisbury's sincerity to think a purely diplomatic arrangement worthwhile. This, it was recognized,

> was not a promise of material support on either side, but was a definition of policy on the part of the two Powers acting in harmony to be pursued by moral and diplomatic means.

Moreover, Kálnoky emphasized, Austrian interests 'were not engaged in the Western Mediterranean but were confined to the Aegean and the Euxine', a point accepted readily enough by Salisbury and to which Corti made no objection.[37]

Nevertheless, despite the casual nature of these agreements—both of which took the form of an exchange of notes rather than

[36] *ibid.* pp. 15–16; Q.V.L. I, 268–73. Docs. 65, 66, 67.
[37] Lowe pp. 17–18.

a treaty—they were of considerable importance. The great advantage of this *entente* with Italy was, of course, as Robilant had pointed out in the course of the neogiations, that by this means 'England would be once more linked to the central powers'. This was evident from the manner of Bismarck's intervention. Unknown to Salisbury, Bismarck had encouraged Robilant towards a Mediterranean understanding with Britain since the previous October and had pressed him directly to open negotiations in January. But from 1 February onwards this interest was overt in the form of Hatzfeldt's support for Corti at London and Bismarck's pressure upon Malet at Berlin, warning him of the dire consequences that would follow if Salisbury turned down the Italian advances.

> He could, for instance, easily patch up matters with France by yielding to her constant solicitations concerning Egypt. He could ward off all apprehension from Russia by reducing his alliance with Austria to its literal engagement to maintain the integrity of the Austrian Empire and allowing Russia to take not Constantinople but the Bosphorus and the Dardanelles.

As Malet commented it was 'a little strong of Bismarck' to suggest going back on his agreement in the previous October to give support in Egypt in return for the favourable settlement in Zanzibar, but the drift of his remarks was clear enough. Either the Italian proposals were accepted or German hostility at both Cairo and Constantinople was to be anticipated, in other words a return to 1885. 'The question is I think a much bigger one that it appeared when first mooted by Ct. Robilant.'[38]

Evidently this view was shared by Salisbury since he told the Queen that this was 'as close an alliance as the Parliamentary character of our institutions will permit' and that it was 'necessary to avoid serious danger'. But the question arises as to what danger he was insuring against. It has been generally assumed[39] that this first agreement with Italy was directed against France; but, whilst this was true in Robilant's case—and even he spoke of the 'paralysing effect these proposals would have upon Russia'—it was certainly not so for Salisbury. There was no quarrel with France which necessitated the support of the Triple Alliance: indeed in the

[38] Malet to Salisbury 2, 5 February 1887, S.P.
[39] Langer, *European Alliances*, pp. 400–401.

same breath as he recommended the agreement with Italy Salisbury put forward to the Queen his proposals on the evacuation of Egypt. Though Flourens had been slightly more pressing than Freycinet, there is nothing in Salisbury's correspondence at this time to suggest any antagonism with Paris. In fact, as he told Malet on 16 February, the natural French fear of Germany 'will be adequate security for us'. Clearly enough, when he encouraged Corti in the first place it was on the assumption that Italy was to be recruited to the defence of Constantinople: certainly he rejected outright 'any promise even of diplomatic co-operation . . . against any single Power such as France'. The danger to Salisbury was not France, or even Russia, but one or both supported by the Triple Alliance. Insurance with the 'League of Peace' averted this, and, by making sure of their support for the renewed Drummond-Wolff negotiations, gave him a sporting chance of achieving a settlement over Egypt which would both improve his relations with France and Turkey and lessen his dependence on Berlin in the future.[40]

Hence the importance of the failure of the Drummond-Wolff negotiations, since the long term result was to make any understanding with France and Turkey impossible. In the autumn of 1886 Freycinet had been trying to settle Egypt by collaboration with London or Berlin and Rome, at this stage avoiding any overtures to Russia on the subject and making clear his lack of interest in Bulgaria.[41] But all his efforts were unavailing. At Berlin Bismarck put him off with platitudes, meanwhile using the French advances to seek concessions from London in Zanzibar: at Rome, Robilant promptly relayed his offers to Berlin and used them to push Bismarck into making a choice between France and England.[42] In London the situation was more complicated. Here Iddesleigh and Salisbury wished to renew the negotiations towards evacuation and assured Freycinet of their good intentions. There was, said Iddesleigh, no English statesman who did not want to put an end to this situation, whilst Salisbury stressed that all he wanted was to get out honourably, since 'the troops that we have there would be much more useful in India'. There can be no doubt that this was quite genuine; apart from anything else

[40] Salisbury to the Queen 2, 10 February, Q.V.L. I, 268–70; to Malet 16 February S.P.; 23 February, Cecil IV, 40–1.
[41] Hornik pp. 610–11; D.D.F. vi. 312, 317, 334, 342, 358.
[42] Lowe p. 12. On Zanzibar see Chapter VI.

it was realized that there was a close connection between Egypt and Bulgaria and that the best way to enlist Turkish sympathies in the latter was to negotiate with the Sultan over Egypt. This, Malet urged, would 'drive Russia back on her haunches'.[43]

But the difficulty was to translate this into action. The other side of the coin of Churchill's policy of abandoning the Straits and an agreement with Russia, was to stick in Egypt at any price. From September onwards Churchill made no secret of his views and told all who would listen to him: in consequence, it was not until January 1887 that Drummond-Wolff could be sent back to Constantinople. But it is significant that as soon as his hands were freed Salisbury took up the question again: the only difference was that the revelation of the Franco-German split made it more possible to stick out for the terms he thought necessary. As he told Drummond-Wolff, 'I do not expect to carry what I want at present but, before modifying these terms, I should like to know what is going to happen in Europe.' Although wanting to avoid 'permanent disagreement with France and Turkey', Salisbury was equally insistent on avoiding any danger to British interests in the stability of Egypt and only intended to retire as far as Cyprus.[44]

It was on this point that the negotiations eventually broke down. Drummond-Wolff and the Sultan managed by 22 May to agree on evacuation after three years, providing there were no sign of internal or external danger, and giving both parties the right to reoccupy if this should arise later. As Salisbury observed, with this 'sword of Damocles' poised over Egypt, British control would be as real whether or not there were any troops in Cairo. But the agreement was subject to ratification by the Sultan and the Mediterranean Powers and here it broke down. Although there was considerable hesitation in Paris, where the Boulanger crisis was at its height, the decision to oppose the Convention in the hopes of getting better terms, when added to Russian pressure and the neutrality of Radowitz as the Re-Insurance negotiations neared completion, made the risks too high for the Sultan to contemplate. Flourens afterwards insisted that there was no French animus against England, that it was merely a question of getting terms

[43] Iddesleigh to White 22 September 1886 F.O. 364/1 (White Papers). Malet to Iddesleigh 16 October 1886, F.O. 343/3 (Malet Papers).
[44] Cecil III, 322, IV, 40; G.P. iv. 865, 866; Q.V.L. I, 272–3; Robinson and Gallagher p. 265. Doc. 68, 69.

more in keeping with French aspirations in Egypt. But there was no doubt that he had miscalculated badly. Salisbury had only agreed to a three year term with very great reluctance and now took the view that he had made his gesture: as Cromer later reflected, the failure of the Wolff negotiations at least 'gave us a fair case for declining to negotiate again—for the time being at all events'. This meant, Staal pointed out to Waddington, that their policy had been completely misdirected; all that mattered was to get the British out; after their past experiences it would be a bold ministry which would contemplate reoccupation, whatever the dangers. Of course, Russian and French interests differed here since the main object of Russian policy, in contrast to the French, was to keep the British in Egypt and thus wreck their relations with the Turks. It was France's misfortune that at this critical conjuncture her policy was conducted by Flourens and Goblet since the result was that they allowed France to be used by Russia, as de Staal acknowledged:

> La question d'Égypt est une grosse question pour vous; pour nous, c'est une carte dans notre jeu.[45]

But it is a mistake to assume that this led to any immediate worsening of British relations with France and Russia. Salisbury himself was undoubtedly irritated by the French action, as his remarks to Lyons about the 'silver lining even to the great black cloud of a Franco-German war' on 20 July indicate; and there was some suggestion that in his mind France had now replaced Russia as the main enemy. But this was fairly short lived. The French made such efforts to repair relations with England in the autumn of 1887 that a series of minor agreements, amongst them the regulation of the Suez Canal, were effected. Moreover, the forceful Goblet was removed in November and by the end of the year relations were no worse than they had normally been since 1882. There was, in fact, a good deal of truth in Salisbury's diplomatic assurances to Waddington in December, 'qu'il n'existe pas d'entente entre nous dirigée contre la France'.[46]

Similarly Anglo-Russian relations were quite normal by the summer. To judge from Giers' overtures in July and September

---

[45] Hornik pp. 618–21; Smith pp. 77–8, 81; D.D.F. vi. bis. no. 44, 51; Meyendorff, *Correspondance Diplomatique de M. de Staal* (Paris 1929) I, 318–19. 351.
[46] Nolde p. 481; Cecil IV, 47–53; D.D.F. vi. bis. no. 68. Docs. 70. 71.

occasioned by the final agreement in Afghanistan, and Salisbury's suggestions to Bismarck in August, there was a sincere desire to avoid a repetition of the former antagonism, which was equally reciprocated in England. Furthermore, neither Salisbury nor the Queen took any interest in the renewed Bulgarian controversy in July, probably because they disapproved of Ferdinand of Coburg; and all that Salisbury wanted in this respect, as he explained to White, was that 'as little should happen as possible'. This was a considerable contrast to the attitude adopted in 1885. But, although Salisbury welcomed this improvement in relations and discounted any 'natural antagonism' there still remained the long term Russian ambitions on Constantinople. This he thought a fatal obstacle to agreement for the present and caused him to look upon 'any cordial friendship as problematical'. De Staal summed up the problem accurately in November:

> Faut il en conclure que Lord Salisbury serait plus porté à se rap-procher de la France et de la Russie? Je ne le pense pas. Les rap-ports de l'Angleterre avec ces deux Puissances se sont assurément améliorés, par suite des arrangements conclus récemment sur deux questions d'une importance considérable, mais de là à une entente générale il y a loin. . . .[47]

But although unprepared to work with Russia in the Near East, Salisbury had no reason to seek support against her after the Drummond-Wolff fiasco. That this was the origin of the December *entente à trois* was due to its effects upon Italy: it was Blanc, not White, who initiated this next development. The idea that the Mediterranean Agreements should be extended to include Turkey as a participant member had been advocated in Berlin in February and March, largely as a means of distracting the Sultan from his current application to join the Triple Alliance. At the time it was not taken very seriously: Kálnoky suggested that he should first compose his differences with England over Egypt before this could be considered. But it was revived in July by the Italians as a means of combating the growing Franco-Russian influence at Constantinople, as demonstrated by their success against the Wolff Convention; it received Austrian support in August as Kálnoky became alarmed at German support for Russia in Bulgaria. Crispi,

---

[47] Smith pp. 85–7, 90–1, 95; Medlicott, 'The Mediterranean Agreements of 1887', *S.R.* 1927 p. 79. Doc. 72.

who finally replaced Depretis at the end of July, was, with Blanc, now ambassador at Constantinople, the main instigator of this scheme. Robilant and Depretis had always tried to keep out of the Bulgarian *imbroglio*, in which they could not see any direct Italian interest, but Crispi regarded it as a question of supporting Mazzinian principles and urged his allies to recognize Ferdinand of Coburg 'as a national demonstration of the wishes of the Bulgarian people'. Assuming that Russia was bound to intervene and that a general war would break out—a war which he thought would be as much to Italy's advantage as the Crimean had been—he thought it a matter of urgency that the allies should make sure of Turkey. Consequently Blanc now drew up a short memorandum which he gave to the Grand Vizier,

> with a view to enlist the sympathies of the Porte in favour of a community of action by the Mediterranean Powers in such a way as to reassure the Sultan as to any dangers he might run from France, even if supported by Russia.[48]

During August and September this scheme was worked on at Constantinople until Austro-Italian agreement was reached on 14 October. On 22 October Bismarck agreed to support it in the sense of recommending it to London, whilst taking care himself to limiting his commitments to keeping the French quiet in the event of a Balkan war; not an arduous task in view of Grévy's insistence in June that France would remain neutral. Simultaneous approaches by the Austrians in London and Herbert Bismarck in Berlin now followed on 25 October to induce Salisbury to join in this league for the defence of Bulgaria. The latter was not initially very forthcoming, suspecting, as in April, that Bismarck was deliberately stirring up trouble in the East in order to have his hand free in the West:

> If he can get up a nice little fight between Russia and the three Powers, he will have leisure to make France a harmless neighbour for some time to come. It goes against me to be one of the Powers in that unscrupulous game.

In so far as the scheme had originated with Crispi he thought it one of the Italian Premier's hare-brained ideas for controlling the Sultan, which would produce 'a close Russo-Turkish alliance

[48] Lowe p. 20; Nolde pp. 523–4; Smith pp. 79–80.

within a week'; the result of his 'longing for some splashy interference in Bulgarian affairs'. Apart from these major drawbacks, in Salisbury's eyes the whole scheme was vitiated by its uselessness in 'building upon the Sultan's fitful and feeble disposition'.[49]

If this was Salisbury's attitude why, nevertheless, did the proposed agreement go through? Because, as he pointed out to the Queen long before he consulted his colleagues, adhesion was the lesser of two evils. Kálnoky in his covering letter and Bismarck in his talks with Malet, made it abundantly clear that if Salisbury were to reject the Austrian proposals it was very probable that Austria would have to seek a settlement with Russia.[50] In some ways of course such a settlement would have been welcomed by Salisbury, but it brought with it the dreaded spectre of the alliance of the three Northern Courts, which had proved in the past so inimicable to British interests. The agreements with Italy and Austria in the spring had offered some guarantee against this old bugbear and, as Salisbury had shown in July,[51] it was worth some trouble to keep it in being. Consequently, if the Austrian price was the extension of the agreement to provide for the specific defence of Turkey in Bulgaria, then it was Salisbury's view that the Austrian proposals would have to be accepted, at least in outline. After all, there was a considerable chance that his fears of Bismarck's intentions might turn out to be imaginary.

But the problem was, even if Salisbury was half converted, to extend this conviction to his Cabinet colleagues. The eight bases were put to them at a meeting on 3 November and the reaction, as far as it can be discerned, whilst not unfavourable in principle, was to seek further clarification of Austrian and German views. Firstly, the Cabinet was eager to extend the principle of the protection of Bulgaria to a guarantee of Turkey in Asia, where much more direct British interests were involved. Secondly, the suggestion that the agreement, when concluded, should be revealed to the Sultan, they thought dangerous. But with modifications of the text Salisbury sought some clarification of German views, in particular some assurance that her new found enthusiasm for opposing Russia would last a change of ruler.

[49] Nolde p. 485; Cecil IV, 70–1. Doc. 73a.
[50] Medlicott pp. 80–1.   [51] *supra*.

This assurance Bismarck was perfectly willing to give since, as Kálnoky had already pointed out, the reliability of any Austro-Italian agreement—such as the proposal under consideration—depended entirely upon whether or not England would adhere to it. Without this adhesion, despite Crispi's fair words and ready promises, Austria could not safely embark upon a war with Russia in the Balkans. Not that Bismarck envisaged this agreement as a preliminary to war, but the whole of his diplomacy at this time seemed to have a much stronger anti-Russian bent than before. British support for Austria, Italy and Turkey would make a good second line of defence should the Re-Insurance Treaty fail. Hence his ready acceptance of the suggestion that he should communicate the essence of the Dual Alliance to Salisbury and Goschen, and the private letter which he wrote for communication to the Cabinet in general on 22 November, a letter in which he stressed that support for Austria was a necessity for Germany. The key figure in the Cabinet was Goschen, and his persuasion, after Bismarck's confidences, swayed the issue. But on one point Goschen was adamant; he could not consent to the Sultan's being made privy to the treaty, as Vienna and Rome suggested, nor would he allow any inspired leakage in order to warn off the Russians. As he explained to Hatzfeldt, any hint of such an agreement in the press would raise a public storm in England, in which the government would be fatally compromised. It was this fact, strongly supported by Salisbury, which determined both Article 9 of the eventual text and the form of the agreement, an exchange of notes. This, thought Salisbury, would cause him less embarrassment in Parliament; a wise precaution in view of later events.

The draft British reply was sent to Rome and Vienna on 25 November and on 5 December Kálnoky, after concerting with Nigra, sent a final Austro-Italian draft to London as the basis for their identical note. This was accepted in its entirety and on 12 December the exchange of notes took place. This time in contrast with those exchanges earlier in the year, the British note was much more specific. Kálnoky's nine points were literally translated word for word and written into the English text. The only difference between the notes lay in the preamble and here it is noticeable that, whereas Kálnoky took his stand on the *entente* of the previous March, Salisbury glossed this over and took as the basis of agreement the Treaty of Berlin; a fairly obvious precaution against internal criticism and a reflection of his view that these were no new treaty obligations.[52]

What was the effect of these agreements upon British foreign policy? This can best be estimated by a comparison of the British position when Salisbury first assumed office in 1885 with what it was at the end of 1887 after the signature of the *entente à trois*. It is clear that an immense change had taken place. The position Salisbury inherited was one of complete isolation in the face of serious friction with Russia in Asia and, to a lesser extent, *vis-à-vis* France in Egypt. In both cases the key lay in Berlin, but his early attempts to change this situation were not particularly successful, especially as friction with Russia increased over Bulgaria. Nor had he been any more successful with Austria in 1886, since Vienna had evaded all his attempts to construct a joint action programme. But, by the end of 1887, the picture was very different. Bismarck, it is true, had still eluded him and remained uncommitted against Russia. But the firm commitment of Austria and Italy in concert with Britain to the defence of Bulgaria and the Ottoman Empire was a considerable advance: as White commented, the situation had undergone 'a complete *vice-versa* at Constantinople from what it was in the spring of 1885'.[53]

Similarly, the British position in Egypt was now guaranteed by this same combination. This was no small advantage. From 1885 onwards Salisbury had sought German support in Egypt, which had been obtained intermittently, but now that he had secured it the tacit abandonment of evacuation became a possibility. This is not to suggest that it was a policy of choice on Salisbury's part; what he wanted, whilst safeguarding essential British interests in Egypt, was to remove the differences with France and Turkey in the hope of recreating the 'Crimean coalition'. But after July 1887 it was demonstrably impossible to place any reliance on the 'sickly, sensual, terrified, fickle Sultan'.[54] Equally, staying in Egypt obviously meant French hostility, which, as it became clear to the French that there was no longer any hope of concession from London or support from Berlin, involved a French alignment with Russia in the Mediterranean. In this way the 1887 agreements both reflected and made more clear cut the potential alignments

[52] Lowe pp. 22–4. Doc. 73b.
[53] White to Salisbury 31 May 1887, in Smith p. 75.
[54] Cecil IV, 50–1.

discernible in 1885: all that remained uncertain was the extent to which Bismarck had committed himself to the Mediterranean *entente*. Against France there was no doubt, but against Russia this was still very much open to question.

How far was this a commitment? Salisbury was as inclined to sceptism in December as he had been in February since, as he wrote to White, any action still depended on the whim of the Cabinet of the day.

> If an emergency should arise during the tenure of a Minister or a Parliament disposed to recognise the obligations of Paris and Berlin, the understanding to which we have just come with Austria and Italy will not be needed to make him act.[55]

This, of course, was true. By Continental standards this was not an alliance since there was no obligation to go to war, only to consult together. But nevertheless it was an important step. As has been pointed out, it was the nearest thing to an alliance that Britain had ever made in peacetime 'and more formal than any agreement made with France or Russia twenty years later'.[56] Moreover, what Salisbury was questioning, both in March and December, was the value of the arrangements to the Triple Alliance, not to Britain. Of the latter he had no doubt, they were 'necessary to avoid serious danger'. In some ways the *entente à trois* represents an evolution in the policy of Berlin and Vienna, not that of London. Salisbury had been after such co-operation since 1885, in 1887 he got it.

[55] Cecil VI, 78–9.
[56] Taylor, *Struggle for Mastery* p. 312.

VI

Salisbury and the Partition of East Africa, 1885–91

Africa is the subject which occupies the Foreign Office more than any other.

Salisbury, Nov. 1889

The Heligoland-Zanzibar Treaty of 1890

The changing balance of forces in Europe from 1887 onwards which lay behind the development of Anglo-German collaboration in the Mediterranean, equally applied to Africa. In 1884–5 Bismarck had felt in a strong enough position to openly attack British predominance in West Africa and take the initial steps in the founding of a German colony in East Africa. But, from 1886 onwards, it was evident that this was not pursued with the vehemence which had characterized his activities over South West Africa or New Guinea, despite the fact that, at least in potential, German East Africa was a far more worthwhile acquisition. Though there were differences over the Sultanate of Zanzibar, at times acute, both Bismarck and Salisbury clearly recognized the importance of not allowing this rivalry to grow into a major controversy and ruin Anglo-German relations in Europe. It was this preoccupation, ultimately, which determined the Heligoland Treaty of 1890, an agreement which in turn produced a series of arrangements with France and Italy which completed the partition of East and Central Africa by 1891.

Effective German penetration of East Africa was a reflection of the lack of British official interest in this region. In the 1870s although German firms had about 20 per cent of the trade of the Sultanate of Zanzibar, British commercial and missionary interests —mainly Scots—were predominant. But attempts by McKinnon to confirm this in the late seventies and early eighties by obtaining

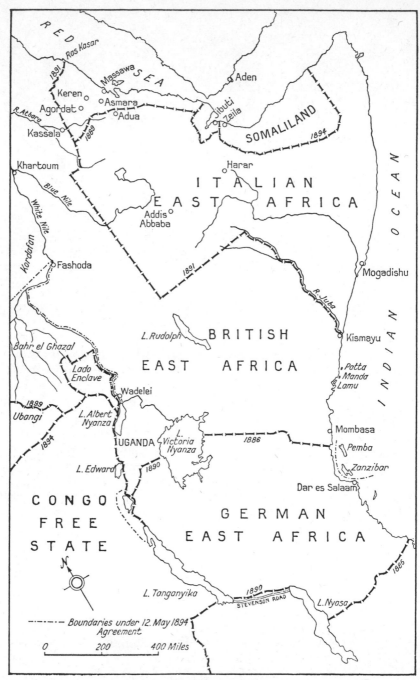

The partition of East Africa

from the Sultan a lease of the mainland to a chartered company, were wrecked by the government in London. It was one thing to acknowledge the importance of Zanzibar itself as a staging post on the route to India via the Cape, a post whose value was enhanced by the French activities in Madagascar, but it was quite another to become involved in the somewhat nebulous claims of the Sultan in the interior. Salisbury had taken this attitude in 1878 and Gladstone repeated it in 1884. Dilke, Chamberlain and some of the Foreign Office officials, smarting at 'being cheeked by Bismarck' in West Africa, wanted to make a stand on East Africa at the end of 1884, and take up the treaties which Harry Johnston had signed with the Kilimanjaro chiefs. But Gladstone ruled this out. Fixed on obtaining German support to get out of Egypt, he would do nothing that could possibly annoy Bismarck and dismissed the scheme on the grounds that it 'savours of annexationism'. In March 1885 Dilke agreed with Herbert Bismarck that in return for respecting the independence of the Sultan in Zanzibar itself Germany should have a free hand in the interior, whilst Gladstone, in the House of Commons, publicly welcomed German interest in the region: 'If Germany becomes a colonizing Power all I can say is God speed her.' When, in April, a scheme was put forward for the formation of a British chartered company to operate in East Africa it was virtually submitted to Berlin to seek German approval. Salisbury, as much in need of German support in 1885 as Gladstone had been, went even further. Assuming from McKinnon's reluctance to move without a government subsidy that the British trade at stake could not be all that great, and failing to appreciate—as Kirk pointed out—that there were 6,000 British Indians in Zanzibar who between them controlled 90 per cent of the commerce, he could not see the slightest grounds for intervention.

> But, if we had no motive for standing well with G.G., I do not quite see our interest in this Zanzibar quarrel. Keeping every other nation out on the bare chance that some day or other our traders will pluck up heart to go in is a poor policy.[1]

This created a clear field for German colonial enthusiasm. Peters' treaties with the chiefs in the interior, which have been

[1] R. Oliver and T. Mathew, *History of East Africa* (Oxford, 1963) I, 355-72; Robinson and Gallagher pp. 179, 190-4; R. Coupland, *The Exploitation of East Africa* (London, 1939) p. 433. Doc. 74.

described as 'a gigantic and deliberate fraud', arrived at an opportune moment for Bismarck who, rather like the Sorcerer's Appren-
tice, found that the colonial movement that he had deliberately
stirred up in 1884, was getting out of hand by 1885. More colonies
were the only sure way to maintain his control of the Reichstag:
as he told Munster, on 25 January, 'the Colonial question is
already, a matter of life and death for reasons of domestic policy'.
Hence his ready acceptance of a policy of annexation in East
Africa, initiated by the *Schutzbrief* of 3 March, culminating in the
enforced submission of the Sultan on 20 December 1885 and
recognition of a German protectorate in the interior and the port
of Dar-es-Salaam.

This occasioned no protest from London. The Sultan was
advised to submit as the only way to maintain his independence
and throughout 1886 Rosebery and Salisbury maintained the line
that the interior was no concern of theirs, and indeed that German
control was preferable since it would open up trade. Even when
the delimitation commission got to work on defining what was
left of the Sultan's dominions in the course of 1886 there was little
trouble. Initial resistance in March from the British and French
commissioners to the German line of confining him to a ten mile
strip was quickly dispelled by hints dropped in London and Paris.
The French commissioner was withdrawn, Freycinet assuring
Bismarck of constant French support in all colonial matters,
whilst Kitchener was simply instructed to give the Germans what
they wanted. A 'unanimous' recommendation of the German view
was signed on 9 June.[2] But Bismarck did not want to push Britain
too far. Even in 1886 there was a considerable contrast between
Bismarck and Peters in this respect. The Kolonialverein wished to
exploit the opportunity to push British influence completely out
of Zanzibar and take over themselves. Peters' object was clear
enough. Experiencing considerable difficulty in raising capital in
Germany, where he had a dubious reputation, he was trying to
obtain it through McKinnon. But obviously McKinnon would not
support Peters if he could get a territory of his own: hence the
attempt to block a British sphere. But although Bismarck had
given some initial support to this idea—in April 1885 he encouraged Rohlfs, the German Consul, to undermine the British

[2] Oliver and Mathew p. 436; F. Müller, *Deutschland-Zanzibar-Ostafrika* (East
Berlin, 1963) pp. 128–30, 140–1, 256–7; Dugdale I, 189.

position with the Sultan—he changed his mind with the advent of Salisbury: instead a policy of collaboration with Britain was initiated which ruled out any question of excluding her from East Africa. As Bismarck noted in August 1885,

> We must support England; we must not start off on a basis of enmity with her; as soon as the Sultan realises this his present complaisance will stop.

Essentially Bismarck was not, as he told the Reichstag in January 1889, 'a colonial man by nature': he simply used colonialism for his own ends. There was a world of difference between him and Peters, who, Bismarck noted on 19 October 1886, 'has an appetite that is far greater than our requirements or our powers of digestion'.[3]

This is why, fundamentally, when the June delimitation agreement was taken up again in October in order to produce a definitive settlement, the idea of partition had an easy passage. It was not that Salisbury or Iddesleigh had shown the slightest interest in East Africa up to this point. The important issues to Salisbury throughout 1885-7 were Egypt, Afghanistan and Bulgaria, where he needed German support and if it were necessary —as Bismarck hinted periodically—he was willing to pay the price in East Africa, which he looked upon simply as one of his sources of credit. As he told Iddesleigh,

> I have been using the credit I have got with Bismarck in the Caroline Islands and Zanzibar to get help in Russia and Turkey and Egypt.

Nor had his interest increased by 1886: he rejected support for the Emin Pasha relief expedition on the grounds that it was a matter for Germany, 'if Emin is a German'. This is not really surprising since even McKinnon was lukewarm about East Africa at this time; it was only when some sort of a British sphere emerged as the result of Anderson, Holmwood and Johnston's labours that McKinnon pricked up interest. Hence the major reason why a British sphere was obtained in October 1886 was less a desperate defence by Salisbury, as Coupland seems to suggest, than Bismarck's moderation. Although stressing to Malet the importance of a settlement favourable to Germany in East Africa for the sake of general Anglo-German relations, and specifically in Egypt, Bismarck showed no signs of wishing to exclude Britain from

[3] Müller pp. 203, 217, 260; Anstey pp. 212-13.

Zanzibar. Already he was thinking in terms of the German position in Europe and had no intention of jeopardizing this for the sake of his own colonial Jingoes. It was in this sense that, whilst he could do what he liked with the Sultan, 'there was a limit to what he could do to Britain'.[4]

If the partition of East Africa in October 1886 introduced what Bismarck later called a 'colonial marriage' it was, nevertheless, a marriage in which Germany was very much the dominant partner. With her spheres of influence extending from the Portuguese frontier in the south to Mount Kilimanjaro, and commencing again at Witu to the north of the British wedge, together with a tacit condominium in Zanzibar, Germany had the lion's share of East Africa. So much so that the Italians, latecomers in this field, for a long time worked on the assumption that it was their German ally, not Britain, with whom they would ultimately have to deal. Why, then, four years later, when a second partition took place as the result of the penetration of the interior, were the roles reversed, with the German territory now a small wedge in a predominately British East Africa?

There were two main factors involved. In the first place, in contrast to 1886, Salisbury now took a serious interest in East Africa: as his biographer tells us, by 1889 maps of Africa had replaced those of Asia and the Balkans in his room at the Foreign Office and his study at Hatfield. This was partly a reflection of European politics: Asia and the Balkans were quiet after 1887. But, more, it was a reflection of the sudden enthusiasm for Africa amongst the British public. It was, apparently, Salisbury's initial instinct that the best solution to the African question was to leave it alone:

> to allow the years to pass over us until the natural progress of civilisation and the struggle for existence should have determined, in a far more effective way than can be done by protocols and treaties, who are to be supreme, and in what parts of that vast continent each nation is to rule.

This was not unconnected with his supposition that, in a free market, British enterprise would emerge uppermost. But this attitude, which had worked well enough in most parts of Africa until the 1880s, had now become impracticable as foreign com-

[4] Cecil III, 230; Coupland pp. 428-9, 473-5. Doc. 75.

petition developed and it was discovered that the system 'had no foundation whatever in international law'. Hence partition.[5]

But whilst partition in 1886 had been possible with very little regard to any British interests—since they were largely non-existent—allowing free rein to the main considerations of British policy in Europe, by 1890 this was no longer the case. In the intervening years two Chartered Companies, the I.B.E.A. and B.S.A.C.[6] had been formed and constituted powerful pressure groups. Of the two the I.B.E.A., chartered in September 1888, was of less importance since it was financially unsound—it collapsed in 1894—and its chairman, McKinnon, was not a particularly forceful personality. Kitchener in 1888 urged that he should be removed whilst Salisbury, even in 1890, thought his 'lack of energy for anything except quarrelling with the Germans' the greatest difficulty in the whole East African problem. But Rhodes' B.S.A.C., chartered in January 1889, was a different proposition. The sheer ebullience of its chairman, the vast public interest in South Africa created by the gold rush, and the increasing imperial fervour evoked by Rhodes' championing of the 'all red route', rapidly created a prevailing view among Englishmen 'that rivalry in any part of the eastern half of Africa was in itself an infringement of their inherent rights'. Moreover, apart from the public interest in the B.S.A.C., it had a good deal to recommend it from the imperial viewpoint, since it offered the best if not the only means of checking the expansion of Kruger's Transvaal. Certainly Salisbury, if Johnston's testimony is accepted, was eager by the summer of 1888 to seize as much as possible of the Nyasa-Zambezi territory and was only deterred from direct annexation by Treasury objections. Supporting the Chartered Company now became the next best solution.[7]

Hence, when this vast public interest was added to the increasing agitation of the missions, who had been in the interior for decades and had no desire to come under German or Portuguese rule, East African interests constituted a considerable pressure group in British politics by the late eighties. Certainly Herbert Bismarck, on a visit to London in March 1889 to discuss the

[5] Cecil IV, 222–9, 254.
[6] 'Imperial British East Africa Company' and 'British South Africa Company'.
[7] Cecil IV, 242–3, 248–81; Coupland p. 469; Robinson and Gallagher pp. 200–1, 226–9, 241–7.

forthcoming Samoa conference and sound out the ground for his father's proposed Anglo-German alliance, was astonished at the manner in which East Africa dominated his conversations with politicians:

> Consistently I met with the anxiety lest East African affairs might take a turn likely to excite public opinion here and threaten the existence of the Government. The other questions, some of them far more important, were made less of, but I was obliged to discuss Zanzibar in detail with Chamberlain, Goschen, Rosebery and Lord Salisbury's two Under-Secretaries of State, each for a good hour.

By 1890 the situation was even worse since, with Stanley returned from his Emin relief expedition and stumping the country, and *The Times* thundering, it would take considerable courage to make any concessions to Germany. But equally, Salisbury thought, if it were simply left to the standard bearers of the natural progress of civilization such as Peters and Stanley, 'men of energy and strong will, but not distinguished by any great restraint over their feelings', the situation 'must constantly degenerate into violence'.[8]

Moreover, apart from the growing public preoccupation with the 'El Dorado' of the East African hinterland, there had been considerable tension over the island of Zanzibar itself. Part of the agreement of October 1886 had been German adhesion to the Anglo-French declaration of 1862 recognizing the independence of the actual island of Zanzibar. But in the course of 1888 this came increasingly in question as with the Arab rebellion on the mainland Bismarck contemplated a bombardment of the island as a means of bringing pressure to bear, possibly to be followed by the 'Tunisification' of the Sultan. But this was more than Salisbury would stand. He had accepted with relative equanimity the almost complete destruction of British influence with the Sultan by the enforcement of the October 1886 partition, but he would not accept German occupation of Zanzibar itself: 'the English and Indian interests are both too strong'. Instead, under the thinly veiled pretence of a joint blockade of the mainland to suppress traffic in arms and slaves, a British squadron remained off the coast throughout the winter of 1888–9. As Salisbury explained to Goschen,

> It keeps our ships by the side of the German ships during the whole of the operation and therefore enforces upon them such moderation as suits our ideas.

[8] Dugdale I, 375.

This, he told the Queen, was about the only way to ensure that the Sultan was not deposed by force since 'on an element where your Majesty's forces are the strongest, we retain a control over them'. That Salisbury's suspicions were not unfounded and that the point was not lost upon Bismarck was demonstrated at the end of December 1888 by the latter's response to pressure to take over the island:

> This would have more of a future if we could gain the island and the Sultan without England, but England is more important to us than Zanzibar and East Africa.[9]

The prompt action on Salisbury's part in 1888 and the response by Bismarck were in considerable contrast to what had happened in 1886, and indeed as recently as the 'Holmwood' incident of April 1887.[10] On both these occasions the 'Egyptian lever' had been brought into play and aquiescence in German demands promptly secured. But, from 1888 onwards, the pattern was reversed, culminating in 1890 in the Zanzibar-Heligoland Treaty with the emergence of Britain as the dominant power in East Africa at German expense. Why was this so? Why, for example did Bismarck in 1888 not employ the Egyptian lever which had proved so effective from 1885–7? Why in the increasing clashes in the interior in 1889 with rival expeditions marching around making treaties was Bismarck willing to negotiate and his successors to concede? This is of considerable importance because part of the explanation of the contrast between Salisbury's concessions in 1886 and aquisitions in 1890 is that the change in the viewpoint of Berlin enabled London to take up a different stance.

That the Egyptian lever was so effective from 1885–7 was a reflection of the weak diplomatic position of Britain and the strength of Berlin. Conversely, after 1887 the British position improved and that of Germany deteriorated. Bismarck depended upon British support for his allies in the Mediterranean, so much so that he thought the moment inopportune in June 1889 for any pressure over Heligoland:

> We must wait for British initiative, and for this, the moment when England needs us. At present we need England, if peace is still to be maintained.

[9] Müller p. 393; Cecil IV, 235–6; Q.V.L. I, 444. Doc. 76.
[10] On the Holmwood incident see E. de Groot, 'Great Britain and Germany and Zanzibar: Consul Holmwood's Papers 1886–7', *J.M.H.* 1953.

Nor was there any change in the general appreciation of the situation in Berlin after Bismarck's fall in March 1890. Dropping the Re-Insurance Treaty placed even more emphasis upon Britain: indeed Caprivi now spoke of her as 'our only natural ally in this inevitable struggle, which will be decisive for the German future'.[11] In these circumstances, with Germany needing Britain at least as much as Britain needed Germany, pressure over Egypt was obviously out: it was no accident that the approach for an Anglo-German alliance in January 1889 came from Bismarck, not from Salisbury, in complete contrast to 1885. Moreover, perversely enough, the Egyptian lever only worked as long as administrations in London were trying to get out of Egypt, since this involved them in diplomatic negotiations. As long as they were content to remain in occupation and as long as there was no deficit in Egyptian finances, then there was little opening for European intervention. Since German interests, in any case, were heavily dependent upon Britain's remaining in Egypt and thus having a stake in the Mediterranean conflict with France, it was difficult to quarrel with Salisbury on this issue after 1887. From the German point of view therefore it was both difficult to find any means of pressure upon Britain in East Africa after 1887 and dangerous to seek to do so. This goes a long way in explaining Salisbury's ability to stand up to Bismarck in East Africa in these years.

Hence, fundamentally, the drastic change in Bismarck's attitude to colonial projects after 1887. His enthusiasm for Peters rapidly diminished as the demands and ambitions of the D.O.A.G.[12] in East Africa began to clash with his own view of the priorities of Germany's needs. Although still playing at *Kolonialpolitik* from time to time—notably in 1888 when he took up the cry that Germany's mission in East Africa was to suppress the slave trade, which brought him useful Catholic support in the Reichstag—it is apparent that Bismarck was no longer very much preoccupied with his majority. The success of the war scare campaign in 1887 in promoting the Septennat had solved most of his electoral problems, whilst the acute illness and death of Frederick removed the Coburg danger. Correspondingly, the German external position was much worse since, despite the Re-Insurance treaty, relations with Russia were uneasy—as was demonstrated by the

[11] Dugdale I, 383; Townsend p. 154. Doc. 77.
[12] 'Deutsche Ost-Afrika Gesellschaft.'

publication of the Austro-German alliance in February 1888. If to this is added that the behaviour of Peters and his Conquistadors —whom the German consul in Zanzibar stigmatized as adventurers of the worst sort—brought a rebellion in 1888–9 which took fairly extensive military operations to suppress, Bismarck's much more restrained attitude after 1887 towards colonization is readily understandable.[13]

This was made absolutely clear in relation to Peters' so-called Emin Pasha relief expedition in 1888–9. Peters in the autumn of 1888 wanted to take advantage of the lack of delimitation in the interior to stage an expedition to the Upper Nile, nominally to rescue Emin, marooned at Lado after the collapse of Egyptian authority in the Sudan, but in fact to annex the territory for Germany. The flights of fancy of Peters and his associates were vast enough: they talked of marching from Wadelai to the Cameroons, thus establishing a vast belt of German territory from coast to coast, and the annexation of Egypt and the Congo together with Belgium and Holland. Africa was to be Germany's India. But all this horrified Bismarck. If he could see little advantage in annexing Katanga, the Upper Nile schemes were positively dangerous: Peters and his associates 'were working for Russia and France'. As he told the explorer Wolff on 5 December 1888,

> This is going too far. The English sphere of interest reaches as far as the sources of the Nile, and I run too high a risk. Your map of Africa is very nice indeed, but my map of Africa lies in Europe. Here lies Russia and here lies France, and we are in the middle, that is my map of Africa.

As Peters in March 1889 set off into the interior—precisely at the moment when Herbert Bismarck was in London—the Chancellor set about disavowing him. Hatzfeldt verbally informed Salisbury to this effect on 25 June and on 19 August a formal note was despatched conveying the view of the German Government that they

> have expressly adhered on the occasion of the project being formed for a German expedition to relieve Emin Pasha, that Uganda, Wadelai and other places to the east and north of Lake Victoria Nyanza are outside the region of German colonisation.

This was reinforced on 19 August by what looked like an inspired

[13] E. Eyck, *Bismarck* (Zürich, 1944) III, 463–8, 487–93; Townsend pp. 114–15; 117–18; Oliver and Mathew p. 447.

article in the Bismarck press to the effect that German foreign policy was determined by the Chancellor, not by the Emin Pasha committee. At the same time, on 11 August 1889, Bismarck told his son that 'the friendship of England is of far greater value to us than anything that this expedition might achieve, even at its most optimistic level'.[14]

This clear-cut attitude on Bismarck's part successfully averted any clash over the Upper Nile hinterland but it left open two issues which were still potential causes of trouble in 1889–90. In the first place the island of Zanzibar. Salisbury's stand in 1888 had averted the German attack on the Sultan and it was more or less true, as Bismarck announced in January 1889, that the two countries were in complete agreement there. Bismarck, 'tired of colonies', even considered selling off Witu in 1889 either to the I.B.E.A. or the Italians, just as he tried to get rid of German South West Africa at this time. But these attempts foundered, basically on the issue of prestige, and by the summer of 1889 the incipient hostility between the rival companies had flared up afresh when the Sultan granted the I.B.E.A. the administration of the island of Lamu, which raised a storm with the D.O.A.G. since they regarded it as within the sphere of Witu. The storm was of such proportions that the question had to be put to a Belgian arbitrator who decided in favour of the I.B.E.A. This was soon followed by the Germans hoisting their flag along the northern part of the Witu coast, which the I.B.E.A. had long since regarded as theirs, and a tariff war ensued in November between the two companies. With this coming on top of the difficulties caused by German military operations, the tacit Anglo-German partnership in Zanzibar pursued since 1886 was wearing a little thin. As Salisbury observed in November 1889,

> The whole question of Zanzibar is both difficult and dangerous, for we are perforce partners with the Germans whose political morality diverges considerably from ours on many points.

During the winter the I.B.E.A. stole a further march by aquiring from the Sultan the administration of the neighbouring islands of Manda and Patta. This brought more trouble, a caution to Euan Smith from Salisbury against further annexations, and a direct

---

[14] Müller pp. 468–9, 474–5, 493; D. R. Gillard, 'Salisbury's African policy and the Heligoland Offer of 1890', *E.H.R.* 1960 p. 635.

hint to Berlin in February 1890 that they should hurry on arbitration, 'as the friction between Germans and Englishmen in Africa whenever they come into contact is increasing'.[15]

Moreover, there was a growing conflict between Rhodes and the Germans in the interior. Taking advantage of the German absorption with the Arab revolt Rhodes had pushed northwards towards the southern end of Lake Tanganyika, encroaching upon the German hinterland. This drew a strong protest from Hatzfeldt on 25 June 1889 on the grounds that Germany, having accepted the British hinterland in the Uganda-Wadelai region, was entitled to the same in her sphere. Though a temporary agreement by Berlin not to press their claims south of 11° parallel averted any immediate clash similar to that with the Portuguese—with whom hostilities had already broken out—it was clear that neither Rhodes nor the missions would be satisfied with this in the long run, since acceptance of this line would cut them off from the Stevenson road and Lake Tanganyika. Certainly the growing British feeling that they were coming up against the Germans everywhere in East Africa worried Hatzfeldt. By the end of the year, he was an ardent advocate of the two governments averting a popular clash 'by coming to a complete understanding one with the other'. But the difficulty in any comprehensive settlement was that both sides would, presumably, have to make concessions. This would be particularly difficult for Salisbury with three elements on his back—the B.S.A.C., I.B.E.A., and the missions, of whom the last were by no means the least. (In June 1890 he told the Queen, admittedly for German consumption, that any attempt to sacrifice the Stevenson Road to Germany 'would certainly help Mr. Gladstone very much'.) Even in March 1889 Herbert Bismarck had found Salisbury practically a lone figure in wishing to stick to collaboration with Germany in East Africa whilst 'the whole Foreign Office, as well as his colleagues, have urged him strongly against it, for fear of its effect on the Parliamentary majority'. Certainly Hatzfeldt thought the position no easier in December.[16]

Hence the idea of the arbitration of 'some of the outstanding

[15] Cecil IV, 247, 279; Townsend pp. 115, 123; Gillard p. 634. In view of this it is difficult to follow the contention of G. N. Sanderson that there was no friction in Zanzibar at this time: 'The Anglo-German Agreement of 1890 and the Upper Nile', *E.H.R.* 1963 p. 70.
[16] Dugdale I, 376; II, 26; Gillard pp. 635–7, 642–3; Robinson and Gallagher pp. 227, 245; Q.V.L. I, 608.

colonial questions, and especially Zanzibar' which Salisbury put to Hatzfeldt on 22 December 1889. The object of the proposition was simple. Salisbury had decided that Uganda and Wadelai must be in the British sphere as part of his 'new found strategy of defending the Valley of the Nile'. This was not really in question; Bismarck had recognized this six months before. But he had made it clear at the time that in return for accepting the British hinterland in the north, he expected similar recognition for the German sphere in the south around Lakes Tanganyika and Nyasa. The only alternative, an argument based on effective occupation, was ruled out because though it suited the British case in the south it would not do so in the north since McKinnon had still not reached Uganda, let alone Wadelai. Hence if a general settlement with Germany was to be reached the sacrifices would have to come from Rhodes and the missions, and in these circumstances an arbitrator would make the ideal scapegoat. As Salisbury told Hatzfeldt:

> He himself would not object if on certain questions more attention was paid to our wishes than would be acceptable to many sections in England, assuming that he could find support with some authority, which would take the responsibility from his shoulders.[17]

This did not mean that Salisbury was putting the claim to the Upper Nile to arbitration: rather the reverse, this was to be exempted from the start. After all his 'first priority' of excluding the Germans from the region would have looked rather odd if the arbitrator had awarded Uganda and Wadelai to Berlin; as he might well have done since, as Salisbury told the Cabinet, German claims were at least as good as British.[18]

This was made quite explicit as soon as negotiation in detail between Anderson and Krauel on what was to go to arbitration commenced in early May 1890, after the delay caused first by Salisbury's illness and then by the upheavals in Berlin surrounding the dismissal of Bismarck. Salisbury refused point blank to include Uganda as a subject for arbitration and, so little were the Germans inclined to press on this point, that within three days Anderson had won 'with surprising ease'.[19] It was not Uganda that caused

---

[17] Dugdale II, 29; Cecil IV, 281; Gillard pp. 633–5.
[18] Robinson and Gallagher pp. 290–1, assume the contrary but their evidence is not convincing.
[19] Gillard pp. 646–8; Cecil IV, 238; Robinson and Gallagher p. 292. It is only 'surprising' if one accepts their initial thesis.

the trouble: as Hatzfeldt was informed from Berlin on 10 May, 'serious difficulties only cropped up concerning the delimitation of spheres of interests to the west of Lake Nyasa'. It was this that produced the Heligoland offer from Salisbury on 13 May, as part of a package deal to avoid serious concessions in the region, to obtain a free hand in Zanzibar and to get rid of the constant bickering over Manda and Patta. British control of the back door to Egypt was certainly important, but it could have been obtained without the offer of Heligoland, at the price of accepting the full German hinterland in the South. It was only *after* Heligoland had been raised, when Salisbury began to waver in the face of Cabinet uneasiness at this bold stroke, that Berlin insisted on all or nothing and talked of 'effective occupation of the disputed territory', as being the only alternative criterion.[20] But, whether Salisbury anticipated this or not, the Heligoland offer was decisive in German eyes: 'by the side of which our East African interests merely come forward as matters for concession'. Now the concessions Salisbury wanted west of Lake Nyasa were obtainable and there is some suggestion that he might have obtained even McKinnon's 'all red route' at the northern end of Lake Tanganyika if he had held out for it. But he did not. If one thing is clear about his attitude to East Africa in 1890 it is that he had no interest in this 'pipe dream'. In his view McKinnon was the one obstacle to a settlement, and should be suppressed; even the latter's attempt to secure his corridor by a private arrangement with Leopold was equally ruled out in case it should annoy Berlin.[21]

By this agreement on 1 July 1890 all possibility of conflicts in East Africa was removed. The Germans obtained their common frontiers with the Congo, the British sole control of Zanzibar and Witu, thus eliminating the major bones of contention between the rival companies. Moreover, British sole control of the Nile watershed was reaffirmed whilst the disputed area around Lake Nyasa was partitioned, Britain retaining the Stevenson Road and thus staving off most criticism. Undoubtedly, from the British viewpoint, it was an extremely satisfactory settlement, virtually

[20] Dugdale II, 32–4, 42; Gillard p. 649. Hence it is only with considerable reservations that one can accept the thesis that the point of the Heligoland offer was to obtain security in Egypt (Sanderson p. 70). See Gillard in *E.H.R.* 1965.

[21] Dugdale II, 38–40; Robinson and Gallagher pp. 296–7; Cecil IV 285. It was this corridor which provoked his celebrated jibe that 'the constant study of maps is apt to disturb men's reasoning powers', *ibid.* 323. Docs. 78, 79, 80.

Salisbury's maximum terms, and not the least of its advantages, as Salisbury pressed upon the Queen on 10 June, was that this had been achieved without any weakening of the 'systems of alliances in Europe'. His fear since 1888 had been that Zanzibar would turn into another Angra Pequena. It was this aspect that most appealed to Berlin. Obviously from the colonial viewpoint they had made most of the sacrifices and they came in for heavy criticism from Peters and his associates on these grounds. But it was, at this time, of little concern to the pilots of the 'New Course'. German Jingoes could be distracted with Heligoland which, particularly to the Emperor and Caprivi, was the 'chief consideration' in view of its importance for naval policy. Moreover, there were the wider issues involved. They, no more than Salisbury, wanted another colonial dispute with England 'likely in incalculable ways to disturb the continuity of European policy'. Hohenlohe's verdict on the Heligoland-Zanzibar treaty was fully representative of governmental circles at the time:

> In this way we were freed from the danger that England might join with France and Russia, which would have been extremely perilous for us.[22]

If this point has been stressed at length it is because recent work on British policy in Africa has shown a marked tendency to explain everything in terms of Egypt and the Upper Nile. Whilst it is not disputed that Salisbury fully intended to keep the 'back door' in 1890, it is contended that this was not the issue in his negotiations with Germany, but its repercussions further south. It may well be true that Salisbury himself thought largely in strategic terms and was sceptical as to the 'El Dorado' of East Africa, a sceptisicm justified by the collapse of both the D.O.A.G. and the I.B.E.A. by 1892. But this does not mean that he was indifferent to the fate of Zanzibar or the Zambezi territories: both had a certain strategic value. Moreover there was public opinion which, worked hard by the interests involved, including the missions, was far from indifferent. Bismarck the *Realpolitiker* felt unable to ignore this sentiment completely, even when he appreciated its serious implications. Salisbury, dependent upon a coalition government, was far more exposed to popular pressures, much as he disliked them and shared Bismarck's apprehensions at the effect this might have

[22] Müller p. 495; Dugdale II, 41; Q.V.L. I, 614.

upon his foreign policy in Europe. Imperial politics were not solely the affairs of governments.

This is not to underrate the importance of this agreement. Without it there was every chance, as both governments feared, that a constant stream of colonial disputes in East Africa would create a mutually hostile public feeling which would wreck the basic Anglo-German alliance. By clearly defining the respective spheres for expansion this particular danger was eliminated. This was why Salisbury pressed the agreement upon a Cabinet and Queen reluctant to part with Heligoland:

> any indefinite postponement of a settlement in Africa would render it very difficult to maintain terms of amity with Germany, and would force us to change our systems of alliances in Europe. The alliance of France instead of the alliance of Germany must necessarily involve the early evacuation of Egypt under very unfavourable conditions.[23]

Clearly, Egypt had its bearing upon this agreement but it was in a more subtle sense than the 'Egyptians' would have us suppose.

The Anglo-Italian East African Agreement of April 1891

The agreement with Germany in July 1890 left Salisbury free to turn to the other main British rival in East Africa, Italy. Anglo-Italian rivalry in East Africa derived almost entirely from the question of the Sudan, though Zanzibar was also a subsidiary source of discord. This in turn depended upon the British attitude towards Egypt. Whilst Salisbury was bent on evacuation he showed little interest in the Sudan and quite cheerfully in May 1887 agreed to an extension of Italian influence up the Red Sea coast from Massowa to Ras Kasar. But, with the failure of the negotiated withdrawal and the gradual realization that the British presence in Egypt was more permanent than had been supposed, there was a visible hardening towards any further Italian extension in the Sudan. This became increasingly marked during 1889–90, when Crispi's drive on Kassala almost produced a complete rupture with Britain, and it was not until he had fallen from power in 1891 that an agreement could be reached.

The decision to remain in Egypt indefinitely, though not

[23] *ibid.* 613–14.

unrelated to developments in the Mediterranean after 1888,[24] was more the product of internal considerations. The basic prerequisite of evacuation, as Salisbury explained in August 1888, had always been that Egypt should be 'strong enough to master internal disorder or to repel an external foe'. Yet neither of these conditions looked like being satisfied. During 1888–9 there were a series of Dervish attacks around Suakin and up the Nile valley which were not finally thrown back until their defeat at Toski on 3 August 1889. Obviously this sort of frontier warfare would remain a running sore until the Sudan was reconquered, but Baring at this time was adamantly opposed to such a step. Having just got Egyptian finances out of the red he had no wish to plunge into a renewal of the disasters that had afflicted them in 1884–5, with all the opportunities that this created for European pressure in Cairo. Moreover, as Salisbury explained to the Queen at the end of 1888, there was no chance of Britain's paying for it: 'the House of Commons would certainly decline to bear the cost'.[25] This 'Dervish' argument was reinforced by the situation in Egypt itself. Here according to Baring hatred of the incompetent Pasha administration was such that revolution was only averted by British bayonets, whilst the only popular leaders were as averse to British rule as to any other foreigners: so much for the Radicals' dream. By June 1889 his conclusion was clear: 'the more I look at it, the more does the evacuation policy appear to me to be impossible under any conditions'. This now convinced Salisbury and all French and Turkish attempts to reopen the question were politely turned aside, although they were now willing to accept the terms they had rejected in 1887. Egypt was not negotiable.[26]

But if Britain were to remain in Egypt the headwaters of the Nile would have to be protected since, Baring explained, whoever held the Sudan 'must by the sheer force of its geographical situation, dominate Egypt'. However, given the financial state of affairs and the fact that the electorate 'shrink instinctively from any proposal to advance into the Egyptian desert', for the present this protection would have to be diplomatic. Hence the announcement of the intention 'to recover the lost Egyptian provinces' to

---

[24] See Chapter VII.
[25] Cecil IV, 134–5; Q.V.L. I, 459; Shibeika, pp. 313–18; For Egyptian finances see the useful table printed in Robinson and Gallagher p. 276.
[26] *ibid.* pp. 278–80, 282–3; Smith 141–2; Cecil IV, 138–9. Doc. 81.

Tornielli and Hatzfeldt in April 1890, since this was the only way to block the current Italian advances near Kassala which so alarmed Baring.[27]

The object and extent of Italian ambitions in the Sudan in 1890 are debatable. Pressure for the occupation of Kassala certainly came from the military commander at Keren, since he was the most exposed to Dervish attack and this habit of the military to demand ever increasing expansion as a means to security was certainly recognized in Rome: in 1888 Bonghi, a leading critic of Crispi's expansionist programme, declared that 'if we leave security to the generals they will want all Africa'. In London, Brackenbury at the War Office, was even more explicit:

> Of course if the Italians are to be judges of what constitutes the 'exigencies of defence' they will be at Kassala in the twinkling of an eye. Once there they will plead, as the Russians have always done in Asia, and as we have found in India, that the exigencies of defence require a further advance which will never stop until they are on the Nile.[28]

But this enthusiasm for expansion on the part of the generals at Massowa would not have got very far but for the support it received from Crispi. Though originally an opponent of Mancini's Massowa expedition, pressure of circumstances had led him to further engagement in Abyssinia. By 1889, Antonelli had converted him to the view that the highlands of Eritrea could be developed as a colony to absorb the emigrants who annually left for America and were 'lost' to Italy. In this way Italy would become one of the great colonial powers and raise her prestige amongst the nations. Since, in his view, it was only by such a policy that Italy's future could be secured, it is not surprising that from 1889 onwards he devoted as much attention to this part of Africa as he had formerly devoted to Tunis and Tripoli. Here, as on the Mediterranean littoral, prestige was at least as important as commercial advantage, as he made clear in a speech in the Chamber in May 1888:

> Italy needs colonies for her future and for her trade and this

[27] Baring to Salisbury 13 March 1890 in Shibeika p. 322; Salisbury to Baring 28 March 1890, S. P.; Dugdale II, 63.

[28] Bonghi in *Atti Parlamentari* (Deputati) 2 May 1888; Brackenbury, D.M.I., to Sanderson 7 October 1890, F.O. 78/4325.

bourgeois habit of always counting the costs is unpatriotic: there is something greater than material interests, the dignity of our country and the interests of civilisation. You have always said that now we are in Rome we must create a new world . . . well then, if these are your wishes you must assist the government, give it the means to succeed in its mission.[29]

Behind the application of this idea to the Sudan in 1889–90 however, there seems to have been also another old idea of Crispi's. He had always bitterly regretted the refusal of Mancini to join in the occupation of Egypt in 1882 since this action, in his view, had lost for Italy the best chance ever offered of creating a solid Anglo-Italian alliance, so essential to Italy's future as a Mediterranean power. Direct assistance in Egypt was no longer a possibility—Salisbury had rejected the offer of troops in 1887—but there was always the 'back door'. Hence the suggestion of joint Anglo-Italian co-operation in the Sudan, as the preliminary to a general scheme of co-partnership in Africa, which would eventually repair the error of 1882. In September 1889 Crispi suggested complete freedom of trade throughout the newly acquired Abyssinian empire in the hope

> that his action in this matter would be duly appreciated by Her Majesty's Government and that they would be convinced by it of the desire of the Italian Government to proceed in the development of their African policy in complete accord with this country.

Neither of these gestures evoked much response from Salisbury so that, in lieu of Crispi's far reaching schemes, relations hinged around the bitterly contested struggle for Kassala.[30]

The Italian attraction to Kassala was due to the fact that, whether it was used as a base for expansion westwards or not, it would give complete control of the Eastern Sudan. This control would certainly remove the danger of Dervish attacks towards Keren or Asmara—and this was to form the basis of the official Italian case —but such attacks were largely mythical. The real reason why Kassala bulked so large in Italian eyes was because it was the centre of the richest of the Sudan provinces and controlled the

[29] Bourguin, *Les politiques d'expansion impérialistes* (Paris, 1949) pp. 137–9; Palamenghi-Crispi, *La prima guerra d'Africa* (Milan, 1914) pp. vi, 2–3.

[30] *ibid.* p. 255; C. Zaghi, 'La Conferenza di Napoli', *Rassegna di politica internazionale* 1936 p. 669. Salisbury to Dufferin 9 September, 30 October 1889, F.O. 170/416 nos. 202, 233.

whole of the trade of the interior. If it could be acquired this trade could be channelled away from the Berber-Suakin route towards Massowa and at last make this expensive luxury pay its way. Emphasis on the commercial importance of Kassala was stressed both by Dal Verme and by Crispi himself. As he explained to Tornielli on 17 October 1890,

> It is true that at one time we did think of renouncing Kassala in exchange for Zeila. . . . But for various reasons we decided not to present the proposal to the English delegates. Above all we were convinced of the utmost importance of Kassala for the commercial importance of Eritrea and, moreover, since the English delegates had no instructions except those concerning the Sudan, we should not have got Zeila and we should have lost the force of our arguments for the possession of Kassala since these were based on the necessity of defending our territory and tribes against Dervish attack.[31]

But unfortunately for Crispi's hopes, Salisbury and Baring had no more intention of giving up Kassala than they had of joining Crispi's African alliance. Baring was well aware of the commercial value of the province, and thought its loss would raise a storm amongst the mercantile classes in Egypt who expected its eventual recovery. Moreover he feared the strategic effects of Italian control of the river Atbara, since it

> gives to the Power occupying it command over one of the main affluents of the Nile, and therefore a power of diverting a portion of the supply which is vital to Egypt.

Whilst not doubting the generally friendly attitude of Italy or the sincerity and the good faith of Crispi, Baring was strongly opposed to allowing any weight to this. In his view quite enough had been done by abandoning Abyssinia to Italy: if she were once allowed a foothold in the Sudan there would be an inevitable drift towards Khartoum.[32]

Generally speaking, Salisbury had been quite favourable to Italian expansion in East Africa. He had been willing to hand over Abyssinia to Italian colonial enterprise in 1888 despite India Office objections, on the grounds that 'the alliance with Italy is a matter of Imperial policy': and, as long as Crispi confined his attentions to this region, Salisbury had accepted the rise of the Italian East

[31] Printed in *Negoziati di Napoli* (Ministero degli Esteri, Rome, 1890), copy in A.S.C. Pisani-Dossi, 18. See also Lyall, *Life of Dufferin* (London, 1926) p. 496.
[32] Cecil IV, 327; F.O. Memorandum of 9 October 1890 in F.O. 170/342, Doc. 82.

African empire with equanimity. As he told Catalani in November 1889, the only thing that concerned him in Abyssinia was that British commercial interests should not be affected: not that these were conspicuous, but 'to avoid complaints in Parliament or the Press'. He had displayed more resistance when Crispi turned to Zanzibar in 1888–9, partly due to the violence of the methods employed, but chiefly because, he told Dufferin, the Italian protectorates at Kismayu and Guardafui 'irritate the Germans and make them even more uncomfortable neighbours that they are by nature'. But even here he had accepted the Italian protectorates eventually and promoted a boundary agreement with the I.B.E.A. in August 1889 which, if it did not fully satisfy Crispi, at least established Italy on the Somali coast. That this region was excluded from the negotiations of 1890, against Crispi's wishes, was mainly because it was tied up with the issue of Zeila and involved a different set of experts, not because Salisbury questioned the Italian title in southern Abyssinia. But the Sudan was a totally different question. Even here Salisbury was willing to make some concessions since he was sceptical of the strategic interests involved on the Red Sea coast which, he thought, 'require the magnifying glass of military theory to be visible at all'. But on the main point he fully supported Baring. An Italian advance on Kassala infringed direct imperial interests and he had 'no wish that their aspirations should be gratified at the cost of any solid sacrifice on our part'.[33]

This became quite clear in the negotiations that followed between March and October 1890 for the settlement of Italian claims in the Sudan. Salisbury and Tornielli reached complete agreement in March on boundaries in the coastal region, partly because Tornielli set no great store on Africa and was anxious to wind up the negotiations before they wrecked the Mediterranean alliance. But Baring insisted on trading this for an Italian renunciation of Kassala, which it proved impossible to obtain. General dal Verme, who went to discuss this with Baring in Cairo in May, saw no point in such a renunciation: Italian forces at Keren were much nearer to Kassala than the British at Suakin and in his view the solution was to present London with a *fait accompli*. But to

[33] Lowe, p. 6.; *Guerra d'Africa* p. 163; Salisbury to Dufferin 15 November 1889, S.P; Salisbury to Baring 15 November 1889, 31 August 1890, in Cecil IV, pp. 326, 331.

Crispi this was too dangerous. Preoccupied at this time with obtaining Salisbury's assistance over Tunis and Tripoli[34] he had no more wish than Tornielli to precipitate trouble over East Africa. The whole point of these negotiations in the first place had been to avert local clashes between the commands at Massowa and Suakin, which was why he had dismissed General Orero in April. As he had told Tornielli in March, 'a cordial understanding between England and Italy is the basis of our policy, in Africa as in Europe'. Hence, instead, a standstill agreement to do nothing until the talks had been resumed at London.[35]

But the difference between Crispi and Tornielli was that whereas the latter, in the interests of the Mediterranean understanding, was eager to drop Kassala, Crispi, convinced of Italy's future in Africa, and perhaps influenced by Salisbury's concessions over Tripoli in August, was optimistic enough to believe that Salisbury would overrule Baring at the forthcoming conference in the interest of the general European understanding. Salisbury on the other hand took the view that this was primarily an Egyptian matter and that he had no 'right' to take the decisions in which London had little interest. Baring should settle with Crispi direct. (Hence Naples instead of London as the meeting place.) Moreover, he saw no reason to override Egyptian interests for objects of wider Imperial strategy, as he had Abyssinian in 1888 or those of McKinnon in June 1890. Abyssiania had been of little concern to him, whilst overruling McKinnon had been essential to reach an understanding with Germany. But a similar agreement with Italy was of little moment to Salisbury in 1890, for reasons which he explained to Baring on 31 August. He was quite content, if Crispi would not accept Baring's terms on Kassala, to let the negotiations be adjourned until Crispi was out of the way and colonial enthusiasm in Italy had diminished. In his view England would not lose by delay since Italy was pressing a policy which was financially impossible. Sooner or later she must recede from it and 'then she will not be so particular about frontiers'.[36]

[34] See Chapter VII.
[35] G.P. viii. no. 1972; Baring to Salisbury 19 April 1890, F.O. 170/430. no. 106; Dal Verme to Crispi 25 May 1890 printed, in *Delimitazione* ... *di Massawa* (Ministero degli Esteri, Rome, 1890), copy in A.S.C. Pisani-Dossi, 18; *Guerra d'Africa*, pp. 198–205, 225–31.
[36] Salisbury to Baring 25 April, 31 August 1890, S.P., partly printed in Cecil IV, 330–1. Doc. 83.

With Salisbury in this frame of mind the failure of the Naples Conference was a foregone conclusion and on 10 October it was broken off since no progress had been made, Crispi blaming it all on the 'ill will of Sir Evelyn Baring'. (This in fact was untrue as it was Salisbury who ordered Baring to break off.) For the rest of Crispi's period of office there was no change since Salisbury simply prevaricated and, although Crispi now apparently considered a *fait accompli* of the 'Kroumir' type, in practice he shrank from the uproar this would provoke in Cairo and London. As Tornielli explained to him, the beneficiary could only be France and, if he wanted to encourage London to think of Rome as a natural ally in the Mediterranean, 'we must move extremely carefully, lest we should create the least suspicion of challenging British supremacy in the Nile valley'. As a final fling Crispi at last resorted to diplomatic pressure, trying to persuade his German and Austrian allies to approach Salisbury. But this was to no avail. Berlin had always taken the view that Italian activity in the Sudan was a mistake and that Rome would do much better to concentrate on the Mediterranean. Deym, the Austrian ambassador, persuaded by Tornielli to raise the subject with Salisbury and in particular to air the Italian complaint that whilst he had made agreements with Germany and France he refused to do so with his Italian ally, was simply told that Crispi's demands were too outrageous. For once Crispi was checkmated and it was not until after the change of government in Rome in February 1891 that Salisbury would agree to reopen the negotiations.[37]

The rapid success of these and the conclusion of an East African agreement with Italy on 31 March 1891 (actually signed on 15 April) was due to the fact that Crispi's successor, di Rudinì, a Sicilian nobleman of the Right, simply accepted Salisbury's terms. Rudinì, in contrast to Crispi, had no interest in East Africa which he wanted to abandon completely in a general retirement to Massowa. Partly this was a question of sentiment: the Right had disliked this African campaign since its very inception. Partly it was a question of economy: his administration depended for its very life on solving the problem of the deficit, and abolishing 'this impossible Africa' would help. This seemed especially true by 1891 since Crispi's legacy, far from being the secure Abyssinian

[37] G. N. Sanderson, 'England, Italy, the Nile Valley 1890-91' *H.J.* 1964 pp. 98, 103-4; Lowe, pp. 63-5. Doc. 84.

Empire that the Treaty of Ucciali of 1889 had suggested, was fast assuming the nightmare proportions of endless military expeditions against Menelik which di Rudinì was determined to avoid. But, above all, it was a question of priorities in foreign policy. To his way of thinking, like Tornielli's, Italy's essential interests lay in the Mediterranean where 'the goodwill of England was in his opinion of far greater importance than any Italian interests that might be connected with these outlying districts (Kassala)'. Hence, in his view, East Africa was ideally suited to become the sacrifice offered up on the altar of an Anglo-Italian alliance, and at one stage he offered to cede the whole of Eritrea 'for a consideration—which I take to be some guarantee of Italy against France'.[38]

In these circumstances there was no difficulty in obtaining Salisbury's maximum terms in the settlement of respective British and Italian spheres of influence from Kismayu, on the Indian Ocean, to the Red Sea.

For Kassala, the principal bone of contention with Crispi, remained firmly in the British sphere and the only reason that Eritrea was not added to it was that Salisbury, for reasons of general European politics, was unresponsive to di Rudinì's hints. As it was, a watered down version of this appeared in a secret protocol by which if Italy were ever to abandon Eritrea—as seemed quite likely at the time—she would 'offer no objection to such abandoned territory being permanently occupied by the Egyptian Government'. The only concession offered at all by Salisbury was an Italian right to a temporary occupation of Kassala if it were necessary for military reasons, on the clear understanding that it would be returned as soon as the Egyptian government were ready to reoccupy it. Even this was more theoretical than practical since di Rudinì assured Dufferin that he had no intention of moving forward: the point was simply that, for parliamentary reasons, he could not accept less than had been offered to Crispi during the conference at Naples.[39] With this agreement the partition of East Africa was completed, apart from a minor rectification in Somaliland in 1894. Salisbury had retained absolute control of the Nile Valley without the breach with Italy that had threatened in 1890,

[38] Sanderson pp. 105–7, 110., Lowe 78–80; Conti-Rossini, *Italia ed Etiopia . . .* (Rome, 1935) pp. 53–6.
[39] Sanderson pp. 108–9.

leaving the Mediterranean alliance intact and thus completing the negotiations he had begun with Germany in 1890. With all danger of a clash over East Africa now removed the way seemed open, in Berlin and Rome at least, for a further development of the alliance in Europe.

VII

Britain and the Franco-Russian Alliance, 1888–92

A war against France and Russia combined might end in
our losing command of the sea, and with command of the
sea, our National existence.

Balfour, 1891

Although to Salisbury the arrangements concluded in 1887 were
as close to an alliance as the British constitution permitted, in
Berlin and Rome the view was taken that this was but the starting
point in the creation of a full scale Quadruple Alliance. Its attain-
ment became the main object of their policies in the Mediterranean
over the next four years. Salisbury, by contrast, had no wish to
take the alliance any further. Apart from the constitutional objection, his dependence upon the Liberal Unionists for a majority
ruled this out and, in any case, as Italian policy developed between
1888 and 1890 he became increasingly unsympathetic to his ally. But
he could not afford to say so openly, or go too far in withdrawing
his support, for the simple reason that he was still dependent upon
the German alliance at Constantinople and in Egypt, especially as
Franco-Russian collaboration became more marked. Consequently
Salisbury's policy in the Mediterranean from 1888 onwards became a tightrope act: on the one hand evading Italian and German
suggestions of a military or naval alliance: on the other building
up their confidence in Britain by large scale naval expansion and
a judicious amount of support when occasion demanded. The last
thing he wanted was any breakdown in his carefully built up connection with Berlin, Rome and Vienna, but, as he told Dufferin in
1891, 'we have to make words do as much work as can be got out
of them'.

The first stage of the campaign to obtain a naval alliance in the
Mediterranean from Salisbury was launched with the war scare of

147

February 1888. This had a dual origin. Franco-Italian relations, remarkably good since 1882, deteriorated suddenly in 1887 over a tariff war until both sides now waged a policy of pinpricks on every possible occasion. The situation was made more serious by Crispi's negotiation of a military convention with Berlin in the autumn of 1887, news of which leaked to the French and convinced them of an impending Italo-German attack. Hence feverish naval preparation at Toulon and the transference of the entire weight of their fleet from the Atlantic to the Mediterranean. That Crispi in fact intended to attack is unlikely: more probable is that, stoking up the war of nerves to obtain tariff concessions, he found that it had got out of control. But an air of extreme urgency was given by the intervention of Berlin. The German military attaché's reports from Paris of unprecedented naval activity at Toulon led both Bismarck and Crispi on 4 February to request British naval assistance in the Mediterranean. Again Bismarck's exact intentions are debatable; there were contradictory indications during 1888 as to whether or not he wanted a Franco-Italian war. But one point was quite clear. Italy would not participate in a war without an assurance of British support, since her own naval weakness gave the French a free hand to bombard Italian ports and ferry troops from Algeria and Tunisia to Italy with impunity. Hence, whether as a prerequisite for a 'preventive' war or as a means of defence if attacked by France and Russia, the major object of policy in Rome and Berlin in 1888 became to obtain a British naval concentration in the Mediterranean and some assurance that it would be used. It was no use waiting whilst the House of Commons debated the justice of the *casus belli* since in the meantime the Italian coastal cities would have been destroyed.[1]

Salisbury's response to this and similar requests in March was a compromise. He did not commit Britain to the defence of Italy, but he did give some assurances. On his instructions the Channel Fleet, which was already in the Mediterranean, was ordered to visit Genoa and La Spezia for a week in February to reassure Italy, a manoeuvre repeated by the Admiralty on their own initiative towards the end of March. But there was no question, as Crispi asserted, of a naval agreement being concluded at this time or even of the demonstrations being a plain warning to the French as current press reports claimed. To Waddington, who came on

[1] See Langer, *European Alliances* pp. 472–6, 479–80; Lowe pp. 27–35.

official instructions to explain that the measures at Toulon were mainly defensive precautions, Salisbury was quite explicit: the visit to Genoa was simply part of the Channel Fleet's spring cruise and, as for Crispi, 'je ne méconnais pas qu'il est inquiet et agité'. As for any engagements with the Central Powers, Salisbury completely denied their existence.[2] In the House of Commons the government spokesman, Fergusson, was much more circumspect when pressed by Labouchere, who had been prompted by Waddington. There were, he stated on 22 February, 'no engagements pledging the employment of the Military and Naval forces in this country, except such as are already known to the House'.[3]

But if this satisfied the French and the Liberal Party it did not satisfy Rome. Not unnaturally Crispi, though appreciating Salisbury's difficult political situation, 'would have preferred some distinct allusion to British sympathies and promises of support towards Italy'. This Salisbury could not provide since, dependent upon the Liberal Unionists' support for the survival of his administration, any such public statement invited trouble. It was for this reason that, throughout 1887, he had taken such care to avoid a treaty since it would need approval by Parliament. It was one thing to agree in secret to do what he considered British interests would compel him to do anyway, quite another to risk a public debate on the subject. But equally some reassurance to Crispi was essential in view of his obvious anxiety and continual German pressure, as Salisbury explained to Edinburgh, the Commander-in-Chief Mediterranean, on 27 March. The only chance of Italy's being able to assist Austria in the event of a Russian attack was that her rear was secure against France. 'Without our naval alliance the Germans always maintain that Italy would count for nothing and be paralysed.'[4]

The solution to the problem of maintaining Italian morale without compromising his own position was simple. Verbal assurances were given to Berlin that in the event of 'a completely unprovoked attack' upon Italy by France 'the English Fleet would immediately come to the help of the Italian Fleet',[5] an assurance whose value was increased by the steady reinforcement of the Mediterranean squadrons. This was a long way from constituting the precise

[2] Waddington to Flourens 25 February 1888, D.D.F. vii. no. 42.
[3] Quoted in Langer p. 467.   [4] Lowe p. 37.
[5] Kálnoky to Károlyi 29 April 1888, *ibid.* p. 40.

naval agreement that Crispi claimed to have obtained but it was some advance upon the mere provision for mutual consultation of the 1887 agreements.[6]

This gradual recognition of some degree of commitment to a naval war in the Mediterranean in 1888 in turn forced a serious review of the capacity of the existing fleet to carry out its obligations. As it became increasingly apparent that existing forces were insufficient even to fight the French with any assurance of success, let alone France and Russia combined, some action had to be taken if Britain was going to maintain her position.[7] For throughout the first half of 1888 foreign policy and strategic planning were proceeding on totally different lines. To Salisbury the most likely source of trouble was still a Russian move on Bulgaria and he told Edinburgh on 27 March that his main task in this event was 'to consider forcing the Dardanelles'.[8] Plainly in his view it was unlikely that France would be as belligerent as Crispi claimed, but he had also committed himself to the defence of Italy if the French were to attack. Both of these considerations required a strong naval concentration in the Mediterranean; the Admiralty, however, was reluctant to provide it. There were two principal reasons for this, the first deriving from their concept of strategy, the second from the physical shortage of ships. Opinion in the Admiralty had long been that the next war with France would take the form of a *guerre de course*, a view advocated by the so-called *Jeune École* in France. Hence they were reluctant to concentrate in the Mediterranean, despite the evidence that the French were doing so, lest the Toulon fleet should give them the slip—as it had done to Nelson—and appear either in the Channel or on the traffic lanes of the world. This was why Hamilton had been reluctant to reinforce Edinburgh in February: a mere demonstration was one thing, but

> if the French mean business it is not to the Mediterranean but to China and Australasia that reinforcements should go, as our commerce can be hit.[9]

Their objection to the demands of Salisbury's foreign policy was simple: they had not the necessary number of ships to blockade

[6] For discussion of this point see Langer p. 481 and Lowe pp. 36–40, 81–2.
[7] See A. J. Marder, *The Anatomy of British Sea Power* (London, 1940) chapter viii.
[8] Lowe p. 37.
[9] Hamilton to Salisbury 5 February 1888, S.P.

Toulon, for which a three to two superiority was needed, and therefore the only sensible policy was to withdraw the Mediterranean fleet and concentrate at Gibraltar, leaving the Italians to their fate. As the implications of the Franco-Russian alliance became obvious this only reinforced their argument.[10]

Oddly enough this did not lead the Admiralty to press for any increase in the building rate. It was quite satisfied with the strength of the fleet for the task it should, in its view, perform and, in any case, was far from sure what it would want to build if given the money. With a vast controversy in progress between the advocates of the battleship and the torpedo it was reluctant to spend vast sums on ironclads which might become obsolete within ten years. The logical answer in this situation was to do nothing and rely on co-operation with Italy whose fleet of ten first class ships, though small, possessed the most powerful then in existence. But the objections to this outweighed the advantages. Apart from the way it would upset current Admiralty strategic thinking, there were adverse reports on Italian naval efficiency: the ships might be good but it was doubted if they could be mobilized quickly enough and it was considered that the personnel were extremely suspect, a factor of importance when it was still thought that naval combat would be decided by grappling and hand to hand fighting with the cutlass.[11]

Nor did Crispi draw any benefit from the French invasion scare that developed in Britain in 1888, if anything rather the reverse. This invasion scare originated with Moltke in Berlin. He gave an interview to the *Telegraph* correspondent and expounded to him how simple it would be for the French to launch an invasion across the Channel, an idea which was repeatedly aired in the British press for months after the original *Telegraph* article of 23 May. Taken in conjunction with Bismarck's current efforts to persuade Salisbury to support Italy, strengthen the fleet or make a German alliance, the Moltke interview—with its heavy emphasis on the French danger—was obviously part of the same alliance offensive. Certainly, it succeeded in creating an impression in London. Salisbury ordered an Admiralty and War Office enquiry from which it emerged in June that, whilst the former discounted any real chance of it happening, both agreed that it was technically

[10] The figures are discussed in Marder pp. 129–31.
[11] *ibid.* p. 141: Lowe, p. 34.

possible. This was sufficient for Salisbury. Hard headed and realistic though he was, in 1888 he appears to have taken seriously Lytton's reports from Paris of the imminence of some Boulangist *coup* and the likelihood that this would lead to an attack upon Britain. As he commented on the Admiralty and War Office report on 29 June:

> it seems to me sufficient for the Government that they agree to think it possible. Our stake is so great that full precautions must be taken against even a distant possibility.[12]

Hence the great review of defence estimates in the autumn, leading to construction of forts and provision of garrison artillery on the south coast, and, above all, attempts to organize the home forces into military districts and army corps.

But this did not induce Salisbury to look any more favourably upon an alliance, either with Italy or with Germany. The N.I.D. view that France and Russia were to be assumed to be acting together and that, if war broke out, 'the balance of maritime strength would be seriously against England' was accepted even by the Admiralty by the autumn of 1888: hence war must at all costs be avoided. Even in the spring Salisbury had been reluctant to promise Crispi naval support, but after a long and weary summer of Franco-Italian incidents provoked, in his view, by Crispi's 'violence and rudeness', he was quite adamant. Crispi's Italy was a danger to peace and any alliance would only encourage him to provoke war with France, a war which in view of the naval position would be a struggle for existence for Britain. Hence his conclusion by December that Crispi should be given 'a wide berth' and that 'if a war were to arise out of one of Crispi's trumpery quarrels, England would certainly stand aloof'.[13]

Instead Salisbury's Cabinet embarked upon naval expansion. In this way the somewhat contradictory demands of naval strategy and foreign policy could be harmonized since the Two Power standard of the Naval Defence Act of March 1889 would provide the force, by the early 'nineties, to contain both France and Russia in the Mediterranean, thus enabling Britain to maintain her links with the Triple Alliance, whilst giving sufficient surplus to enable the Admiralty to pursue its global commerce protection policy.

[12] Cab/37/21/18. Docs. 85–91.
[13] Lowe pp. 49–51; Marder p. 132. Doc. 92.

Moreover, the most important consideration, although expansion at this rate was more expensive than an alliance, it had none of the latter's disadvantages: the decision for peace or war lay completely in British hands.

The fact that this decision had already been taken on 11 December probably influenced the non-acceptance of Bismarck's sudden offer of an Anglo-German alliance in January 1889. Bismarck's intentions in this move have been the subject of considerable discussion but without any real conclusion. Certainly he had doubts about his Russian alliance at this time and had even hinted in October that if Britain joined the Triple Alliance 'Germany would willingly have accepted any risk of displeasing Russia'.[14] In view of his current difficulties with William II and Waldersee this may have been simply reinsurance in reverse. But it is much more likely that he intended to run the two in harness and direct his real animosity against France, not Russia. This, taken in conjunction with his professed readiness in May 1888 to let the next petty dispute with France lead to war and the support given to Crispi in the Massowa affair in July, suggests a possibly sinister side to his projects.

If so, Salisbury blocked it. He had steadily refused to support Crispi's activist leanings in Massowa and Tunis where his sympathies were almost entirely with the French: now he equally rejected Bismarck's anti-French alliance. This was not due so much, as was certainly the case with Crispi, to the fact that he suspected Bismarck of belligerent intentions. On the whole his reading of the oracle in 1888–9 was that, if only because of the Lebel rifle, 'Germany does not want war just now'. But if he later missed the older man's 'extraordinary penetration' he was certainly critical of his judgment in 1888. 'The Chancellor's humours' he told Malet in April, 'are as variable as those of the French Assembly.' If Bismarck advocated an Anglo-German alliance on the grounds that, although France wanted peace the Republican government was so unstable that it might do anything, then this argument told equally against Germany under the Iron Chancellor in Salisbury's eyes.[15]

Moreover, after his accession in 1888, the whims of William II were added to the humours of Bismarck. Whereas Frederick III

[14] Cecil IV, 112.
[15] Salisbury to Malet 11 April, 1 September 1888, Lowe p. 47. For Bismarck's intentions in 1888–9 see the discussion *ibid.* pp. 45–6, in Langer pp. 486–7, and in N. Rich, *Friedrich von Holstein* (London, 1965) I, 216–19, 246–9.

was generally admired in London, William was rapidly distrusted and detested: his fantastic behaviour lent weight to the general supposition that he was bent on emulating Frederick the Great, that he had 'a very unhealthy and unnatural state of mind'. Though this impression sprang originally simply from his lack of filial piety, by the end of the year Salisbury was sufficiently alienated to classify him with Crispi as a menace to peace: to the Queen, with her evident approval, he stressed the 'similarity of the Young Emperor's behaviour and that of the Germans in Zanzibar'. Salisbury was no democrat but both he and the Queen were appalled at the trend in Germany in 1888, 'quite of an age gone by!' In these circumstances, though both he and Bismarck were careful to emphasize that the glacial relations between the two courts should not affect Anglo-German understanding, it was extremely difficult to contemplate making an alliance when the Queen adamantly refused to even receive the Emperor.[16]

It is evident that Salisbury had little enthusiasm to be the horse to Germany's rider. It was one thing to co-operate with her in naval operations off Zanzibar, as he agreed in October, since 'where your Majesty's forces are the strongest, we retain a control over them'.[17] But it was quite another to become committed to a war against France in circumstances he could not control, when in his view British interests demanded no such step. Bismarck might stress that France was Britain's real danger but Salisbury did not agree: his reading of the European situation in 1888 was very different. The only thing he feared, he told the Queen in August, was a Russian descent upon Constantinople. But, he thought, Austria would oppose it and Germany and Italy would have to follow suit: 'the alliance with Austria covers the only weak point in the English position'. Admittedly France was 'and must always remain' the greatest potential danger, but this was dormant for the present and would remain so whilst French relations with Germany and Italy were so strained. There was no sense in forcing the French to turn against Britain in company with Russia, which Bismarck's alliance would make a certainty. 'Let sleeping dogs lie' was always Salisbury's outlook. Naval expansion on a scale sufficient eventually to place Britain 'in a completely commanding

[16] Q.V.L. I, 398, 441, 450, 467; Salisbury openly voiced his distrust of the Emperor to the French in October: Lowe p. 47.
[17] Q.V.L. I, 444.

position'[18] was a much safer and more popular decision for his government to take in their peculiar domestic position: what soundings were taken with his parliamentary allies on the projected German alliance indicated that the moment was 'inopportune', which in the circumstances of 1888-9 was sufficient to make it a non-starter.[19]

Despite this decision however, Salisbury was none the less eager to continue the existing policy of close co-operation: and, since Bismarck thought likewise, extolling in a speech in the Reichstag on 29 January 1889 the ancient virtues of the English alliance, it is not surprising that over the next two years Anglo-German relations were at their peak, what has been called 'the honeymoon of the flirtation between Britain and the Triple Alliance'.[20] Extreme care was now taken in Berlin to avert any clash over colonial issues, whether in Samoa or Zanzibar, an attitude culminating in the Heligoland Treaty of July 1890. With her expanding naval power Britain became once more an ally worth cultivating and a force which was still thrown on the side of the Triple Alliance. This alignment was given added emphasis in July 1889 when Salisbury, yielding to Bismarck's argument that 'England and Germany should appear friendly before the world, as Italy would derive courage from that belief', pressed the Queen into an Imperial visit to Osborne.[21] For this reason, evidently, he was at some pains to soothe Rome at this time. During the July scare, when Crispi again claimed that the French were about to attack him, Salisbury gave him a measure of assurance. Though denying that there were 'any engagements between this country and Italy pledging either to material action', a statement which refutes Crispi's claim of 'a written promise' of support, he did announce that 'in view of the present state of Mediterranean politics' the British fleet would shortly be strengthened.[22]

This pattern of assurances without engagement was to remain the constant basis of his Mediterranean policy and relations with the Triple Alliance and was quite evident in the related questions of Bizerta, Tunis and Tripoli in 1890. The Italian War Office from 1888 onwards had been worried by the French fortification of

[18] *ibid.* 437-8, 456.
[19] See Langer p. 494: Marder pp. 141-3. Doc. 77.
[20] W. Hermann, *Dreibund, Zweibund, England* (Stuttgart, 1929) p. 25.
[21] Q.V.L. I, 477, 484.
[22] Salisbury to Dering 25 July 1889, Lowe p. 81. Doc. 93.

Bizerta as providing a secure base from which the French could attack Sicily, and appealed via Berlin for British representations at Paris to stop this as contrary to the assurances given in 1881. In fact the Admiralty was totally unconcerned. In its view 'the more spent on Bizerta the better for England and Italy', the supposition being that it simply ate up the French naval budget.[23] But Salisbury thought the appeal too dangerous to ignore completely. As on the Tunis and Tripoli issues, he thought it necessary for his relations with Germany to maintain at least a dialogue with Rome. But he was very careful not to let this go to the lengths of annoying the French, for reasons he explained with some feeling at the time, and he finally rejected Crispi's proposed course of action on Bizerta in January 1891. The Italian connection was 'an unprofitable and even slightly onerous corollary on the German alliance'. Germany and Austria were 'very useful friends' and for their sake Britain had to make some gestures to preserve the alliance with Italy:

> But, by itself, it makes our relations with France more difficult: and it is of no use anywhere else. . . . It is a very difficult position for us. We have to make words do as much work as can be got out of them . . .[24]

The German concern over these related questions of Bizerta, Tunis and Tripoli in July 1890 was partly genuine fear that if Crispi were not supported he might carry out his threats to leave the alliance and partly an extension of the idea pursued since 1887 of pushing Salisbury into a more definite anti-French stance in the Mediterranean. Salisbury's lukewarmness over Bizerta had puzzled Caprivi considerably. Unaware of the Admiralty view he assumed that the indifference was feigned for diplomatic purposes. Hence his reasoning that if only it were made clear in London that Germany would not take the lead in this then the British interests at stake would force Salisbury into more positive opposition to the French. A similar consideration governed his attitude over the Tunis question. When Crispi threatened to leave the Triple Alliance unless he got support against supposed French intentions to formally annexe Tunis, Caprivi's first reaction was to let him do so. He assumed from Crispi's invocation of the *casus foederis* that Italy wanted war, a war which would turn into a struggle for

[23] Hamilton to Salisbury 28 January 1891, S.P.; Marder pp. 150–2.
[24] Salisbury to Dufferin 16 January 1891, Lowe p. 72.

existence against France and Russia, and which Caprivi would not contemplate over a trifling question like this. But, as it emerged that all Crispi wanted was compensation in the shape of Tripoli, this opened up very different perspectives since it offered an opportunity to cement the understanding with Britain. Salisbury would never participate in a war over Tunis but he might well be persuaded to join in diplomatic representations to the French in view of the supposed British interest in Bizerta. The major idea behind the German sacrifices in the Heligoland Treaty had been that they would prepare the way for the Quadruple Alliance: now therefore was the moment, Holstein appealed, for a joint diplomatic offensive in the Mediterranean 'to snub the pretensions of France by a display of concert between the four powers'.[25]

Hence the appeal on 1 August 1890 for Salisbury to save the alliance. But in London it was not believed that the crisis was anything like as severe as Berlin assumed. Salisbury rightly saw that Crispi was bluffing in his threats of deserting the alliance and rejected the written guarantee of Tripoli that Hatzfeldt advocated. This would be bound to find its way to Constantinople and confirm the Sultan in his suspicion that 'among the European Powers, Russia is the one that will despoil him least'.[26] The most Salisbury would do was to write Crispi a reassuring letter on 4 August, full of platitudes almost innocuous enough for the Sultan to read, but which did state that British interests as well as Italian 'cannot allow Tripoli to share the fate of Tunis'.[27] According to Catalani, Crispi's personal envoy, in conversation Salisbury went a good deal further, envisaging an eventual Italian occupation of Tripoli as 'an absolute necessity', a statement that Crispi repeated to Berlin as a verbal and written promise of Tripoli.[28]

This is unlikely. In August 1890 Salisbury saw no good reason to make any real concessions to Italy, 'even in African square miles'. His priorities were quite evident. In the agreement of 5 August with France, to compensate for the British acquisition of Zanzibar, he cheerfully gave away the central Sahara without

[25] Malet to Salisbury 22 July 1890, quoted in T. Bayer, *England und der neue Kurs* (Tübingen, 1955) p. 18. The most recent discussion of German aims in 1890 is in N. Rich, *Friedrich von Holstein* I, 322-30.
[26] Doc. 94.
[27] Crispi, *Politica Estera* pp. 370-1.
[28] *ibid.* 368-9; G.P. viii. no. 1896.

fixing any eastern boundary to French expansion in the Tripolitanian hinterland, an action which occasioned considerable protest from Rome 'against the tendency in the English Cabinet to make concessions to France at the expense of Italian interests'.[29] In his correspondence with Crispi and Dufferin all the stress was laid upon the ill effects of any Italian activity in Tripoli in Constantinople lest Italy 'might compromise us irrevocably with the Sultan'.[30] All Salisbury had done was to recognize the legitimacy of the Italian interest and their joint concern that it should not fall to France. That Crispi expressed his satisfaction with this meagre statement of interest was, in all probability, because he expected to use this to actually obtain Tripoli from the French. Certainly when this manoeuvre collapsed in September, after Salisbury's denial in Paris that he had promised Crispi anything, the Italian diplomatic campaign on Bizerta and now the Tripolitanian hinterland was resumed in full force. This suggests that Crispi was not really so satisfied as he claimed to be.[31]

Thus the German expectation that their considerable concessions in Africa would lead to a more definite commitment from Britain against France in the Mediterranean was largely disappointed in 1890. True, Salisbury had given some guarded assurances over Tripoli, but the value of this was considerably lessened by his simultaneous gift to France of the Tripolitarian hinterland. Nor did Crispi's renewed protests over Bizerta achieve anything. In fact they only tended to increase Salisbury's exasperation: certainly in January 1891 he finally expressed his all but complete disinterest in the subject and suggested Crispi should leave it alone. Nor was this simply, as Tornielli assumed, the result of Crispi's threats to the British position on the Nile. Rudinì, who, in the hope of a Mediterranean alliance, gave way in East Africa in April 1891 as completely as Caprivi had done in July 1890, in fact obtained no more from Salisbury than his predecessor had done. He, no more than Tornielli, could appreciate that Salisbury's basic purpose in his relations with Italy was to maintain the line to Berlin. Moreover, whereas Rudinì needed a British alliance to protect his parliamentary position, for Salisbury this would be the ruin of his coalition. Hence in May and

[29] Crispi, *Questioni Internazionali* pp. 37–8.
[30] Salisbury to Crispi 4 August, *supra.*
[31] See Lowe pp. 68–70.

June 1891 when Hatzfeldt put Rudinì's proposals to Salisbury for an alliance with Britain to protect their mutual interests in the Mediterranean, he was turned down flat. On 18 May Salisbury was willing to consider a rewording of the British Note of 12 February 1887 but even this was abandoned after a storm in the House of Commons and the press following Labouchere's accusations that the government had joined the Triple Alliance. On 8 June he told Hatzfeldt that he could not enter into any more definite engagements in view of the nervousness of his colleagues. Rudinì was persuaded, in view of this, to postpone the negotiations until a more favourable moment, but in fact this never materialized.[32]

In the face of increasing difficulties Salisbury now tried to hold together the threads of his Mediterranean policy. On the one hand it was as important as ever to maintain the link via Rome to Berlin, a consideration which led him to emphasize to Vienna that although he could not make any more definite commitments, the recent airing of public opinion made it apparent that 'Italy can count on British support whether or not there is any previous agreement'. There was now, he thought, no doubt that Rosebery would endorse this policy, for no government 'could permit the balance in the Mediterranean to be altered in France's favour'.[33]

But it is equally apparent that he was more careful than ever not to alienate the French. At the same time as he spoke to the Austrians he assured Waddington that he had no commitments to Italy and lent weight to this by his rejection of an Italian royal visit, instead inviting the French fleet to visit Portsmouth on their return from Cronstadt. As the realities of the Franco-Russian alliance became increasingly apparent during the summer after the Cronstadt visit, Salisbury's reaction was to draw in his horns still further. As he told the Queen on 22 August, though British interests still lay with the Triple Alliance 'it is most important to persuade the French, if we can, that England has no antipathy to France, or any partisanship against her'.[34] This dual consideration dominated Salisbury's attitude to Mediterranean issues for the remainder of his period of office and was particularly evident in

[32] *ibid.* 77–83; Sanderson, *England, Italy* pp. 109–15.
[33] Doc. 95.
[34] Q.V.L. II, 65.

159

the two questions, Morocco and the defence of the Straits, which forced themselves on his consideration during 1891–2. British interest in Morocco at this time was slight. The only real point of concern was lest Tangier should fall into the hands of another power, since this would impair the effective control of the entrance to the Mediterranean conferred by the possession of Gibraltar. But there was never the slightest intention, as was widely suspected on the Continent, of taking Tangier: Salisbury's preference was simply to preserve Moroccan 'independence and territorial integrity'.[35] In Morocco, as elsewhere, Italian ambitions under Crispi were much more forceful than this and from 1887 to 1891 Crispi tried to pursue an active anti-French campaign at Fez with the backing of an Italo-Spanish-British alliance. But Salisbury was unwilling to contemplate any such step. He took the attitude that Italy, with the greater interest at stake in the Mediterranean, should take the lead in Morocco, not Britain; and that he personally preferred 'to let sleeping dogs, that is France, lie'.[36]

This, part of his general attitude of not clashing with the French in the Mediterranean more than was strictly necessary, led to growing Anglo-French tacit co-operation in Morocco over the next few years, based on the conviction in London that Crispi, not France, was the main disturber of the peace. The Anglo-Italian alignment against France in Morocco therefore was never strong at the best of times but it received a death blow in 1891 when Rudinì, in conformity with his general policy of improving relations with France, completely abandoned Crispi's activist tendencies in Morocco as elsewhere. His alliance with Spain was eventually renewed in May but it was almost meaningless: Rudinì decided that Morocco was 'too far away from us' and should be left to Spain and England, whilst in Madrid the government openly went over to France.[37] Hence Salisbury's surprise and incomprehension when from September 1891 onwards Hatzfeldt constantly urged him to lead Italy and Spain into action against French pretensions to Tuat, an oasis in the Algerian-Moroccan desert of indeterminate status. As he explained to Malet, he was

[35] Salisbury to Euan Smith 16 May 1891 in A. J. P. Taylor, 'British Policy in Morocco...', *E.H.R.* 1951 p. 353.
[36] Tornielli to Crispi 1 January 1889 in F. Curato, *La questione marocchina* (Milan, 1964) II, 39.
[37] *ibid.* 198.

curious as to why Germany should display 'such an unusual interest in a country from whose affairs they have hitherto ostentatiously held aloof'.[38]

The explanation of the mystery lay in the deterioration of the German position in Europe. In a memorandum of 24 March 1891 Holstein exposed the principal German difficulty which lay at the root of his Moroccan policy. The whole point of a colonial understanding with Britain had been the supposition that these issues were the only obstacle to a complete understanding between her and the Triple Alliance: but instead they were getting nowhere and indeed there were signs that Salisbury was contemplating a settlement with France. Hence the object of German policy should be 'to recall England to the consideration of her European interests', since it was 'precisely these European interests which unite us with England'. Assuming, wrongly, from the appointment of Euan Smith to Tangier that Salisbury was about to embark on an annexationist policy in Morocco, he thought the time ripe to push him forward in conjunction with Italy and Spain in opposition to the French seizure of Tuat. This, if it could be achieved, would put new life into the Mediterranean alliance, visibly shaky after Cronstadt, and a source of worry after Rudinì's interview with Giers at Monza on 13–14 October.[39]

But the scheme misfired completely. Salisbury thought a *démarche* in Paris only likely to spur on the French and, considering Tuat of very slight importance, denied that any British interest was involved.[40] At first he displayed some sign of willingness to support Italy and Spain (as distinct from taking the lead) for the sake of the alliance, but even this disappeared when he discovered it was but a German manoeuvre, that Rudinì had no interest in Tuat either and was 'perfectly prepared to leave it to the French'.[41] Promptly Salisbury covered himself with the French, and Holstein's hopes of using Morocco to drive a wedge between London and Paris collapsed. But the manoeuvre did have one useful result. Recognizing that behind the German action lay considerable anxiety concerning their Italian ally he now began a campaign of reassurances in Rome. After all, as he now instructed Dufferin, it was 'better that Germany should be reassured by Italy by means

[38] Salisbury to Malet 13 November 1891 in Bayer, p. 21
[39] G.P. vii. nos. 1922–32; *The Holstein Papers* III, 374–5, 390.
[40] *ibid.* 393.   [41] Dufferin to Salisbury 24 November 1891, S.P.

of endearments with us, than by means of bickerings with France'.[42] Hence at last an exchange of correspondence with Rudinì, whose value was lessened by the fact of its being private rather than official, but in which Salisbury did at least state on paper that 'public opinion in England would support Italy as long as it was not alienated beforehand by alarms on matters of secondary importance'.[43]

Clearly at the end of 1891 Salisbury saw no point in taking unnecessary risks in the face of the growing strength of the Franco-Russian alliance. He would support Italy if attacked but he would not oppose France unless he had to. If for no other reason, this was obviously advisable in view of the delicate balance of naval forces, an argument which was simultaneously reinforced from the other end of the Mediterranean. The central keystone of Salisbury's arch had always been that it was an essential British interest to defend Constantinople. But when this policy had been reaffirmed in 1887 it had been assumed that the Sultan would support the *entente à trois*, an assumption which was increasingly doubtful by 1891. In view of the critical importance of Turkey, Salisbury had devoted almost as much care to the susceptibilities of the Porte as to those of the Quai d'Orsay. He repeatedly warned off Crispi from his various reckless schemes of aggrandizement at Ottoman expense, notably in Crete in 1889 and Tripoli in 1890, on the grounds that these would drive Turkey entirely into the arms of Russia. But nothing could get round the stubborn facts of the continued British occupation of Egypt and the Franco-Russian alliance, both of which no doubt impressed the Sultan as his immediate problems. After the rejection of the Drummond-Wolff convention in 1887 Salisbury had no intention of reviving the subject, but this was obviously the major cause of Anglo-Turkish discord. Whilst this lasted there was little hope of military co-operation between them, a fact that so impressed Hatzfeldt that in September 1891 he embarked on an attempt to mediate for a new Egyptian convention. But Salisbury would offer nothing of substance. Completely accepting Baring's argument he had no intention of evacuating, whilst the Sultan, convinced he would get better terms from Gladstone, equally preferred to do nothing.[44]

[42] Cecil IV, 383.
[43] Salisbury to Rudinì 11 December 1891, S.P.
[44] Rich, I. 343–5.

But this meant in practice, as White warned in October 1891, that in a crisis the Sultan was not to be relied upon: there was a 'growing disposition to adopt obligations towards Russia of strict neutrality on his part'.[45]

This gradual collapse of British influence at Constantinople after 1887 over Egypt had serious repercussions upon naval strategy. According to the Admiralty, British strength was inferior to that of France and Russia combined but, as long as the Straits were closed, some of the best Russian ships were locked up in the Black Sea. The question was how much longer this would last. It took four years to build an ironclad but it was likely, given the predominant Russian influence at Constantinople, that it would take 'much less than that time to give free access to the Mediterranean of the full Russian strength now cut off at Sebastopol'.[46] Moreover in 1891 the French and Russian building rate increased sharply, by 1893 exceeding that of Britain. The question therefore arose whether, desirable though it might be to forestall any Russian coup, this was still technically possible if the Sultan, as well as France, had to be considered hostile.

Salisbury still accepted that it was. In October 1891, after a *Standard* article had proclaimed that Britain would never 'suffer Russia to obtain command of the Dardanelles', he confirmed to Berlin and Vienna that this represented official policy. But this was seriously questioned by the Admiralty. Hamilton, pressed for his views, told Salisbury that 'now it is much more difficult than it was two years ago since the French Fleet at Toulon is much stronger'.[47] Ever since Hoskins had been to Constantinople in 1889 to report on the Turkish defences it had been clear that the Sultan, whilst neglecting the Bosphorous, was fortifying the Dardanelles. Hamilton's conclusion in April 1890 had been that it made current policy invalid and that the Mediterranean should be virtually evacuated. At the time he was overruled, presumably in the interests of British relations with the Triple Alliance, but in November 1891 he returned to the charge. With Hoskins now First Sea Lord the Admiralty and War Office embarked on a study of the question of forcing the Straits, and their conclusions were embodied in a joint report of 18 March 1892. This stressed Hoskins' view that to attempt to pass the fortified Dardanelles

[45] Lowe p. 86.   [46] Balfour to Hamilton 29 December 1891, *ibid.* p. 87.
[47] Hamilton to Salisbury 19 November 1891, S.P.

with the Russians in front of them and the French behind risked the loss of the entire British fleet, and, with this, command of the sea. It could not even be contemplated until the French at Toulon had been destroyed: 'unless we are acting in concert with France, the road to Constantinople lies across the ruins of the French fleet'.[48] If the French chose to stay in port British naval strategy would collapse and Constantinople would fall to Russia.

This conclusion however was by no means accepted by Salisbury and the report, together with a Foreign Office counterblast of 4 June, was put before the Cabinet. Although there was no immediate likelihood of any Russian move, the position was evidently serious since, Salisbury pointed out, foreign and naval policy 'have been proceeding on lines as far divergent as it is possible for lines of policy to diverge' and, if persisted in, would bring 'discomfiture to all who trust in us and indefinite discredit to ourselves'.[49] But by the summer of 1892 the sands were running out for the Conservative administration and, whatever Salisbury personally thought, this was no time to reach a decision one way or the other. Clearly he was highly reluctant to see the results of six years' work thrown away, either because the 'experts' said his policy was impossible or because he was going out of office. Since 1885 he had been striving to break out of the isolated position in Europe that he had inherited from Gladstone and had achieved considerable success. His attempts to improve relations with France and the Sultan had been a complete failure, but his moves in the other direction had proved much more fruitful.

From 1887 onwards he had attained the policy of co-operation with the Triple Alliance that he had sought since 1885, a development of the utmost importance in his eye. To keep this up he had usually supported Italy in the Mediterranean even when, under Crispi, this had become wearisome and had an adverse effect upon his relations with France. Since it was important to Berlin to keep a strong naval force in the Mediterranean he had done so, despite a fairly constant pressure from the Admiralty to withdraw: and had even given guarded assurances of British naval support in the event of war. But he had always been careful not to commit himself to a naval alliance: to have done so would only have misled his allies, a point appreciated by Bismarck but not by his successors.

[48] Doc. 96.   [49] *ibid.*

In 1892 as in 1887 the essential point in Salisbury's eyes was to use Rome as a link with Berlin in order to avoid the danger of isolation. This meant, in practice, an obligation to defend Constantinople against Russia and Italy against France, a policy which entailed a strong Mediterranean fleet if it were to act as a credible deterrent and make England a worthwhile alliance partner. Although Salisbury was reasonably sure that Rosebery would follow this line he tried to make certain. In 1886 he had briefed Rosebery personally before leaving office: this time, in view of their strained personal relations, he did it indirectly. In a long letter to the Permanent Under-Secretary at the Foreign Office, Currie, he put on record the central points of his policy, presumably for Rosebery's benefit. The 'key to the present situation in Europe' lay in 'our position towards Italy and through Italy to the Triple Alliance'. If this policy of limited support were to be abandoned by the Liberal administration then catastrophe would follow: 'a reconstruction of the *Drei-Kaiser-Bund* and Russia on the Bosphorous'. The past, he hoped, would be sufficient warning to avoid this.[50]

[50] Lowe p. 90.

VIII

Liberal Foreign Policy, 1892-5

> . . . the Queen will *resist any* attempt to change the
> foreign policy, any attempts to abandon our obligations
> towards Egypt & any truckling to France and Russia.
>
> *The Queen,* 13 July 1892

The general expectation in Europe was that Salisbury's retirement
from office in 1892 would lead to a considerable change in British
foreign policy. The Mediterranean Agreements had been founded
on the assumption that they were good only for the life of Salisbury's administration and this seemed to be confirmed as, during
the election campaign, Gladstone made no secret of his desire to
evacuate Egypt and his disapproval of European alliances. The
French certainly saw themselves as the beneficiaries of the new
régime which, it was thought, would rapidly re-establish the old
entente cordiale. Yet, in practice, nothing changed. Salisbury's
policy of co-operation with the Triple Alliance was not discarded
by the Liberal government: Grey, who was Parliamentary Under-
Secretary for foreign affairs in Gladstone's last administration,
was quite clear that, initially at least, policy 'was to side with the
Triple Alliance as being the stable power in Europe'.[1] Despite
Gladstone, it had become apparent by January 1893 that Egypt
would not be evacuated; by the following summer Rosebery
announced that the French attitude over such issues as Uganda
and Siam was 'driving England into the arms of the Triple
Alliance'; a state of affairs with which the Central Powers had
every reason to feel contented. It is erroneous to assume therefore
that the swing away from Germany towards France owed anything

[1] L. Penson, 'The New Course in British Foreign Policy', *T.R.H.S.* 1943, p. 121.
For Sanderson's and Hardinge's opinions see B.D. ii, 92; viii, 2, 17. The explanation
of the discrepancy is probably that Sanderson was not aware of Currie's and Rosebery's secret conversations with Hatzfeldt, Deym and Tornielli.

to Liberal principles: Rosebery was far more anti-French than Salisbury ever was. It was not until much later, after the summer of 1894, that this relationship broke up and Rosebery embarked upon an attempt to work with Russia and France, leading his former allies to long for the return of Salisbury. The reasons for this development, the initial collaboration with the Triple Alliance and its abandonment in 1894, need explanation; for here were the roots of the drift towards France and Russia which became the keynotes of foreign policy ten years later.

That Liberal foreign policy from 1892 to 1895 in fact bore little or no resemblance to the Gladstonian principles enunciated during the election campaign was due—apart from the usual transition from principle to expediency once in office—to its early domination by one man, Rosebery. It was far from self-evident that he would be appointed Foreign Secretary since, despite his previous brief experience, he had no desire to accept office and far preferred the seclusion of private life. But neither the Queen nor the Party could do without him. The Queen was adamant. Though more or less resigned to having 'that dangerous old fanatic thrust down her throat', she practically dictated the rest of the composition of Gladstone's Cabinet and absolutely refused to take 'either Sir C. Dilke or that equally horrid Mr. Labouchere'. On Rosebery she was absolutely insistent as 'necessary to quiet the alarm of the F. Powers' and sent streams of private persuasions via Ponsonby and the Prince of Wales, whilst actively canvassing other likely members—Spencer and Kimberley—that they should promise to always support Rosebery in the Cabinet. Nor could the Party do without him. With a majority of only forty including the Irish members it would be sheer folly to embark on Irish legislation—on which Gladstone was bent—without him in the government: there was sufficient disunity among the other members without having Rosebery sniping from the sidelines. As Harcourt accurately put it 'without you the Government would have been simply ridiculous; now it is only impossible'.[2]

It is this situation which explains the extraordinary position of Rosebery in this Liberal Cabinet. Having no interest in the survival of the administration and having been, as he told the Queen, most reluctant 'to throw in his lot with these people', he could

[2] R. R. James, *Rosebery* (London, 1963) pp. 234–7, 242, 247–50; A. Ponsonby, *Henry Ponsonby* (London, 1942) pp. 215–17.

state his own terms for becoming Foreign Secretary and keep his colleagues up to them by weekly threats of resignation. In retrospect Gladstone bitterly regretted his appointment as the greatest mistake of his career, but it is difficult to see what else he could have done in the circumstances of August 1892. Certainly, to judge by events, there seems to have been some sort of private understanding between the two of them, for Rosebery largely conducted foreign policy without reference even to the Prime Minister. The result of this situation was soon apparent in questions such as Uganda and Egypt and was well summarized by Esher, after a visit to Rosebery in September 1892:

> He is absolute at the F.O. He informs his colleagues of very little, and does as he pleases. If it offends them he retires. We shall remain in Egypt and the continuity of Lord S's policy will not be disturbed.

For if Rosebery had made one thing clear since 1885 it was his devotion to the continuity of foreign policy, a doctrine which amounted in practice to simply carrying on that of Salisbury. This was so well known that Labouchere publicly labelled him Salisbury's representative in the Liberal Cabinet; so that, in fairness to Rosebery, it is quite apparent that Gladstone must have known what a bed of thorns he was preparing for himself when he asked him to take the Foreign Office.[3]

Rosebery and the Mediterranean Entente

The effects of this were first made apparent in the delicate relationship with the Triple Alliance in the Mediterranean. There had been considerable alarm in Rome and to some extent in Berlin at the prospect of a Gladstonian administration, particularly whilst there was considerable uncertainty as to whether Rosebery would take office. Kimberley, the only alternative, was an unknown quantity whilst the thought of Labouchere as Under-Secretary was not endearing. But this anxiety largely evaporated after Hatzfeldt's conversations with Rosebery and Currie from 6 to 11 September. These, almost certainly, were the repercussion of Salisbury's 'Political Testament', which had been explicit enough and, as if to give added weight to its contents, Rosebery was immediately greeted by trouble with Russia in the Pamirs. Hence the extent to

[3] James p. 250; Ponsonby p. 276, Esher I, 162; Q.V.L. II, 141-7.

which he went out of his way to assure the Germans of the continuity of British policy in the Mediterranean, a continuity on which some doubt had been shed by a recent letter from Gladstone published in the *Corriere di Napoli* complaining of Italy's 'enormous military expediture and its embarrassing alliances'.

Although Rosebery in his final written version of this interview for transmission to Berlin and Rome stated that he was only expressing his 'personal view' and insisted upon the insertion of 'groundlessly' in the case of a French attack upon Italy, it is quite evident that this was a very watered down version of the original conversation. In view of what he in fact said and of possible indiscretions at Rome getting back to London, it is not surprising that he took these precautions. What he told Hatzfeldt was that, though he was not yet sure of the consent of some of his colleagues,

> he, Lord Rosebery could assure me without exaggeration that he was now almost indispensable to the inherently weak Ministry, and was therefore much stronger than formerly. Added to this was the fact that any Government, even Gladstone's, was bound to help Italy in the event of an attack.

Not surprisingly, Hatzfeldt was more than satisfied with this at the time, as he had not expected to get anything like this from Rosebery so quickly. Attributing, probably correctly, Rosebery's reserve solely to his current difficulties with his colleagues, he was quite content with Currie's suggestion to leave more extensive declarations until 'the Minister's position became better established'.[4]

This was equally acceptable to Berlin. As early as 20 August Caprivi assured Vienna that the appointment of Rosebery had removed all doubts: that as long as the foreign policy of England remained in his hands 'the position she has assumed in relation to the Triple Alliance will be unaltered'. Nor was this simply a case of Hatzfeldt exaggerating in order to reassure the German allies. Deym, who saw Rosebery on 3 November, was slightly more cautious than Hatzfeldt but did not doubt from Rosebery's conversation and Currie's assurances that 'in principle' there had been no change in outlook towards the Triple Alliance or the Eastern

---

[4] Rosebery's version, for communication to Berlin and Rome, is in Dugdale II, 175; Hatzfeldt's account and comments, pp. 169–74. Compare B.D. viii, 4–10.

Question. In Rome, Brin was at first not so easily convinced by the German assurances: he pointed out that the term 'groundlessly' was all important for Italy since what would happen if France attacked Germany, and Italy, by virtue of the *casus foederis*, joined her ally? Vivian, whom he had consulted on this point, had thought it 'very questionable' if he would get British support in this eventuality and it was of the first importance for this to be quite clear. But he was eventually satisfied by the new found optimism of Tornielli. Since 1890 the latter had been increasingly gloomy as to the prospects of British support being effective, so it was the more reassuring when he now acknowledged that 'there was no reason to doubt Rosebery's sincerity and goodwill' or that he 'would maintain his policy towards Italy along the same lines as his predecessor'; although he could not resist this final jibe, no doubt inspired by Salisbury's tergiversations,

the latter was such a negative policy that it can easily be continued as long as circumstances do not impose another one.[5]

Thus it is quite clear that, whatever may have happened later, initially there was at least as much confidence in Rosebery as there had been in Salisbury among Britain's Mediterranean allies. Rosebery had given a written statement of his views which, though not binding the Cabinet, was serious declaration of intent which, it was supposed, would be amplified later when the political situation permitted. The honeymoon continued throughout 1892–3. Italian anxieties over Bizerta were partially allayed by the initiation of an exchange of intelligence on developments there, since this at least showed that Britain took some interest. In Morocco Rosebery, though no more willing to take the lead in opposing France over Tuat than Salisbury had been, regained his allies' confidence by the recall of the errant Euan Smith, and the plain adoption of the old policy of maintaining the Moorish Empire. At Madrid the Italian alliance with Spain, aimed at keeping her within the monarchical orbit, was supported against the French, though with decreasing effect.

But most important of all was Rosebery's stand on Egypt. The main fear amongst the Triple Alliance powers concerning the new administration had always been the professed eagerness of

[5] Lowe pp. 93–4; Dugdale II, 174–6; Tornielli to Brin 12 October 1892, A.M.E. *Seria politica*, Inghilterra, 487/4674.

Gladstone and the Radicals, openly expressed during the elections, to seek an understanding with France over Egypt: evidently this would have considerable repercussions on the Italian position. Hence the importance of Rosebery's stand. In November he assured Deym that 'at present England cannot possibly think of evacuation', whilst he bluntly told Gladstone who was pushing the issue that it was 'a pernicious waste of time and energy'. In January 1893, when Cromer became involved in a clash with the new Khedive and the French inspired the Turks to launch a new conference offensive, Rosebery insisted on the despatch of more British troops to emphasize the determination to remain. Gladstone opposed this vehemently. He told Harcourt, who was similarly apoplectic, that 'they might as well ask him to set a torch to Westminster Abbey as to send more troops to Egypt'. But they went. Rosebery's threats of resignation were as potent as ever with the Home Rule bill in the offing and all Waddington's attempts to work behind his back with the eager Gladstone and Harcourt only ended in Rosebery's having him declared *persona non grata*.[6]

This preoccupation with Egypt naturally drove Rosebery closer to the Triple Alliance: as he told Gladstone in February, 'Italy is the key to the situation'. As long as they were sure of Italy they could ignore the French, an attitude which gained ground with the ominous developments of 1893 in the Mediterranean. The establishment of a Russian squadron at Toulon after the demonstrative fleet visit in October strengthened the argument for maintaining the Italian connection. Not that it would produce any worthwhile naval support; the naval view generally by 1893 was that the Italian fleet was more of a liability than an asset. But it had important political connotations: quite simply, Italy was now more exposed than ever and unless given adequate backing would be forced to gravitate to the Franco-Russian bloc. This would be fatal to British interests and Rosebery strongly urged a fleet counter demonstration at Taranto or Spezia on the obvious grounds that 'in the face of the Russian-French action it behoves us to cultivate friendships with Italy'. But he would not go much further than this. When approached by Deym at the end of the

[6] Deym to Kálnoky, 3 November 1892, S.A.W. viii, 112. Brief. Doc. 97; T. B. Miller, 'The Egyptian Question and British Foreign Policy, 1892–4', *J.M.H.* 1960 pp. 5–7; Robinson and Gallagher pp. 323–4.

year with the suggestion that he should make an Italian alliance, he rejected this out of hand: it was 'a course which was entirely opposed to British policy'. As he explained to Malet on 3 January 1894, the current weakening of the Triple Alliance in face of the Franco-Russian bloc was a development 'which I most truly deplore', but the idea of restoring the balance by British entry or making a secret alliance with Italy was to ignore the realities of the situation in London. 'Neither of these however is in the range of practical politics for a British minister at this time.'[7]

Rosebery's answer to this was twofold. In the first place, since the Italian fleet was a dubious asset, there had to be further naval expansion in Britain. This, put forward in Spencer's naval estimates of November 1893, which provided for a minimum programme of seven additional battleships by 1898, provoked a storm of protest from Gladstone which ended with his forced retirement on 1 March 1894 and Rosebery's becoming Prime Minister. But already by the end of December it was clear that the battle had been won when Harcourt, however reluctantly, accepted Spencer's arguments: hence Rosebery's reassurances to Deym at this time that the fleet was being considerably strengthened. But this in itself did not answer the problem, which was in 1894 the same as it had been in 1892, the unreliability if not downright hostility of the Sultan, making it impossible to force the Straits. In November 1893 Currie took it as axiomatic that 'when the war breaks out Russia will be in possession of the Bosphorus'. Rosebery, putting it even more bluntly, called British naval strategy in the Mediterranean 'a policy of bounce'; if the Russian Black Sea fleet came out the Levant squadron would have to run for Malta. Hence his new interest in the Austrian approaches in December 1893 for a definite agreement over co-operation at the Straits, since it offered a chance to obtain a means of keeping France neutral, which in turn would make a naval passage of the Dardanelles possible.[8]

The driving force behind Kálnoky's approaches to London in December 1893 lay in Italy. He had always been eager to cement the rather vague understanding of September 1892 when the occasion permitted and, indeed, had made further approaches to Rosebery in June 1893 when unusually warm public praise of

[7] Marder pp. 172, 177; Temperley and Penson p. 482; Miller *ibid*; Bayer p. 116. Doc. 99.

[8] Temperley and Penson pp. 477–80; Bayer p. 115, Marder pp. 191–202, 219–22. Doc. 98.

Austria by the retiring British ambassador led him to believe that this might be a hint from London. At the time he was put off by Rosebery's insistence that he could still not afford to consult his colleagues and that it should be left to time and the French, who were in any case gradually 'driving England into the arms of the Triple Alliance'. But by December he could afford to wait no longer. It was feared in Vienna that not only would there be serious upheaval in Italy as the result of the financial crisis, the revolt in Sicily and the Aigues-Mortes riots, but that this would have external repercussions. To make matters worse the whole Italian crisis was given an anti-Austrian flavour when the King, on the fall of Giolitti at the end of November, refused to include a leading irredentist as foreign minister in the new Cabinet.

This, coming on top of the steady German drift towards Russia which had become marked since the Siam crisis of July and the Toulon visit in October, considerably weakened the Austrian position in the Balkans and worried Kálnoky. If he could persuade Rosebery, on the strength of the Italian crisis, that he should assume more positive obligations in the Mediterranean, then this might not only bolster up Italy and Austria but also check the German drift towards Russia which was so unwelcome in Vienna. Hence Kálnoky's stress in December that the

> psychological moment has come for England not only to increase her navy, but also to make up her mind whether she intends to assert her traditional political authority or whether she will allow herself to be crowded out of the Mediterranean, where British power has hitherto been predominant.[9]

What he wanted, apart from reassurances to Italy, was made clear in January and February when he tried to get a clear definition of British policy in regard to the Straits. Kálnoky now raised the spectre of an Austrian abandonment of the Balkans and Constantinople unless Rosebery, *with Cabinet agreement*, would make a firm guarantee that England would, in case of need, stand by her former policy of defending Constantinople against Russia. As far as Vienna and London were concerned they seemed likely to reach an understanding since Kálnoky, recognizing 'that England could not bind herself like the Continental monarchies', seemed willing to waive any formal treaty; whilst Rosebery was perfectly agree-

[9] Quoted in Langer, *Franco-Russian Alliance* p. 368. Temperley and Penson pp. 472–7; Hermann pp. 92–3; Farini, *Diario* I, 349–62.

able to guaranteeing to defend Constantinople. Now Prime Minister, with Kimberley at the Foreign Office following his lead, this was a safe enough bet from the political viewpoint. But the Admiralty demanded the prior neutralization of the French and to this end Rosebery proposed that Kálnoky should induce his German ally to agree to apply pressure in Paris. It was here that the whole negotiation broke down and created the beginning of the fatal breach between England and the Triple Alliance. For Berlin was not persuaded that negotiations were worth while. Since the previous autumn the Germans had embarked on their own methods of safeguarding themselves from the Franco-Russian bloc and saw no reason to drop these unless Rosebery were willing to join the Triple Alliance, a condition they knew to be impossible.[10]

The root of this attitude lay in the conviction that Rosebery and the Liberal government in England were unreliable, a belief that stemmed from the Siam crisis on 31 July 1893. This, a pure 'storm in a tea cup', derived from a wrongly deciphered telegram which gave the impression that the French had ordered a British gunboat out of the Mekong river, created a flurry of alarm, made more portentous by the fact that Rosebery sent for Hatzfeldt and made what appeared to be an appeal for the assistance of the Triple Alliance. In fact the crisis was over the next day when the signal was corrected. But the German Emperor, who was at Windsor when the crisis started, either because he was genuinely alarmed at the manner in which he had nearly been involved in a general war by British action, or because Rosebery had retreated in the face of France, now abandoned the entire trend of German policy of the previous three years on the grounds that the Liberals were unreliable. Now Germany, Marschall concluded, 'would have to find other means of keeping the Franco-Russian alliance in check'. This was echoed by Caprivi. Long convinced that the first shots in the next war must be fired by Britain he added, 'this is militarily correct and to this end diplomacy must work'.[11]

It was only logical therefore, now that the policy of encouraging Rosebery to oppose France had failed, to turn to the alternative of

[10] Hermann pp. 94–113; Temperley and Penson pp. 481–7; Marder p. 219.

[11] A. J. P. Taylor, 'Les premières années de l'alliance russe', *Revue historique* 1950 p. 68; Hermann pp. 46–51; Israel pp. 52–3; N. Rich, *Friedrich von Holstein* I (Cambridge 1965) pp. 350–5.

separating France and Russia and pushing the former into an open clash with England. To this end Caprivi and the Emperor concentrated on improving relations with Russia by a commercial treaty, the activity that so alarmed Kálnoky, whilst Marschall and Kayser embarked on a colonial understanding with France over the Cameroons in March 1894 whose main object was to encourage her expansion in Africa and wreck Rosebery's attempt to make Germany a buffer between England and France. Since this was accompanied by a resurrection of the Samoan question in April, in which Marschall adopted the unrealistic attitude of wanting the lot, and then by deliberate obstructiveness over the Congo in June, it is obvious that by 1894 Berlin was not greatly concerned on whose corns it trod—in London or Vienna. Rosebery's fairly accurate deduction in January 1895 that 'Berlin or he who guides Berlin has been actuated by hostility to the Liberal Government in England' was endorsed by Malet.[12]

Although it is frequently stated that the object of German obstructiveness over the Congo was to force Britain into the Triple Alliance[13] there is in fact no evidence to support this. On the contrary, the German correspondence suggests strongly that this policy had been abandoned for the present and that all they were concerned with was to obtain Samoa.[14] Nor is this particularly surprising. By 1894 Holstein had completely reversed his tack of 1890 and now advocated going far beyond what Bismarck ever dreamt of in giving Russia a free hand in the East, whilst Caprivi's basic objection to any negotiation along Rosebery's lines was that 'we should risk failure if we made it possible for England to report to Russia any words of ours unfavourable to her on the Dardanelles question'. Lacking any interest in Constantinople they saw no further reason to humour British colonial susceptibilities, as they had done since 1890, and felt free to pursue German colonial interests without reference to the British *entente*. Moreover this offered definite advantages to Caprivi by 1894 since the active pursuit of *Kolonialpolitik* would appease his critics in the Reichstag who were ever opposed to his subservience to England in colonial affairs. Caprivi, it is true, always added the limitation that he would do nothing to attack the British position in Egypt;

---

[12] Hermann pp. 117–26; Israel pp. 61–3; Bayer pp. 85–8, 123; G.P. viii. no. 2031. Doc. 101.
[13] e.g. Taylor, *Struggle for Mastery* p. 349.   [14] G. P. viii. nos. 2035, 2039.

their presence there was an essential German interest, the very basis of Anglo-French discord; but apart from this his policy over the Congo suffered from a 'lack of any clear objective and the muddled diversity of purpose'.[15]

But this had more serious effects than had been anticipated as, for the mirage of Samoa, Germany embarked on a dispute with Britain over the Congo in which her actual interest was negligible and whose only effect was to wreck what remained of the Mediterranean *entente*. Nor when it came to the point could Caprivi even pursue his policy to its logical conclusion of outright support for France, lest it should lead to Rosebery's openly abandoning Italy: under pressure from his allies he had to retreat and the only result was an infuriated Rosebery, no Samoa and the promotion of an Anglo-French attempt to settle their differences. It is true that it did not lead to the complete breakdown in Anglo-German relations that at first seemed likely. Rosebery initially took great exception to the German tone 'which she might properly use in addressing Monaco' and threatened that if she continued to pursue an anti-British policy in Africa then he would be obliged to change his Mediterranean policy. But within two days he had changed his mind; it was not worth changing his foreign policy for twenty-five kilometres of Africa; like Caprivi, he had too much at stake. But the patching up of the Congo quarrel by 22 June was only skin deep. In October there was a further row over Mozambique in which Kimberley 'all but threatened war', whilst Marschall was incensed by Rosebery's Guildhall speech in November in which he stressed his good relations with Russia and France. It was very noticeable that for all Rosebery's assurance that these did not preclude cordial terms with the Triple Alliance, the latter were conspicious for their absence, and there was no further discussion whilst he was in office of any closer links in the Mediterranean.[16]

This cooling off was equally apparent in his relations with Italy. From the first moment of his return to office in December 1893 Crispi had embarked on a series of attempts to create a hard and fast alliance with Britain. Though taking no part in Kálnoky's negotiations with Rosebery, of which he was not informed, he was as conscious as the former of Italy's precarious position in the

---

[15] Rich I, 364–7; G.P. viii. no. 2023; ix. no. 2155.
[16] Hermann pp. 126–8; Temperley and Penson pp. 489–92; Bayer pp. 122–3. See also next section. Doc. 100.

face of the Franco-Russian alliance in the Mediterranean. Hence his advocacy of working together in all African questions, a campaign that was initiated in January 1894 when Blanc showered London with memoranda denouncing the equivocal policy of his predecessors in this region, emphasizing the absolute loyalty of the new régime, and suggesting that Britain should seize Tangier. To this end they should come to a 'lasting understanding'. The point of this move, taken in conjunction with similar offers of support in Egypt, where Crispi wanted to resurrect the idea of a joint campaign in the Sudan, was quite simple: the British occupation of Egypt had been a boon to Italy in getting support in the Mediterranean; if England could now be induced to occupy Tangier, then not only would she be separated from France for good, but Italy could also claim her compensation—Tripoli.[17]

But, unfortunately for Blanc's schemes, Rosebery and Kimberley showed no signs of swallowing the proffered bait. In Morocco the Liberal government was working closely and happily with the French, and vastly preferred the *status quo* to any adventure in Blanc's company. In Egypt, Cromer and his military advisers were opposed to any advance in the Sudan on the grounds that it was beyond Egyptian resources; also because, with memories of 1890, they had no wish to become involved in joint operations which might compromise Egyptian rights in the Sudan. Of all Blanc's schemes for a general alliance with England based on a series of local agreements the only one to materialize by the summer of 1894 was an agreement for co-operation in the Abyssinian province of Harar. Blanc, the perennial optimist, set great store by this very limited concession: he thought it indicated the abandonment of Gladstonian policies and heralded 'a new positivism on the part of Rosebery, aligning Britain with Italy against France'. He was to be disillusioned swiftly since the agreement unfortunately coincided with the Congo crisis and, as soon as he tried to make practical use of it for a joint Anglo-Italian mission to the Harar to counteract French activities, Kimberley refused point blank. 'We have enough on our hands already without adding fuel to the fire.'[18]

[17] G. P. viii. no. 1896; Ford to Rosebery 31 January 1894, F.O. 45/716. nos. 28–32, Sanderson minute 'they seem to be a bid for an English alliance'.
[18] A. J. P. Taylor, 'British Policy in Morocco, 1882–1902', *E.H.R.* 1951 pp. 361–2; Shibeika, pp. 328–30; C. J. Lowe, 'Anglo-Italian Differences over East Africa, 1892–5', *E.H.R.* 1966 pp. 323–5.

As the Anglo-German divergence became apparent after June 1894 Blanc desperately tried to keep in with both sides: since Tornielli now insisted that Rosebery was moving towards France and that Blanc's efforts were a waste of time, he was recalled to please Berlin and a new desperate offensive was mounted to create a separate Anglo-Italian understanding. On 15 July Kassala was taken by Italian forces and on 6 August Blanc sent another appeal to London for a joint campaign against the Dervishes and a general Mediterranean alliance which, so he told Bülow, was inevitable now that Italy was a co-occupant of Egyptian territory. This argument had little influence in Cairo or London. The last thing Cromer wanted was the premature overthrow of the Dervishes whilst Kimberley, with memories of 1885, shied instinctively from any Sudan campaign.

> Apart from the merits of the case it is necessary to bear in mind that the public in this country has an instinctive dread of a fresh Soudan expedition.

Nor could the argument of general imperial policy move Rosebery. Though he still talked of Italy as 'the central keystone of the situation', in his mind the boot was now on the other foot. With the development of the Armenian *Dreibund* it was the Triple Alliance which needed Britain, not vice versa, a conclusion which led him to oppose any assistance to Italy in the Sudan on purely realistic grounds:

> It would of course assure the Italians of our friendship which is very desirable. But our first duty is to Egypt and our own interests . . . (this move) might divert the Dervishes from the Italians to ourselves.[19]

The last straw came in January and February 1895. Blanc and Crispi, increasingly alarmed by the growing signs of Franco-Russian support of Abyssinia when they were becoming involved in open warfare with Menelik, pressed in London for some declaration of British solidarity with Italy in the Red Sea; preferably taking the form of facilities at Zeila. But it brought a point blank refusal. Sanderson and Kimberley, whilst denying that their collaboration with Russian and France extended to this area, emphasized how important it was to them to maintain good relations with Russia, 'especially in view of the contiguity of the two

[19] *ibid.* pp. 318–20; Bayer p. 123.

powers in Asia'. Italy, whilst she could still probably expect British assistance in the Mediterranean, should not presume on this to expect England 'to share in her aggressive action in Africa, thereby getting into conflict with other powers'. Kimberley was not going to throw away any prospect of his collaboration with Russia and France's bringing a solution to the Armenian problem for the sake of Italy in Abyssinia. All that Blanc could do was to sit down and wait for the return of Salisbury: then, it was hoped, 'England may become true to herself and her traditions'.[20]

Plainly enough by 1895 the old *entente à trois* was at a low ebb. Blanc's policy of 'with Germany on land, with England on the sea' was now torn in two directions; whilst Kálnoky, with his hopes of a British commitment in the East wrecked by German policy, became bitterly critical of Berlin; he told Eulenberg in November 1894, no doubt for his master's consumption, that German policy since the fall of Bismarck had lacked any sense of overall direction and had been run by 'third or fourth rate clerks'. Rosebery, equally resentful, ascribing all the difficulties to the anti-Liberal prejudices of the German rulers, thought 'much harm has already been done'. Whilst there was some force in the German view that Rosebery himself was the root of most of the trouble, with his bland assumption, visible in Siam and his Cameroons diplomacy, that he could simply play off Germany against France whilst avoiding any commitment himself, this state of affairs could not help the long-term prospect of British relations with the Central Powers. Hatzfeldt himself fully realized this. As he pointed out to Holstein in December 1894, it was all very well to write off Rosebery, but

> even Salisbury will not be able to contend with it if, by the time he returns to office, public opinion has turned decisively against the Triple Alliance.[21]

Rosebery and France—the Wadelai Stakes

Although both Siam and the Niger contributed their share to the tension in Anglo-French relations during Rosebery's direction of foreign policy, there was never any doubt that the main issue lay in the problem of Egypt and the Upper Nile. Armchair strategists in Simla and London armed with small scale maps talked airily

[20] Lowe pp. 326–7. For the Armenian question see pp. 191–3, 196–203.
[21] Hermann pp. 135–7; Bayer p. 123; *The Holstein Papers* III. no. 430. Doc. 102.

during this period of the danger of France's joining Russia in a pincer movement on India by sweeping from Indo-China through Siam and Burma, but Rosebery, apart from his momentary aberration on 31 July 1893, never took this seriously. Negotiations with the French to define the Siamese boundaries dragged on until January 1896 (and to some extent until February 1904) but the basic principle, establishing Siam as a 'territorial buffer between her [France's] frontier and our own', was settled in July 1893. Certainly the French foreign minister of the day, Develle, assured Dufferin on 9 August that 'he regarded the Siamese question as buried'.[22]

West Africa also presented difficulties. There were some half a dozen disputes which were not settled until 1898—some not until 1904—but until Chamberlain's arrival at the Colonial Office in July 1895 they were regarded as the small change of diplomacy. When Hanotaux told Phipps in August 1894 that there was no chance of England and France's 'going to war on account of Sierra Leone or any other corner of Africa'[23] this was also a reflection of the attitude of Rosebery and Kimberley. The difference between them and Salisbury in this respect however, though slight in theory, was important in practice. With the exception of the Upper Niger, Salisbury had shown not the slightest interest in the hinterland of the West African colonies from 1889 to 1892 and made no attempt to secure them against the inroads of the French. In his view the colonies' revenues were too precarious for them to pay for the occupation of further territory themselves and 'the sanction of Parliament was not to be expected for the employment of Imperial resources'.[24] But whereas Salisbury determined his own African priorities and kept the Office under control, Rosebery took his African policy from Anderson. This was fatal for the prospects of Anglo-French agreement since, lacking any overall perspective, Anderson tended to look at foreign policy solely from the viewpoint of his African empire. Kimberley, after the failure of the Paris negotiations in December 1894, might urge that the important thing was 'that molehills should not be magnified into mountains . . . and should not

[22] Dufferin to Rosebery 31 July, 9 August 1893, Cab/37/34/42, 46. Doc. 106.
[23] Phipps to Kimberley 11 August 1894, G. N. Sanderson, *England Europe and the Upper Nile* (Edinburgh, 1965) p. 191.
[24] Salisbury to Dufferin 30 March 1892, Robinson and Gallagher p. 383.

prevent agreement in larger questions of policy',[25] but he showed little sign of being able to impose this sensible idea upon his own subordinates.

The only real point of substance in West Africa was the struggle for control of the Niger and its tributary, the Benue, largely because the trade of this region was considered worth while and because Goldie's Royal Niger Company formed an effective pressure group in London. In theory the problem had been solved in 1890 when Salisbury, in compensation for the loss of French rights in Zanzibar, acknowledged their control of the Sahara as far south as a line drawn from Say on the Upper Niger to Barrawa on Lake Chad, the assumption being that the territory to the south of this was to be British. But in practice this did not work since the western and eastern flanks were undefined and subject to both German and French pressure, which was one reason why Anderson advocated making a boundary agreement with the German Cameroons. At least this would keep the French out of the eastern flank,

> as in future troubles with France about her push to Lake Chad, which are certain to come, Germany will have to be accounted with, and we shall be quit of the danger of collision.[26]

This scheme collapsed however in March 1894 when Marschall, in whose interest it lay to encourage an Anglo-French clash in Africa, gave France access to the Benue river; so that Kimberley was thrown back upon direct negotiation with Paris. Since the French held all the advantages of physical occupation of the ground this was an unenviable prospect. The sensible course to have pursued in this situation would have been that which Kimberley advocated, giving away paper concessions in West Africa to achieve the main object, which was to keep the French off the Nile. But Anderson completely misread the situation. Taken in by Goldie's assurance that he controlled the ground, he adopted the line that an agreement on the Niger was a British concession to be offered against a French promise to keep out of the Bahr el Ghazal.[27] This had the effect that, although a

[25] Kimberley to Dufferin 4 December 1894, K.P.
[26] Anderson to Currie 8 August 1893, Bayer p. 85. Both he and Robinson and Gallagher (pp. 329, 392) assume this was aimed at keeping the French off the Nile, but Sanderson (pp. 108–10) shows this was unlikely.
[27] *ibid.* 203–4. For Goldie's activities see J. E. Flint, *Sir George Goldie and the Making of Nigeria* (London, 1960).

compromise agreement on the Niger was reached in October 1894, it went back into the melting pot with the collapse of negotiations over the Nile.

The reason why the question of the Upper Nile became all important during 1892-5 was its connection with the evacuation of Egypt. As the Quai d'Orsay realized that, despite Gladstone's utterances, there would be no withdrawal, they gradually came to accept, however reluctantly, the dangerous projects of the Colonial Ministry for the physical occupation of the provinces of the Upper Nile between Fashoda and Wadelai, so that by the mere threat of building a dam they could force the British into an Egyptian conference. Since Rosebery was equally determined to prevent this, as Grey eventually made clear in March 1895, an Anglo-French clash on the Upper Nile appeared inevitable sooner or later.

The problem was created by the fact that although Germany and Italy had recognized the British claim to the Nile Valley in 1890-1, neither France nor the Belgian Congo State had done so, an omission which left them free to push on to the Nile at Wadelai whenever they felt inclined. The situation was made worse by the parlous financial condition of the I.B.E.A. which in 1892 announced its impending withdrawal from Uganda: this, if implemented, would leave the French and Belgians a free hand, especially since the French already had a footing in the area through the White Fathers. Salisbury, in an effort to avert this, had tried, unsuccessfully, to push the Treasury into paying for a Uganda railway, leaving the problem for Rosebery to cope with. Almost the first thing Rosebery found on taking office was a memorandum from Anderson advocating the direct annexation of Uganda and its administration by the Foreign Office. Since such a step involved action, as distinct from writing a Note, Rosebery had to consult the Cabinet, and found that he had raised a hornet's nest. The majority, intent on the evacuation of Egypt, could see no point in the protection of the Upper Nile and all Rosebery's attempts to work the slave trade and the missionaries were to little effect. Harcourt, with his customary eloquence, summed up the results of Anderson's project as 'nothing but endless expense, trouble and disaster', a sentiment fully echoed by Gladstone and Morley.[28]

[28] Robinson and Gallagher, pp. 307-10, 315-16, 320-1. Doc. 103.

The best that Rosebery could obtain for the moment therefore was a temporary stay of execution for three months whilst the Company should effect an orderly withdrawal. But by November, by exploiting his threats of resignation, he managed to extend the period by the despatch of Portal, ostensibly to 'report' on the situation, but with private instructions from Rosebery to maintain the British position until his 'report' had been considered, a state of affairs which drifted insensibly into occupation since Portal and his Hotchkiss gun effectively controlled Uganda. Clearly, therefore, despite opposition from the majority of the Cabinet, Rosebery had no intention of abandoning Uganda and, as his victory in the Cabinet on Egypt in January and Labouchere's resounding defeat in the Commons on Uganda in March revealed the strength of his position, he increasingly treated Portal's report as a foregone conclusion. This, when it arrived and had been suitably edited, was all that could be desired from Anderson's viewpoint whilst the crisis over the Party leadership arising from the Spencer Programme in December 1893, from which Rosebery emerged as Prime Minister, made it inevitable that he got his way over Uganda. Thus, long before its annexation was approved by Parliament in May 1894, Rosebery could work on the assumption that the protection of the Upper Nile had become an accepted axiom of Liberal foreign policy.[29]

This protection seemed all the more necessary in view of alarming news of French and Belgian expeditions to the Bahr el Ghazal during 1893 but, since Portal was in no condition to occupy anything beyond Wadelai and the Uganda railway no more than an idea, it had to be diplomatic. Since it was clear that whatever hopes Rosebery had placed on the Anglo-German Cameroons Agreement protecting the back door to the Nile had been dashed by the Franco-German collaboration, there was now little alternative but to fall back on Leopold's Congo. As Kimberley pointed out on 13 March everything pointed to the probability of a coming Franco-German offensive: 'we should prepare ourselves promptly in all possible points so as to be ready to meet what may be a very serious attack'.[30] Hence the rushed, almost panic-stricken, approaches by Rosebery to Leopold on 5 March which led to the ill-conceived Anglo-Congolese Treaty of 12 May 1894, for if the

[29] *ibid.* 326–8.
[30] Minute by Kimberley 13 March 1894, Bayer p. 120.

Belgians also joined the French then the British position would be hopeless. The idea behind this was simple enough. Taking Leopold's claims to have occupied the area in force at their face value, Rosebery hoped to use him as a barrier against the French whilst neutralizing his own claims by extracting a recognition of the British right to the Nile watershed in exchange for the cession of the 'Lado enclave': an idea that Kimberley simplified for Harcourt's benefit as 'to prevent the French . . . from establishing themselves there and to settle with the Belgians who are there'.[31]

By 15 April Leopold had accepted this in return for a lease of the left bank up to Fashoda but the difficulty was to make him stick to this in the face of concerted French and German opposition after its publication on 21 May. French opposition was only to be expected in view of the current ambition in Paris to send Monteil through the Bahr el Ghazal and, despite his expression of pained surprise in June, it is obvious that Kimberley had expected German support for France on this: Anderson acknowledged on 17 April that 'our real object is to anticipate a joint attack by Germany and France'.[32] This would explain the casual way in which Anderson threw in Article III, the British lease from the Congo of a twenty-five kilometre strip behind German East Africa. He must have been well aware that this would bring forth strong German objections since Salisbury had rejected a similar agreement in 1890 as contrary to the spirit of the agreement with Berlin: but, if there were going to be a row anyway, perhaps he thought that he might as well obtain his 'all red route'. The major mystery in what has been described as 'one of the wildest pieces of diplomatic jugglery on record' is how Rosebery hoped to get away with it: since, even if England could afford to brave it out, secure in the knowledge that Germany would not go too far in view of the Italian position, it was obvious that Belgium was completely exposed to her two most powerful neighbours.[33]

But the fatal flaw in the treaty was that, on top of arousing French and German opposition, Rosebery could not even carry his own Cabinet with him. Harcourt, since Gladstone's departure the main bulwark of the government in the Commons, was more

[31] M. P. Hornik, 'The Anglo-Belgian Agreement of 12 May 1894', *E.H.R.* 1942 p. 232.　　　　　　　　　　　　　　　　　　　　　　[32] Bayer p. 89.
[33] Anstey pp. 227–8; Hornik p. 243; Sanderson pp. 165–6.

insistent than ever in his opposition to 'Jingoism'. As Kimberley mournfully explained to Dufferin:

> Harcourt insists, very naturally, in having his finger in the pie. It is not the same as it was when Rosebery was at the Foreign Office. He is very difficult to get on with.[34]

From the start he had opposed this treaty on the grounds that 'it creates a most dangerous situation with regard to France' and as soon as it became a question of whether England would 'go to war with France to maintain the Anglo-Belgian convention', he became violent. Nor would he hear of simply buying off Germany by dropping Article III: this was 'an impolitic course which only exposes us to fresh humiliation'.[35] In his view the whole treaty should be scrapped and, since he had the support of Morley and Asquith, he had to be listened to.

To a large extent this was simply Harcourt's 'Little England-ism', in which he had been consistent since at least 1885, but the element of personal hostility to Rosebery and his secrecy in the conduct of foreign affairs increasingly came to the fore. As Rose-bery commented to the Queen on 14 May,

> He himself (Rosebery) is only able to guide this tumultuous party through a leader, bitterly hostile to himself, and ostentatiously in-different to the fate of the Government.[36]

In fact Harcourt, with his weekly threats of resignation, was now simply repeating Rosebery's tactics of 1892–3. Obviously in the face of the internal opposition, added to that of France and Germany who now began to talk of an Egyptian conference, Rosebery could not maintain his position. On 22 June he conceded that Leopold should drop Article III, thus pacifying Berlin, whilst he raised no objections to simultaneous Belgian negotia-tions with France. This resulted in a Franco-Belgian agreement on 14 August by which Leopold abandoned most of his leases under the May treaty, thus almost completely destroying their object from the British viewpoint. All that survived, and this was slight con-solation, was Belgian recognition of the British 'sphere of influence' on the Upper Nile.

[34] Kimberley to Dufferin 3 July 1894, K.P.
[35] Hornik pp. 232–5.
[36] Crewe, *Lord Rosebery* (London, 1931) II, 456.

In this way Rosebery's attempts to build up buffers—first Germany, then Belgium—against French penetration of the 'back door' to Egypt had failed and he was forced back on what he had hitherto avoided, direct negotiations with France. The object of these, which lasted from June until November 1894, was 'a review' of all African questions pending between the two governments (excluding Egypt), in the hope that, in exchange for a promise to settle all other African questions 'in a spirit of conciliation', Hanotaux might be induced to accept British supremacy in the Nile Valley. But this was a little optimistic. Hanotaux maintained that French rights there were 'as serious as those of England' and, although himself inclined to be conciliatory, was in turn pressed from behind by the impatient colonial minister Delcassé. He, convinced of the French ability to get there first now the Belgians were neutralized, was eager to launch Monteil on his expedition. Unable to prevent Monteil's despatch in July, Hanotaux did however manage to insist on one point: not, for the present, to penetrate 'into the basin of the Nile', an act which gave him a breathing space to pursue his negotiations with London. But these were completely fruitless. A series of agreements on minor boundary questions in West Africa still left the major issue, the Nile watershed, as far as ever from settlement. Hanotaux in October offered a mutual disengagement: neither side to enter the disputed area, but this was rejected alike by Rosebery and Delcassé who both seemed convinced they could get there first. On 17 November the French government broke off negotiations and whatever promise there had ever been in the Phipps-Hanotaux discussions for an Anglo-French settlement on Africa in 1894 now faded away.[37]

This effectively put Rosebery back where he had started as far as keeping France off the Upper Nile by diplomacy was concerned. Nor was there any substitute in direct action. By May 1895 it was clear that the idea of penetration via Uganda was a mirage, at least until the railway was built, whilst the approach from the north involved first defeating the Dervishes, a project for which the Liberals had little inclination. Hence, in the face of growing rumours of the progress of a French expedition, the administration's desperate final fling, what Hanotaux sarcastically described as diplomacy by parliamentary statement. For Grey's declaration

[37] A. J. P. Taylor, 'Prelude to Fashoda', *E.H.R.* 1950 pp. 61–7, 70–4. Cf. Sanderson, pp. 188–211. Doc. 104.

in the House of Commons on 28 March that any French attempt to penetrate the Upper Nile would be an 'unfriendly act' effectively created a Monroe Doctrine for the Nile Valley, which Salisbury referred to in 1898 as a fair warning to France. At the time Kimberley, in the interests of good relations with France in the Near East, tried to whitewash Grey's proceedings as the utterances of 'a simple Under-Secretary' and offered bromides such as his suggestion of a moratorium on expeditions: 'we were not moving forward, why could not the French remain quiet and let the question sleep'.[38]

But this was pure guile: it would have suited British interests admirably if the Dervish had remained in control of the Upper Nile in perpetuity. It was not lost on Courcel that Grey's statement was fully representative of government policy and he, for one, was considerably impressed by 'the dominant position acquired by England through the declarations of Sir Edward Grey'. Grey was not disavowed by the Cabinet, despite what Rosebery called

> a small but important section . . . the keynote of whose policy is that France is always right and Great Britain always wrong.[39]

The circumstantial evidence strongly suggests that Grey had been put up to this by Rosebery himself as a means of circumventing Harcourt's veto: certainly both he and Kimberley strongly supported Grey after the event.[40]

Rosebery and Russia—the Pamirs and Armenia

The key to the swing in Liberal policy towards working with Russia and France in the autumn of 1894 lay in the settlement of outstanding Anglo-Russian difficulties in Central Asia, since this effectively removed the main current cause of dissension between the two countries. The centre of this had lain in the Pamirs, the desolate terrain to the north-east of the Hindu Kush. Essentially the Pamirs crises of 1891–3 were a continuation of the same problem that had beset Gladstone's government in 1884–5, the closing of the frontier in Asia. The problem in the Herat region had been

[38] Taylor pp. 77–9.
[39] D.D.F. xi. no. 429; Rosebery to the Queen 2 April 1895, Q.V.L. II, 492. Doc. 105.
[40] James pp. 374–5; Temperley and Penson pp. 501–2. Cf. Sanderson pp. 214–16.

finally resolved by the settlement of the boundaries in 1887, but this left the extension eastwards open, apart from the vague 1873 agreement that it should follow the line of the Oxus. Nobody had any real claim to the area, which was inhabited only by nomad Kirghiz in the summer months, and whose delimitation was not assisted by the prevalent habit of all concerned in removing or defacing each other's claim stones.

Alarm on the Pamirs started in Simla as Younghusband's explorations of the passes on the northern frontier in 1891 revealed both that it was perfectly feasible to launch an invasion of Chitral with a sizeable force and that Russian exploratory missions were well established in the area concerned. This all culminated in August 1891 with the forcible expulsion from Bozai Gumbaz of Younghusband and the arrest of one of his assistants by a Russian party on the grounds that this was Russian territory. In the course of the next two years with increasing tension on both sides, Bozai Gumbaz, in fact a deserted waste 'marked by the existence of a small mud tomb', became magnified into an important issue until Rosebery, in November 1893, nominated it the 'Gibraltar of the Hindu Kush', with all the wealth of association that this involved.[41]

Although there were some elements in India which advocated making a *casus belli* of this—notably Roberts—on the whole British policy was conditioned by hard facts. These were unpleasant enough. In the first place it was difficult to reply in kind to the expulsion of Younghusband since the approaches from the south made it impossible to keep any sizeable force in the area, whilst, secondly, 1892–3 was patently the wrong time, in view of the naval position, to risk a war with Russia and France. Hence both in Simla and in London they were reduced to diplomacy, the object of which was to stretch Afghan claims as far as Chinese Turkestan and persuade the Russians to delimitate this frontier, which would effectively keep them away from the Hindu Kush. There were three major obstacles: the lack of interest on the part of the Amir, Abdur Rahman; the initial reluctance of the Chinese, then their total preoccupation in Korea; and finally the strength of the military party in St. Petersburg, who did not want a settlement of any sort. That Rosebery succeeded in the face of these difficulties in obtaining an agreement by 1895 was no small tribute to his persistence. Equally important however was the advocacy by

[41] Alder pp. 225–7. See also Chapter iv. Doc. 107.

Giers and de Staal of a settlement with England. The military were strongly opposed to a settlement because as long as the area was open they could push forward their effective occupation until they achieved their ultimate goal, control of the passes of the Hindu Kush and the ability to debouch on to the Indian plain at their convenience. But, useful as this might be for Russian diplomacy, Giers, and even more de Staal, opposed it as a double edged weapon. The objection, as de Staal put it concisely was simple:

Le jour où une pareille prétention serait émise, la Quadruple Alliance serait faite.[42]

It was unfortunate for Rosebery that he inherited the Foreign Office at the precise moment when this crisis reached its height. At one stage, in February 1892, it had seemed that the foreign ministry in St. Petersburg had gained the upper hand with their proposal for a commission of enquiry on the Pamirs. Salisbury had welcomed this with open arms on the general principle that 'it will occupy a great deal of time': anything which deterred the Russian military from action was an advantage, given the complete inability of Simla to respond in kind. But gradually in the spring and summer of 1892 this prospect receded as Giers became ill and the military, in the general ascendent with the signing of the Franco-Russian alliance, became once more the dominant force in Russia. Hence more expeditions to the Pamirs, the defeat of the Afghans at Somatash in August 1892, and the prospect for Gladstone of commencing his fourth administration as he had ended his second, with an Afghan crisis in which the Russians once more started off with the initial advantage of possession of the ground.

Rosebery's reaction to this situation was to threaten to send British counter expeditions to forestall the Russians. As popular interest in the Pamirs developed, and with memories of the effect of Pendjeh on Liberal fortunes, he urged Kimberley on 25 August that 'Her Majesty's Government cannot remain purely passive'. But in fact this was all they could do, in view of the geographical facts. Nor did Rosebery have any better luck with Abdur Rahman or the Chinese. Both in the autumn of 1892 withdrew from the Pamirs and gave no signs of any enthusiasm to be used as British catspaws: so that, in the end, Rosebery was reduced to urging

[42] *ibid.* pp. 232-5; de Staal to Chichkine 31 May 1892, quoted *ibid.* p. 249.

St. Petersburg to negotiate 'the completion of the frontier delimitation commenced in 1885'.[43]

Why they agreed is a mystery. As far as local conditions were concerned all the advantages lay in Russian hands and if they had chosen to occupy the passes into Chitral nothing could have stopped them. The explanation must lie in European affairs rather than Central Asia and here Caprivi's Reichstag speech of 11 January 1893 with its emphasis upon the two front war was probably not without its effects, particularly at a time when France was engulfed in the Panama scandals.[44] This was not a suitable moment for risking a forward movement which might precipitate a European conflict with Britain, particularly as it seemed that they could obtain most of their demands by negotiation. Hence, presumably, the Tsar's decision in favour of the diplomats rather than the soldiers in March 1893.

The initial Russian terms were, not surprisingly, stiff: the line of the Oxus and its southern tributary the Wakham-su, which would bring them within twelve miles of the passes into Chitral and make it impossible for the British posts to be established on the northern slopes of the Hindu Kush, which Simla thought essential. But Rosebery, largely because he lacked any alternative, though to some extent misled by Simla's emphasis on the Hunza passes at the conjunction with Chinese Turkestan, decided in July 1893 that the line of the Oxus would have to be accepted in exchange for concessions around Lake Victoria. This of course meant enforcing upon the Amir the loss of his provinces beyond the Oxus, Roshan and Shignan, but both Rosebery and Simla were resigned to this: what upset the apparent agreement in July 1893 was a last minute stand by the Russian military for their full demands in the Pamirs. Not until December was this dropped and the detailed surveying on the spot started, a process which dragged on until October 1895.[45]

But by 1894 it was clear enough that the war danger was over and that the main object of the Indian Government—the prevention of Russian encroachment upon the passes of the Hindu Kush in peacetime—had been achieved. This in turn made possible the new phase of Anglo-Russian co-operation in the Near East, made

[43] *ibid.* pp. 247–54.
[44] See for example J. N. Nichols, *Germany after Bismarck* (Harvard, 1958) pp. 277–278.
[45] Alder pp. 263–4, 267–9, 272.

public by Rosebery's Guildhall speech in November, which centred around the Armenian question. Great hopes were originally placed on this, Harcourt in particular viewing it as the solution to the main problem in foreign policy:

> The key to the enigma is a good understanding with Russia, a thing we have never yet tried but which is now happily within our reach.[46]

Nor is there reason to doubt that, if it could have been made to work, the Eastern Question could have been settled in 1895. But it was doomed from the start. British and Russian interests in the Armenian problem were far from identical and to some extent diametrically opposed.

In Britain public opinion was so roused by the cruelties perpetrated in the suppression of the Armenian revolt in the autumn of 1894 as to demand the carrying out of the serious and effective reforms promised by the Treaty of Berlin, a project which the Cabinet fully accepted. Harcourt, not normally an advocate of gunboat diplomacy, was strongly in favour of action, if only on the grounds that

> we should . . . not allow our nose to be tweaked by the Grand Turk, unless we mean to allow ourselves to be the laughing stock of Constantinople and of Europe.[47]

But action had to be regulated by what Russia would accept, since otherwise, as Kimberley realized from the start, the Sultan would simply play off the two powers against each other: 'if we can keep Russia with us he will not dare to resist'.[48] But in St. Petersburg there was no desire to do anything. The Armenian revolt, if successful, would have dangerous repercussions in Russian Armenia; and Lobanov, Giers' successor, only joined in the British sponsored Commission of Enquiry in order to prevent it accomplishing anything. This Commission pursued its laborious task throughout the winter and finally came up with recommendations for reform, but by the time this materialized Anglo-Russian cooperation was as good as dead.[49]

The *coup de grâce* to the temporary association of England, Russia and France was delivered by events in the Far East. The

[46] Gardiner II, 325 (no date).
[47] To Kimberley 2 December 1894, *ibid.* 327–8.
[48] Kimberley to Currie 29 January 1895, K.P.
[49] Langer, *Diplomacy of Imperialism* pp. 162–3.

Japanese attack on China in August 1894 raised important British interests since 70 per cent of the foreign trade of China was in British hands and was bound to suffer from a Sino-Japanese war. Hence Kimberley's initial response was to propose the joint intervention of the Great Powers to stop the war, a proposal which he launched on 6 October 1894 as part of his programme of collaboration with Russia. As he told Lascelles at the time,

> I am inclined to believe that Russia is sincere in wishing at present to maintain the status quo in the Far East. She is not ready for action and would prefer to wait for the completion of the Siberian railway. . . .[50]

But this scheme collapsed on the refusal of Germany and the United States to participate and the war ran on until the spring of 1895. The Japanese occupied southern Manchuria, captured Port Arthur, the main Chinese fortified area, and imposed peace at Shimonoseki on 17 April on the basis of the cession of the Liaotung peninsular, Formosa and further large scale opening up of China to foreign trade. This time Russia took the lead in suggesting intervention since her interests in Manchuria were directly affected and on the same day Lobanov in turn appealed to the powers. In Berlin, partly due to Holstein's eagerness to close the Chinese question before the Kaiser decided to embark on territorial acquisitions, but also because this offered the best way to replace Britain and France in Russia's good graces, Lobanov's proposal was taken up with alacrity. Paris followed, willy nilly, but London now held back.[51]

The explanation of this *volte face* in London was simple. Public opinion in Britain had undergone one of its violent changes in the course of the war and was now fairly pro-Japanese, in contrast to its position during the previous autumn. Moreover it was quite apparent that the terms of Shimonoseki did not conflict with British interests, indeed that the further opening up of China to foreign trade assisted them. If, then, the Cabinet were to join Russia in intervention it would be in the face of public feeling and without even, as Kimberley explained to Lascelles, pressure from the China trade as an excuse:

> There are really no two opinions here on the subject. We should

[50] Kimberley to Lascelles 16 October 1894, K. P.
[51] Rich II, 438–9; Langer pp. 174, 185.

have much preferred the status quo before the war, but our interests are not so much concerned. . . . We have not had a word on the subject from the commercial bodies in the country who are not slow to cry out if they think the interests of British commerce are menaced.[52]

Rosebery himself, recognizing that 'our separation from Russia in this matter must have a prejudicial effect on the understanding between the two countries', still wanted to go ahead, but the divisions in the Cabinet made this impossible. Harcourt told Kimberley that he was 'quite as much against entering upon active operations in concert with Russia in this matter as I am against going into partnership with the Triple Alliance', an attitude which put an end to all discussion.[53]

The result was simply that the Continental powers went ahead on their own in forcing the Japanese out of Port Arthur by an agreement signed on 8 May and what remained of the Anglo-Russian understanding now collapsed. This in turn made any settlement of the Eastern Question impossible: on 11 May an outline reform plan was put to the Sultan which Currie thought he might accept if joint pressure were kept up, but already by the end of the month it was clear that the Russians were withdrawing.[54] The only consolation for Rosebery was that he no longer had to cope with the situation. In June the administration, dependent on the Irish for its majority, committed the final folly of proposing a memorial to Oliver Cromwell, and on the 21st reaped the appropriate reward. The next day Rosebery, to his 'immense relief',[55] resigned and left the problem to Salisbury.

Rosebery's achievements as a Foreign Secretary were considerable. The last of the Whigs—if one excepts Lansdowne—he had the natural gift for dealing with foreign affairs which went with the manners of the *grand seigneur*. Handicapped by his singularly morose disposition after the death of his wife, he had to be practically dragged to the Foreign Office but, once in harness, showed no eagerness to drop it. It was Gladstone who was forced out, not Rosebery, and for a long time—until apparently the

[52] Kimberley to Lascelles 1 May 1895, K.P.
[53] Rosebery to the Queen 23 April 1895, Q.V.L. II, 496–7; Gardiner II, 338. Doc. 108.
[54] Currie to Kimberley 30 May 1895, K.P.
[55] Rosebery to the Queen 22 June 1895, Q.V.L. II, 522.

success of Harcourt's budget in 1894—he worked on the expectation that Harcourt would follow him. Only after this did the long drawn out struggle prey on his nerves to the extent of welcoming defeat in 1895. Obviously, compared with his predecessor, Rosebery had a more difficult task. Inheriting Salisbury's mantle at a time when British naval supremacy was regarded as dubious and her main enemies had just joined forces, Rosebery had also to cope with considerable opposition within the Cabinet. Yet, despite this, he continued the main lines of Salisbury's policy in their entirety: he supported the Triple Alliance in the Mediterranean, pursued 'Die Wacht am Nile' and backed this up in the Spencer Programme by further naval expansion.

How did he achieve this in the face of Cabinet opposition? Largely by ruthlessness and secrecy. Rosebery had a habit of presenting the Cabinet with a series of *faits accomplis*, a habit which naturally infuriated the Opposition and did more to break up the Liberal party than any other single factor. By 1895 he and Harcourt and Morley were not on speaking terms. But Rosebery achieved results. By not telling his colleagues anything he managed to retain the connection with the Triple Alliance that Salisbury had so laboriously built up; that this broke down in 1894 was not all Rosebery's fault. By sleight of hand he held on to Uganda and promoted the Anglo-Belgian agreement, at a time when most of the Cabinet were in favour of abandoning Egypt, not acquiring the Upper Nile. In this respect Rosebery's tenure of office is an object lesson in what a strong-minded Foreign Secretary could achieve given a certain amount of support by key personnel, notably Kimberley and Spencer.

Essentially what Rosebery was trying to do in Africa was to complete Salisbury's work of 1890–1 by a settlement with France. In this he failed, partly because Hanotaux could not control his Colonial Office as Salisbury later could not control his. But Rosebery did at least succeed in posing the problem clearly: by the Grey declaration he staked the British claim to the Nile and gave Salisbury an unequivocal basis to stand on after 1895. In Central Asia he scored a signal, if limited success: the settlements with Russia and France in the Pamirs and Siam stood the test of time and if his handling of the Sino-Japanese war was less happy, it can at least be argued that in retrospect Rosebery was right for the wrong reasons.

His greatest failure, apart from relations with Germany, lay in Armenia. Rosebery's handling of Germany in 1894 shows a growing exasperation with Berlin which, if understandable, was out of proportion. Making all allowances for the devious game Marschall was playing, Rosebery's outburst to Deym on 17 June was unwarranted: the Germans had good reason to complain of Anderson's treaty and Rosebery's threats to abandon the Triple Alliance have the air of wounded self-esteem. No doubt, after the trouble he had gone to to hoodwink Harcourt, it was infuriating to see the treaty collapsing around him. But this had serious consequences. Rosebery inherited a clean sheet in Anglo-German relations but he left them in a state of considerable disarray, a series of minor running sores in Africa and, more important, basic doubts as to the whole purpose of British policy in the Mediterranean. Rosebery's marked tendency to work with Russia and France from the autumn of 1894 onwards, partly deriving from his irritation with Berlin, only made things worse.

Rosebery, of course, was not responsible for the Armenian massacres or the violent feelings they aroused in Britain, but it was he who decided to try to solve the problem by working with Russia. Had it been successful Rosebery would probably have been hailed as the greatest foreign minister of the nineteenth century—the man who solved the Eastern Question. But it was not, and of all his legacies this was the one Salisbury least appreciated. Again Rosebery was not entirely to blame: he could see, as the little Englanders could not, that obtaining Russian co-operation in this was partly a question of going along with them in opposition to Japan. But this was not the whole story: there were solid reasons why Russia would never contemplate a policy of coercing the Sultan and it took Rosebery and Kimberley, in their slightly naïve enthusiasm for the new policy of working with Russia, rather a long time to see this. Rosebery has always suffered by comparison with the great Salisbury whose pupil he avowed himself to be but, as the inventor of the principle of the continuity of foreign policy, he deserves considerable credit for the manner in which he carried this out, given the Cabinets he had to contend with.

IX

The Near East and Africa

We certainly wish to be good friends with Germany: as
we were in 1892. That is to say we wish to lean to the
Triple Alliance without belonging to it.

Salisbury, 1896

The Abandonment of Constantinople

The assumption behind the German policy of using Rosebery as
a stopgap was that once Salisbury returned to office British
relations with the Triple Alliance would resume where they had
left off in 1892. Yet this did not happen. Although there was no
definite break, by the end of 1897 relations were at least as cool
as they had been under Rosebery, whilst the general drift was
much more towards an understanding with St. Petersburg than
with Berlin. Though the prospects of this faded after 1898 and a
German alliance returned to favour it was found, when subjected
to rational analysis, that in the intervening years the basic common
interest which had been so strong up to 1894 had disappeared.
Once this was realized the British alignment with the Central
Powers in Europe, traditional since 1887, faded away, to be replaced
by the state of flux that Chamberlain labelled 'splendid isolation'.

The initial reason for this lay in the further development of the
Armenian question. In Armenia Salisbury inherited from Rosebery the policy of collaboration with France and Russia to introduce reform, but without any real idea of how this was to be
accomplished, The basic difficulty, as he outlined it to Currie on
1 July, was that they were trying to impose terms which no
independent sovereign would accept unless force was used: 'and
how are we to apply it in the absence of allies?' For the next twelve
months, until Salisbury finally abandoned the problem as beyond

solution, this remained the simple basic issue. In Britain support for the unfortunate Armenians was strong, with an agitation in their favour reminiscent of the Bulgarian movement of the seventies which 'approaches to frenzy in its intensity'. But on the Continent this feeling did not exist. It was Salisbury's impression that 'from Archangel to Cadiz' nobody cared whether the Armenians were exterminated or not. Certainly it was quite clear to him after a month in office that there was no hope of Russian or French agreement to the application of pressure at Constantinople and that the German powers were equally opposed: 'they think it quixotic and dangerous'. Hence there was no point even in dropping Rosebery's Armenian *triplice* in favour of a general European conference after the pattern of 1876, as Currie urged:

> The only result of calling a Conference will be that we shall be politely bowed out by six Powers, instead of two, as now.[1]

If collaboration with Russia and France or a European conference were a waste of time, what other means of pressure upon the Sultan remained open? Salisbury pursued two at this stage, neither of them very effective. The first was to fly the kite of partition of the Turkish Empire, both in his private discussions with ambassadors and his public utterances, notably in the House of Lords on 15 August. How far he took it seriously at this stage is a matter of opinion. Hatzfeldt's views varied, at first he thought it was something which Salisbury would only come to as a last resort; later, particularly after Salisbury's suggestion on 30 July that the Italians should turn their eyes towards Tripoli and Albania, rather than their embarrassing preoccupation with Zeila, he changed his mind. Now he thought that Salisbury envisaged a fairly imminent partition and was ready to offer Constantinople to Russia. Almost certainly he was wrong, for when from 29 August onwards the Kaiser made a series of advances to Salisbury making precisely this suggestion it was carefully evaded. As has been pointed out, Salisbury never said at this stage that he would abandon Constantinople to Russia, this was simply 'what Hatzfeldt fancifully conjectures'.[2] But was he altogether to blame for

[1] Salisbury to Currie 1 July, 27 August, 17 December 1895, Lowe pp. 99–101. Docs. 109, 111.

[2] J. A. S. Grenville, *Lord Salisbury and Foreign Policy* (London, 1964) pp. 30–6, 40–3. Grenville is unduly critical of Hatzfeldt: for a more favourable interpretation see Rich II, 452–6.

making this mistake, with Salisbury continually talking about the impending collapse? Undoubtedly Hatzfeldt made an error of judgment here, since Salisbury later vigorously denied that he had ever hinted anything of the kind, but in view of his remarks about Tripoli and Albania it is not surprising that Hatzfeldt assumed Salisbury was serious in talking of partition. If it were only intended to frighten the Sultan it was ineffective: but it is not impossible that Salisbury originally meant it seriously, then dropped it as too hazardous. Instead, by the end of August, dropping all idea of action at the Straits as liable to lead Russia 'to pacify the Armenians after her own fashion', Salisbury had embarked on a new project, a military expedition to Arabia. This had the great advantage of not leading to any conflict with Russia but might well 'bring down the Turkish Empire with a run'. However this could not have worried Salisbury unduly for he was quite prepared to take the chance. As he told Currie when announcing this scheme,

> We cannot cook so very unsavoury an omelette as that which has been bequeathed to me by my predecessors without breaking a monstrous number of eggs.[3]

That the idea of action at the Straits revived in November was the result of the new wave of massacres in Constantinople at the end of September, which so horrified the resident ambassadors as to produce a momentary spasm of unity. On 17 October they forced the Sultan to issue an *iradé* granting all the reforms which had been pressed on him since May. Encouraged by this Goluchowski even suggested on 11 November that the Powers should jointly force the Straits and actually put into effect the reform of 17 October. This immediately revived Salisbury's interest since it now seemed that he would at least have Austrian backing and, since Crispi had been urging British action since the summer, he was already assured of Italian support. On 17 October he told Deym that he was perfectly willing to renew the former understanding, and that British policy was certainly to uphold the Turkish Empire, since its collapse was bound to be detrimental to British interests. This and his keen interest in forcing the Straits in the next two months, show quite clearly that, whatever he had been considering in July, he was, by October, until events and his

[3] Salisbury to Currie 27 August, 13 September, 1895, S.P.

own Cabinet conspired against him, as eager as he had been in 1892 to pursue the old policy. The difference was, however, that maintaining the Turkish Empire did not necessarily mean supporting Abdul Hamid II. If this fear crazed maniac could be removed he thought the Empire might well gain a new lease of life. Obviously Salisbury underestimated the talents of the Sultan, for in 1897 this Empire which he thought on the verge of collapse managed to smash the Greeks with ease.

But Salisbury's hopes in November of any sort of concerted action against the Sultan quickly collapsed. Goluchowski retreated as rapidly as he had advanced: with no interest in the Armenians the whole point of his policy had been to avert any possible Anglo-Russian deal over Constantinople (which Berlin told him was imminent) by drawing Salisbury back into the *entente à trois*. But it was no part of his intention to risk a war with Russia over this, in which he would get no German support. Hence, as soon as Lobanov made it clear on 20 November that in no case would he agree to the opening of the Straits, Goluchowski abandoned the whole project, since there was now not the slightest chance of any Anglo-Russian deal; whilst perseverance might well 'have led to war and that for interests the importance of which to herself Austria cannot recognize'. This killed any chance of action because Salisbury could not persuade the Cabinet to agree to forcing the Straits without Austrian support. The Admiralty stuck to its view, held since 1892, that it could not be done without French neutrality: Goschen, now First Lord, with support from Chamberlain, Balfour and Hamilton, would not overrule them without guarantees of Austrian and Italian support. Although Crispi was as ready as ever and even offered troops at this juncture, plainly Goluchowski was not, with the result that, as Salisbury petulantly complained, 'In Armenia I have been told by the Cabinet practically to sit still'.[4]

This determined the failure of Goluchowski's attempts to redefine the *entente à trois* in February 1896. After the collapse of his one initiative in November, Goluchowski showed no particular interest in negotiation with London, but if the Austrians were satisfied the Italians were not. Apart from Crispi's own Mazzinian sympathy with the subject peoples of the Ottoman Empire, which had the effect of Rome's being much more in tune with London

[4] Grenville pp. 44–51; Langer pp. 206–8; Lowe pp. 101–5. Docs. 110, 112.

than with Vienna over Armenia, Crispi was desperately afraid by the end of 1895 of an Anglo-French-Russian understanding. All the signs had pointed to this since 1894 and Italy had been its first victim in the Red Sea: hence the constant urging from Rome ever since Salisbury's return for the old *entente à trois* to be resurrected. Until January Goluchowski took very little notice: with Berlin constantly emphasizing the dangers of involvement with Britain he could not afford to do so. Even the Kruger Telegram[5] episode had little effect on his confidence in Berlin, but Crispi, now more alarmed than ever, threatened that unless negotiations were opened with London he would have to demand more support in the Mediterranean when it came to the renewal of the Triple Alliance in the summer. This at last stirred Goluchowski into action.[6]

But, in contrast to Crispi and Salisbury, he was unwilling simply to renew the former agreement. Part of his reluctance to negotiate at all at this stage was due to this. What he wanted, on all or nothing basis, was a hard and fast alliance in the Mediterranean and, as he told Crispi, the way to obtain this was to await the outbreak of the inevitable Anglo-Russian war. This dogma, which originated in Berlin's assumption that 'unless a binding convention can be arrived at . . . England will not honour her obligations',[7] wrecked the negotiations that followed and hopelessly compromised all the attempts at an Anglo-German alliance in the succeeding years. It was Goluchowski's fatal mistake since Salisbury was perfectly willing to renew the existing arrangement, which would thus have continued and afforded a much better basis for the later discussions of British entry into the Triple Alliance. But the timing, as Goluchowski himself surmised, was all wrong for an alliance proposal in January 1896. The Kruger Telegram was not yet a month old and public opinion was still bitterly anti-Turk and pro-Armenian. This was decisive. As Salisbury explained to the Queen on 15 January, when she half advocated accepting German overtures, it was almost impossible for an English government to enter such an alliance. When the decision for peace or war had to be taken,

the Parliament and people would not be guided in any degree by the

[5] See pp. 216–18.
[6] Lowe pp. 108–10.
[7] Lascelles to Salisbury, quoting Marschall, 21 December 1895, *ibid.* p. 105.

fact that the Government had some years before signed a secret agreement to go to war, but entirely by the cause for which it was proposed to go to war and their interests and feelings in respect to it.

The great difference between what Goluchowski now wanted and the agreements of 1887 was that the latter 'contained no sort of promise to go to war'.[8]

What Salisbury wanted and offered was to simply renew the old understanding and continue to work closely with Austria, on the assumption that in time the public would forget the Armenians and oppose any Russian seizure of Constantinople. Even this was a good deal more than some members of the Cabinet wanted. Chamberlain certainly, probably also Hamilton and Balfour, now wished to throw over the Triple Alliance in favour of Russia since they completely accepted the Admiralty case that we 'cannot keep Russia out of Constantinople'. In Hamilton's view, the only result of trying to had been to consolidate the Franco-Russian alliance: 'a mere recital of our past policy is a heavy indictment of the policy pursued'.[9] Salisbury, the obvious recipient of the brunt of this criticism in view of his single-handed conduct of foreign policy over the past ten years, not unnaturally disagreed. In his view, with which Goschen concurred, cutting Austria adrift was dangerous: 'It would reconstitute the Drei Kaiser Bundnis, a state of affairs which must be injurious to this country.'[10]

Goluchowski however thought otherwise and the effect of the Armenian crisis was therefore to bring about the end of Anglo-Austrian collaboration in the Eastern Mediterranean. Although in March he told Hohenlohe and the Kaiser that he still wanted to maintain the best possible relations with Britain despite the failure of the February negotiations, this did not amount to much in practice and the renewal of the Armenian massacres in August only served to emphasize the increasing rift. In September Goluchowski told Currie that on three of the four points which had been fundamental to the *entente à trois* British policy was now at best equivocal, whilst the Russian policy of maintaining the Sultan was much more in accordance with Austrian interests. As the crisis

---

[8] Q.V.L. III, 22. For a detailed analysis of these negotiations see J. A. S. Grenville, 'Goluchowski, Salisbury and the Mediterranean Agreements', S.R. 1958 pp. 351–9. Doc. 116.
[9] Hamilton to Balfour 12 January 1896, Lowe p. 108.
[10] Salisbury to the Queen 19 February 1896, *ibid.* p. 113. Doc. 117.

deepened towards the winter Goluchowski made one final effort and renewed the question he had posed point blank the year before: would Salisbury defend Constantinople? On the latter's refusal to commit himself, the game was abandoned and Austria explicitly resumed full liberty of action. Clearly by January 1897 British policy had changed: Goluchowski rightly detected a weakening of Salisbury's attitude even since the previous year. In January and February 1896 Salisbury had been at pains to emphasize that though he could not commit himself to a military alliance to defend Constantinople, he thought the overwhelming probability was that Britain would certainly fight if Russia should move. Now short of saying that Britain had completely lost interest, he all but admitted there was very slight chance of any British action. In fact he as good as told the Tsar as much in September 1896 on the latter's visit to Balmoral. Admitting that he had now abandoned the former theory that it was necessary for British security in India to keep Russia out of Constantinople, he even added that British interest in the Straits 'was not so large as others and was purely maritime'. His only proviso was that Russia should not execute a *coup de main* and that she should reach prior agreement with Austria. As he repeated to Goluchowski in the following January, he 'could not admit that England had an interest more vital that that of Austria and France'. In practice, in contrast to Goluchowski, all Salisbury's efforts from the autumn of 1896 onwards were bent towards getting a European conference whose main task would be to depose the Sultan, not to defend him against Russia.[11]

In view of the momentous consequences of this change in British policy, it is worth making two points. Firstly, it seems clear that Salisbury's attitude on this question was the product of gradual evolution. He did not come back to office in July 1895 with any determination to partition the Ottoman Empire, as the Germans only too readily assumed. His remarks on this subject in July and August, when not kite-flying, were in all probability a bluff to impress the Sultan,[12] since at quite an early stage he was well aware of the general opposition to any such action. Certainly he did not intend to give Russia Constantinople at this stage. The

[11] Grenville pp. 79–83. Docs. 113, 114.
[12] This was certainly Deym's impression: to Goluchowski, 17 October 1895, S.A.W. XXV/463/30B.

change in policy was the result of renewed massacres in September 1895 and August 1896. The first stirred him to revive the *entente à trois* and press the Cabinet for naval action to pass the Straits: their refusal made it impossible to agree to Goluchowski's extension of the agreement. The second made plain once and for all that the policy of supporting the Turkish Empire had now reached the end of the road and Salisbury as good as told all concerned that Britain had no further interest.

Secondly, although it is a point of some importance that the decision to end the *entente à trois* came from Goluchowski, this should not be taken too far. Certainly, in 1896–7, it was he who posed the question as either Britain made a binding alliance or Austria would resume a free hand, whilst Salisbury was averse to anything that would 'cut Austria adrift'. In view of the long term consequences for British relations with the Triple Alliance this was a mistake, since Goluchowski had not in fact anything better to put in its place. But he was not altogether wrong in his perception of the drift of British policy and attempts to arrest it. Although Salisbury by nature was always opposed to any change in foreign policy and certainly, even in 1897, showed no signs of actively wanting to partition the Turkish Empire, Goluchowski was quite correct in assuming that British policy had changed since the agreements were originally made. Salisbury himself said so in January 1897.[13] The swing of the Sultan away from Britain and towards Russia, noticeable even by 1892, was confirmed by the Armenian massacres and the reaction these produced in Britain. By 1897 it was both technically impossible and morally unthinkable that Britain would fight to defend Turkey: even Salisbury, at this time the only defender of the traditional policy left in the Cabinet, was much more inclined to collaborating with Russia than to fighting her. It is extremely doubtful whether Britain would have done anything if Nelidov's scheme for seizing the Bosphorus had been put into operation in January 1897. Ten years before this would have been unthinkable but, by 1897, Salisbury had written off Turkey and was moving in another direction, as he told Currie in October.[14]

[13] Salisbury to Rumbold 20 January 1897, B.D. ix (i) pp. 775–6. It is in this sense that the conclusions of Grenville's otherwise excellent analysis (supra pp. 367–9) are most open to criticism.
[14] Grenville *Lord Salisbury* p. 94. Doc. 115.

Towards Fashoda: the reconquest of the Sudan

Tempting though it is from the logical standpoint to infer that the decision to advance to Dongola was the natural corollary of that to abandon Constantinople, it was by no means so straightforward. Although the D.N.I. urged this course from November 1895 onwards, in March 1896 the Cabinet was far from decided on the question of the abandonment of Constantinople, though it was plainly moving towards it. It was not until late in 1897 that the decision had been reached and the natural corollary accepted —the decision to reconquer the Sudan with all that this implied, not only in Africa but also in Asia. From 1896–8 Salisbury preferred to let things drift to see what happened rather than reach a decision. In these years he kept as many irons in the fire as possible. He attempted to reach a settlement with Russia over Turkey and China and with France over Africa; but he also kept up his relations with the Triple Alliance and made the first tentative moves for an advance in the Sudan. But he did not commit himself to anything until January 1898. It was not until then, when British troops were sent to take Khartoum, that an irrevocable decision was taken. It is significant that this action, which implied a willingness to risk a confrontation with France over Egypt and the Nile Valley, was simultaneous with his approaches to St. Petersburg. This fact has been obscured by the advance to Dongola in March 1896 and the supposition that it represented a decision to 'forestall the French', who had ambitious plans for an East-West pincer movement. In fact it was nothing of the kind. The advance to Dongola was the offshoot of Salisbury's relations with the Triple Alliance.[15]

It derived initially from the Italian defeat at Adowa on 1 March 1896 and the whole complex of Anglo-Italian recrimination which preceded it. Since July 1895 Crispi and Blanc had been trying to obtain help over Zeila in East Africa against the growing Franco-Russian support for Menelik in Abyssinia. Salisbury, as intent on keeping French and Russian goodwill in the Mediterranean and Far East as his predecessor, rejected these requests, even when they were supported by Germany. This in turn led to growing German distrust towards Salisbury which, coming on top of their

---

[15] For the basic arguments on this point see Taylor, *Struggle for Mastery* pp. 367–8; J. Hargreaves, 'Entente Manquée', (*C.*)*H.J.* 1953 p. 85; Robinson and Gallagher pp. 349–51; Grenville p. 119; Langer pp. 284–8.

dislike of his Turkish policy and the Emperor's personal pique after the Cowes interview, contributed to the explosion of the Kruger Telegram. This and the projected Continental League which followed had been explicitly designed to frighten England into joining the Triple Alliance but turned out to be a complete fiasco. Public opinion in Britain swung into a violently anti-German phase which, added to its Turcophobia, made closer relations with the Central Powers all but impossible, as Salisbury had been obliged to admit to Vienna in February. But this was an extremely dangerous situation since, despite improved relations with France, those with Russia were as distant as ever. Hence the importance of Adowa since it provided a sort of test case: if Britain failed to support Italy now any connection with the Triple Alliance was a dead letter.[16]

The immediate effect of the Italian defeat at Adowa was to cause alarm at Vienna and Berlin for the fate of the monarchy. Goluchowski, unable to rely on British support in the Mediterranean and alarmed by the increase of Russian influence in Bulgaria and at Berlin, was now faced with a serious possibility of the collapse of his southern flank. If the republican agitation were to continue in Italy it was only too probable that a wave of irredentism would bring in a pro-French ministry which would denounce the Triple Alliance. At Berlin the reaction was very similar. If Marschall remained indifferent to possible developments, the Kaiser, for whom the danger to a crowned head was of emotional importance, took a more serious view. Since it seemed possible that intervention might still save Crispi's ministry and avert the danger of a Francophile successor, it was an obvious move to appeal to the one power who could give effective assistance to Crispi in Africa—England.

Moreover there was an added advantage to be derived from such a move. Despite the breakdown of the 'Armenian Triplice' the improvement in Anglo-French relations had continued unabated: Salisbury, it was reported, was contemplating concessions to France in Egypt. This, if true, would ruin all German calculations that an Anglo-French understanding was impossible and, quite clearly, would strengthen any tendency in Italy to desert the Triple Alliance. If this were to occur it would bring a most unwelcome addition to French strength in Europe, when the French had

[16] See Lowe, *Anglo-Italian Differences in East Africa* pp. 328–36.

shown themselves utterly irreconcilable by their rejection of the Continental League. Yet by one simple gesture all this could be avoided, since if Salisbury could be induced to assume the offensive in East Africa to save Crispi, this would also nip the incipient Anglo-French understanding in the bud. Small wonder that William II afterwards congratulated himself on his triumphant diplomacy. If it were true, as he thought, that an Anglo-French understanding had been imminent and that the advance to Dongola had been the result of his intervention, then indeed he had achieved a triumph on a par with that of Björko.[17]

But had William's assumptions any validity? The first was certainly wrong since it must be doubted that Salisbury was considering any serious concessions to France in Egypt. In February Courcel, with an agreement on Siam behind him and negotiations on West Africa in progress, was optimistic: and consequently all the more depressed in March. But in fact it emerges from Salisbury's correspondence with Cromer that all he was thinking of was some gesture in Egypt to show his goodwill—the appointment of Frenchmen to a few minor administrative posts. This would have been hardly sufficient to create an Anglo-French *entente*. The precondition of such an alignment, as Courcel himself ruefully pointed out, was that France should be in a position to act as a brake upon her Russian ally: as she was not it was essential to England to keep the Triple Alliance in being. But William's second assumption—that he was responsible for the advance to Dongola—had rather more substance. It is generally accepted that, before Adowa, Salisbury had no intention of assuming the offensive in the Sudan, either to forestall the French or to relieve the Italians at Kassala. Cromer, preoccupied with the effect of operations upon Egyptian finances, was not keen; Salisbury, afraid lest a premature move should provoke a French counter-advance, preferred to wait until the Uganda railway was complete. With this preoccupation in mind it is not surprising that Italian appeals for assistance at Kassala should have fallen on deaf ears. Cromer, with many hesitations, was prepared to give limited approval to a scheme for an advance from Tokar, but when this met with disapproval in London on military grounds the idea was dropped. As Salisbury put it:

[17] G.P. xi. nos. 2673, 2681, 2713, 2769; Langer pp. 281–2; Rich II, 474–5.

The Power of the Khalifa tends steadily to diminish, and a waiting game is the obvious policy. Whenever we are masters of the valley of the Nile Kasalah will be easily dealt with. Till then it has little value.[18]

This attitude was maintained in London for a full week after Adowa. The general feeling in England at first was that Crispi's extravagant policies had come home to roost: that this disaster might induce a more sane policy in keeping with Italy's position in Europe. William's appeal on 3 March for either military action against the Franco-Russian conspiracy in the Red Sea or at least financial assistance met with no response from Salisbury: even his own sovereign could not move him. Hatzfeldt's hints that Italian naval co-operation in the Mediterranean might not be available in future if this appeal were turned down brought only the typical reply that England would rely on her own strength. As late as 8 March Ferrero insisted to Hatzfeldt that there was no hope of any assistance from Salisbury who, he thought, wanted an Italian defeat so that he could annex Eritrea himself! Needless to say Ferrero's suspicions were absurd. The main reason why Salisbury was showing such reserve lay, in all probability, in the extended Cabinet crisis in Rome for, until this was resolved, any more forward in London was unlikely. Salisbury, in contrast to the German powers, certainly had no interest in the preservation of Crispi in office, as at first seemed possible, so there was no call for urgency. In fact the Italians had not, as yet, made any appeal for assistance themselves and it was only on 10 March, when Rudinì had taken office, that this was made. Certainly Salisbury was far more likely to assist Rudinì than he was Crispi.[19]

Yet, despite his silence until 12 March on the subject of support for Italy, Salisbury was showing signs of response to William's theatricals as early as the 4th. On this date, after receipt of Lascelles' telegraphic report of his interview with the Kaiser, Salisbury had a very long interview with Hatzfeldt. In the course of this he emphasized his strong desire to re-establish the old terms of friendship with the Triple Alliance and strongly denied any intention of reaching an understanding with France. The recent difficulties over the renewal of the Mediterranean Agreements had been due, he insinuated, to his Cabinet colleagues. Whilst in Russia it was easy to follow a constant line in foreign policy, all

[18] Hargreaves pp. 83–4; Shibeika pp. 350–4.
[19] G.P. xi, nos. 2673, 2681, 2713, 2769; Langer pp. 281–2; Rich II, 474–5.

parliamentary states had to pay some attention to the necessity of ensuring the support of public opinion. His own views, he maintained, were the same as ever; a point which he emphasized in a personal letter to Lascelles, penned on 10 March, for communication to the German Foreign Office.[20]

Quite plainly Salisbury regarded the Emperor's overtures as a means to rebuilding the link with the Central Powers, a link which had been seriously weakened in January and February. Just as in February Salisbury had been anxious not to 'cut Austria adrift' lest it should lead to another *Dreikaiserbund* so now it was important to avoid the impression gaining ground that he had no interest in the maintenance of the Italian position in the Triple Alliance. As always when concessions to Italy were concerned it was largely a question of the price. In the case of Zeila the price, the direct antagonism of France, was too high: now, in the case of Kassala, there was a good chance that relations with France might not be affected whilst the returns, in the shape of renewed German benevolence, were high.[21]

In addition to these European considerations there was a certain amount of danger from the African standpoint. Hatzfeldt, Courcel and Ferrero expressed their scepticism on this point, considering that Salisbury was acting from motives based entirely on the European alignments. Whilst there was a good deal to be said for this point of view it was not entirely true. The preference for a waiting policy in the Sudan had been based on the assumption that Dervish power would diminish: but increasingly in the first fortnight in March it became doubtful if this assumption were valid. The strong probability of Dervish collaboration with Menelik, coupled with increasing Italian weakness, made it likely that they could, unless checked, gain a considerable increase in prestige through the infliction of a defeat upon a European power. As Queen Victoria put it: 'It will lower Italy and encourage these wild African tribes . . .' and Salisbury himself acknowledged this. He told the reluctant Cromer on 13 March that a military advance was necessary since 'it would not have been safe, either from an African or European point of view to sit quite still while they were being crushed'.[22]

---

[20] Doc. 118.
[21] G.P. xi. nos. 2694. 2779; Robinson and Gallagher p. 345.
[22] Salisbury to Cromer 13 March; The Queen to Salisbury 15 March 1896, S.P.

It was the combination of these considerations, backed by an Italian appeal for assistance on 10 March, that determined the Cabinet's decision two days later to order the advance to Dongola. Italian scepticism, based on the obvious fact that Dongola was some distance from Kassala, was unjustified. When on 14–15 March Rudinì, doubting the utility of holding Kassala, decided to withdraw, Salisbury promptly cancelled the Dongola expedition and only put it on again when Rudinì reversed his decision the next day: a point which Salisbury rammed home in May when Rome began to talk of payment for remaining at Kassala. The remoteness of Dongola from Kassala was immaterial since the whole point was that a large scale Egyptian advance along the Nile would draw off Dervish forces from Kassala just as effectively as any move from Suakin or Tokar. Besides, since the whole project had to be dressed up as an Egyptian decision for sound political reasons—to delude Egypt, the Powers and the House of Commons—Dongola made much more sense as an objective:

> we desired to kill two birds with one stone and use the same military effort to plant the foot of Egypt rather farther up the Nile . . . I forgot to add that a mere demonstration (as Cromer urged) is almost impossible under our form of government. The House of Commons asks questions which must be answered. If we say that our movement is a mere demonstration and that we mean to return without doing anything Osman Digma will not be frightened.[23]

Curiously enough the one consideration that would appear to have been absent from Salisbury's mind in this move was any idea of forestalling the French. This is not so surprising as it might seem at first for, at the time, reoccupation of the Upper Nile was envisaged via Uganda, not Dongola. It was only in the course of the next eighteen months, as the sheer technical difficulties of the Uganda railway unfolded and operations on the Nile proved easier than expected, that the Uganda project was abandoned for the Northern route: in 1896 any expectation of going beyond Dongola was confined to 'the more remote future'. In any case Salisbury was totally unconcerned with the prospect of a race to the Nile. In his view it was immaterial if, as seemed only too likely, some French expedition should arrive at Fashoda before the British. What would decide the issue of the Nile Valley, as he

[23] Salisbury to Cromer *ibid.* (partly quoted in Zetland, *Lord Cromer*, p. 223); Shibeika pp. 354–8.

shrewdly told Lansdowne as late as October 1897, was not whether a French explorer had induced some chief on the Nile to sign a treaty, but the diplomatic situation in Europe:

> The diplomatic question will be interesting and difficult, but the increase of those qualities conferred by a French adventurer's 'effective occupation' will not be serious.

Even at this stage he still thought there was a good deal to be said for leaving the Dervishes in occupation south of Dongola, a policy which had a strong appeal to the Chancellor of the Exchequer, oppressed by the thought of the financial and electoral consequences of 'a forward policy in too many places at once'. In November 1897 an advance on Khartoum was rejected by the members of the Cabinet, despite their knowledge that the Uganda project had collapsed, and all that Salisbury could do in December was to repeat Kimberley's tactics of 1895, a stern warning to Paris that Britain rejected 'any claim to occupy any part of the valley of the Nile'.[24]

Evidently there was still much hesitation in embarking on a full scale Sudan expedition to which Cromer was still averse, yet suddenly, in January 1898, Salisbury reversed the November decision, sent the troops Kitchener required and undertook to pay the bill. There is no evidence to account for this sudden abandonment of all hesitancy on Salisbury's part, but an explanation can be inferred from events. All along he had looked upon the problem of a confrontation with France on the Nile Valley as a question of timing and, since 1896, had sought to postpone this as long as possible. To this end he had deliberately played down the Dongola advance and, whilst saying nothing about the Nile, had endeavoured to promote a settlement in West Africa where he was far more prepared to make concessions. To Salisbury's way of thinking and to most of the Cabinet's West Africa was to provide the makeweight to sweeten the French on the Nile and in this period he was certainly prepared to concede far more in this region than Rosebery in 1894.[25] If it had been left to Salisbury, who was convinced that in West Africa there was 'no loot to get except in Goldie's dreams', all these trivial border disputes would have been

---

[24] Sanderson pp. 241–63. Robinson and Gallagher pp. 350–1, 357–8, 362–4. Docs. 120–3.
[25] e.g. the remarkable assurances to France contained in D.D.F. xi. no. 341.

settled in 1896; but there were two important obstacles. The first was Chamberlain. Deprived of the natural outlet for his radical instincts in internal politics by his attitude towards Home Rule, Chamberlain after 1895 embarked on his new imperialism. The consequence of this emphasis upon Imperial development was that every piece of British colonial territory or claim was regarded as a potential gold mine. Hence, in complete contrast to Salisbury, Hicks-Beach and Goschen, who were inclined to look upon West Africa as light soil and mangrove swamp, he insisted on disputing possession of even the most obscure piece of territory. Since his position in the Cabinet was too strong for him to be ignored this meant that these relatively simple questions were the subject of a long drawn out debate which dragged on until June 1898.[26]

This situation seriously prejudiced Salisbury's strategy of linking concessions in the West with a settlement in the East, but the process was completed by Hanotaux. There is no doubt that Hanotaux genuinely wanted an Anglo-French reconciliation in Africa, but, pushed by the Colonial Ministry and lacking the political strength to ignore their pressure, he was not prepared to accept French exclusion from Egypt and the Nile Valley without adequate compensation; an attitude which became increasingly inflexible as the Dreyfus case roused nationalist fervour in Paris. Precisely what he hoped to achieve in East Africa by the various expeditions he launched in his pincer movements of 1896–8 is difficult to assess, since he had acknowledged in 1894 that he was not going to fight Britain for the Bahr-el-Ghazel. In so far as there was any definite idea behind Marchand's expedition it was to force another Egyptian conference and perhaps here, as was certainly the case in West Africa, he and Delcassé worked on the assumption that a physical French presence on the Nile would assist France at the conference table.[27] Hence his unwillingness to accept the idea of a package deal on East and West Africa and insistence on separation of the two, particularly since in view of Chamberlain's attitude he doubted whether he would get much in West Africa anyway. That an agreement on West Africa was signed at all in

[26] For the West African negotiations generally see Robinson and Gallagher pp. 393–407.
[27] Sanderson thinks that the object of the Colonial Ministry was to force a contest with Britain, but cannot prove it as the archives have been 'weeded'. See pp. 312–13, 272, 287–9.

June 1898 must be attributed mainly to his knowledge of his own impending fall, coupled with extreme Cabinet pressure on Chamberlain. But the end result of Hanotaux's policy was that France got the worst of both worlds. She did not obtain the concessions in West Africa which would have been forthcoming for a renunciation in the East whilst, when it came to the point, Marchand's expedition achieved none of the objectives which Hanotaux envisaged and simply left his successor, Delcassé, a very unpleasant situation. In fact all that Hanotaux and Delcassé obtained for France in 1898–9 had been offered to them in 1894–5.[28]

The most probable explanation of both French and British policy in the Nile valley from 1896 to 1898 is that both expected to exploit the general diplomatic situation. At the time the new phase was initiated by the advance to Dongola in March 1896, the Anglophile Berthelot was undecided whether or not to oppose it. But there was considerable pressure upon him from St. Petersburg to do so; there, as in Berlin, any sort of Anglo-French understanding whether on Siam or Egypt was viewed with the utmost suspicion. It was therefore with reasonable expectation of Russian support in Egypt that Marchand was finally despatched in June 1896, an assumption lent colour by the co-operation of Leontiev's semi-official mission with Lagarde in Abyssinia in 1897–8. But in fact when it came to the Marchand-Kitchener confrontation at Fashoda in September 1898 this support was not forthcoming, as Delcassé, now Foreign Minister, discovered.[29]

Although it is not known why Russia failed to support France an explanation may be deduced. From the autumn of 1896 onwards Salisbury had bent all his efforts to reach an understanding with Russia over Constantinople, whilst Hanotaux went out of his way to emphasize that there would be no French support in the event of war over the Straits. The decision to reject Nelidov's schemes at the end of 1896 for Russian seizure of the Straits in favour of Witte's project for the 'peaceful penetration' of China was a logical development of this: why risk war in these circumstances?

---

[28] For French criticism of Hanotaux see P. Renouvin, 'Les origines de l'expedition de Fashoda', *Revue historique* December 1948, and *La politique extérieure de la 111ᵉ république* (Paris, n.d.) pp. 277–84; T. Iams, *Dreyfus, Diplomatists and the Dual Alliance* (Paris, 1962) pp. 40–3, 55–63; Sanderson pp. 322–3.

[29] There is little or no explanation in the French documents on this point. See D.D.F. xii. no. 365 xiv. pp. 657–8: Robinson and Gallagher pp. 354, 359–60; Sanderson pp. 355–7.

This concentration in the Far East received dramatic impetus from the German seizure of Kiao-chow in November 1897, which in turn led to the Russian action at Port Arthur in December. Significantly, in January 1898 Salisbury renewed his offer of an Anglo-Russian understanding, this time to include both the Ottoman and Manchu Empires. The pattern in this is reasonably apparent. With Russia's concentrating on the Far East it was safe to despatch British troops to Khartoum in the certain knowledge that this would produce a crisis with France about six months later. As long as Russia was left alone in the Far East she would not support France in Egypt: this at least seems to have been Salisbury's assumption. As he put it succinctly, 'I don't think we carry guns enough to fight them and the French together'.[30]

Similarly in the case of Franco-German collaboration. Despite the fiasco of the Continental League in 1896, Hanotaux set considerable store by French exploitation of Anglo-German divergences in South Africa. In June 1898 he linked it with the tension in China as a hopeful sign for France in the forthcoming clash on the Nile. But the Anglo-German agreement of 30 August 1898 killed this, since it actually created a limited Anglo-German alliance; certainly Delcassé dismissed any possibility of assistance from that quarter.[31] Consequently, when Salisbury simply refused to negotiate on Kitchener's conquests in September–October 1898 and insisted on Marchand's withdrawal from Fashoda, prepared if necessary to starve him out, and coupled this with the mobilization of the reserve fleet, the question reduced itself to one of counting battleships.[32] This made it a foregone conclusion. The Spencer Programme of 1894 and subsequent expansions in 1896–7 had put Britain in an unassailable position. With 18 British battleships to 15 French in the Mediterranean, plus infinitely superior reserves, Delcassé had no doubts as to the outcome of such a conflict and sought only to escape from the situation without sacrificing national honour, a precious consideration at the height of the Dreyfus affair.[33] This was difficult in view of Salisbury's blunt insistence on evacuation but eventually, at the end of October, after a partial compromise in the sense of hints of some concessions *after* evacuation, Marchand was recalled.

[30] Taylor pp. 368–9; Renouvin p. 288.   [31] D.D.F. xiv. no. 329.
[32] Doc. 124.
[33] Marder pp. 320–3.

In March 1899 an agreement finally delimitated the Anglo-French boundary in the Sudan leaving the entire Nile valley east of Darfur to British rule, thus finally closing the issue which Salisbury had opened in 1890 with the Heligoland Treaty. That this had been brought to a solution favourable to British imperial interests without a war was fundamentally a tribute to the good sense of Salisbury and Delcassé: it would have been easy enough in the jingo atmosphere of the autumn of 1898 for either of them to have provoked a war. In this respect it was fortunate that Delcassé had replaced Hanotaux at the Quai d'Orsay for, although he was responsible for launching the march on Fashoda in the first place, Delcassé—in contrast to Hanotaux—had the parliamentary strength to insist on accepting Salisbury's terms when he appreciated the gravity of the position. It was equally fortunate that Salisbury, not Chamberlain, conducted British foreign policy at this juncture, for the evidence suggests that the latter would have fought the French gladly in 1898: Salisbury certainly thought this his object at times.[34] But this was the fundamental difference between them. Whereas in 1898 Chamberlain wanted a German alliance and was even willing to pay a limited price for it if it came to the point, Salisbury's major object was to avoid the Anglo-French war into which, he strongly suspected, it was the Kaiser's if not Chamberlain's object to push him.

Anglo-German Rivalry in South Africa 1895-8

The Anglo-German friction over South Africa which so encouraged Hanotaux in June 1898 was the product of rivalry in the Transvaal which dated back to at least 1894. When Gladstone, by the conventions of 1881 and 1884, had established Boer Home Rule subject only to British scrutiny of any treaty relations with a third party, the Transvaal had been a backward agrarian state of no particular importance, and which certainly posed no threat to the strategic base of Cape Town. But the gold and diamond discoveries on the Rand changed this completely: by the nineties the Transvaal was easily the most prosperous part of South Africa, bent not only on complete independence, but threatening to absorb by attraction the British provinces into some sort of

[34] Robinson and Gallagher pp. 371-5.

federal republic. Hence for those in Cape Town and London who thought it essential to retain British imperial supremacy in South Africa, the problem now became how to control and contain the Transvaal. Two principal measures were envisaged to this end, both interconnected. The first thing was to obtain complete control of the Transvaal's external trade outlets, then this could be used as a means of forcing Kruger to grant an adult male franchise. If this were done, swamped with recent immigrants mostly of British extraction, Boer nationalism and intransigence could thus be outvoted. Hence the importance of the railway to Delagoa Bay in Portuguese East Africa (Mozambique) since this was Kruger's only independent link with the outside world.

It has been argued that this was simply a question of economic imperialism, Rhodes fearing that the Delagoa Bay railway would ruin Cape Town and Durban, the terminal points of the two existing lines. But this is to mistake means for ends. It may well have been this consideration which moved Rhodes, though even in his case dreams of empire were important, but what moved London was the long-standing strategic importance of the Cape. The thesis of economic imperialism only holds good if it is assumed that the pressure to act against the Transvaal came from Cape Town, not London. In fact London was as much involved in the Jameson affair as Cape Town. No British government was going to watch idly whilst the Transvaal became a threat to its control of the Cape, especially as German interest in the area became more pronounced. Hicks Beach, the least jingoistic of Salisbury's Cabinet, summed up the real issue succinctly: the Cape was 'perhaps the most important strategical position in the world and one of the main links of our great Empire'.[35]

Although German immigrants and capital had moved into the Transvaal steadily in the late eighties they were still a small minority among the *Uitlanders* in the nineties and, in fact, there was no sign of any official German interest in the Transvaal until 1894. Then in June and November Hatzfeldt twice officially warned Kimberley against any pressure on Kruger in favour of the *Uitlanders* or any attempt to seize Delagoa Bay which, he said, 'Germany could not permit'. In 1895 this interest seemed to

---

[35] Quoted in Robinson and Gallagher p. 461. For contrasting views see *ibid.* pp. 411–21; Langer, *Diplomacy of Imperialism* pp. 216–21; Taylor, *Struggle for Mastery* p. 363–4.

increase after Kruger's open appeal on 27 January for closer relations with Germany, provoking an Anglo-German exchange in February from which it emerged that Marschall insisted there should be no attempt, commercially or politically, to change the status of the Transvaal. All this of course, given the assumption in London that Kruger was not permitted independent relations with foreign states, was like a red rag to a bull: as *The Times* reasoned on 22 November 1894, it was difficult to understand this concern unless Berlin 'takes an extraordinary paternal interest in the Transvaal'.[36] Kimberley now repeated Rosebery's tactic of June over the Congo in complaining to Vienna of German conduct in South Africa, stressing that 'Cape Colony was perhaps the most vital interest of Great Britain'.[37] To Hatzfeldt he was quite blunt and all but threatened war in the event of German interference in Delagoa Bay: there was no question of what Germany could permit in relation to the Portuguese colonies, since 'this country with its great sea power would be able to speak the strongest word'.[38] Small wonder that with this question coming on top of the great row over the Congo Malet concluded in July 1895 that colonial questions were the main source of animus in Anglo-German relations and himself saw fit to warn the German Foreign Office that 'national feeling in England was just as susceptible over Delagoa Bay as over Egypt'.[39]

Thus long before the storm over the Jameson Raid and the Kruger Telegram in January 1896 made apparent the depth of Anglo-German hostility over South Africa, both governments had given fair warning of their intentions. Germany did not intend to allow the Transvaal to be annexed by Britain: Britain would resent any German 'interference' in her vital concerns. Just why, in these circumstances, Berlin chose to continue this course is something of a mystery, as indeed is the whole of German policy in relation to the Transvaal, but there are one or two pointers. Firstly, it had obvious connections with *la haute politique*. Whilst there is very little evidence that Berlin thought in terms of blackmailing Rosebery into the Triple Alliance in 1894, there can be no doubt that this idea was very much to the fore at the end of 1895.

[36] *History of 'The Times'* III, 164.
[37] Deym to Kálnoky 1 November 1894, Penson, 'New Course', *T.R.H.S.* 1943 p. 128.
[38] Kimberley to Malet 5 December 1894, printed in Bayer p. 122. Doc. 125.
[39] Malet to Salisbury 7 July 1895, *ibid.* p. 124.

This is obvious from the schemes of Holstein who, totally uninterested in the Transvaal but very much concerned with the European alliance system, thought in terms of some great *coup* with which to frighten Salisbury into line. If he himself did not view the Transvaal as the ideal début for this line of action, Hohenlohe and the Kaiser certainly did.[40]

At the same time the colonial ambitions which had prompted German policy in the Congo affair remained unabated and received new emphasis with the return to work of Dr. Kayser in July 1895. Whether the scheme for obtaining Mozambique was related to that of intervention in the Transvaal is uncertain, but what is quite clear is that Germany now wanted the Portuguese colonies, as well as Samoa. Moreover, these projects were now enthusiastically supported by the 'All Highest', less for their own sake than for the argument they afforded for a High Seas Fleet, but none the less effectively for that. No doubt the latter's personal pique played a large part in the promotion of the Kruger Telegram, as his reaction to Malet's friendly warning against intrigue in the Transvaal with 'we are not Venezuelans' suggests,[41] but there was method in his madness. It is difficult to avoid the suspicion that behind German policy in the Transvaal all along was the conscious thought of building up a claim to compensation elsewhere: Gosselin suggested even in December 1894 that this was what Berlin was driving at and quite certainly that had become the major object by 1898–9.[42]

But this was precisely what successive Foreign Secretaries, Kimberley as much as Salisbury, would not admit. In all probability there would never have been a South African crisis with Germany if they had been willing to pay for a free hand in the Transvaal, but London had no intention of launching into a second partition of Africa if it could be avoided. Anderson recognized in August 1895 that 'unless we arrive at an African settlement with her (Germany) we must be prepared for increasing friction in Imperial as well as in local questions',[43] but Salisbury thought otherwise. From July 1895 onwards Chamberlain and Rhodes worked together to solve the Transvaal problem by a *fait accompli* with no objection from Salisbury. Admittedly he had other

[40] Rich II, 464–71. [41] Grenville p. 105.
[42] Bayer pp. 103, 107–9.
[43] Anderson Memo 31 August 1895, *ibid.* p. 109.

217

preoccupations and there were basic political objections to checking Chamberlain's new found enthusiasms, but he made no attempt to do so. When finally apprised by Chamberlain in December 1895 of the arrangements for the rising in Johannesburg, he recognized that this would bring a clash with Germany, but had no thought of buying her off: 'Of course Germany has no rights in the affair, and must be resisted if the necessity arises.'[44] If the whole affair of the Jameson Raid had not been so badly bungled there would have been no resistance on his part to annexing the Transvaal and braving it out, secure in naval supremacy. It was failure, as Jameson rightly surmised, that led to his disavowal and the temporary abandonment of a military 'solution' to the Transvaal question, not fear of the German reaction. Once failure was apparent Salisbury was careful to be conciliatory to Berlin, as he demonstrated with the Dongola expedition; this was obvious diplomacy. The British press might rave at Germany and make Jameson a hero but Salisbury was simply philosophical: 'If filibustering fails it is always disreputable'.[45]

But the effect of this failure was to put off any quick solution to the Transvaal problem for the present because Jameson's activities had completely alienated the Cape Dutch. This in turn forced Chamberlain to revert to diplomacy over the next two years, despite the growing intransigence of Kruger who was now openly arming, apparently convinced of German support. Inevitably this brought him back to the issue which had baffled Ripon and Kimberley in 1894: obtaining control of Delagoa Bay. As Selbourne put it in an important memorandum on South Africa of March 1896, this would force the Transvaal to 'renounce their foreign intrigues as of no further practical utility, and they would come to terms with us'.[46] Milner in July 1898 put it even higher: possession of Delagoa Bay was the best chance there was 'for the mastery in South Africa without a war'.[47] But the principal difficulty was the same as before: the attitude of Germany. The Portuguese government, however much in need of money, were far too

[44] Salisbury to Chamberlain 30 December 1895 in E. Drus 'Report on the papers of Joseph Chamberlain. . . '*B.I.H.R.* 1952 pp. 36–7. See also 'The question of imperial complicity in the Jameson Raid', *E.H.R.* 1953.
[45] *ibid.* 31 December, Grenville p. 102.
[46] Selborne Memorandum 26 March 1896 printed in Robinson and Gallagher p. 436.
[47] Garvin III, 311.

frightened of Berlin to sell the line to a British nominee without German consent. Hence despite Chamberlain's anxious pressure on Salisbury for results, the Portuguese negotiations remained in the doldrums during 1896–7. Moreover, since Salisbury and the older members of the Cabinet refused to contemplate a war in the Transvaal with its attendant risk of a collision with Germany at the same time as the maturing crisis in relations with Russia and France, this meant that pressure on Kruger had to be relaxed. By the end of 1897 Chamberlain was resigned 'to let the Boers 'stew in their own juice'.[48]

Why then the Anglo-German agreement of 30 August 1898 providing for an abandonment of German interest in the Transvaal in return for a substantive half share of the Portuguese colonies? What had occurred in six months to produce this? This new found Anglo-German concord on South Africa was a by-product of the worsening situation in the Far East.[49] Chamberlain's alarm at Russian expansion in China during the Port Arthur crisis in March 1898, added to his existing troubles with France in West Africa, convinced him that the only way out was a German alliance. Hence he, for one, was at last willing to compensate Germany for the abandonment of her interest in the Transvaal, for the sake of the wider harmony that might flow from this. As he later told Balfour it was 'worth while to pay blackmail sometimes'.[50] In Berlin, though there was little enthusiasm for an alliance at that particular moment, there was no objection to an agreement on South Africa if the terms were sufficiently favourable, as Bülow was convinced that the time was now ripe to exploit this new found eagerness in London to obtain German colonial demands.

A start was to be made with the Portuguese Empire. Getting wind of renewed Anglo-Portuguese negotiations in June and finding Salisbury unreceptive to hints that Germany should be admitted to them, on 18 June Bülow applied pressure in Lisbon to have them broken off. Instead he now substituted the prospect of a joint Anglo-German loan guaranteed on the customs of the Angola and Mozambique, together with an agreement to divide the Portuguese Empire in case of default and some fairly substantial British colonial concessions to Germany. This proposition,

[48] Robinson and Gallagher pp. 442–5.   [49] For this see Chapter X.
[50] Garvin III, 315.

which Salisbury found totally unreasonable, was in Bülow's eyes a generous concession. As he told Hatzfeldt in a stream of instructions in June and July, by giving England 'a free hand regarding Delagoa Bay' they were in effect abandoning the Boers, since this was 'the key of the Transvaal'. Such a renunciation could only be justified to German public opinion if Germany 'has gained evident advantages'.[51] In German eyes this agreement was to provide a sort of test case for the sincerity of the supposed British eagerness for a German alliance and, assuming that Britain intended to take over the Portuguese colonies herself, it was not unreasonable to demand a share. But the assumption was misplaced. Salisbury had no wish to acquire the Portuguese Empire, all he wanted was to exploit her fear of Germany to get effective control of Delagoa Bay in return for a British guarantee. If in the late eighties he had been somewhat contemptuous of Portugal's vast claims and inclined to gunboat diplomacy when these conflicted with Rhodes' ambitions on the Zambezi, by 1898 he was reverting to Granville's tactics of 1883. Bolstering up a weak Portugal was infinitely preferable to having a strong Germany for a neighbour in South Africa. Nor did the theme of the general Anglo-German alliance seem to hold any inducement for him: as he told Hatzfeldt later 'the time for general alliances was past in any case'.

Why then did he give in? There are two answers to this. The first is in terms of the general diplomatic situation: with a row with France on the Nile imminent and Bülow threatening to collaborate with France and Russia in Africa and the Far East, it was obviously politic not to exacerbate Berlin. If this did not alarm Salisbury unduly it certainly did his colleagues, who insisted on 22 June that German interests should be consulted. This Cabinet revolt by the younger element which was to become increasingly critical of Salisbury's traditionalist outlook over the next few years, was the major explanation of the Anglo-German agreement of 1898. Chamberlain and Balfour took the view that the Prime Minister was unduly suspicious of Germany and, thinking mainly of the Far East, thought that a general alliance could be built upon co-operation in Africa. Though Chamberlain's enthusiasm for this dwindled considerably when he discovered the extent of the German demands—which he, as Colonial minister, would have to pay—he still thought it necessary to pursue the

[51] *ibid.* p. 318.

negotiations. Whilst he would have preferred these to have been part of a general settlement and alliance it was sufficient of a start to get rid of the Transvaal controversy which had dogged British policy in South Africa for so long. Balfour, who had complete charge of these negotiations in August and concluded them quickly before Salisbury's return, evidently thought the same. An Anglo-German alliance in South Africa against any third party was a useful achievement in 1898 and, even if he expressed some scepticism at Hatzfeldt's assurances that it was but the prelude to 'a new era of Anglo-German co-operation in other parts of the world',[52] he was one of the foremost supporters of it in London over the next three years.

The essence of the agreement of 30 August 1898 was, as Bülow had originally proposed, that if Portugal approached either power for a loan it would only be granted jointly on the security of the customs of her colonies of Mozambique, Angola and Timor. Moreover, in a secret convention, it was agreed that the manner in which the customs receipts were divided, e.g. those of Delagoa Bay to England, Northern Mozambique to Germany, should be the basis of partition of the Portuguese Empire if 'unfortunately' it were found impossible to maintain its integrity. Any third power was to be kept out of South Africa. As it stood this was pure gain for England because Balfour had obtained a withdrawal of German patronage from the Transvaal without paying the price of having Germany as a neighbour. The drawback lay in the future: they had still not laid their hands on the Delagoa Bay railway and could not now do so without the dreaded partition with Germany. The Germans obviously calculated that this situation would hurry on the partition that they eagerly awaited, but here they made a mistake.

Pressures in South Africa by 1899[53] made it unlikely that diplomatic methods could still produce a solution and, in any case, when it came to force, British requirements were adequately covered by the separate secret agreement with Portugal. This, the so-called Windsor Treaty of 14 October 1899, closed Delagoa Bay to munitions for the Transvaal in return for a British guarantee of the Portuguese Empire but, since none of the conditions envisaged by the 1898 treaty were involved, Germany was given no case to

[52] Balfour Memorandum September 1898. Doc. 126. See Grenville pp. 196–7.
[53] For a good analysis of these, see Robinson and Gallagher pp. 452–61.

221

claim her share. Delagoa Bay remained under Portuguese control and no loan was advanced by Britain: in fact Salisbury took good care to drop appropriate hints in Lisbon and a loan was obtained from France. Obviously enough this was sharp practice since it infringed upon the intention, if not the letter, of the 1898 agreement and in this particular instance, Holstein was perfectly correct in his suspicion of what he called Salisbury's 'little jokes'. The only defence of the Windsor Treaty is that Salisbury had not wanted to make an agreement with Berlin in the first place and preferred that Germany, rather than Portugal, should be the dupe. The reasons for this were not due to notions of morality in politics—Salisbury had few of these and it is only in comparison with his German counterparts that he assumes this aura—but because it best suited British interests.[54]

Nevertheless, despite the fact that it never became operational, the 1898 agreement had a certain importance. In the first place it prevented any chance of Franco-German collaboration over Africa in 1898. Obviously Bülow was insincere in his approaches to Paris in June and Hanotaux wrong in thinking that Delcassé missed his chance of promoting a Franco-German agreement: Bülow stood to gain far more from an agreement with London and was only using Paris to push up the price. But if, as Salisbury wanted, his terms had been rejected he might well have taken up the approaches to Paris seriously, which would have made a considerable difference to the French position at the time of Fashoda. Certainly the Russians, like Delcassé, assumed it to be a waste of time to approach Berlin on African questions after the Anglo-German agreement.[55] Also, assuming that the reports of Chamberlain's bellicosity at the time of Fashoda were true, his desire to reach agreement with Germany first was a sensible one: Salisbury strongly suspected that behind the project of a German alliance lay the idea of a French war, which was perhaps one reason why he was so averse to it.

Secondly, this agreement of August 1898 made the South African war possible since it 'isolated the Transvaal from European aid'.[56] Although Salisbury might have been willing to ignore

---

[54] For two very different assessments of the morality of the Portuguese negotiations see Grenville pp. 193–8, 261–2; Rich II, 586–9, 600.
[55] D.D.F. xiv. no. 347.
[56] Robinson and Gallagher p. 448. For a contrary view, Grenville p. 197.

the German claims to an interest in the fate of South Africa in 1895-6, this was not feasible in 1898-9. At odds with France in Africa and Russia in Asia it would have been courting disaster to ride roughshod over German interests as well. Salisbury, of course, was not a protagonist of a South African war, 'all for a people whom we despise, and for territory which will bring no profit and no power to England',[57] which perhaps partly explains his lack of interest in the August agreement. But the suspicion is not absent that this was in Chamberlain's mind when he urged the payment of blackmail. Bent as he was in 1898 on 'Imperial expansion now or never'[58] to redress the decline of British might, what better than a war to achieve it? Even if this was not his prime consideration in August 1898, it served as an essential preliminary to increasing the pace in 1899. This is not to suggest that it was this agreement alone that kept Germany neutral during the war that followed: no doubt British naval supremacy and the hesitancy of France and Russia were more important factors. Besides, Chamberlain was forced to pay twice: in November 1899 he had to cede the British share of Samoa in return for a German state visit to Windsor, the equivalent of a declaration of neutrality.[59]

But, after this, what incentive was there for the Government in Berlin to do other than remain quiet? It had got all that it wanted in Samoa and the reversion to half the Portuguese colonies and now had a vested interest in keeping third parties out of South Africa. If Salisbury was right in his general view that a German alliance would be 'all *do* and no *des*', on this occasion Balfour and Chamberlain were more far-sighted. It is difficult to suppose that the Imperial government in Berlin would have continued to fly in the face of German sentiment, as it did throughout the Boer war, if Salisbury had had his way and rejected any concessions to Germany either in South Africa or Samoa. Moreover, Berlin was not totally insincere in its assurances that these colonial agreements were to be the starting point of an Anglo-German alliance. Given the view that Britain needed an alliance far more than Germany, it was not an unreasonable standpoint that outstanding colonial differences should first be settled in the German favour. At least it can be said that by 1899 colonial problems offered no obstacle to

[57] To Lansdowne 30 August 1899, Robinson and Gallagher p. 454.
[58] Esher's note 29 January 1898, *ibid*. p. 460.
[59] Cf. Rich II, 600, 611-18; Taylor pp. 401-2; Grenville pp. 272-3, 287-9.

such an alliance, a very different prospect from that of 1894–5. The only trouble was that settling colonial rivalries, important though it was, was insufficient in itself to lead to an alliance: some positive outside pressure was needed to force the two sides to combine. With British interest in Constantinople at such a low ebb by 1898 this pressure could only come from the new area of conflict, the Far East.

X

The Far East

We may push too far the argument that because we have
in the past survived in spite of our isolation, we need
have no misgivings as to the effect of that isolation in the
future.

Lansdowne, 1901

The essence of the Far Eastern problem at the end of the nineteenth century as seen through British eyes was summed up in
Salisbury's 'dying nations' speech to the Primrose League on
4 May 1898. The world, he maintained, was composed of living
and dying states in which

. . . the living nations will gradually encroach on the territory of the
dying and the seeds and causes of conflict among civilised nations
will speedily appear.

China seemed eminently qualified for the second category since, as
had been shown since 1894, it was completely unable to resist
attempts at spoliation on the part of Japan and the European
Great Powers. This brought up a fundamental problem for those
conducting British foreign policy: should they, in the face of these
facts, continue to support the maintenance of an integral Chinese
Empire as they had done for the previous half century, or should
they seek to protect their interests by obtaining their 'slice of the
melon?' In practice policy hovered somewhere between the two
with the result that here, as elsewhere, as Curzon bitterly lamented,
it consisted of 'anxiously waiting to see what will turn up next'.
On the one hand Salisbury's Cabinet sought American and German support for the principle of the 'Open Door': on the other
they sought to neutralize Port Arthur by leasing Wei-hai-wei,
negotiated with Russia for a 'sphere of interest' agreement and,
under pressure from British mercantile interests banded together

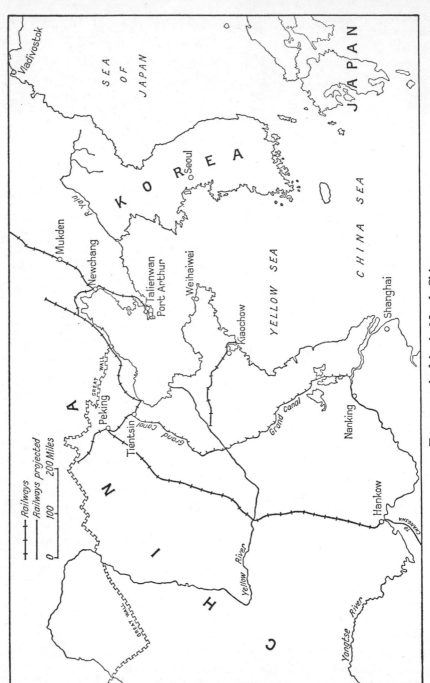

European rivalries in North China

in the China Association, added Kowloon to Hong Kong. That this was inconsistent is obvious enough but perhaps the best defence of it as a policy is that it is difficult to see, in the circumstances in which Britain found herself in world politics from 1898–1902, what other course could have been pursued. At least it avoided the two extremes of fighting Russia and France over China or outright annexation of the Yangtse valley, both of which courses had their advocates in London.[1]

In China British interests were commercial, not political. From the seizure of Hong Kong in 1842 until 1898 the object of British policy was confined to the opening up of China to trade. This in fact had not been particularly successful. Although British merchants in Shanghai and Hong Kong controlled 70 per cent of what Chinese external trade there was, dominated the river trade and even carried half the purely coastal trade, the overall volume of this was small considering the size of China. In the mid-nineties it was not significantly greater than British trade with Japan, for Manchester it was no better as an outlet than Turkey, whilst, despite the sharp drop of cotton exports to India during the eighties, they were still five times as great as those to China. Nor was there any sign in fact, as opposed to prediction, that trade with China was increasing: it remained static throughout the nineties. Why then was seemingly disproportionate importance attached to the Chinese market in the late nineties? The answer would appear to be that the 'Old China hands', the business community in general, and even politicians like Chamberlain and Hicks Beach, were obsessed by the *potential* market of the empire of four hundred million Chinese. As Hicks Beach, Chancellor of the Exchequer, expressed it in a speech at Swansea on 17 January 1898:

> We look upon it as the most hopeful place of the future for the commerce of our country and the commerce of the world at large, and the Government was absolutely determined . . . if necessary, at the cost of war, that the door should not be shut against us.

If only it could be opened up to trade and investment, and other powers prevented from obtaining exclusive spheres, it was

[1] This is certainly Grenville's conclusion: 'Salisbury was thus following the only possible course open to him'. Grenville, *Lord Salisbury* p. 135. Curzon to Hamilton 6 September 1899, *ibid.* p. 297.

thought that it would solve all the problems inherent in the decline of British industrial supremacy at the turn of the century: nobody seemed to realize, as Hobson pointed out in 1903, that in developing China they might be sowing dragon's teeth.[2]

But the crux of the problem lay in the commercial and strategic ambitions of other powers. There was no objection from the China Association to the Japanese attack on China in 1894 as Japan was not taken seriously as a rival and the main effect was seen as helping to force the Chinese to open up trade. But their views rapidly changed as the after effects of this war—notably the provision of the loan to pay off the Japanese indemnity—brought increasing Russian and French pressure upon Pekin for concessions in Manchuria and Szechuen. Once these regions came under their control and protective tariff systems British trade in the area concerned would be dead:

> if once Germany, Russia and France take possession of portions of China . . . a system far more exclusive than any Chinese system ever was will be imposed, and imposed mainly against the commerce of this country.

Hence from 1896 onwards mercantile interests pursued two policies which were increasingly incompatible. The Foreign Office was pressed both to continue the old policy of squeezing Pekin to open up China to trade by the removal of internal restrictions and more treaty ports and simultaneously to counter Russian and French concessions and loans with British counterparts. This quickly became a vicious circle and led quite naturally to the second phase, the idea of a deal with Russia, a division of China into 'spheres of preponderance' in which the British sphere would be the Yangtse valley.

How far this was a conscious departure from the 'Open Door' is a moot point. Balfour seemed to think negotiation with Russia perfectly compatible with this doctrine and certainly, in the very limited agreement on railway concessions that emerged from this, it is difficult to see anything in the nature of a partition of China. Salisbury too always distinguished sharply between a 'sphere of

[2] P. Joseph, *Foreign Diplomacy in China 1894–1900* (London, 1928) pp. 228–9, 238: N. A. Pelcovits, *Old China Hands* (New York, 1948) pp. 192–3, 264: J. A. Hobson, *Imperialism* (3rd ed. London, 1938) pp. 307–9, 312–13: Langer, *Diplomacy of Imperialism* pp. 388–9.

influence' and a 'sphere of interest' and it was his unwillingness to go beyond the latter that made negotiation with Russia difficult in 1898. Although the China Association constantly pressed for it he always rejected point blank the suggestion that the Yangste should be brought under direct British administration on the Indian or Egyptian model. Here there was certainly a great gulf between commercial opinion and Foreign Office policy. But, when this is said, it is difficult to avoid the conclusion that, although they disliked it, the Foreign Office was moving towards a conscious recognition of 'spheres of influence' by Lansdowne's time. After all, the purpose of the Anglo-Japanese alliance from the British viewpoint was not to drive the Russians out of Manchuria but to protect the Yangste. Moreover, though the leasing of Wei-hai-wei and Kowloon was a reaction to the German and Russian moves rather than the initiation of a change of policy, it is difficult after this to draw any sharp line of distinction between British policy in China and that of other states. Salisbury might claim that all Britain wanted was trade, but this was equally true of the others. Certainly Americans, whose interest in the 'Open Door' was undiluted by the distraction of a well staked out claim to a 'sphere of preponderance', thought that 'England is as great an offender in China as Russia herself'.[3]

All this does not detract from the fact that the British policy of preference was the preservation of Chinese territorial integrity. The explanation for this is not unique moral virtue but simply that Britain already possessed more territory outside China than she could administer and would gain nothing from assuming responsibility for China's untold millions: whilst if China were partitioned she would lose the trade she controlled in conditions of open competition. In contrast Russia, France and Germany saw no virtue in a system that simply guaranteed British commercial predominance now that they were in a position to challenge it. The challenge was extremely difficult to resist since, despite Hicks Beach, it was evident that Britain was in no condition to fight a war in the Far East without an ally even in 1898. By 1900, with 300,000 troops engaged in South Africa, it was a plain impossibility. Hence British Far Eastern policy was one of manoeuvre:

[3] Pelcovits, 168–9, 188–9, 215, 218: C. S. Campbell, *Anglo-American Understanding 1898–1903* (Baltimore, 1957) p. 168: J. T. Pratt, *War and Politics in China* (London, 1943) pp. 114–18.

on the one hand attempts to reach an understanding with Russia coupled with forceful diplomacy at Pekin: on the other, attempts to find an ally to counteract the Franco-Russian alliance.[4] That the outcome of this in January 1902 was an alliance with Japan was the least likely prospect in 1898.

The turning point for British Far Eastern policy was the Port Arthur crisis of December 1897 which lasted until March 1898. Up till then British opinion either in the China Association or in the Foreign Office had not been unduly perturbed by Russian activities in North China; if anything they were much more worried by French concession hunting in Yunnan and Kwantung. Nor was there any reason why they should have been. Although the Russo-Chinese Treaty of 3 June 1896 provided for the construction of the Trans-Siberian Railway through Manchuria and was intended to lay the basis of Russian commercial dominance of North China and political influence at Pekin, construction work did not even begin until the spring of 1898. In 1896–7 Russian penetration of Manchuria was 'more theoretical than actual'. Nor had the Russians any desire to annex Chinese territory themselves, since this could only induce a general scramble to their own disadvantage. Though Witte, the Minister of Finance, and Muraviev the Foreign Minister, differed over the tactics to pursue, their end was the same: to preserve China intact until the completion of the Trans-Siberian Railway in 1905 would put Russia in such a strong military position in the Far East that she could exercise a complete preponderance at Pekin. This identity of interest was reasonably apparent to Salisbury. In 1895 he had welcomed Russian involvement in China as a distraction from the Near East and, as he made clear to the Japanese in 1896, he did not intend to oppose Russia there unless she began 'to occupy territory which did not belong to her'.[5]

Hence the shock induced by the Russian occupation of Port Arthur on 11 December 1897, coupled with the knowledge that she was negotiating for a lease of the Liaotung peninsular. This change of policy in St. Petersburg was the result of the personal decision of the Tsar. Irritated by William II's impulsive personal

[4] G. F. Hudson, *British and American Policies in the Far East since 1900* (Leeds, 1955) p. 7; G. W. Monger, *The End of Isolation* (London, 1963) p. 15.
[5] A. Malozemoff, *Russian Far Eastern Policy, 1881–1904* (Berkeley, 1958) pp. 73, 83, 112; Grenville p. 136.

diplomacy and seizure of Kiao-Chow in November, which ran completely contrary to all previous German policy in the Far East, the Tsar was determined on some tangible compensation to uphold Russian prestige. The Russian Admiralty was not particularly impressed with Port Arthur—which was not ice free—and Witte vehemently opposed the move as upsetting the whole basis of Russo-Chinese relations. But the will of the Tsar, perhaps encouraged by Muraviev, was sufficient to overrule them. Even so the decision of 11 December was not final since the Chinese still had to be persuaded to grant the lease, hence the crisis until it was finally settled on 27 March 1898.[6]

It was this uncertainty which prompted Salisbury to attempt at this stage to reach the sort of agreement with Russia which the China lobby was urging. His instructions to O'Conor in St. Petersburg of 17 and 25 January show clearly enough what he had in mind: an Anglo-Russian agreement on their respective aims in China and Turkey so that the 'sick men' could not continue to play them off against each other, 'neutralizing each other's efforts much more frequently than the real antagonism of their interests would justify'. At this stage evidently this was regarded as perfectly compatible with the 'Open Door' since, as Balfour told Goschen on 26 February:

> our desire was to combine the policy of a friendly understanding with Russia with that of a defensive arrangement with the U.S. . . . there seems no reason why the two policies should not properly be run together.

But there was an important proviso in Salisbury's conception of a deal which wrecked its chances from the beginning. Whilst welcoming the partition of spheres of commercial influence and concessions, he would not admit anything which would 'impair the integrity of the present empires'; which effectively excluded any agreement on Russian control of Port Arthur or Talienwan as closed ports. Whilst these ideas were not necessarily in conflict with those of Witte, they were a flat contradiction of those of the Tsar and made an agreement highly unlikely. In any case the issue was decided by the outcome of the simultaneous struggle at Pekin to finance the third instalment of the indemnity to Japan. Muraviev was prepared to withdraw from Port Arthur if the

[6] Malozemoff pp. 99–102.

Russian loan conditions—providing for complete Russian economic control of Mongolia and Manchuria together with the right to select a Manchurian port—were accepted. But the success of the Anglo-German syndicate by 1 March 1898, with corresponding concessions in the Yangtse region, ended all chance of an alternative policy and on 27 March the lease of Port Arthur for twenty-five years was announced.[7]

This was the point of departure for British policy in two ways. In the first place the Cabinet decided that in order to uphold British influence in China it must have a makeweight for this and similar French concessions in South China. Hence the leases of Wei-hai-wei and Kowloon in April, which made it increasingly difficult, as Balfour recognized, to distinguish between 'spheres of preponderance' and 'spheres of interest'. Secondly, it was the Port Arthur crisis in February and March 1898 which started Chamberlain's quest for a German alliance, a mirage which became an obsession over the next three years. The quest for a German alliance was important because although it finally emerged that this was a red herring, the psychological effects of inducing the Cabinet to think in terms of an alliance for the Far East made it easier for Lansdowne in 1901–2 to introduce an alliance with Japan.

In the search for an alliance in China, Chamberlain reflected popular opinion in believing that the events of March were a serious setback for British interests. The evidence suggests that Salisbury was far more sanguine, but from March until May he was convalescent, leaving Balfour and Chamberlain in charge. To a considerable extent they had a very different conception of foreign policy from that of Salisbury. Balfour, if somewhat contemptuous of Chamberlain's efforts, shared his view that nonparticipation in the Continental alliance systems made it likely that the British Empire would simply become the object of attack. Both he and Chamberlain favoured what the latter termed the 'Anglo-Saxon alliance', but American preoccupation with the impending war with Spain made any effective support from this source in the Far East out of the question, despite the similar interest in the 'Open Door'. McKinley's response to Balfour's tentative sounding in March 1898 made this quite clear. Plainly

[7] *ibid.* pp. 103–6; Grenville pp. 138–40; Balfour to Goschen 26 February 1898, B.M. Add. Mss. 49706. Docs. 127, 128.

the successive declarations that came from Washington in favour of the 'Open Door' were of no practical significance and, in any case, given the depth of basic anti-British feeling in the United States, no administration, however Anglophile, would embark on a British alliance for the small American interests at stake. Hence with the Russians unwilling to negotiate on British terms and with the U.S.A. out of the running, Balfour and Chamberlain now turned to Germany, whose interests in China Balfour assured the House on 5 April were 'absolutely identical' with those of Great Britain.[8]

There could have been no greater misconception. Two fundamental flaws ran throughout the spasmodic negotiations for an Anglo-German alliance over the next three years. Anglo-German interests in China were far from being identical. The object of British policy from March 1898 onwards was to check the consolidation of Russian control of Manchuria and certainly to prevent her expansion southwards, a policy identified as that of the 'Open Door'. The British interest in this was obvious enough in view of the enormous trade which was at stake. But the Germans had no trade to speak of and what they had was menaced far more by the British stranglehold on the Yangtse than the Russian on Manchuria.

Moreover there was not the slightest intention of opposing Russian expansion in China: on the contrary in 1898 as in 1895 the greater the Russian concentration on the Far East the better as far as Berlin was concerned. The seizure of Kiao-chow was an aberration, the whim of the Kaiser, the offshoot of *Flottenpolitik* rather than a consciously thought out rational policy of German expansion in China and, as such, was bitterly opposed by Holstein. Certainly he was quite adamant that Germany was not going to fight Russia in the Far East for the sake of British interests: in China, he told Hatzfeldt on 26 March 1898, Germany was neutral. Bülow, if more inclined to wobble under the influence of court politics and the necessity of making his views conform to those of the erratic William, was no more favourable. Like Holstein he assumed that time was on Germany's side, that a British alliance could be obtained on German terms if only they played their cards correctly, and certainly that they were not going to oppose Russia

---

[8] C. S. Campbell pp. 19–20; A. E. Campbell, *Great Britain and the United States, 1895–1903* (London, 1960) pp. 166–8. For a detailed analysis of Balfour and Chamberlain's foreign policy see Grenville pp. 149ff.

over Manchuria. In his eyes Chamberlain's advances simply created the opportunity to operate a colonial squeeze, as proof of British good intentions.[9]

To the basic divergence of purpose was added the confusion created by the Kaiser's personal interventions and Eckardstein's fantasies. Eckardstein, First Secretary at the London embassy, in charge for long periods owing to Hatzfeldt's illness, was listened to largely because for a long time he was taken to be what he claimed to be, the personal reflection of Emperor William, whose views were important in the peculiar nature of German politics. Like Hatzfeldt he had the best of motives and genuinely wanted to promote an Anglo-German alliance, but his ingenious device of by-passing the tedious methods of diplomatic negotiation by telling both sides that the other wanted an alliance defeated its own object. In fact none of the statesmen involved, with the possible exception of Balfour, wanted the sort of alliance Eckardstein was pushing, and the only result of his activities was to spin out the farce for a longer period since both sides waited for advances which never came.

If the Anglo-German negotiations had been confined to the question of a Far Eastern alliance, this incompatibility of interests would have emerged at an early stage and saved a lot of trouble. But they were not. Though primarily impressed with the Russian menace in China, in March 1898 Chamberlain took a pessimistic view of British chances all over the world. In a *coup d'oeil* which embraced his current squabbles with the French in West Africa, with the Germans over the Portuguese colonies, the Russians in China, the perennial trouble on the North West frontier and the campaign against the Dervishes in the Sudan, he declared:

> We may emerge from all these troubles without a war, but I cannot conceal from myself that the prospect is more gloomy than it has ever been in my recollection.

Consequently in his discussions with Hatzfeldt on 29 March Chamberlain frankly told him that the whole basis of the British policy of non-alignment was up for review and that he favoured an Anglo-German alliance. This was rendered by Hatzfeldt as Britain would 'join the Triple Alliance' and the basis of much subsequent confusion was laid. In fact Chamberlain had no

[9] Rich, *Friedrich von Holstein* II, 561–6, 570–4; Grenville pp. 152–5.

intention of joining the Triple Alliance, as he made clear on 25 April, but by then Eckardstein had become involved and the damage was done.[10]

But if Eckardstein added to the confusion, both then and subsequently, the main reason for the failure of Chamberlain's approaches lay elsewhere. For Bülow's unwillingness to conclude an alliance was at least equally matched by Salisbury's. Unimpressed by the dangers of the situation, Salisbury cheerfully told the Primrose League on 4 May that 'we shall maintain against all comers that which we possess'. Approached by Hatzfeldt a week later, he roundly told him that he

> could not recognise that Germany had any claim that we should purchase her support by concessions to which, except for the consideration of that support, we should be averse.

Clearly Hatzfeldt's conception of an alliance via limited colonial agreements by which all the concessions made came from London found no support with Salisbury, and even Balfour's (Eckardstein inspired and mythical) report of the Kaiser's enthusiasm only made him more suspicious. Always wary of the unstable William, he told Balfour on 9 April that his one object since had he been on the throne had been 'to get us into a war with France'. Despite the trouble with the French on the Niger and impending difficulties on the Nile he had no wish to insure against such a war by a German alliance, even if it could be obtained, 'for Germany will blackmail us heavily'.[11] Moreover, as Salisbury realized and Chamberlain did not, there was a fundamental difficulty in an Anglo-German alliance in that it would oblige Britain to defend German interests in Europe. It was no longer possible to contemplate supporting the Ottoman and Habsburg Empires, on which Germany would insist, since the next stage in the Eastern Question was confidently expected to be the dissolution of the Austrian Empire itself. An Anglo-German alliance in these circumstances was not an attractive proposition.

This view, which he expressed clearly enough in 1898, remained the basis of Salisbury's attitude towards a German alliance as long as he retained control of foreign policy and his Memorandum of 21 May 1901 was no more than an extension of it. This is not to

[10] Rich, II, 575–9, 589–90, 628; Garvin III, 367–8; Grenville pp. 161–2.
[11] *ibid.* 165–7; B. Dugdale, *Life of Balfour* I, 257–8.

say that co-operation with Germany, in China or elsewhere, was impossible. Over the next three years there were a number of local agreements: the Portuguese Colonies Convention[12] of August 1898 was followed almost immediately by one on Shantung Railways in September, whilst two years later followed the famous 'joint' declaration on the 'Open Door' in the Yangtse Valley. But these agreements were far from constituting the Anglo-German alliance against Russia that Chamberlain had been seeking and in fact British problems in China over the next three years were solved largely without recourse to Berlin.

The immediate problem in 1898 of Russian encroachment upon the British sphere was checked by an Anglo-Russian railway concession agreement in April 1899, establishing the Great Wall as the boundary for their respective concession hunting. For the rest of the year the China Association, despite its pressure for effective occupation of the Yangtse on the Russian or German model, had to remain content with this. In June its programme was openly repudiated by the government, on grounds that were simple enough:

> We cannot make the Yangtse Valley a province like Shantung or Manchuria, first because it is infinitely larger, and secondly, we are not prepared to undertake the immense responsibility of governing what is practically a third of China.

With its growing preoccupation in South Africa there was no room for an active policy in the Far East and, once hostilities with the Boers commenced with a series of staggering defeats, this consideration rapidly outweighed all others. If it forced Salisbury, grudgingly, to pay the German price in Samoa in November 1899, it made him equally averse to any action likely to provoke the Tsar, an essential precaution if the tales of Muraviev's attempt to create a Continental League had any substance. Hence in India, where fears of Russian activity in Afghanistan grew in 1899–1900, Curzon was forced to abandon his schemes for a forward policy. Salisbury put it succinctly:

> Curzon always wants me to talk to Russia as if I had five hundred thousand men at my back, and I have not.[13]

[12] See Chapter IX pp. 220–1.
[13] Pelcovits pp. 241, 255, 258; Grenville pp. 299–302. Doc. 129.

Fortunately for British interests the Russians were similarly preoccupied. Despite active consideration of a move in Turkey, Afghanistan, or China, the failure of Muraviev's efforts to raise an anti-British coalition in Berlin was discouraging, and instead they decided to do nothing until the completion of the Trans-Siberian railway. That a Manchurian crisis in fact materialized before this, in March 1901, was the result not so much of deliberate Russian action as a by-product of the seizure of the initiative by the Chinese court in the Boxer rising.[14] The Boxer movement, rumbling since January, reached its full flood from 14 June–14 August 1900 with the siege and relief of the legations in Pekin. Though this was the most dramatic part of the revolt it was by no means the end. Punitive expeditions under the overall command of von Waldersee tramped around North China until April 1901, whilst in Manchuria the Russians were engaged in open warfare with Chinese regular forces until October and with 'bandit suppression' until the following March.

Although it caught the public imagination, in itself the rebellion was of no serious consequence to Britain. There was a large number of her nationals in Pekin, and British owned railway lines and trade in North China were damaged, but the Yangtse provinces took no part in the Boxer movement and trade there was comparatively unaffected. This was reflected in the government's attitude in London, where, in contrast to Berlin, there was no great enthusiasm for intervention. But what did matter was the aftermath, the effective occupation of large tracts of North China by foreign troops and the threat that this conveyed of an effective partition of China, contrary to all British interests. This was why Salisbury had opposed military intervention in the first place. With as little concern for European missionaries as he had for the Chinese, his main preoccupation was that any sort of military action would spark off a partition of China at a time when Britain, fully absorbed in South Africa, would be in a poor position to claim her share. As he told the Queen on 10 June 'Russia, not China, seems to me the greatest danger at the moment'. Though it is possible to criticize his policy on humanitarian grounds, as most of the Cabinet did, Salisbury's fears were amply borne out by events. Admittedly it was a Russian led force which saved

[14] For the Chinese background see C. Tan, *The Boxer Catastrophe* (New York, 1949).

Tientsin from the Boxers and cleared the railways to Pekin, but recovering control of the British owned lines and installations at Tientsin from his late ally had become Lansdowne's major problem by 1901.[15]

Initially the Russian attitude was remarkably similar. Giers, the Russian minister at Pekin, opposed German pressure to land troops in May on the grounds that it 'threatens to partition China': even when on 7 June Muraviev advocated sending part of the Manchurian garrison to Tientsin this was largely to forestall the Japanese. Having no missionaries, the only Russian concern was their prestige at Pekin, a concern which led them to adopt the convenient fiction that the Boxer movement was a revolt against the Dowager Empress and to offer Russian troops for its suppression. Hence, once the Russian dominated force had relieved Pekin in August, it quickly withdrew, took no part in Waldersee's expeditions and played a minimal role in the formulation of the joint demands of the Powers for compensation. Instead it concentrated on Manchuria, initially on defeating the Chinese forces, deploying 100,000 troops in the process, then, after October, on exploiting their *de facto* control of the province to establish a system of indirect rule, as Alexeiev put it, 'similar to that of the British advisers to the native rulers in India'. It was this, formulated in the Alexeiev/Tseng agreement of 26 November, published in *The Times* of 3 January 1901, which sparked off the Manchurian crisis, since it was taken to be a thinly disguised Russian annexation of the province. Though technically this view was mistaken since it was only in the nature of a temporary working agreement for the administration of the province, Russian official terms as formulated by Lamsdorff, Witte and Kuropatkin in January–February 1901 were not very different. Though Manchuria was still recognized as a Chinese province it was to be firmly under Russian control.[16]

It was this state of affairs in China which prompted the most serious attempts at Anglo-German collaboration in the Far East: the Yangtse Agreement of October 1900 and Lansdowne's approaches to Berlin for a joint guarantee to Japan in March 1901.

[15] Grenville pp. 286–9, 303, 306–8; Malozemoff pp. 120–3. In retrospect the attitude of the European powers towards China in 1900 appears ludicrous and explicable only in terms of their complete lack of any attempt to understand Chinese problems: see Pratt pp. 19–22, Langer p. 704.
[16] Malozemoff pp. 126–8, 134–5, 149–50, 153, 157–8.

This, if ever, was the moment when the two governments came nearest to considering a mutual alliance and it is instructive to observe how far apart they were. The Yangtse Agreement was the product of two forces. Originally Bülow and Holstein were alarmed lest the evident intention of Russia to absorb Manchuria should lead the British, unable to resist her in view of the South African War, to agree to partition of China in which their share would be the Yangtse. If this occurred Germany would be bottled up in Shantung with no possibility of expansion. Hence the idea of an agreement, the main purpose of which was to rule out any British annexation of the Yangtse valley, by adhering to the principle of the 'Open Door' re-enunciated in Hay's circular of July 1900. There never was in their mind the idea that it should commit Germany in any way against Russia, though Holstein did not exclude the thought that this might encourage Britain to 'make Russia leave Manchuria'.

> A Yangtse agreement, binding both sides to respect freedom of trade, would be completely unobjectionable to us, as it would not be directed against Russia.[17]

But the scheme was complicated by the Kaiser's intervention. Infuriated by the Russian intimation they they did not intend to support Waldersee's peregrinations in North China—thus making him look rather foolish after his 'Attila' speech—on 22 August he gave vent to his feelings to the Prince of Wales and Lascelles at Wilhelmshöhe. The report of these remarks to the Cabinet and the growing Russo-German differences in Pekin over the Kaiser's insistence on a policy of reprisals not unnaturally created the impression in London that he was in one of his anti-Russian moods and wanted a British alliance. Chamberlain, backed by Lansdowne and Goschen, now penned a memorandum which reached the epoch making conclusion that 'in China and elsewhere it is to our interest that Germany should throw herself across the path of Russia' (the principle on which Salisbury's policy had been based for the last ten years) and urged that they should take him up. Salisbury, long convinced that the Kaiser was more than slightly mad, was inclined to be sceptical but eventually, pushed by his colleagues, drafted an agreement which he described as 'unnecessary but innocuous' which was signed on 16 October.

[17] Rich II, 619–21; Grenville p. 312. Doc. 130.

The importance of this agreement lies not so much in what it contained as in what it was thought it might lead to. As far as the agreement itself is concerned it was clearly not a preparation for action, as Holstein commented at the time. The first clause ruled out any attempt to check Russian economic penetration of Manchuria since it confined their support for freedom of trade in China to 'as far as they can exercise influence'. The second, intended certainly by Salisbury to stop Russian territorial annexation, was similarly innocuous, since Salisbury's direct language was watered down in the German drafting. This, as Holstein pointed out, made it quite safe for Germany to sign:

> As Russia officially disclaims any intention of annexation, the expanded English version is not directed against Russia if the Amur is excluded.

Salisbury himself seems to have recognized this fact and placed little reliance upon it: the Cabinet in general however thought they had at last concluded an Anglo-German *entente* for the Far East. Hence their corresponding disappointment when it collapsed at the first signs of pressure upon it in March 1901.[18]

During the winter Holstein regarded this agreement as a means of getting 'again within calling distance of England' and by no means dismissed the idea that it might lead to something bigger. Nor was the time inappropriate: the Kaiser's visit to London to the deathbed of Queen Victoria in January 1901 made him more popular than he had ever been before in Britain. Moreover, in November 1900, Salisbury, whose opposition to a German alliance had been increasingly resented by his more impatient colleagues, was persuaded to hand over the Foreign Office to Lansdowne, who was certainly much more open minded on this than his predecessor.

But the basic gulf remained. What Lansdowne wanted, as his proposals to the Cabinet in March demonstrated, was a Far Eastern alliance. But this was of no interest to Berlin. More than ever convinced, particularly after Eckardstein's fabrication of more alliance proposals from Chamberlain in January 1901, that the British were coming round to their terms, Holstein, Bülow and the Kaiser simply waited for proposals that never came and did

18 Rich II, 621–3; Grenville pp. 313–18, 335. The text of the agreement is printed in B.D. ii. pp. 12–13.

not even bother to cultivate the agreement they already had. In the growing Anglo-Russian tension over Russian attempts to control Tientsin in February, Bülow airily ignored his ally and made a separate arrangement with Russia, crowning it all with his declaration in the Reichstag on 15 March of Germany's 'absolute indifference' to the fate of Manchuria, a statement which was certainly contrary to the spirit, if not the letter, of the October agreement. This timing was particularly unfortunate since it came precisely at the moment when Lansdowne was drafting an Anglo-German Japanese alliance which, in consequence, was never put to Berlin. While Bülow's preoccupation with the anti-British state of German public feeling and Holstein's insistence that they must not risk a breach with Russia without a prior commitment from Britain are understandable, it is equally apparent that this action removed most of the incentive in London for a German alliance. From March 1901 onwards Germany was regarded as useless as far as the Far East was concerned and Lansdowne gradually turned to negotiation with Russia and Japan instead.[19]

Until 1901 there is nothing to suggest that Britain envisaged Japan as a possible ally in the Far East. Relations had always been fairly cordial, particularly since 1895, and the Japanese were not thought of in any way as rivals to British interests in China: it was significant that when Salisbury did at last accept the need for military intervention in June 1900 his idea was to persuade Japan to send troops. But this did not mean more than the assumption that they were harmless. It is true that Chamberlain had advocated an understanding with them as early as December 1897 but it had never amounted to anything: after all, at one time or another Chamberlain suggested an alliance with everybody. At the time the Japanese preferred to negotiate with Russia for the sharing of influence in Korea (the Nishi/Rosen agreement of 28 April 1898) as Salisbury had always assumed they would do, and as he advocated as the preferred policy for Britain. Although Goschen recognized in February 1898 that the Japanese fleet was formidable and 'their two battleships superior to any others in that region', this was not considered of any immediate application: Japan would not do anything until her military and naval build up had

---

[19] Rich II, 627–32. Grenville pp. 333–5, 339–43, Monger pp. 17, 23–9. Docs. 131–134.

been completed and, in any case, until March 1901 Germany was a far greater prize. Nor did Japanese conduct during the Boxer rebellion do anything to change these assumptions. It was only British persuasion which led them to send troops to Tientsin and take the lead in the march on Pekin: they were extremely careful not to arouse suspicion and as soon as Russian forces were withdrawn to Manchuria, their main force left for Japan. The extent to which they formulated plans for their 'slice of the melon' at this stage showed no intention to oppose Russia: the object of their acquisitiveness was the province of Fukien, opposite Formosa. Even as they grew alarmed at Russian activities in Manchuria the Japanese did not turn to Britain: as in 1898 they preferred to negotiate with St. Petersburg and even with Berlin.[20]

Hence Japanese adherence to the Yangtse agreement of October 1900 is not necessarily a sign that they were moving towards Britain. In August they had made several approaches to Berlin for mutual support in Korea and Shantung on the assumption that Russo-German relations were breaking down in China, of which the Anglo-German October agreement seemed confirmation. The Japanese certainly assumed from this that Germany would now oppose a Russian annexation of Manchuria in which, of the three powers concerned, Japan had the prime interest. Hence from October onwards it was Japan who tended to take the initiative, particularly after the publication of the Tseng/Alexeiev agreement in January 1901. Lansdowne did not appear too concerned with the fate of Manchuria at first: from October to March his main preoccupation was Tientsin, 'for parliamentary and other reasons', and he turned a deaf ear to Japanese proposals in February that they should jointly offer China material assistance to oppose Russia in Manchuria. Before he would move he wanted to be sure of German support. With the British army still tied up in South Africa it was as essential as ever to regulate any advance in China by the pace of Berlin, and the general reluctance there to do anything to oppose Russia obliged him, as he told Lascelles on 9 March, 'to proceed with extreme caution'. Hence the crucial importance of Bülow's declaration on Manchuria, since the effect of this was to leave Japan and Britain alone to face Russia. Now

---

[20] Pelcovits pp. 188–9; Garvin III, 248–50; I. H. Nish, 'Japan's Indecision during the Boxer Disturbances', *Journal of Asian Studies* 1961 pp. 449–50, 455–9. Goschen Memorandum 1 February 1898, Cab/37/46/17.

they had no option but either to reach agreement with Russia separately or to combine together.[21]

On 10 March 1901 Hayashi informed Lansdowne that Tokio had been told by Berlin that Germany would observe 'benevolent neutrality' in the event of a crisis in the Far East and asked how far he thought they could rely on this and how far Britain would support them? In view of recent German refusals Lansdowne considered the prospects poor but, afraid that a blunt rejection of this, the last of a long line of Japanese proposals since January, most of which had been turned down, would turn them towards Russia again, thought the effort should be made to 'elicit from Germany a distinct statement of her intentions'. Hence the draft declaration he prepared for the Cabinet on 12 March, to which it was intended to invite German adhesion, announcing the intention of Britain and Germany to remain neutral in the event of a Russo-Japanese war but to give naval assistance to Japan in the event of intervention by a second power. In fact this was never sent to Berlin since Salisbury, dragging his feet as usual where any question of a German alliance was concerned, persuaded his colleagues the next day that on tactical grounds it would be better to sound out the Germans before presenting it. Since in response to Lascelles' enquiries Berlin announced that 'benevolent neutrality' meant the 'strictest and most correct neutrality', an announcement which was followed the next day by Bülow's 'absolute indifference' speech, Lansdowne regretfully concluded that he could only advise Japan that the British attitude would be the same:

> our South African entanglements make it impossible for us to commit ourselves to a policy which might involve us in war, unless we can assure ourselves that any obligation which we might incur would be shared by another power.[22]

The German objection to Lansdowne's Japanese inspired scheme of a Far Eastern *triplice* was obvious enough: as Holstein pointed out on 18 April, it would be

> directly contrary to our interests, because this would put an end to the necessity for England to link herself by a general treaty with Germany, or rather with the Triple Alliance.

[21] For this and for much of what follows on Japanese aims I am indebted to my colleague Dr. I. H. Nish who very kindly allowed me to read the typescript of his book on the Anglo-Japanese Alliance.

[22] Monger pp. 21–9; Grenville pp. 340–1. Doc. 131.

But, equally, Lansdowne was only interested in a Far Eastern alliance. His objection to the schemes which Eckardstein now hawked around again from March until May for a general alliance against France and Russia was fundamental:

> it would oblige us to adopt in all our foreign relations a policy which would no longer be British but Anglo-German.

Hence there was not much of a contrast between his attitude and that of Salisbury. In the choice of either joining the Triple Alliance or nothing, as Hatzfeldt posed it on 23 May, they were by no means in opposite camps. If Salisbury adamantly opposed it on the grounds that 'the bargain would be a bad one for the country', Landsowne was far from being its ardent advocate: its real supporters were Hamilton, who simply thought we should 'throw our lot in, for good or bad, with some other Power', and probably Balfour, the most European minded of them all. As far as Lansdowne is concerned it is difficult to avoid the conclusion that he was at this time as much an isolationist as Salisbury as far as concluding a European alliance was concerned. The real turning point for him in relations with Germany was the collapse of his Far Eastern *triplice* in March. After this, though he at no time closed the door on a German understanding and continued desultory negotiations from time to time, he abandoned any hope of getting what he wanted in the Far East from Berlin. As he in fact told Eckardstein on 18 March 1901, Bülow's statement on Manchuria

> put an end to any idea which might have been entertained as to the possibility of England and Germany combining for the purpose of 'keeping a ring' for Russia and Japan.[23]

In fact during the spring and summer of 1901 most of the tension went out of the Far Eastern crisis. Japanese pressure in St. Petersburg on 25 March, combined with Chinese resistance, persuaded Russia to drop the proposed Russo-Chinese agreement on 5 April rather than risk a war. Encouraged by this, Lansdowne even took the opportunity to attempt an Anglo-Russian settlement in China, rejecting Japanese approaches for a separate understanding. It was not until this project had collapsed

---

[23] Rich II, 647; Monger pp. 30, 36–7; B.D. no. 77. For a different view of Lansdowne see Grenville pp. 33–4, 46–9. Docs. 132, 133.

and the German alliance had again been shelved that he turned once more to Japan, noting, not surprisingly, that 'she is a little sore with us and inclined to think that we have not supported her sufficiently against Russia'. Nor is there any reason to suppose that at this stage Lansdowne contemplated the sort of military alliance that finally emerged; indeed only three months before he had specifically rejected a military alliance with Japan alone as too dangerous. All he wanted, having lost the Germans, was to find some way of keeping the remaining partner and thus avoid the danger of a Japanese settlement with Russia which would leave Britain completely isolated in the Far East. Consequently, although he raised the question of an 'understanding' in July with Hayashi, the Japanese minister, there was no question of an offensive-defensive alliance at this stage. In fact Lansdowne was very careful to emphasize his view of Russian rights in Manchuria and rule out any assistance against her unless she violated Chinese territorial integrity. It was only when the negotiations really got going in October and acquired a momentum of their own that it was realized what a commitment to Japan would mean in practice, and by then the attractions far outweighed the drawbacks.[24]

Japanese policy was equally hesitant. In Japan there was virtual unanimity among leading ministers as to the objects of her policy, which were clearly outlined by Katsura soon after he became Prime Minister in May 1901:

> to place Korea outside the scope of foreign countries' expansion policies . . . any extension of Russian power in Manchuria beyond the rights stipulated in existing treaties, would constitute a menace to Korean independence.

But on the manner in which this should be achieved there was considerable divergence. Some, notably Ito, considered the most effective method to be negotiation with Russia; others, particularly Kato, thought more in terms of an alliance with England. Nor were these ideas mutually exclusive. It was obvious that an alliance with London would materially improve Tokio's prospects in negotiation with St. Petersburg. Hence to a considerable extent Japanese policy from July 1901 to January 1902 was empirical, trying to find out what sort of an alliance, if any, they could get with Britain, then weighing this against their chances in immediate

[24] Malozemoff pp. 160, 167; Monger pp. 33–4, 46–9; Grenville p. 399.

negotiations with Russia. Even when the decision in December went in favour of a British alliance, this did not mean an end to negotiation with Russia, as Ito was careful to confirm with Lansdowne in January 1902. Hence it is a mistake to look at Japanese policy in terms of Russophils and Anglophils; it was a debate as to means not to ends. Certainly Ito approved of approaches to London in August but he doubted, in view of the fate of previous approaches that year, whether they would bring any better result. After all it was a notorious fact that Salisbury did not like to commit himself in advance, but if Japan was to be able to negotiate with Russia with any certainty she must have behind her something more than a vague *entente*.[25]

The major question in relation to the Japanese alliance from the British viewpoint is why the Cabinet, once engaged in negotiation, abandoned all its former reservations about prior commitment and made a full blown naval alliance. As Balfour pointed out, this made nonsense of all the arguments that had been used against a German alliance, and what was the point, if they were going to have an alliance, of choosing the weaker military power? The answer to this seems twofold. In the first place the concern of the Cabinet was almost exclusively for the Far East and it had been shown time and again by October 1901 that Germany would not oppose Russia for the sake of British interests in China. It was significant that Bertie, who soon became the leader of the anti-German section of the Foreign Office, served his apprenticeship in the Far Eastern department and was certainly extremely suspicious of German policy there by October 1901. In a memorandum of 22 September he opposed any further negotiation with Germany on this subject on the grounds that Berlin would simply make use of it in St. Petersburg. Japan, in contrast, had her own interests in China to defend and showed every intention of doing so.

Secondly, a Japanese alliance would save increased naval expenditure. Whereas joining the Triple Alliance was a financial liability in the sense that Britain would take on more commitments to defend, a Japanese alliance would enable the Admiralty to cut naval expenditure. As Custance, the D.N.I., remarked in February 1902, the Japanese alliance grew 'out of arguments and facts which emanated from the Naval Intelligence Department'. The

[25] Katsura to Inouye 8 August 1901, quoted in Nish, p. 159. See Grenville pp. 392–8, 409–11 for a rather different interpretation of Japanese policy

246

essence of this lay in battleship strengths in the Far East. Selborne, the First Sea Lord of the Admiralty, emphasized in a crucial memorandum on 4 September 1901 that a Japanese alliance would give joint superiority over France and Russia in the Far East which otherwise could only be maintained by an increase in naval construction. Nothing could be more calculated to appeal to Hicks Beach, the Chancellor of the Exchequer and Salisbury's main supporter in opposition to a German alliance, since this would enable him to wield the economy axe upon the naval estimates.[26]

Thus when in October rumours reached Lansdowne of renewed Russian pressure on China and a repetition of the Manchurian crisis of the Spring, he and the Cabinet were already thinking in terms of a naval understanding with Japan, not Germany, as the solution. After discussion with Hayashi on 16 October Lansdowne drew up a draft treaty, for which he obtained Salisbury's approval, and which he put to the Cabinet on 5 November. But, characteristically, he simultaneously tried to negotiate with Russian on a joint Persian/Chinese settlement: he, like the Japanese, saw nothing incongruous in running the two together. It was Lamsdorff's rejection of his offers, and the virtual Russian refusal to negotiate with Ito, that made an Anglo-Japanese alliance a certainty. How far Lansdowne seriously expected Lamsdorff to take up his offer is a moot point: probably his main object, as he explained to the Cabinet, was that

> our position would, I believe, be strengthened, especially with the public here, by the fact that we had made proposals of this kind.

This was an important consideration since the Liberals were already mounting a strong press campaign for a Russian settlement in preference to an anti-Russian alliance. But with Lamsdorff's refusal, on the 6 November Lansdowne's draft treaty was given to Hayashi and accepted in principle in Tokio a week later. On 12 December, having waited almost a month to obtain Ito's approval, the Japanese Cabinet went ahead without him and presented its counterdraft in London.[27]

---

[26] Monger pp. 59, 63–5; Custance to Bridge 25 February 1902, Nish, pp. 153–7, 174–7; Z. S. Steiner, 'Great Britain and the creation of the Anglo-Japanese Alliance', *J.M.H.* 1959 p. 31. Doc. 135.

[27] Monger pp. 54–7; Steiner pp. 32–5. Doc. 136.

This, whilst accepting Lansdowne's basic premise of mutual support if either were attacked by two powers, had two novel features. Firstly an emphasis on Japanese interests in Korea, reserving themselves, as Lansdowne told the Cabinet on 16 December, 'a free hand to make a *casus foederis* out of any Russian encroachment in Corea'. Secondly, a demand that both parties should keep naval forces in this theatre at least equal to those of any other power. Neither of these proposals was welcome to the Cabinet. Balfour criticized the first as likely to involve Britain in a struggle for existence 'over some obscure Russo-Japanese quarrel in Korea', whilst the second robbed the alliance of all its value from the naval viewpoint. Consequently some modifications were insisted on, though the treaty that emerged was still fundamentally the Japanese draft. The naval clause was made into a simple statement of intent by the addition of 'as far as possible', whilst on the subject of Korea the Japanese were persuaded to add the meaningless statement that they had no aggressive aims. In addition, compensating recognition of British concern was given by agreeing that China was an area in which a threat to their interests might raise the *casus foederis*. Evidently there was still only grudging acceptance in the Cabinet, as was clear from the pressure to include India and Siam, whilst Salisbury still thought that it would 'not be sanctioned by Parliament'. But he did not definitely oppose it. This lack of definite opposition from Salisbury combined with Lansdowne's insistence that if the Cabinet wanted Japanese support these were the best terms obtainable, against the background of the vague general feeling in the Cabinet by the end of 1901 that some fundamental change of policy was necessary, and was sufficient to carry it through. It was signed on 30 January and ratified by Parliament on 11 February 1902.[28]

Traditionally the Anglo-Japanese alliance has been regarded as the great divide in British foreign policy in this period, on the grounds that it marked the turning from 'splendid isolation' to the policy of understandings and limited commitments which became the basis of British policy in the decade before 1914 and created an increasing involvement in Continental politics. More recently this view has been challenged to the extent of being stood on its head: 'the alliance did not mark the end of British isolation; rather it

[28] Monger pp. 50, 58–61; Grenville pp. 412–16; Lansdowne, Cabinet Memorandum 16 December, Nish, pp. 204–18. Docs. 137–9.

The Far East

confirmed it'. Which is true? There is no doubt that contemporaries were extremely conscious that this represented a considerable change in foreign policy. Salisbury clearly so: the whole tenor of the argument of his memorandum of 7 January 1902 against the Japanese alliance was that this was a perilous and untried path, contrary to British traditions. This attitude can also be seen in Lansdowne's recommendation of the alliance to the House of Lords, when he appealed to them to forget 'musty formulas' and 'old fashioned superstitions as to the desirability of pursuing a policy of isolation'; a view reflected in the *Spectator*'s obituary on the passing of the 'fixed policy of not making alliances'. There can be no question that this was correct: the alliance certainly involved an obligation to go to war in circumstances which were largely outside British control which was a commitment which had not been made since the 1830s in Europe.[29]

But it is misleading to confuse this alliance with the British position in Europe. The Anglo-Japanese alliance made no appreciable difference here and it certainly did not end British 'isolation' from the Continent. The Japanese agreement was a regional pact to cope with the situation in China and in particular the presumed danger from Russian ambitions in North China. It was not a general alliance: in fact this was precisely Balfour's criticism of it. Obviously it had repercussions on the British position in Europe: if nothing else it averted any weakening of the British fleets in European waters. But the effect of this was to make a European alliance less necessary. This was why *The Times*, the most vociferous opponent of a German alliance, welcomed that with Japan with open arms: now there was no reason at all to seek support from Berlin. But, unfortunately, both at the time and subsequently, this has been obscured by the jargon of 'splendid isolation', with its inherent assumption that this was an accurate description of Salisbury's policy over the preceding decades. As has recently been shown, 'splendid isolation' was a term invented not by Salisbury but by his opponent, Chamberlain, in 1898, when he airily declared that Britain had pursued a 'policy of strict isolation' since the Crimean War. In a sense of course he was right. Britain, in contrast to the Continental Great Powers, had undertaken no military commitments until the Japanese alliance of 1902, and the latter

[29] A. J. P. Taylor, *Struggle for Mastery in Europe* p. 400; Monger p. 61; C. Howard, 'Splendid Isolation', *History* 1962 p. 41; Nish pp. 241–4.

249

were naval rather than military. But in this sense British policy remained isolationist until 1914. Despite the understandings with France and Russia there was no obligation to go to war, which makes nonsense of the thesis that there was a deliberate change in British policy towards greater commitments in Europe and that this was initiated by the replacement of Salisbury by Lansdowne and his Japanese alliance of January 1902.[30]

In fact Salisbury's policy never had been isolationist. 'Isolationist' was a term which he disliked and rarely employed. From 1886 to 1897 he had worked more or less closely with the Triple Alliance, in an *entente à trois* which was just as real as the more publicized Triple *Entente* of the years before 1914. If the expected general European war had broken out during this period there was as much reason to suppose that Britain would have supported the Central Powers as there was in 1914 to presume that she would support France and Russia. That the *entente* collapsed after 1897 was due to a variety of reasons, but not because Salisbury suddenly became isolationist. In fact from 1897 until 1900 he had tried just as hard as Lansdowne and Grey did later to reach an understanding with France and Russia, as his son pointed out to Balfour in 1905:

> The French agreement (of 1904) was in its inception not a departure from our previous foreign policy, but strictly in accordance with it. For the last twenty years we have been engaged with different Powers, notably with Germany and with France, in adjusting conflicting claims, and in bargaining so as to get rid of causes of friction . . .[31]

Thus the general significance of the alliance of 1902 has been overestimated as a turning away from a policy of isolation towards one of alliances: it was the exception, not the rule. Yet there is one sense in which this development was decisive. There can be no doubt that by 1900 there was a strong party in the Cabinet in favour of a German alliance, with some members prepared to go

---

[30] Howard p. 34; *History of 'The Times'*, III, 373–4; J. M. Goudswaard, *Some Aspects of the End of Britain's Splendid Isolation* (Rotterdam, 1952) p. 121: 'There is nothing . . . to support the view that any definite decision to end the policy of "splendid isolation" was ever made at any specific moment by the British Government'.

[31] Salisbury to Balfour 9 November 1905. B.M. Add. Mss. 49758, I am indebted to Dr. Nish for drawing my attention to this letter. Doc. 140.

whole hog for a military alliance which would certainly have put an end to not only isolation but also independence. It was this group which was defeated by the Japanese alliance, a compromise between doing nothing—which was still Salisbury's policy of preference—and accepting the dictation of Berlin. Certainly Chamberlain, by October 1901, had abandoned all hope of a German alliance and was fast moving in a totally different direction. Moreover, it was significant that although he opposed a German alliance tooth and nail, Salisbury was by no means so adamant when it came to one with Japan.

The explanation is reasonably obvious. Whereas the Japanese alliance did not make relations with Russia any worse and indeed, according to *The Times*, could 'only tend in the long run to promote a satisfactory understanding', an alliance with Germany would lead to permanent hostility with France and Russia. This it had always been the major object of Salisbury's policy to avoid, and there was little difference between him and Lansdowne in this respect.[32] Lansdowne never had been an ardent advocate of a general German alliance: the lead in this had been given by Chamberlain and to some extent Balfour with Lansdowne in support. What he wanted once he became Foreign Minister was some form of insurance in the Far East, not a commitment in Europe. Whilst he was undoubtedly the architect of the Japanese alliance he was not the assassin of 'Splendid Isolation'. The sense of detachment from Continental affairs long outlived Lansdowne: even after participation in the last two European wars there is still a sizeable element in Britain who do not think of themselves as part of Europe!

[32] *History of 'The Times'*, III, 374; Monger pp. 65–6. For an excellent discussion of this point see Grenville pp. 434–6.

Bibliography

The object of this bibliography is simply to help students who wish to pursue more specialized reading on British foreign policy in this period. Accordingly it does not list the principal archival material available: for this the reader is referred to some of the bibliographies contained in the monographs listed below. Those in Hargreaves, Sanderson, Greaves and Monger are particularly useful. Nor does it list the great printed collections of documents referred to occasionally in the text: they are well known to scholars and no student is likely to use them without expert guidance. Similarly in the case of unpublished theses: these are conveniently listed in the Thesis Supplements of the Bulletin of the Institute of Historical Research, London. Books published before 1937 may be found in the excellent bibliography in R. W. Seton-Watson, *Britain in Europe*, published in that year. The place of publication is London unless otherwise stated.

ALDER, G.J. *British India's Northern Frontier 1865–1895* (1963)
ANDERSON, M. S. *The Eastern Question* (1966)
ANON. *History of 'The Times'* vol. III 1884–1912 (1947)
ANSTEY, R. T. *Britain and the Congo in the 19th Century* (1962)
AYDELOTTE, W. O. *Bismarck and British Colonial Policy* (Philadelphia, 1937)
BAYER, T. *England und der neue Kurs* (Tübingen, 1955)
BENIANS, E. A. (ed.) *The Cambridge History of the British Empire* vol. III (Cambridge, 1959)
BLACK, C. *The Establishment of Constitutional Government in Bulgaria* (Princeton, 1943)
CAMPBELL, A. E. *Great Britain and the United States, 1895–1903* (1960)
CAMPBELL, C. S. *Anglo-American Understanding 1898–1903* (Baltimore, 1957)
CROWE, S. E. *The Berlin West Africa Conference 1884–5* (1942)
EYCK, E, *Bismarck* vol. III (Zürich, 1944)
FLINT, J. E. *Sir George Goldie and the Making of Nigeria* (1960)
FRASER-TYTLER, W. K. *Afghanistan* (Oxford, 1950)

Bibliography

GIBBS, N. H. *The Origin of Imperial Defence* (Oxford, 1955)

GOOCH, G. P. *Studies in Diplomacy and Statecraft* (1942)

GOSSES, F. *The Management of British Foreign Policy before 1914* (Leiden, 1948)

GOUDSWAARD, J. M. *Some Aspects of the End of Britain's 'Splendid Isolation'* (Rotterdam, 1952)

GREAVES, R. L. *Persia and the Defence of India 1884–1892* (1959)

GRENVILLE, J. A. S. *Lord Salisbury and Foreign Policy* (1964)

HALE, O. J. *Publicity and Diplomacy with special reference to England and Germany, 1890–1914* (New York, 1940)

HARGREAVES, J. *Prelude to the Partition of West Africa* (1965)

HINSLEY, F. H. (ed.) *The New Cambridge Modern History* vol. XI (Cambridge, 1962)

HUBATSCH, W. *Die Ära Tirpitz* (Göttingen, 1955)

ILIAMS, T. *Dreyfus, Diplomatists and the Dual Alliance* (Paris, 1962)

JOHNSON, F. A. *Defence by Committee* (Oxford, 1962)

KIERNAN, E. V. *British Diplomacy in China, 1880–1885* (New York, 1939)

LOWE, C. J. *Salisbury and the Mediterranean* (1965)

MALOZEMOFF, A. *Russian Far Eastern Policy 1881–1904* (Berkeley, 1958)

MARDER, A. J. *The Anatomy of British Sea Power* (1940)

— *Fear God and Dread Nought: the Correspondence of Admiral of the Fleet Lord Fisher of Kilverstone* (3 vols. 1952–9)

MEDLICOTT, W. N. *The Congress of Berlin and After* (1938)

— *Bismarck, Gladstone and the Concert of Europe* (1956)

MONGER, G. W. *The End of Isolation* (1963)

MÜLLER, F. F. *Deutschland-Zanzibar-Ostafrika* (East Berlin, 1959)

NISH, I. H. *The Anglo-Japanese Alliance, 1894–1907* (1966)

OLIVER, R. and MATHEW, G. (eds.) *History of East Africa* vol. I (1963)

PELCOVITS, N. A. *Old China Hands and the Foreign Office* (New York, 1948)

PENSON, L. M. *Foreign Affairs under the Third Marquess of Salisbury* (1962)

PERHAM, M. *Lugard, The Years of Adventure* (1956)

POEL, J. VAN DER. *The Jameson Raid* (1961)

RASSOW, P. *Die Stellung Deutschlands im Kreise der grossen Mächte 1887–1890* (Wiesbaden, 1959)

RENOUVIN, P. *Les Politiques d'Expansion imperialistes* (Paris, 1949)

— *La Politique exterieure de la IIIe République* (Paris, n.d.)

RICH, N. *Friedrich von Holstein* (Cambridge, 1965)

RICH, N. and FISHER, M. H. *The Holstein Papers* (1959–63)

ROBINSON, R. and GALLAGHER, J. *Africa and the Victorians* (1959)

RÖMER, A. *England und die europäischen Machte im Jahre 1887* (Aarau, 1957)

SALVATORELLI, L. *La Triplice Alleanza* (Milan, 1939)

SALVEMINI, G. *La politica estera dell'Italia 1871–1914* (Florence, 1944)

SANDERSON, G. N. *England, Europe and the Upper Nile* (Edinburgh, 1965)

Bibliography

SARKISSIAN, A. O. (ed.) *Studies in Diplomatic History* (1961)
SERRA, E. *L'intesa Mediterranea del 1902* (Milan, 1957)
SETON-WATSON, R. W. *Britain in Europe, 1789–1914* (Cambridge, 1937)
SHIBEIKA, M. T. *British Policy in the Sudan, 1882–1902* (1952)
SMITH, C. L. *The Embassy of Sir William White at Constantinople, 1886–1891* (Oxford, 1957)
TAYLOR, A. J. P. *Germany's First Bid for Colonies* (1938)
— *The Struggle for Mastery in Europe* (Oxford, 1954)
— *The Trouble Makers* (1957)
TEMPERLEY, H. and PENSON, L. *A century of Diplomatic Blue Books* (Cambridge, 1938)
— *Foundations of British Foreign Policy* (Cambridge, 1938)
THORNTON, A. P. *The Imperial Idea and its Enemies* (1959)
WARHURST, P. R. *Anglo-Portuguese Relations in South-Central Africa* (1960)
ZAGHI, C., P. S. *Mancini, L'Africa e il problema del Mediterraneo* (Rome, 1955)

ARTICLES IN LEARNED JOURNALS

BROCKWAY, T. P. Britain and the Persian Bubble, 1888–92. *J.M.H.* 1941
COWLING, M. Lytton, the Cabinet, and the Russians: August to November 1878. *E.H.R.* 1961
GIGLIO, C. I negoziati italo-inglesi per Massaua dal 25 dicembre 1884 al 5 febbraio 1885. *Il Risorgimento* 1952
DRUS, E. The Question of Imperial Complicity in the Jameson Raid. *E.H.R.* 1953
EDWARDS, E. W. The Japanese Alliance and the Anglo-French Agreement. *History* 1957
GILLARD, D. R. Salisbury's African Policy and the Heligoland Offer of 1890. *E.H.R.* 1960, 1965
GRENVILLE, J. A. S. Goluchowski, Salisbury, and the Mediterranean Agreements. *S.R.* 1958
— Lansdowne's abortive project of 12 March 1901 for a secret agreement with Germany. *B.I.H.R.* 1954
DE GROOT, E. Great Britain and Germany in Zanzibar: Consul Holmwood's Papers, 1886–7. *J.M.H.* 1953
HARGREAVES, J. D. Entente Manquée: Anglo-French relations 1895–6. *(C).H.J.* 1953
HINSLEY, F. H. Bismarck, Salisbury and the Mediterranean Agreements of 1887. *H.J.* 1958
HORNIK, M. P. The Mission of Sir Henry Drummond Wolff to Constantinople, 1885–7. *E.H.R.* 1940
— The Anglo-Belgian Agreement of 12 May 1894. *E.H.R.* 1942

Bibliography

HOWARD, C. Splendid Isolation. *History* 1962

JELAVICH, C. The Diary of D. A. Miliutin, 1878–1882. *J.M.H.* 1954

KLUKE, P. Bismarck und Salisbury. *H.Z.* 1953

LOWE, C. J. Anglo-Italian Differences over East Africa, 1892–5, and their Effects upon the Mediterranean Entente. *E.H.R.* 1966

MEDLICOTT, W. N. The Gladstone Government and the Cyprus Convention. *J.M.H.* 1940

— The Powers and the Unification of the Two Bulgarias, 1885. *E.H.R.* 1939 (In two parts)

MILLER, T. B. The Egyptian Question and British Foreign Policy, 1892–4. *J.M.H.* 1960

MONGER, G. L. The End of Isolation: Britain, Germany and Japan, 1900–1902. *T.R.H.S.* 1963

NEWBURY, C. W. The development of French Policy on the Lower and Upper Niger, 1880–1898. *J.M.H.* 1959

PALMER, A. W. Lord Salisbury's Approach to Russia, 1898. *Oxford Slavonic Papers*, 1955

PARSONS, F. V. The North-West Africa Company and the British Government, 1875–1895. *H.J.* 1958

— The Proposed Madrid Conference on Morocco, 1887–8. *H.J.* 1965

PENSON, L. M. The New Course in British Foreign Policy, 1892–1902. *T.R.H.S.* 1943

RAMM, A. Great Britain and the planting of Italian Power in the Red Sea, 1868–1885. *E.H.R.* 1944

RENOUVIN, P. Les origines de l'expédition de Fachoda. *R.H.* 1948

ROBINSON, R. and GALLAGHER, J. The Imperialism of Free Trade. *Econ.H.R.* 1953

SANDERSON, G. N. The Anglo-German Agreement of 1890 and the Upper Nile. *E.H.R.* 1963

— England, Italy, the Nile Valley and the European Balance. *H.J.* 1964

SETON-WATSON, R. The Foundations of British Policy. *T.R.H.S.* 1947

STEINER, Z. S. Great Britain and the Creation of the Anglo-Japanese Alliance. *J.M.H.* 1959

— The Last Years of the Old Foreign Office, 1898–1905. *H.I.* 1963

STENGERS, J. L'Impérialisme colonial de la fin du XIXᵉ siècle: mythe ou rèalité. *J.A.H.* 1962

TAYLOR, A. J. P. Prelude to Fashoda. *E.H.R.* 1950

— British Policy in Morocco, 1886–1902. *E.H.R.* 1951

— Les premières années de l'alliance Franco-Russe. *R.H.* 1950

TEMPERLEY, H. British Secret Diplomacy from Canning to Grey. *(C.)H.J.* 1938

THORNTON, A. P. British Policy in Persia, 1858–90. *E.H.R.* 1954 and 1955 (Two parts)

Bibliography

WALSH, W. B. The Imperial Russian General Staff and India. *Russian Review* 1957

WALTERS, E. Lord Salisbury's refusal to revise and renew the Mediterranean Agreements. *S.R.* 1950, 1951

DOCUMENTS

Contents

II. THE EASTERN QUESTION, 1878–82

Salisbury formulates British objectives in the Near East

Salisbury changes the British interpretation of the Rule of the Straits

Salisbury and Disraeli welcome a German alliance to defend the Balkans

Salisbury's conditions for defending Asia Minor

The object of the Cyprus Convention

Salisbury admits reform in Turkey is a hopeless prospect

Contents

III. THE EGYPTIAN LEVER

Contents

263

Contents

IV. THE DEFENCE OF INDIA

Contents

Contents

Salisbury's anxiety to preserve peace

The negotiation of the First Mediterranean Agreement

The negotiations for an Egyptian Convention in 1887

Salisbury rejects Russian overtures and reluctantly extends the Mediterranean Agreements

VI. PARTITION OF EAST AFRICA, 1885–91

Gladstone rejects annexationism in East Africa

Bismarck applies the Egyptian lever in Zanzibar

British interests clash with those of Germany and Italy in Zanzibar

Contents

Salisbury rejects a German alliance

Negotiations for an African Settlement with Germany in 1890

The protection of the Nile

VII. BRITAIN AND THE FRANCO-RUSSIAN ALLIANCE 1888–92

British Military Weakness

The invasion scare of 1888 and the origin of the Naval Defence Act

The development of the policy of limited support for Italy in the Mediterranean

Contents

The Defence of Constantinople

VIII. LIBERAL FOREIGN POLICY

Rosebery gives assurances on the continuity of foreign policy

Naval Expansion and Foreign Policy in 1893

The deterioration of relations with the Triple Alliance

Rosebery urges the retention of Uganda

Kimberley suggests concessions in West Africa in return for an agreement on the Nile

Kimberley supports the Grey Declaration

Contents

IX. THE NEAR EAST AND AFRICA

The Armenian problem and the Straits

Relations with the Triple Alliance

The reconquest of the Sudan

Contents

The Portuguese Colonies

X. THE FAR EAST

Salisbury seeks an understanding with Russia

The Cabinet decides against war over Port Arthur

Balfour opposes a forceful policy over Manchurian railway concessions

Chamberlain advocates an agreement with Germany on the Open Door

Negotiations with Germany on the Far East in 1901

Negotiations with Japan

II

The Eastern Question, 1878–82

SALISBURY FORMULATES BRITISH OBJECTIVES IN THE NEAR EAST

1. (*Salisbury to Disraeli 21 March 1878, in Cecil II, 213–14*) *Extract*

Of course, we have a right to object to all [of the Treaty of San Stefano] as all are contrary to existing Treaties, but it would be doubtful policy to do so in view of English opinion. At all events, I think we should put in the forefront of our objections:

(1) Those articles which menace the balance of power in the Egean.
(2) Those which threaten the Greek race in the Balkan Peninsular with extinction.

And that we should indicate the necessity of either cancelling, *or* meeting with compensatory provisions, the portions of the Treaty which, by reducing Turkey to vassalage, threaten the free passage of the Straits, and also menace English interests in other places where the exercise of Turkish authority affects them.

I am, as you know, not a believer in the possibility of setting the Turkish Government on its legs again, as a genuine reliable Power; and, unless you have a distinct belief the other way, I think you should be cautious about adopting any line of policy which may stake England's security in those seas on Turkish efficiency. I should be disposed to be satisfied with war or negotiations which ended in these results:

(1) Driving back the Slav State to the Balkans—and substituting a Greek province; politically, but not administratively, under the Porte.
(2) Effective securities for the free passage of the Straits at all times, as if they were open sea.

(3) Two naval stations for England—say Lemnos and Cyprus, with an occupation, at least temporary, of some place like Scanderoon; for the sake of moral effect.

(4) Perhaps I would add reduction of indemnity to amount which there would be reasonable prospect of Turkey paying without giving pretext for fresh encroachment.

These are merely suggestions for your consideration and require no answer.

SALISBURY CHANGES THE BRITISH INTERPRETATION OF THE RULE OF THE STRAITS

2. (*Derby to Shuvalov 6 May 1877, F.O. 65/986. Printed in Lee, p. 195*)

Extract

The existing arrangements made under European sanction which regulate the navigation of the Bosphorous and Dardanelles appear to them (Her Majesty's Government) wise and salutary and there would be, in their judgment, serious objections to their alteration in any material particular.

3. (*Report of the Cabinet Committee on the Treaty of San Stefano, 27 March 1878. Confidential Print, No. 3548. Printed in Temperley and Penson, p. 369*)

3. The Straits

Article XXIV. What would best suit the interests of Great Britain, in the altered state of circumstances, would be that the Straits should be free to ships of war, as well as of commerce, and that all forts and batteries should be removed.

This would be unacceptable to the Porte; but it might possibly be made acceptable by an engagement to maintain the defence and guarantee the safety of Constantinople from the sea with an adequate naval squadron.

If this cannot be done, and if the present rule of the closing of the Straits is continued, we should make it clear, by a statement placed on record at the Congress, that we do not assent to Article XXIV in so far as it would prejudice or limit any right by way of blockade or otherwise which, in the event of war, we, as a belligerent, should be entitled to.

The Eastern Question, 1878–82

4. (*Salisbury at the Congress of Berlin, 11 July 1878, F.O. 78/2911, printed in Lee, p. 197*)

Je déclare donc de la part du Gouvernement de sa Majesté qu'en acceptant le renouvellement des stipulations du Traité de 1841 confirmées par la Traité de 1856 avec une disposition semblable a celle de l'article 2 du Traité de 1871, Sa Majesté s'engage seulement envers le Sultan et nullement envers aucune autre Puissance, et que Sa Majesté ne prend aucune obligation envers une autre Puissance quelconque qui l'empêcherait, s'il semblait nécessaire à Sa Majesté, de donner l'ordre à sa flotte d'entrer dans les détroits dans le cas que l'indépendance du Sultan serait menacée.

5. (*Salisbury 7 May 1885 in the House of Lords, Hansard, vol. 297 col. 1826*)

The object of the declaration which I had to make on behalf of Her Majesty's Government I understood to be to establish the principle that our engagements in respect of the Dardanelles were not engagements of a general, European, or International character, but were engagements towards the Sultan only; the practical bearing of that reservation being that if, in any circumstances, the Sultan should not be acting independently, but under pressure from some other Power, there would be no International obligation on our part to abstain from passing through the Dardanelles.

SALISBURY AND DISRAELI WELCOME A GERMAN ALLIANCE TO DEFEND THE BALKANS

6. (*Salisbury to Disraeli 15 October 1879, in Cecil II, 368*)

Münster is here now and I have had a long talk with him about our matter. The reason of his not speaking to me was that he had not heard from B.; that Russia was putting some water into her wine and that therefore he thought there was no hurry.

I stated to him our view—that Austria's position in Europe was a matter in which we took deep interest, and considered essential: that if Russia attacked Germany and Austria, Germany might rely on our being on her side. I said, 'I suppose the service you want of us would be to influence France and Italy to observe neutrality'. He replied, that was their object: that Metz and Strasburg made them tolerably safe from an attack on the south part of the frontier, but that they were open through Belgium. Of that,

273

I said, he might feel confident; and I was pretty sure we could prevent any French Government from joining Russia against him; but that he might rely on our goodwill and assistance in the contingency of an attack on Austria and Germany.

It was all very much in the sense and tone of his conversation with you, but it left the impression on my mind that, since he had spoken to you, there had been a slight change of mind and that B. is not so keen now as then . . .

7. (*Northcote to the Queen 4 November 1879, Cab/41/13/12*)

Extract

. . . no proposal having come from either of the German Powers that this Country should enter into the new alliance, he and Lord Salisbury looked on the matter as *non avenu* and that it might very well rest as it does.

At the Cabinet Lord Salisbury said that M. Waddington seemed satisfied that there was nothing intended which could annoy France; and that M. Waddington disclaimed for France generally, as well as for his own Ministry, the idea of a Russian alliance. France desires peace for a generation.

SALISBURY'S CONDITIONS FOR DEFENDING ASIA MINOR

8. (*Salisbury to Layard 16 May 1878, in Cecil II, 269*)

Two conditions, however, are indispensable. If our defensive alliance is to be worth anything, we must not be hampered by divisions at home, and we must have every facility for exercising vigilance and giving assistance in Asia.

To meet the first object it will be necessary that the Porte should give us specific assurances of good government to Asiatic Christians, similar to those given in the Treaty to Russia; and should thereby invest us with a special privilege of advice and remonstrance in case of any gross abuse.

To meet the other, the Porte should concede to us the occupation of Cyprus. It has the double advantage of vicinity both to Asia Minor and Syria; it would enable us without any act of overt hostility and without disturbing the peace of Europe, to accumulate material of war and, if requisite, the troops necessary for operations in Asia Minor or Syria, while it would not excite the jealousy which other Powers would feel at any acquisitions on the mainland.

We should not desire to acquire it in any way which could indicate hostility to the Porte, or any acquiescence in partition. We should therefore propose to hold it as part of the agreement by which we undertook to defend the Asiatic Empire against the Russians; and we should distinctly stipulate that, as both these engagements were consequent on the Russian annexations in Armenia, as soon as these should cease, both our defensive alliance and our occupation of Cyprus should cease also.

THE OBJECT OF THE CYPRUS CONVENTION

9. (*Memorandum by General Simmons, War Office 26 July 1878, F.O. 78/2893. Printed in Lee, pp. 199–201*)

Extract

By obtaining possession of the Turkish provinces adjoining Persia, Russia would acquire the means of applying pressure on the whole of the northern & western frontiers of Persia which would be irresistible and render the latter power a passive if not an active ally in the extension of her influence and territory towards India.

In speaking lately to a high Persian diplomatist relative to the Anglo-Turkish convention of the 4 June he expressed himself in the highest terms as to the result it would have in Persia by placing that country in a favourable position both as regards trade and the influences which might be brought to bear for the improvement and civilization of that country. His expressions as to the supineness of Great Britain in the past as regards her influence in Persia were equally strong and the satisfaction amounting to delight evinced by him point strongly to the apprehension under which he was that Persia might pass entirely under the influence of Russia.

By the eventual and almost certain extension of her influence and power, if not of her conquests, in Asia Minor, Russia might obtain practical possession of Turkish territory down to the Gulf of Skenderoon and along the shores of the Mediterranean, and if once there it would be difficult to arrest her progress to the Straits of the Dardanelles and the Bosphorus when the Black Sea would be closed against the ships of war of other powers & her position in Asia Minor would be consolidated and the flow of British commerce into the rich countries lying between the Black and Mediterranean seas might be prejudiced.

If the power of Russia were consolidated in Asia Minor either directly by conquest or indirectly by the country passing under her protection she would obtain the power of raising and provisioning armies which by the aid of conscription would become so powerful that no European power dependent upon the sea for its communications could expect to maintain an army in the field at such a distance from home sufficiently strong to resist further conquests.

Syria would then, under this supposition, come under the control of the Power that had obtained possession of the resources of Asia Minor and eventually the Suez Canal & Egypt might feel its influence.

It results from the above considerations that if the progress of Russia through Asia to the Dardanelles and the Mediterranean is to be checked at all it must be before she has acquired the means of forming and maintaining larger armies than she at present possesses to the South of the Caucasus.

The best method and in fact so far as I can see the only probability of effecting this object is to resist all progress or attempt at extension beyond her present limits which cannot reasonably be expected to be done by Turkey unaided by some other power or powers. In fact whether the Anglo-Turkish convention existed or not, it is more than probable that Great Britain in the event of Russia again attacking Turkey in Asia Minor would be compelled to take measures and even go to war to prevent the extension of Russia on this side.

The military means by which Russia is to be resisted require careful consideration. There can be no doubt that the first thing is to secure the Dardanelles & Bosphorus from attack on the European side because unless the free entrance of H.M's ships into the Black Sea is secured the most vulnerable point in the dominions of the Czar viz: his Transcaucasian possessions will be guarded against attack, the best route by which reinforcements can be brought to the theatre of war in Asia Minor by the Black Sea would remain open to Russia, and the defence of Asia Minor against further aggression will become almost impossible.

The other measures to be taken are to obtain order and security for life and property in Asia Minor and to open up the country by making such roads and communications through it as will not only serve the purposes of commerce but will be capable of being used as military roads for the movement of troops and stores to the vicinity of the frontiers and to organize the country militarily for defence by improving its financial position, by enrolling and training the inhabitants as soldiers and by constructing such defensive works as the careful examination of the country might dictate.

If the entrance into the Black Sea were absolutely secured and the native population organized in sufficient strength to oppose the progress of Russian arms in the elevated region of Armenia a force by threatening invasion up the valley of the Rion would jeopardize the whole of the Russian possessions to the South of the Caucasus or if not in sufficient strength to do this a British force landed in the Gulf of Skenderoon, if a line of railway were constructed thence up to Diarbekir and Erzinghan, would be as near to the theatre of war as any reinforcements coming from Russia and arriving there fresh without the fatigue of long marches be in a favourable position to aid the forces of the country in repelling attack.

SALISBURY ADMITS REFORM IN TURKEY IS A HOPELESS PROSPECT

10. (*To Major Trotter 16 September 1879, in Cecil II, 321–2*)

Extract

The evils you depict are terrible and the prospect of a remedy is not near. The majority of the population being Mussulman, Armenian 'Autonomy' is impossible, and if the Armenians are at all like the Bulgarians, the remedy if possible would be worse than the disease. A cure would at once be found if there were a capable Government at Constantinople. But the Sultan's feebleness of character puts that hope out of the question, and if he were dethroned or if he were an able man, it is doubtful if he could find ministers of energy among the class by which he is surrounded. There is therefore little to hope for from Constantinople.

GOSCHEN EMPHASIZES THE LIBERAL GOVERNMENT'S INTEREST IN REFORM IN TURKEY

11. (*Goschen to Granville 21 June 1880, Cab/37/2/30*)

Extract

The substance of Musurus Pasha's remarks to me has been that he had prepared everything most pleasantly for my reception; that the Sultan had at first been alarmed at my mission, but that he had represented to His Majesty that I should certainly be most conciliatory; that Her Majesty's Government were most friendly and that there would be no difficulty whatever in an amicable arrangement satisfactory to all; that the Montenegrin difficulty was not created by the Porte; that in the Greek Frontier question the Porte would not object to giving a large slice of territory to Greece, provided Janina, Larissa (which was a forest of minarets) and Metzovo, all-important for purposes of communication, were left to the Turks, and that as to reforms the Asiatic provinces could be brought under a similar arrangement to those prepared for the European provinces, where the Commissioners were now at work preparing Statues. He repeated continually: 'Tout cela s'arrangera.'

I need not trouble your Lordship with my replies beyond stating that I declined to discuss the Greek frontier, and that as to the reforms, the Commissioners dealing with them were being thwarted by interminable delays, while the 'Project de Loi' itself was, I believed, very unsatisfactory. But I dwelt on the evidence, which I discovered at every turn, of an absolute indifference, if not worse, as to the reforms, the breaking up of the English Gendarmerie, the recall of Valis who were working well; the impunity of those who were committing abuses, the impossibility of transacting any business with the present Ministers; above all, the constant appointment of officials and great officers undeserving of confidence. Musurus Pasha replied, with some anxiety, that he had understood from your Lordship that my mission was to deal with the unexecuted portion of the Treaty of Berlin, and he greatly regretted and deprecated the language I was holding.

I answered to the effect that it was the most essential point of my mission to bring home to the mind of the Sultan and the Porte that the desire of England to see the maintenance of the present territorial limits of the sovereignty of the Sultan was dependent on the execution of reforms, and that, if reforms were not made, England had no special and separate interests to lead her to save Turkey from her ruin. I have little hope that any important part of this conversation will reach the Sultan's ears, but as, apparently, Musurus Pasha sees the Sultan constantly, and has been chosen on these two or three occasions by the Sultan to see me on his behalf, I thought it right to be very explicit, so as to remove, if possible, from Musurus Pasha's own mind, his very erroneous impressions as to the nature of the situation.

GLADSTONE SEEKS TO MAINTAIN CONTINUITY IN FOREIGN POLICY, WHILST CHANGING THE EMPHASIS TO THE CONCERT

12. (*Memorandum of conversation with Granville 23 September 1880, B.M. Add. Mss 44764, printed in Ramm I, 181*)

Extract

Those of us who sit in the House of Commons (and we are in thorough agreement with the Ministers who are Lords) were certainly not returned to Parliament to carry forward the Foreign Policy of the last Government.

And this was known throughout the country, and beyond it.

Nevertheless, sensible of the expediency of maintaining as far as might be a continuity in Foreign Policy, we sought for a ground of action which might be common to both political parties.

We found this ground in the unfulfilled Clauses of the Treaty of Berlin which for all reasons it was urgent to press forward.

We hold an international title to demand as a single power the fulfilment of those clauses.

Probably a perfect international title, evidently a far better one than the title of the late Government to conclude the Anglo-Turkish Convention.

Instead of using this liberty we placed ourselves under great restraint by endeavouring to organize a European Concert.

Our policy thus was only as follows: to require what Europe had decided, and to require it through the agency of Europe.

BISMARCK OFFERS ADVICE ON THE EASTERN QUESTION

13. (*Ampthill to Granville 20 December 1881, Cab/37/6/36*)

Extract

What France might do no one could foretell, but he believed that Tunis was as much as she could digest, and that her appetite would not extend to Tripoli.

The Eastern policy of England he believed to be based on the absolute necessity to keep the road to India free, the earnest desire to maintain the political *status quo* in Turkey, in Asia, and in Egypt, and the philanthropic wish to improve the material condition of the Sultan's subjects. His Majesty had, therefore, every reason to confide and rely in the policy of England, whilst Germany had every reason to support that policy, because it was conducive to the maintenance of peace and order in Europe.

He looked upon the breaking up of the Turkish Empire as so great a danger to Europe, that he was prepared to go great lengths to keep it together, at least as long as he lived himself, for what happened after his death he had no means of controlling, and as the Turks, as a military nation, had proved themselves to be the race best able to keep order among the various nationalities composing the Empire, he would support the Turkish Government for the sake of keeping the Empire together.

In regard to Egypt, he also agreed with England, that the *status quo* should be maintained, and he thought England right to resist the interference of any other Power in Egypt, and he held that England would be justified in going to war to resist any foreign interference with Egypt, and if ever he should be consulted about a foreign occupation of Egypt, he would give his opinion in favour of a Turkish occupation, and would object to any other but a Turkish garrison for Egypt.

He agreed in all points with the policy of England, except in one, and that was, the philanthropic side of her policy. He believed that pressure for reforms could be overdone, and actually did more harm than good, because the irritation produced on the Turkish mind by high foreign pressure manifested itself by increased procrastination, and led to the very result it was so desirable to obviate.

He could, therefore, not give his support to a policy of pressure for reforms, and believed that better results could be obtained by leaving the Sultan alone, and giving the Pashas time to reflect on the advice already tendered by the Powers since the Congress of Berlin which, he flattered himself, had really laid the foundation of lasting peace in Turkey.

I thanked Prince Bismarck for his friendly communication, and said that he had rightly interpreted our policy in regard to the road to India, and the maintenance of the political *status quo* in Turkey, Asia, and Egypt; but that we could never cease to press for reforms in Turkey, and for the improvement of the condition of the Sultan's subjects, because we knew from experience that if we ever relaxed our efforts, the Ottoman Administration would become more corrupt, and the condition of the people more abject and hopeless than it was even now, as he might learn, for instance, from our Blue Books on Armenia.

I therefore took this opportunity of renewing to him my earnest appeal to Count Hatzfeldt, that he would urge the Sultan, through his emissaries, Ali and Reschid, to send, without further delay, a Governor-General to Armenia, with full powers to improve the condition of the people, as recommended by Lord Dufferin and his colleagues.

CONSERVATIVE POLICY IN TUNIS AND EGYPT

14. (*Salisbury to Lyons 7 August 1878, Cab/37/5/11*)

I have the honour to inclose to your Excellency a copy of a despatch from the Minister of Foreign Affairs in France, which was handed to me on Saturday by the French Ambassador.

The subject to which it relates was referred to more than once in the very satisfactory conversations which I had with M. Waddington at Berlin. They were of a private character, and did not differ in their circumstances from those which daily took place between the various Plenipotentiaries. I did not, therefore, at the time make any note of them, or transmit any summary of them to your Excellency, as it is usual to do after conversations of importance taking place at the Foreign Office. I am consequently unable to affirm that M. Waddington has reproduced the precise words made use of then either by himself or me. I am rather disposed to think that, though he has used the form of quotation, he merely desired to indicate the general bearing of our communications, and especially the amicable feelings towards France by which my language was inspired. So far, and without being able to confirm the exact phrases attributed to me, I have great pleasure in bearing witness to the general justice of his recollections.

Instead, however, of offering any verbal criticisms upon them, it will be simpler to state in a few sentences the views which Her Majesty's Government entertain upon this subject.

They have witnessed with lively satisfaction the success of the experiment conducted by France in Algeria, and the great work of civilization which it is accomplishing in that country. They have never been unaware that the presence of France on those shores, supported as it is by an imposing military force, must have the effect of giving to her, when she thinks fit to exercise it, the power of pressing with decisive force upon the Government of the neighbouring Province of Tunis. This is a result which they have long recognized as inevitable and have accepted without reluctance. England has no special interests in this region which could possibly lead her to view with apprehension or distrust the legitimate and expanding influence of France.

On the future destines of this province it is unnecessary to speculate. I think M. Waddington must have misconceived me in understanding that I foreboded an early fall to the existing Government of Tunis. My information would rather lead me to expect that, if it is disturbed by no external shock, it may last for a considerable time. With respect, therefore, to an event which may be distant, I will only say that it will not alter the attitude of England. She will continue to recognize, as she does now, the natural results of the neighbourhood of a powerful and civilizing country like France, and she has no counter-claims of her own to advance.

There is one consideration, however, to which I drew the attention of M. Waddington in conversation, and to which I ought not to omit all reference upon the present occasion. France is not the only country which lies in close proximity to Tunis. I have no means of knowing the exact views of the Italian Government upon this question, but I have grounds for believing that it is one to which their attention has been drawn. Her Majesty's Government must not be understood as having arrived at any opinion upon the position which Italy may take up in reference to the region under discussion; for as no communications have passed between the two Governments on this matter, any such opinion would have been formed in entire ignorance.

15. (*Salisbury to Layard 29 October 1878, Cecil II, 332*)

What happened was this: In the course of our intercourse at Berlin, which was necessarily familiar, Waddington and I often discussed the events which were taking place in the Mediterranean and their effect on the balance of power in the European States. While I maintained our right to a dominant influence in Western Asia and especially in Mesopotamia, I disclaimed any intention of establishing an exclusive footing in Egypt; and with respect to Tunis, I said that England was wholly disinterested and had no intention to contest the influence which the geographical position of Algeria naturally gave to France. Lord Beaconsfield held similar language to him. Sometimes also we discussed the possibility of the Turkish Empire going entirely to pieces. In that case, I told him, he must not hold us bound to any promise as to Egypt; but that, as to Tunis, England would not hold herself bound to interfere with any course which France in such an event might choose to take.

16. (*Disraeli to the Queen 21 February 1879, Cab 41/12/7*)

A short Cabinet but a satisfactory one on Egyptian affairs. England and France will act together. If it were not for the South Africa affair we sh^d prepare for the military occupation of Egypt. Let us hope it may not be necessary or may be postponed—now the advantage of Cyprus may be recognized. In 4 & 20 hours almost in a night a couple of Y^r Majesty's ships might carry a couple of thousand men from that island to Alexandria.

17. (*Salisbury to Northcote 16 September 1881, Cecil II, 331–2*)

As to our policy—the defence of it lies in a nutshell. When you have got a neighbour and faithful ally who is bent on meddling in a country in which you are deeply interested—you have three courses open to you. You may renounce—or monopolize—or share. Renouncing would have been to place the French across our road to India. Monopolizing would have been very near the risk of war. So we resolved to share.

GRANVILLE AND GLADSTONE ACCEPT SALISBURY'S COMMITMENTS ON TUNIS

18. (*Granville to Lyons 17 June 1880, Cab 37/5/11*)

Extract

The French Ambassador spoke to me on the 9th instant on the subject of Tunis.

His Excellency said that the interests of France in Africa did not permit her to be indifferent to whatever affected the condition of Tunis. The Government of that country was weak, and it would be unwise to ignore the possibility of its coming to an end. It was far from the desire of the French Government to accelerate such an event, and to profit by it to obtain an extension of territory. On the contrary, they were desirous of preventing any such contingency. But, at the same time, they found it necessary to exercise a certain amount of influence over the Tunisian Government themselves, and they were jealous of the establishment of any preponderating influence there by other Powers.

His Excellency said that at Berlin Lord Beaconsfield and Lord Salisbury held very friendly language on the subject of Tunis. They had repudiated the notion of any jealousy on the part of England of the growing influence and civilizing effects of French administration in Africa; and they seemed rather to encourage than to deprecate the very sensible increase of French influence over Tunis, even if it were to be pushed to a degree greater than was intended or desired by France.

The French Government did not wish to press Her Majesty's Government on the subject, but they would be glad to know as early as convenient whether the present Government shared the views of their predecessors.

I saw M. Leon Say again on the 12th instant, and returned to the subject.

I stated to his Excellency that in the correspondence which is preserved in this Office respecting the communications which passed between Lord Salisbury, Lord Beaconsfield, and M. Waddington at Berlin on the subject of Tunis, I found that there was some discrepancy between what was originally mentioned in private conversation and what was afterwards recorded officially to your Excellency as the opinion of the late Government. I found also that Lord Salisbury in that despatch had distinctly reserved any opinion upon the position which Italy might take up in reference to Tunis.

I said that, in the view of Her Majesty's Government, Tunis was a portion of the Ottoman Empire, to dispose of which Great Britain had no moral or international right. But Her Majesty's Government had no jealousy of the influence which France, from her greater power and her high civilization, exercised, and is likely to exercise, over Tunis.

Her Majesty's Government, I said, were in the same position as their predecessors as regards the position which Italy may take up in reference to Tunis.

19. (*Gladstone to Granville 22 April 1881, Fitzmaurice II, 236*)

Extract

It appears to me that our position for resisting the French intrigues in Tunis—which are but too palpable—has been frightfully weakened: *first* by the acquisition of Cyprus in utter defiance of the Treaty of Paris, *secondly*, to a degree not yet quite cleared up, by Salisbury's declaration: which, whatever it may have been, I suppose binds us.

The first point I think most grave, and in fact the position seems to me not tenable beyond the point of friendly remonstrance in case of need.

Nothing could I think possibly be better than your letter to Menabrea.

You will have understood that I do not retract my approval as to sending ships, and if the occasion arise I would send a sufficiency.

The possible harbour is a grave fact but I do not see that it neutralizes Malta more than it is neutralized by Malta. The other side is in other hands: and there is another access by Tacursia say 20 to 100 miles round.

THE LIBERALS AND THE OCCUPATION OF EGYPT

20. (*Gladstone to Granville 13 September 1881, P.R.O. 30/29/124. Printed in Ramm I, 291*)

I have telegraphed to you to-day that I am in readiness to meet you in town on Egyptian matters should there be, in your judgment, occasion for it.

My opinions however as at present advised are in conformity with what I believe to be yours. I sum up thus

1. Steady concert with France.
2. Turkish General to go if need be.
3. Turkish troops, in preference to any others.
4. No British or French force, unless ships be needful for *bona fide* protection of subjects.

21. (*Granville to Dufferin 26 January 1882, Cab/37/7/9*)

Extract

The policy of Her Majesty's Government has undergone no change since the date of my despatch to Sir E. Malet of the 4 November, and they are as anxious as they were then for the progress and well-being of Egypt, for the continuance of the sovereignty of the Porte over it, and for the maintenance of the liberties and administrative independence secured to it by the Sultan's Firmans.

They desire to promote the financial and material improvement of the country, and the introduction of necessary reforms in the various branches of the Administration; but they have no ambitious designs, and no wish to secure for themselves an exclusive influence, nor would they willingly see such an influence in the hands of any other single Power. They have every reason to believe that the Government of France holds similar views, and is equally free from any designs of self-aggrandizement.

But Her Majesty's Government cannot be indifferent to events which might plunge Egypt into anarchy, and destroy the results of the efforts which have been successfully made during the last few years to improve the condition of the country, and it was with a view of warding off such a catastrophe that they thought it advisable, in conjunction with the French Government, to forward, through their respective Agents, a Declaration which should have the effect of showing the complete accord of the two Governments in carrying out the policy which I have described.

The course of events in Egypt during the last few months tended to show that the recent movement, though it may have beneficial effects if kept within proper limits, might, if pushed too far, lead to a limitation of the Khedive's authority, as existing in virtue of the Firmans granted by the Sultans and communicated to the Powers, and might also result in an interference with those international arrangements in which England and France are primarily interested by reason of their situation and specially interested in virtue of the Decrees of the Khedive, negotiated by and with them alone, by which they were invited to reorganize the administration of the finances in Egypt, but to which the other Powers of Europe have also become parties.

22. (*Memorandum by Gladstone 21 June 1882, P.R.O. 30/29/125. Printed in Ramm I, 381*)

1. Propose in Conference that Sultan should send troops.
2. Support proposal with reasons.
3. Intimate that if Conference decline, or if Sultan decline, we shall invite Conference to concert effectual means for the re-establishment of legality and security in Egypt.

4. So far as we can at present judge, the form of this invitation will be to ask the Powers to provide for or sanction a military intervention other than Turkish under their authority.

23. (*Gladstone to the Queen 3 July 1882, Cab/41/16/33*)

The hesitation and vacillation of the French policy, due to the inherent weakness (as seemed probable) of the position of the Government, has retarded and disconcerted proceedings in the East, and has given encouragement to the party of military domination in Egypt.

In the opinion of the Cabinet, the circumstances required that decisive instructions should be given to the Admiral at Alexandria 'to authorize him to destroy the earthworks and fortifications of that point in case any attempts should be made to resume the construction of the works or any operation to strengthen them, or to block the harbour and enclose the fleet'.

24. (*Gladstone to the Queen 27 July 1882, Cab/41/16/40*)

Extract

Mr. Gladstone reports to Your Majesty with his humble duty that the Cabinet met for a short time today to consider in what way it would be proper to treat the offer of the Sultan to send troops to Egypt, which has evidently been drawn from him by British action.

It appeared to the Cabinet that the time had come for explaining to the Conference that the *force majeure* used in the Bombardment for the defence and safety of the Fleet had been followed by a state of things in Egypt which rendered immediate action necessary, and entailed on the British forces the obligation of taking steps to uphold locally the authority of the Khedive, and secure his person from danger, while the country in general passed under the sway of action by lawless military tyranny, in resistance to the lawful ruler. While this was done on the spot, it was determined to dispatch an expedition from this country to restore order and tranquillity in Egypt. The co-operation of the Sultan with us would be welcome, in conformity with all the declarations which had heretofore been made: but a decided pressure ought to be made to bring the Sultan at once to issue a proclamation against the Rebels, so that there might be no mistake as to his intentions.

III

The Egyptian Lever

BRITAIN DETERMINES TO END THE DUAL CONTROL

25. (*Malet to Granville 5 September 1882, Cab/37/9/84*)

Extract

The dual system has had a great deal to do towards bringing us to our present pass. You will have observed in Arabi's letter to the Porte (Confidential Print, August 10, Section 3) that he says that the French Consul has told him, confidentially, that the French are aware of the views of the English, and that, though obliged to act in concert with us for the moment, the French Government will not fail in the end to come to Arabi's assistance. I have every reason to believe that this was the general tone of French utterances, and I should not be at all surprised at the very words having been used. The French have intrigued against us ever since I have been in Egypt, while we have behaved with thorough loyalty towards them. We shall perhaps never have another legitimate opportunity of enforcing our own preponderance, and I hope that it may be taken advantage of.

To my mind, the really most important point in the reconstruction before us is the establishment of justice to the natives; till this is done there will be no security in Egypt of a durable and solid character. If they will not give it to themselves it should be forced upon them.

26. (*Gladstone to Granville 3 October 1882, P.R.O. 30/29/126. Printed in Ramm I, 440–1*)

Extract

I am far from thinking the Controul has entirely failed. But it seems to me that in the face of France we are entitled to say it has failed, and for this reason. It afforded Arabi the pretext, & in the face of the world, the justifying reason, on which he founded his movement, disturbed Europe, & cost us our lives & our millions. This being so the parties to the Controul, did not act jointly in upholding it, and in meeting the consequences it had entailed. Therefore I think we are in a condition not to go before France with a request, which would involve us in much risk, but in the most delicate manner to convey to them our full belief that they with us will see it cannot be maintained. Affording a pretext for disturbance in Egypt—justly irritating to any genuine national feeling that may exist—tending to excite jealousies in some European quarters—and having entirely failed to sustain itself by force against force—this provisional arrangement has been tried and found wanting. After the great disintegration in Egypt we have had to consider what is the safest basis for the future as against the dangers encompassing (us) on so many sides; we have concluded that this basis is to be found in freedom & self-development, as far as may be, for Egypt, & we ought to anticipate the concurrence of France which has often done generous acts in a generous policy. I have made rather a long story of it.

THE LIBERAL GOVERNMENT ANNOUNCES ITS INTENTION TO WITHDRAW FROM EGYPT

Extract

27. (*Granville, Draft Circular 14 December 1882, Cab/37/9/107*)

The course of events has thrown upon Her Majesty's Government the task, which they would willingly have shared with other Powers, of suppressing the military rebellion in Egypt, and restoring peace and order in that country. The object has been, happily, accomplished; and although for the present a British force remains in Egypt for the preservation of public tranquillity, Her Majesty's Government are desirous of withdrawing it as soon as the state of the country, and the organization of proper means for the maintenance of the Khedive's authority, will admit of it. In the meanwhile, the position in which Her Majesty's Government are placed towards His Highness imposes upon them the duty of giving advice with the object of securing that the order of things to be established shall be of a satisfactory character, and possess the elements of stability and progress.

The Egyptian Lever

28. (*Report of Cabinet Committee 4 November 1882, Cab/37/9/103*)

Extract

In the present state of things there is, moreover, always the possibility of the Canal being destroyed or blocked by an enemy, with the object of inflicting a blow on Great Britain, which, of all the Maritime Powers, derives by far the greatest benefit from its use.

The Committee are therefore against the proposal to leave matters as they are.

The Neutralization of the Canal

This is a proposal to close the Canal absolutely against all vessels of war at all times.

The Committee are against it, on the ground that it would tie the hands of this country, and that, in their opinion, it is of the highest importance to the interests of Great Britain to secure the power of sending her naval and military forces at any time through the Canal for the protection of her Eastern possessions.

Proposal to close the Canal against the Vessels of War of Belligerents

This proposal would, under most circumstances, be detrimental to the interests of Great Britain as a belligerent, and the Committee, therefore, do not recommend it.

Proposal to close the Canal against all War Vessels in event only of a War between any two European Powers

The Committee are against this proposal, for the reason already stated in dealing with the second proposal. They consider that the Canal should be open at all times to British ships of war.

Proposal to guarantee the Free Navigation of the Canal for all Vessels and at all times—

(a) By a British Protectorate over Egypt or the Canal
(b) By an Agreement among the great Maritime Powers

As regards the first alternative (a), it appears to the Committee that a British Protectorate in Egypt or on the Canal, though effectually securing the passage of the Canal, would involve great responsibilities and the employment of a large force, which, in certain contingencies, might be isolated, and to which grave political objections exist. It would seem also to be unnecessary, if less costly but effectual means of obtaining the required security can be found.

The Committee have, therefore, directed their attention more particularly to the second alternative (b), and they are of opinion that it would be to the interest of Great Britain that an international agreement should be concluded respecting the Canal.

29. (*Lyons to Granville 5 June 1883, Cab/37/10/42*)

In my Secret despatch No. 327 of the 18th ultimo, I observed that while M. Challemel-Lacour himself (according to his wont) showed very little disposition, when conversing with me on diplomatic questions, to go beyond the matter actually in hand, subordinate French officials did not hesitate to let it be known that courtesy in minor questions would not exclude strenuous resistance to England in matters strongly affecting French feelings or French views of the interests of the country.

It is my painful duty to report to your Lordship that during the period of nearly three weeks which has elapsed since I wrote the despatch referred to, irritation against England has been on the increase. As ill-feeling has grown among the public, the language held in official quarters has (as I am credibly informed) become plainer and stronger. M. Challemel-Lacour, in his communications with me, has continued to be perfectly correct, and, I may say, even cordial: but your Lordship will not fail to have observed that even in the cautious speeches he has made in the Chambers, he has not been altogether able to refrain from letting suspicion of England and unfriendly feeling towards her ooze out. For instance, it can hardly be doubted that it was to England he intended to allude when, three days ago, in his speech respecting Tonquin, he said, 'Nous savons, Messieurs, qu'on travaille à exciter la Chine, et nous savons qui l'excite.'

The immediate cause of the present increase of the irritation against England is the language of the English press respecting the Tonquin expedition and the Suez Canal Company.

And here, perhaps, I may repeat that the question of the Suez Canal Company is the really hazardous point in the relations between England and France. It is the question in which the pecuniary and sentimental interests of the French most closely meet. It is the ground which those who desire a quarrel with

England would choose for one. To a spirited treatment of this question a Government driven to extremities would resort to recover popularity and to divert public attention from home difficulties. It is on this question that even a moderate and prudent Government might be turned out of office, or be forced by public outcry to resort to language and to measures which might lead to serious dangers.

There are unhappily several other matters which, in the present excitable state of public opinion in France, may require delicate handling; but it is with regard to the Suez Canal Company that French feeling is most of all sensitive.

GRANVILLE TRIES TO SOLVE THE FINANCIAL PROBLEM BY A EUROPEAN CONFERENCE

30. (*Granville Draft Circular 9 April 1884, Cab/37/13/24*)

Extract

I transmit to your Excellency herewith a brief statement of the present condition and prospects of the finances of Egypt.

Her Majesty's Government wish to invite the careful attention of the Great Powers of Europe to this question, both in virtue of their important though not uniform participation in the particular arrangements which are at present in force in regard to it, and also on account of their common concern in the welfare of Egypt.

The finances of Egypt have been brought into very serious difficulties:

1. By the destruction of property at Alexandria, and by the awards of the International Commission for compensation of the sufferers, amounting in all to a sum of upwards of four and a-quarter millions of pounds.

2. By the cost, as now sufficiently known, of the protracted endeavour of Egypt to hold the Soudan; by the attempt made to suppress the insurrection in that region; by the disaster which befell the Egyptian forces in October last, and by the measures which it has been necessary to take in view of the dangers thus created. The expenditure already incurred, and to be incurred, under this head, cannot be estimated at less than one and a-half millions.

3. By the excess, for some years past, of the current administrative charges over the available revenue of the country; and by the necessity of considerable expenditure on works of irrigation.

The Egyptian Lever

THE DIFFICULTIES OF ADMINISTERING EGYPT

31. (*Baring Memorandum 4 July 1884, Cab/37/12/34*)

Extract

I repeat what I have often said before, viz., that we cannot obtain at the same time the advantages of a policy of annexation and those of a policy of withdrawal. This is what we have been endeavouring to do since the battle of Tel-el-Kebir. The sooner we abandon the endeavour the better.

I do not mean to say that we are to abandon all attempts at introducing reforms into Egypt. Far from it. All I mean is, that we must be content with slow and moderate progress, that we must leave a wide latitude to the native Ministry as to the time and method of carrying out internal reforms, that we must give the various Englishmen employed in the Egyptian service to understand that they must rely mainly on their own tact, ability, and force of character, rather than on diplomatic support, that we must leave the Egyptian Government to govern Egypt really as well as nominally, and that we must decline to take the responsibility of governing the country on our own shoulders.

I am aware of the difficulties, from the point of view of Parliament, and of English public opinion, of carrying this policy into effect. But I submit that those difficulties must be faced if the British garrison is to be withdrawn in three and a-half years. I firmly believe that any other policy that that which I have sketched out is foredoomed to failure. . . .

Let me add that I do not ask for any public declaration of policy in the sense which I am now advocating. My special business, of course, is to represent to the Government the local view of Egyptian politics, and from that point of view I maintain that, whilst wishing to withdraw from Egypt, we have, as a matter of fact, been acting in a manner which, in one way or another, has taken us far along the road to annexation. But I fully recognize the Parliamentary difficulties of the situation. I am keenly alive to the fact that we are treating a subject which, whether it be regarded from the English or the European standpoint, is probably more complicated and more fraught with possible dangers in the future than any question of foreign policy which an English Government has had to deal with for the last half-century or more. All, therefore, I ask is that Her Majesty's Government should tell me distinctly, for my own guidance, whether the principles I have advocated meet generally with their acceptance, and whether I shall be supported should I act on those principles. If I know this my task on my return to Egypt will still indeed be one of very great difficulty, but I should at all events feel that I had some practical guide by which I might regulate my conduct in the daily work of Egyptian affairs.

THE PROBLEMS OF EVACUATION DIVIDE THE CABINET

32. (*Northbrook Memorandum 9 August 1884, Cab/37/13/38*)

Extract

I think it most desirable that we should act with the Sultan, if he can be brought to enter into a cordial understanding with us. We should thereby not only put ourselves, so far as the circumstances admit of it, in a sound international position, but obtain the command of some excellent troops if we should be compelled to defend Egypt by arms.

It is also very desirable that we should obtain the cordial support of Italy.

England, Italy, and Turkey would have naval strength in the Mediterranean sufficient to deter the French from any temptation to try a *coup* on the Canal.

2. Our objects being to settle Egypt, to withdraw our army within a reasonable time, and to preserve the peace of Europe, the following seem to me to be the main lines of policy which are most likely to attain those objects.

3. No one can be more opposed to the annexation of Egypt, or to any step in that direction, than I am; but I may have to recommend that we should remain in Egypt for a term of three or five years; with the consent and at the request of the Sultan, if possible. During this time we should undertake, as now, to protect the country, and our advice must be followed by the Khedive's Government upon all matters which we consider necessary to our position. At the same time, the internal administration of the country should be conducted upon the lines recommended by Sir Evelyn Baring in a recent Memorandum.

The Egyptian Lever

33. (*Harcourt Memorandum for the Cabinet 16 November 1884,*
Gardiner I, 603–5)

Extract

Egypt has long been the focus of European intrigue and will be
more than ever so under an English administration. Russia,
France, Germany would be for ever tripping up our heels. We
should always be in hot water with the Powers. We should have
all the evils of becoming a Continental State. We should be for
ever in quarrels, perhaps on the verge of war. And all for what?
Added to that, the Administration of Egypt will always afford to
the Opposition in Parliament, as it now does, a constant and convenient weapon with which to harrass a Government. Half the time
of Parliament will be taken up with Egyptian discussion . . .

Then what are we to do. I answer, Retire from Egypt, quam
celerrime.

That is the policy we have always declared and to which we are
pledged. But it will be asked, when and how soon. I admit that
our present engagements for the relief of Gordon and the general
situation make our instant withdrawal impossible. We must per-
force wait till we have got Gordon out and we cannot let the
whole fabric of Egyptian administration tumble to pieces at once.

34. (*Gladstone to Granville 6 January 1885, P.R.O. 30/29/29. Printed*
in Ramm II, 314)

Extract

If we reach that point, I am disposed to admit that the conduct of
the Powers (except Italy), active only in thwarting, and absolutely
useless in helping, the execution of a task, which we undertook
with their approval and greatly for their advantage, has given to
this country (whether to this Ministry or not) rights and claims
beyond what, if enjoying their co-operation, it might have been
entitled to: rights and claims growing out of the necessity of the
case.

It is I suppose an indisputable proposition that we should maintain the peace of Egypt while we remain there.

Is it possible to do this, at the same (time) leaving finance
prospectively to the Egyptian Government, and declaring our
stay to be provisional, and prolonged only as in your draft dispatch
of Sunday.

On the other side there lies guarantee, assumption of financial control, and abandonment of definite ideas of withdrawal: in brief, what Hartington has repeatedly described, including I suppose the maintenance of the Law of Liquidation.

Some ingenious brain may devise some other method.

GLADSTONE SEEKS A SETTLEMENT WITH BISMARCK

35. (*Gladstone to Granville 31 December 1884, P.R.O. 30/29/128. Printed in Ramm II, 309*)

Extract

If the French are paltering with us, as there was already some reason to believe, it cannot I presume be submitted to.

Through their fault not ours Bismarck will gain his not unnatural purpose of keeping us widely apart.

Close co-operation with Germany, though I do not say indispensable, thus becomes of immense importance.

I for one am ready for it because I think that as far as I understand the matters at issue the Germans are on most of them substantially right.

36. (*Malet to Granville 24 January 1885, Cab 37/14/6*)

Extract

I then said to the Prince that the whole situation was undoubtedly a very unsatisfactory one, and that it gave me great pain, as it had been my hope and endeavour and my duty, under instructions from your Lordship, to bring about a more cordial understanding between the two Powers; that I knew that it had never been the intention of Her Majesty's Government to thwart the colonial aspirations of Germany, and that, in my opinion, our action had repeatedly shown this desire; but I said that it would be impossible for us to act so as to meet his wishes, even where it was easy for us to do so, unless we knew what those wishes were, and I therefore begged him to tell me what now, at this moment, he wanted; was it the parts of New Guinea which we were now annexing? Was it Zululand? I said that the knowledge of his wishes, whatever they might be, was better than that we should go on mutually acting in the dark, and consequently running against each other.

The Prince replied that the understanding which he had arrived at with France in consequence of his failure to come to one with us, put it out of his power to take up the question now, as he had expounded it to us in May, and that he could no longer make any particular bargain. The long conversation came to an end by his saying that he had been anxious to explain to me the series of circumstances that had preceded the present phase of the political relations between the two countries, which he was sure I must regret as much as he did.

The general impression which I derived from the conversation was that the Prince does not desire that relations between the two countries should improve at present.

It is only hazarding a guess if I venture to suggest that his object is to have a sufficient excuse for recalling Count Münster, whom he genuinely believes to have been remiss in his duties, and that a change of Ambassador may be succeeded by a more satisfactory state of affairs.

BISMARCK EXPLAINS HIS COLONIAL POLICY

37. (*Currie, Notes of a conversation with Prince Bismarck 28 September 1885, S.P. Printed in Greaves, pp. 246–7.*)

Extract

In the morning I walked with the Prince alone.

He said that he was glad to have an opportunity of talking openly with a person in the confidence of Lord Salisbury though he regretted that this conversation did not follow the elections instead of preceding them. Though he hoped that the present Gov[ernment] would remain in office it was possible that Mr. Gladstone might become Prime Minister again & he was a man who had no knowledge of foreign affairs & with whom it was impossible to do business.

But what he was about to say had reference to England as a nation.

Friendship with England had been the traditional policy of Prussia. The first thing that had interrupted it was the conduct of England during the Franco German War—Her neutrality had a leaning on the French side, and this the German nation had not forgiven. Later had come the Colonial questions. But the policy which he had pursued and which had been considered as unfriendly to England was not inspired by any feeling against her or wish to injure her. It related only to questions where England & France were at variance and he had sided with France in order to try and extinguish the animosity of that country against Germany. He had thought, (mistakenly, as he now saw) that in time it would be possible for France to be so far reconciled to Germany that she would give up seeking constantly for an opportunity of revenge—Such had been the case after Waterloo, & France which had been on the most hostile terms with England in 1840 had been close friends with her 10 years later.

With this view he had humored and made love to the French. He had helped them in Egypt & Madagascar and had indulged them in the Congo affair. He had persevered in this policy for 15 years, but it had entirely failed and he had now finally made up his mind that he had been following a wild goose chase. The game was beyond his power to catch. All his efforts had been thrown away & France was as ready to seize any opportunity of attacking Germany as ever. The Spanish affair had been the last drop in the balance which had decided him. He now washed his hands of France and was prepared to side with England in questions between the 2 Countries. There were now no points of difference between England & Germany. As far as the Colonies went, he had got all he wanted, and more than he believed Germany could digest. He had never favored the Colonial idea himself, but opinion in Germany ran so strongly in favor of Colonial enterprise that he could not resist it, or rather that he could not refrain from turning the Colonial stream into the main channel of his Parliamentary policy.

THE SOUDAN PROBLEM

38. (*Baring to Granville 26 March 1884, Cab/37/12/18*)

I cannot say whether it will be possible for me to communicate your Lordship's message to Gordon, but in any case I cannot reconcile myself to making the attempt to forward such a message without again addressing your Lordship. Let me earnestly beg Her Majesty's Government to place themselves in the position of Gordon and Stewart. They have been sent on a most difficult and dangerous mission by Her Majesty's Government. Their proposal to send Zebehr, which if it had been acted on some weeks ago would certainly have altered the situation, was rejected. Consequences which they foresaw have ensued. If they receive the instructions contained in your Lordship's telegram, they cannot but understand them as meaning that they, and all who are with them, are to be abandoned, and to receive no help from the British Government.

Coëtlogen, who is here, assures me that so long as rebels hold banks of river about Sixth Cataract it will be quite impossible for boats to pass. He does not believe Gordon can cut his way through by land. Coëtlogon ridicules the idea of retreating with garrison, &c., to the Equator, and we may be sure that Gordon and Stewart will not come away alone. As a matter of personal opinion, I do not believe in the impossibility of helping Gordon, even during summer, if Indian troops were employed and money was not spared. But if it be decided to make no attempt to afford present help, then I would urge that Gordon be told to try and maintain his position during summer, and that then, if he be still beleagured, an expedition will be sent as early as possible in the autumn to relieve him. This would, at all events, give him some hope, and the mere announcement of the intentions of Government would go a long way to insure his safety by keeping loyal tribes who may be still wavering.

No one can regret more than I do the necessity of sending British or Indian troops to the Soudan, but having sent Gordon to Khartoum, it appears to me that it is our bounden duty, both as a matter of humanity and policy, not to abandon him.

39. (*Granville to Baring 29 March 1884, Cab 37/12/16*)

His [Gordon's] instructions, drawn up in accordance with his own views, were to report to Her Majesty's Government on the military situation in the Soudan, and on the measures which it might be advisable to take for the security of the Egyptian garrisons still holding positions in that country, and for the safety of the European population in Khartoum; and, further, upon the best mode of effecting the evacuation of the interior of the Soudan, and upon the manner in which the safety and good administration by the Egyptian Government of the ports on the sea-coast could best be secured. He was, in addition, authorized and instructed to perform such other duties as the Egyptian Government might desire to intrust to him, and as might be communicated to him by you.

The circumstances with which it was necessary to deal were, no doubt, difficult, and might change from day to day, but it certainly was not in contemplation that the duties to be assigned to General Gordon should be of a nature which would require the dispatch of a British expedition to support or to extricate him.

It was left for you and him to decide in concert whether he should proceed to Suakin, or go himself, or dispatch Colonel Stewart to Khartoum via the Nile. Your opinion was that it was useless that they should proceed to Suakin, and they were accordingly dispatched to Khartoum, with further instructions from you, in which General Gordon again expressed his entire concurrence.

In those instructions you impressed upon General Gordon that the main end to be pursued was the evacuation of the Soudan, adding that this policy had been adopted after very full discussion by the Egyptian Government under the advice of Her Majesty's Government; that it had the full approval of the Khedive and of his present Ministers, and that you understood that General Gordon also concurred in it, and thought it should on no account be changed.

40. (*Report of Cabinet Meeting of 12 March 1885, Cab/41/19/20. Printed in Letters of Queen Victoria 2nd series, III, 623. See also p. 638*)

The Ministers found it necessary to examine in connection with this matter the somewhat menacing state of the questions connected with the frontier of Afghanistan, and especially the considerable advances of Russian troops beyond but towards that frontier. Upon the whole they are of opinion that the possible necessity of a rapid reinforcement of the British Army in India, although it is only possible, yet stands related to an Imperial duty of so high an order, that it might conceivably at this juncture, come to override the present intentions as to the Soudan or part of them, and that it would consequently be imprudent to do anything which would practically extend our obligations in these quarters, as it is the entanglement of the British forces in Soudanese operations which would most powerfully tempt Russia to adopt aggressive measures.

IV

The Defence of India

CONSERVATIVE POLICY TO PARTITION AFGHANISTAN

41. (*Disraeli to the Queen 5 December 1879, Cab/41/13/16*)

Extract

It is clear that Lord Lytton would like to fall back on the Treaty of Gundamuk, but feels that is impossible: he, therefore contemplates a group of quasi-independent chieftains under the influence or protection of the Imperial Crown of India, but combining this, for some time, with adequate military occupation of the Country by Y^{r.} Majesty's forces. If this were affected, and Candahar, for example, in possession of Y^{r.} Majesty's army, & in two years time connected by a rail-way with Herat, Ld. Lytton would not be unwilling to see the Shah of Persia Lord of Herat on the same terms as the chiefs of Candahar, Cabul, Ghasnee etc. Such arrangements cannot be made off hand.

Lord Salisbury, on the other hand, tho' not disapproving of this general policy, wishes to close with Persia at once, from the fear that Russia will forestall us.

Lord Cranbrook, who from his office, as well as his character, naturally exercises much influence on this question, looks upon the disintegration of Afghanistan as inevitable, & is in favor, generally, of the V-Roy's views, but more strongly in favor of the Persian Convention than Ld. Lytton, & wishes to hasten the general settlement of Afghanistan, so that we may meet Parliament with a distinct policy.

After the Cabinet unanimously agreeing, that the treaty of Gundamuk shd be looked upon as abrogated, & that disintegration must be accepted as a fact by Your Majesty's Government, Lord Beaconsfield guided the Cabinet to a decision on Wednesday, which substantially adopted the views of Lord Cranbrook, but authorized Lord Salisbury to continue negotiating with Persia.

It is the opinion of Lord Beaconsfield, that Persia will wait, &, so, that we may be able to effect a safer & more satisfactory arrangement, than the Shah now would propose or accept.

AGREEMENT TO DEFEND AFGHANISTAN

42. (*Griffin to Abdur Rahman Khan July 1880, Cab/37/2/36*)

To His Highness Sirdar Abdul Rahman Khan, Amir of Kabul
After compliments,   July 1880

His Excellency the Viceroy and Governor General in Council has learnt with pleasure that your Highness has proceeded toward Kabul, in accordance with the invitation of the British Government. Therefore, in consideration of the friendly sentiments by which Your Highness is animated, and of the advantage to be derived by the Sirdars and people from the establishment of a settled government under your Highness' authority, the British Government recognizes your Highness as Amir of Kabul.

I am furthered empowered, on the part of the Viceroy and Governor General of India, to inform your Highness that the British Government has no desire to interfere in the internal government of the territories in the possession of your Highness, and has no wish that an English Resident should be stationed anywhere within those territories. For the convenience of ordinary friendly intercourse, such as is maintained between two adjoining States, it may be advisable that a Muhammedan Agent of the British Government should reside, by agreement, at Kabul.

Your Highness has requested that the views and intentions of the British Government with regard to the position of the ruler at Kabul in relation to foreign powers, should be placed on record for Your Highness' information. The Viceroy and Governor General in Council authorizes me to declare to you that since the British Government admits no right of interference by foreign powers within Afghanistan, and since both Russia and Persia are pledged to abstain from all interference with the affairs of Afghanistan, it is plain that your Highness can have no political relations with any foreign power except with the British Government. If any foreign power should attempt to interfere in Afghanistan, and if such interference should lead to unprovoked aggression on the dominions of your Highness, in that event the British Government would be prepared to aid you, to such extent and in such manner as may appear to the British Government necessary, in repelling it; provided that your Highness follows unreservedly the advice of the British Government in regard to your external relations.

BIG VERSUS LITTLE ENDIANS

43. (*Memorandum by H. C. Rawlinson 25 September 1880, Cab/ 37/3/51*)

Extract

The really important questions involved in the proposal to abandon Candahar to Abdur Rahman and to retire precipitately to Pishin or Sinde, refer to the effects which such a proceeding would have upon our general position in Europe and Asia. To say that we should be stultified would very imperfectly represent the situation. In real truth, we should abdicate our position as a first-class Asiatic power, and must be content hereafter to play a very subordinate part in the history of the world. Already the first result of our vacillating Afghan policy has shown itself at Teheran, where our staunch supporter the late Prime Minister has been driven from office to be replaced by a notorious Russia partizan, and where accordingly we may expect to see Russian influence completely dominant in the future. The natural results, indeed, of our retirement from Afghanistan under present circumstances, which are, in truth, not favourable to our military reputation, and which will assuredly be magnified by report to our disadvantage, would be to leave the field completely open to Russian ambition and intrigue. Assisted actively by Persia, she would have no difficulty in occupying Merv in the course of one or, at most, two more campaigns. Bokhara, at the same time, would be absorbed and the Russian would march with the Afghan frontier along the line of the Oxus. At the same time, Persian nominees would be established at Herat and Candahar, Ayub probably, or one of the Meshed refugees, at the former and Mir Afzal at the latter; and Abdur Rahman, whether he wished it or not, would be obliged, in order to maintain his position, to enter into friendly relations with his old friends at Tashkend and Samarcand. Whether all this would constitute any real danger to India must be

303

a matter of opinion. According to my present lights, without anticipating any attempt at immediate invasion, or even any serious offensive demonstration, I think that the evidence of our recoil before the advancing power of Russia, such as our withdrawal from Candahar would be considered to be, would have a most disquieting effect on the Native mind in India, and would predispose many of our large feudatories to listen to intrigues against the stability of our rule; and it is further important to remember that difficulties in India, any popular discontent or show of weakness upon our part, would react on the position at home and seriously diminish our influence in the Councils of Europe.

. . .

I have only now to say a few words in conclusion on the subject of the Candahar railway.

Of all possible political short-comings connected with Afghanistan, the most fatal, as it seems to me, would be the abandonment of this most promising undertaking. The railway was the most efficient arm of defence hitherto devised against Russian agression, far more efficient than the conquest of Cabul, or the establishment in power of a friendly Amir, for its effect when completed would have been to transfer our military base from the Indus to within 350 miles of the threatened point of attack, namely Herat. If we now abandon the work as a sequel to the withdrawal of our troops from the upper country, it must be remembered that we virtually deprive ourselves of the power of protecting the Afghan frontier from Russian aggression, and that the promises accordingly of assistance against external attack, which we recently volunteered to Abdur Rahman at Cabul, are rendered impossible of performance, for we could not and should not, whatever the emergency, march troops again from the Indus to the Oxus.

44. (*Memorandum by Northbrook 15 October 1880, Cab/37/3/59*)

Extract

By the last mail I have received from Lord Ripon a copy of a memorandum which he has written, explaining his reasons for wishing to retain Pishin and Sibi; and as I have a strong opinion against the permanent retention of Pishin, I think the time has arrived when I should put it forward for consideration.

In doing so I will just say, by way of preface, that in my opinion the late war with Afghanistan was unjust and impolitic. Even if the war had been just, I think the policy of the late Government since its commencement has been for the most part unwise. I hold 'the scientific frontier' to be a delusion, and I disapprove of the plan of dividing Afghanistan and of ceding Herat to Persia It is therefore naturally my object to prevent the policy of the late Government from being carried out, and to remedy as far as possible the injurious effects of the war.

Fortunately, since the accession of the present Government to office, circumstances have enabled us to make considerable progress in this direction. The negotiation with Persia concerning Herat broke down, and we have reverted to the provisions of the Treaty of Paris of 1867, under which Persia has undertaken not to interfere with Afghanistan. Abdul Rahman has been received by the people of Cabul, and generally in Eastern Afghanistan, without opposition. Our troops have been withdrawn to the Khyber Pass without a shot having been fired at them. We have decided to abandon the Kurram Valley. On the side of Candahar the want of power or of good faith, or of both, on the part of the Wali Shere Ali Khan which resulted in the defection of his troops and brought about the disaster of Maiwand, has freed us from the obligation which the late Government unwisely undertook to establish him as an independent ruler of Candahar supported by British troops. Although the defeat of General Burrows at Maiwand is deeply to be deplored, the successful march of Sir Frederick Roberts from Cabul to Candahar and his decisive victory over Ayub Khan have retrieved this disaster, and in Lord Ripon's opinion our military reputation in Afghanistan has been amply sustained.

CANDAHAR TO BE ABANDONED

45. (*Hartington to Ripon 11 November 1880, Cab/37/3/69*)

Extract

It is not contended that there is now, more than in the past, anything in our relations with the tribes on our frontier, or the more powerful tribes which inhabit Kandahar and the surrounding province, which makes it necessary for us to establish a military post or a military protectorate at Kandahar. It is as a measure of defence against some power far more formidable than any Afghan race that the extension of our military frontier is recommended; and it is both as to the existence of such a danger, and as to the expediency of this mode of resisting it, if it does exist, that it is deprecated.

Her Majesty's Government, sharing the opinions of some of the most eminent Indian statesmen of past and present times, and up to a very recent date of every Minister of the Crown responsible for Indian policy, consider that there exists no such danger or apprehension of danger to the security of India from possible foreign invasion as would justify the Government in taking measures which must certainly lead immediately to very heavy additions to their large military expenditure, which will cause a constant strain on the organization of the Native Army, and which will almost certainly involve us in future complications and difficulties, the nature of which it is easy to anticipate though their exact form cannot be predicted. They are of opinion that recent experience has done nothing to strengthen the arguments of those who desire, as a military measure, to advance the Indian frontier, and much to verify the forebodings of those who were opposed to that policy. The advances of the Russian frontier which have taken place in recent years were foreseen, and their influence upon our position in India was deliberately considered, by Lord Lawrence and other Indian statesmen, on whose advice the Home Government repeatedly declined to permit itself to be committed to a policy of military extension. Those advances, although they have been continuous and steady, have not been effected without great difficulties both of a military and administrative character. They have secured to Russia no position of formidable strength; they have added nothing to her military resources; and they have been and are still attended by all the disadvantages which had been anticipated, as the result of an indefinite extension of her military position in an unproductive region inhabited by uncivilized and hostile tribes.

Her Majesty's Government are unable to admit that the mere fact of the existence of Russian military positions some hundred miles nearer to the North-Western frontier of India constitutes in itself any cause for anxiety, or for apprehending the possibility of an invasion of India from that quarter.

The Defence of India

46. (*Ripon Memorandum 2 September 1881, Cab/37/5/17*)

Extract

I have no dislike and no fear of Russia; I have always thought that it was altogether unnecessary to seek for an explanation of Russia's advance in Central Asia in any far-reaching scheme of Indian conquest; the circumstances in which she has been placed seem to me quite sufficient to account for that advance without supposing her to be animated by any special hostility to England, or by any deep designs against our Power in the East. I can scarcely conceive it possible that any Russian Government can seriously desire to acquire the position of a vast territory like India lying at an enormous distance from their own country, and I have the fullest confidence that England could successfully defend herself against any attack which Russia could possibly make against her Indian dominions. But I hold that Russian interference in Afghanistan is to be deprecated in the interests of England and of Russia alike, and I am prepared therefore to accept Lord Hartington's declaration, and will proceed to review the present situation from the point of view which it involves.

That situation is very different from what it was when Lord Derby transmitted towards the end of 1875 the Memorandum which was drawn up by the English Foreign Office in reply to Prince Gortschakoff's Memorandum of April in that year, and which, if I mistake not, is the last formal attempt at anything in the nature of a friendly understanding with Russia on the subject of Central Asia. The annexation of the Akhal country has brought the Russian frontier so close to Merv as to render it almost certain that the next collision with the Tekke-Turkomans will lead to an expedition against that place, and will practically render the sphere of Russia's influence in Central Asia, if not her actual possessions, conterminous with the northern boundary of Afghanistan. It has long been the endeavour of wise English statesmen to postpone the existence of this state of things, but it is, I think, impossible any longer to doubt that it will now be realized in a very short time, not improbably in the course of next year. When this happens, and Russia is practically conterminous with Afghanistan, the danger of that interference with Afghan affairs, which Lord Hartington's declaration binds us to resist, will, if nothing is done to obviate it, become very imminent.

The Defence of India

47. (*Hartington Memorandum for Cabinet 22 May 1882, Cab/37/8/35*)

Extract

I do not think that the spirit in which our overtures on the Persian boundary question have been met by the Russian Government offers any hope that they would enter into any engagement which would give us any real security, or would in any way limit their power of using Afghanistan as a means of giving us trouble whenever circumstances would make it convenient. I must admit that my opinions as to Russian policy in Central Asia have been somewhat modified by the course of recent negotiations. I was disposed to attach a good deal of importance to the 'imperious necessity' argument, and to believe that their advances and annexations had been forced upon them by the conduct of their Turkoman neighbours, or by their own officers using that conduct as a pretext. But it does now appear that they have reached a point where it would, if they wished it, be so easy to obtain a comparatively settled frontier, and to impose a limit to further annexations, that I cannot but look on their reluctance to entertain any proposals in this direction as a proof that they prefer to take the chances of possible complications with us in Afghanistan, in order to secure the advantage of a position in which their power of giving us annoyance and bringing pressure to bear on us will be increased.

AFGHAN BOUNDARIES

48. (*Notes by Currie 25 April 1883, Cab/37/10/29*)

Extract

M. de Giers informed Sir E. Thornton in April last that he considered it to be of great importance that the boundary of Afghanistan from Khoja Saleh to the Persian frontier in the neighbourhood of Sarakhs should be 'formally and definitely' laid down, and that he had instructed Prince Lobanow to endeavour to induce Her Majesty's Government to agree to the adoption of measures for this purpose.

M. Zinoview, the new Director of the Asiatic Department of the Russian Foreign Office, has recently spoken in the same sense to Mr. Kennedy. He talked of the Central Asian question as 'now confined to questions of frontier towards Persia and Afghanistan, and expressed his hope and wish of settling that question in a manner satisfactory to England'. He said that the present moment was favourable, and that Russia's sole aim was to obtain and exercise moral influence over the nomadic and thieving Turkomans, in order to render secure the commercial routes between the Caspian and Russian Turkestan. The most important question was to define the Persian frontier from Baba Durma to Sarakhs, which concerned solely Russia and Persia. From Sarakhs the frontier [of Afghanistan] would be drawn eastwards to Khoja Saleh on the Oxus.

The object of the Russian Foreign Office in making these protestations may be only to keep the British Government quiet while they are settling the boundary question with Persia, and annexing the Ateks and Merv, with a view to a fresh departure in the direction of Herat as soon as that process is accomplished. But, on the other hand, it may be observed that the position which Russia is now on the point of attaining is the one which she has been, more or less openly, aiming at for years past.

M. de Giers says that his Government 'would have no particular objection to Candahar being occupied by Her Majesty's forces, or even British authorities exercising controlling influence at Herat, but they had a right to expect that Russian influence should be allowed to prevail in the countries to the north of Afghanistan and Persia, with which they were encouraging the establishment of commercial relations in the hope of imbuing their inhabitants with ideas of civilization'.

49. (*F.O. Memorandum by Barrington 11 March 1885, Cab/37/14/13*)

Extract

In regard to the questions raised as to the Sarik Turkomans, Her Majesty's Government have to observe that according to the information in their possession Badgheis, including Penjdeh, has formed a part of Afghanistan ever since Afghanistan became a kingdom; that those districts were, as dependencies of Herat, under the rule of Shere Ali Khan; that the tribes who have settled at Pendjeh during the last quarter of a century have fully acknowledged that they are within Afghan territory, that they have paid revenue in some form or other to the Herat authorities; and that a Naib, or Deputy of the Governor of Herat, has, as a rule, resided amongst them both before and since 1873. When the Ameer, therefore, on account of the approach of the Russian power, began, some considerable time anterior to the Russian occupation of Merv, to establish his hold more firmly on Pendjeh, he was merely exercising rights which he considered to belong justly to him.

In the opinion of Her Majesty's Government, the Ameer's title to the sovereignty of the tract in question cannot be vitiated by the presence within his frontier of a tribe the other part of which is in territory now claimed by Russia. It happens not infrequently on other Asiatic frontiers that tribes are divided by territorial boundaries, and Her Majesty's Government see no reason why a division should be impracticable in the present instance or serious difficulties arise on that account in the case of the frontier now to be demarcated between Russia and Afghanistan.

On these and other grounds Her Majesty's Government think it right at once to say that they are unable to give their adhesion to any understanding by which Pendjeh or other districts claimed as Afghan shall, without enquiry on the spot, be excluded from Afghanistan.

It now remains for Her Majesty's Government to deal with the new proposal contained in the concluding portion of M. de Giers' Memorandum, namely, that failing an agreement as to the limits of a zone, the two Governments might endeavour to come to an understanding in regard to an actual line of frontier, the direction of which is described in the following terms:

'Starting from a point on the right bank of the Heri-Rud about 10 versts south of Zulfikar, the line would pass by Kehrizi Elias and Hekrizi Soume to the rivulet of Yegri Gruek, would follow the heights bordering on the right bank of that rivulet to the ruins of Tchemenibid, and thence the chain of hills on the right bank of the Kuschk to Havuzi Khan, whence it would run to a point situated to the north of Meruchak, which would be left to Afghanistan. Starting from this point, the line of demarcation would follow the crest of the heights on the north of the valley of the Kaisor and on the west of the valley of Sangalak, and leaving Andkhoi to the east would run to Khoja Saleh on the Amou Daria.' This line to be conditional on the Ameer undertaking not to build fortifications which might become a menace to the populations on the other side of the frontier.

Her Majesty's Government regret that they are unable to agree to the proposed line or to the conditions annexed to it.

HERAT MEANS WAR

50. (*Gladstone to the Queen 25 March 1885, Cab/41/19/18. Printed in Letters of Queen Victoria 2nd series, III, 630*)

Extract

The Cabinet also thought that Lord Granville should communicate with the Russian ambassador and point out to him the necessary consequence of any design upon Herat, in bringing about a case of war between the two countries, according to the policy of the British Empire, as it has now been understood and established for nearly half a century . . .

GRANVILLE STANDS ON ZULFICAR, HAVING ABANDONED PENDJEH

51. (*F.O. Memorandum 18 June 1885, Cab/37/15/22*)

Extract

Lord Granville replied on the 11 June as follows:
'M. l'Ambassadeur,

'I have the honour to acknowledge the receipt of your Excellency's communication of yesterday.

'I will not fail to give the information contained in it to my successor as soon as his appointment is made.

'In the meantime, the Russian Government will have clearly understood that the limit of our demand is to secure Zulfikar to the Afghans in exchange for Pendjeh, which arrangement you were authorized by the Emperor to agree to on the 17th April.

'This authority was given in answer to the statement made by Lord Kimberley at our interview on the 14th April, which your Excellency will remember, that it was a *sine qua non* that the Zulfikar Pass should be left in possession of Afghanistan.'

On the 13th instant the Viceroy of India telegraphed:

'As I have already informed Ameer on the strength of your telegram of the 4th May, that his frontier would be drawn to north of Zulfikar Pass, as well as of Maruchak, and as he has made a corresponding announcement to his Sirdars it would be difficult for this Government to acquiesce in any modification of that line in a sense adverse to interests of Ameer without his free consent. We therefore strongly deprecate any further concessions of the kind for which Russian Government now appears to be contending. They would discredit our character for constancy and good faith in eyes of Ameer and of his people, and my Council is united in opinion that surrender on Pendjeh entitles us to vindicate at all hazards the line that has been already accorded to Ameer. The reason of His Highness attaching so much value to Zulfikar Pass was on account of its commanding the roads to Gulran.

SALISBURY MAINTAINS GRANVILLE'S POLICY ON ZULFICAR

52. (*Salisbury to Thornton 1 July 1885, Cab/15/37/42*)

Extract

M. de Staal entirely concurred with me in the importance of expedition, and promised to represent my views on the matter to his Government.

I further pointed out to him that the questions between us depended not so much on the intrinsic value of the localities (which, even in a strategic point of view, were variously estimated), but on the promise which England had made to the Ameer of Afghanistan. We had promised that the boundary-line should go to the north of the Zulfikar Pass; we had made that promise in reliance on the consent of Russia, when Pendjeh was yielded by England, that the Zulfikar Pass would be yielded by Russia; and from that engagement which we had so made it was not open to us to recede.

DUFFERIN EXPLAINS THE DIFFICULTIES OF MAINTAINING AFGHANISTAN AS A BUFFER STATE

53. *Dufferin to Churchill 30 July 1885, Cab/37/16/46*)

Extract

I have never personally felt very cordially inclined to the 'Buffer' policy, and I have often had misgivings as to the wisdom of the engagements into which we entered with the Amir under the auspices of my predecessor. In spite of the cautious wording of the agreement, its obligations are very absolute and specific, especially as entered into by a Power like England with a weak and uncivilized Government. Under this stipulation, we are bound to assist the Amir to the best of our ability, though in whatever manner we may think expedient, in the event of the integrity of his dominions being threatened by a Foreign Power. Now, what are his dominions? A range of thinly populated and open frontier many hundred miles in length, destitute of strategical positions, and of defenders skilful enough to use them to advantage if they did exist, exposed at all points to the incursions of every neighbour, and so distant from our own military base as to make it out of the question for us to send any troops to protect what we have undertaken to defend. This condition of affairs compels us to combine such efforts as it may be possible for us to make with those of an ignorant, jealous, and boastful, though resolute and intelligent Chief, whose own position and freedom of action are endangered and hampered by circumstances and considerations which render it difficult for him to comply with our wishes or follow out any programme we may trace for him, even when it is in accordance with his own ideas and obvious interests. Unfortunately in many instances some of our recommendations are naturally opposed to what he or any one else in his position might fairly consider to be advantageous to the maintenance of his own authority and independence. Even supposing that the Ruler himself were to prove as docile and subservient as we could desire, his subjects consist of a conglomeration of divided and insubordinate tribes, or else of subservient and alien races hating his rule, and ready to welcome the first comer who will advance to their liberation, while most of the subordinates through whom he administers his provinces are either incompetent, disobedient, corrupt, or disloyal, and sometimes all these things at once. It is evident that an offensive and defensive alliance with a person so situated possesses every sort of uninviting characteristic; but when we have further to take into account the duplicity natural to every Afghan, the facilities possessed by Russia for intrigue, and the consequent chance of all our friend's professions being insincere and his turning out a traitor on our hands, the advantages to be derived from the 'buffer' policy become very attentuated. . . .

But I would most earnestly deprecate attempting to exact from him concessions which he could not grant without risking his hold over his people, or which would drive him into the arms of Russia. As I said at the beginning of this letter, though by no means a warm advocate of the 'buffer' policy, I think that it should have a fair and full trial, and that it would be a thousand pities if, through any impatience or unreasonable demands, we should revive the bitter ill-feeling between ourselves and the Afghans which successive invasions of their country have very naturally created, but which might, by skilful management on our part, be made rapidly to disappear. We have everything to gain and nothing to lose by being friends with them, whereas their declared enmity and their co-operation with Russia would force upon us a policy which, though perhaps not disadvantageous in its ultimate result, should, if possible, be avoided, or at all events postponed to the last moment, on account of the fierce political controversies it would excite in England, as well as on account of the great strain it would impose upon our resources here.

SALISBURY SEEKS GERMAN ARBITRATION

54. (*Paper shown to Herbert Bismarck 3 August 1885 by Currie, enclosed in Currie to Salisbury 4 August, S.P. Printed in Greaves, pp. 240–1*)

Extract

The position is critical and, if a settlement is not arrived at within the next few months, is very likely to lead to war. The Russian Commanders are enterprising and are eager for a dash at Herat. The Afghans are rash, and another Pendjeh affair may occur at any moment. Either of these contingencies would inevitably produce a rupture between England and Russia, which would lead to hostilities, not only in Central Asia, but in every part of the world where England could deal a blow at her antagonist. The point on which we should concentrate the greatest part of our energies would be the cutting of the communications between Russia and her Central Asian possessions. For this it would be an absolute necessity for us to obtain an entrance to the Black Sea for our ships, and this we should unquestionably do by some means or other, whatever view Europe might hold as to the localization of the war.

In order to avert this calamity, the only plan seems to be to make an appeal to Prince Bismarck to mediate between the two Countries. The question at issue being now reduced to the one point of Zulficar, all that would be required to bring about a settlement, would be that H. H. should adjudicate upon the interpretation of the words of M. de Giers's Telegram of April 16 agreeing to cede Zulficar in exchange for Pendjeh . . .

The Prince would be adding lustre to his renown, and it would not be the least of his great achievements that his moderating and pacific influence should have secured peace between two of the great Powers of Europe, when all other hopes of agreement had failed.

If he were to effect this, he would secure for himself and his Country the lasting gratitude of England, and he would be laying the foundations of a closer and more intimate alliance between the two Countries.

The present Prime Minister of England is known to be favorable to such an alliance in the fullest sense of the terms, and once established, the English people, who have the strongest leaning towards their old Protestant ally, would not allow their Government (from whatever party it might be taken) to swerve from it. A close union between the greatest military power and the greatest naval power would produce a combination that would not only secure the peace of the world, but would also be in the highest degree advantageous to the interests of the two Countries. It would put Germany at ease as regards the safety of her Colonial possessions in the event of European complications, and it would leave England free to defend her interests in the event of unprovoked aggression on the part of Russia against her Indian Empire, without fear of hostile neutrality on the part of the European Powers.

THE PROBLEM OF DEFENDING INDIA

55. (*Brackenbury Memorandum, Intelligence Branch War Office 25 January 1887, Cab/37/19/8*)

Extract

I have before me the Russian plan (Kuropatkin's) for an advance into Afghanistan or on India, with the notes of the Indian Intelligence Department upon it; also the proposals for the defence of the north-west frontier, by the Defence Committee in 1885, with notes by Sir Charles MacGregor, Sir T. D. Baker, and Sir Frederick Roberts. I find an universal concurrence of opinion that it is impossible to defend India on the Indus; that it is essential that we should reoccupy Candahar at the first available opportunity, such as the first intimation of the Russians crossing the Afghan frontier, or—should it happen first—the death of the Ameer.

And there is universal concurrence of opinion that our communications with the frontier are still gravely deficient for defensive purposes.

My own opinion is that the one true means of defending India is to strike at the Russian communications with her Trans-Caspian dominions. This can only be done from a base on the Black Sea; from a base in the Mediterranean, through Turkey in Asia; or from a base in the Persian Gulf, through Persia. The last operation, which would be far the most effective, would require railway communication from the Persian Gulf; the second, railway communication from the Mediterranean to the interior.

Yet, little by little, we have let Persia slip out of our hands into the grasp of the Czar, to an extent which the most recent despatches from Tehran have emphasized. We have taken no steps for the construction of a railway from the Mediterranean into the interior of Asia Minor. We have allowed Batoum, the one open port which would have given us a base on the Black Sea, to be strongly fortified by Russia; and now we have the best reason to know that Russia is devoting her efforts to securing the northern end of the Bosphorus against all comers. Thus, our position for any such operations is in no way improving; while, on the other hand, Russia is hourly strengthening hers in the Black Sea, in Transcaucasia, in Persia, and in Central Asia.

56. (*India Office Memorandum November 1891, Cab/37/20/29*)

Extract

Lord Salisbury agreed in the expediency of obtaining the best technical opinions as to the point at which Russian aggression could be most advantageously met, but doubted the advantage of instructing the Commission to trace a military frontier beyond which Russia should not be allowed to advance.

Firstly, His Lordship believes such a course to be impossible in practice, for it implies a continuity of policy, which has not been shown in recent times, and is scarcely likely to be shown in the future, in the conduct of Government by successive administrations in this country.

Secondly, the settlement of such frontier appears to be superfluous. If Afghanistan is to be the only, or the principal, theatre of war, the point where Russian aggression is to be directed must depend largely on the circumstances of the moment. The contents of Major-General Brackenbury's memorandum tend to show that the alternative course of making war with Russia all over the world is an empty phrase unless Great Britain has the command of the Turkish army, and, in Lord Salisbury's opinion, it is as certain as any diplomatic forecast can be that Great Britain will never have that command.

Lastly. Although this is a military objection which Lord Salisbury offers with great diffidence, he would ask whether the idea of a military frontier line does not ignore the character which the struggle between Great Britain and Russia, whenever it comes, must assume. That struggle will be a war, not of battles, but of devastation. The security of British India will be, not to defeat Russia, but to make it impossible for a Russian army to live within reach of the British possessions. And this implies not a frontier line, but a frontier region.

V

The Mediterranean Alliance

CURRIE AND BISMARCK DISCUSS CONSTANTINOPLE AND EGYPT

57. (*Currie, Notes of a conversation with Prince Bismarck 28 September 1885, S.P. Printed in Greaves, pp. 251–3*)

Extract

He admitted that he could not get the Austrians to agree with him as to the unimportance of the acquisition of Consple by Russia, but said that people in Germany who had thoroughly studied the question took his view.

Austria would no doubt be disposed to resist the advance of Russia if she could count on the alliance of England. I said it was difficult for any one who had been brought up in the English view of foreign policy to admit that the possession of Consple by Russia would not be a misfortune for the rest of Europe. Surely her increase of prestige and the stimulus it would give to her energies would alone be a menace to Germany and still more to Austria, while it would inevitably bring the Slav populations of the Balkan peninsula under her rule. As far as England was concerned the evil result was perhaps confined to the loss of the only vulnerable point where we could strike at Russia in the event of her attacking India and by occupying the Black Sea with our fleet could cut her communication in the Caucasus.

He would not admit that it would strengthen Russia in any way. She had already more population than she could manage . . .

I pressed him on this question of the Russian possession of Consple in the hope of discovering what his real intentions are in the matter. He gave me the impression of having labored, with only partial success, to convince himself that Germany could stand aside and leave Consple either to fall into Russian hands, or to be kept out of them by an Anglo-Austrian alliance.

His language occasionally betrays distrust of Austria. Towards Russia his tone is one of dislike and contempt and he dwells with pleasure on stories of Russian corruption, and dishonesty.

The conversation then turned to Egypt. He said the existence of the Canal made it essential for England to hold the Country. I asked if our naval superiority would not enable us to secure the use of the Canal in time of war. He said that was not enough as the banks might be occupied and the canal blocked.

I said that your view was that our occupation should not be permanent, but that you could not fix a date for evacuation, and that you considered that we ought to retain a privileged position, and that the task of sending troops if necessary to restore order should be confined to us. Did he think that the Powers would agree to our having such a position? He said he saw no reason why the German Powers should object. Russia or France might do so, and our danger would be that Turkish troops supported by Russia, or the French fleet might arrive before us—I said your idea was that we might have troops in Cyprus for the purpose. He said that our principal difficulty would no doubt be with France, but we need not so much mind her, as she could not go to war with us, without security on her Eastern frontier which he did not intend to give her. I spoke of the efforts we had made and were making to improve the condition of the people. He seemed to look upon this rather as an amiable weakness on our part, and said that in Egypt they complained that we had abolished the courbash and that the peasants would not work.

SALISBURY SEEKS AN ANGLO-TURKISH SOLUTION TO THE EGYPTIAN PROBLEM

58. (*Salisbury, Draft to Drummond-Wolff 7 August 1885, Cab/ 37/16/48*)

Extract

These considerations make it a matter of high importance both to the welfare of Egypt and to the objects which Her Majesty's Government have had in view, that the military co-operation of the Sultan should be obtained in maintaining order in some portions of the Egyptian territory which are no longer protected by the Egyptian troops. Such a step on his part would do much to establish his hold over the country and the maintenance of his just rights as ascertained by Treaty, and it would add lustre to the prestige which the name of his Government enjoys in the more distant provinces of his Empire.

From communications, however, which have been made to Her Majesty's Government by the Turkish Ambassador in London, it appears probable that the Sultan would insist, as a condition of any such co-operation as that of which I have spoken, that his troops should not only be stationed in the south of Egypt, but also in the capital of the country, in Cairo itself; the object of His Majesty being that, so long as the English occupation continued, the Turkish occupation should continue side by side with it.

Objections may be raised, in principle, to this arrangement from many points of view, but if it were guarded against misapprehension, if precautions were taken that the arrangement was not turned to objects for which it was not designed, the proposal does not seem to Her Majesty's Government inadmissible in itself.

Objections taken by other Governments, especially by the Government of France, to any such proposal, are well known to His Majesty. I do not venture to forecast how far those objections may go, and to what extent they are to be looked upon as insuperable. There is no doubt that they will constitute a material obstacle to the accomplishment of the Sultan's wishes. If they are to be overcome at all, it can only be by the lapse of time.

It is possible that other considerations may arise which may modify the view which the French Government takes upon this subject. I do not think it is necessary to abandon all hope of some such change in their policy, but in the meantime it will be your duty to impress upon the Sultan that the best road to the accomplishment of what he desires is the introduction of Turkish troops into those parts of Egypt where apparently they will not meet with any objection on the part of the Government of France. From this point of view, as well as from others, it will not be difficult for you to show to the Sultan that his real interest lies in the acceptance, on his part, in principle at all events, of the policy of co-operating in the military protection of the southern territories contiguous to Egypt.

For the present, the view of Her Majesty's Government is that the direct dominion of the Khedive should not be carried further in the valley of the Nile than the region which may be undeniably controlled from a military station at the furthest terminus of the railways.

59. (*Drummond-Wolff to Salisbury 16 January 1886, Cab/37/17/4*)

Extract

I am informed that his Excellency Moukhtar Pasha has written to Constantinople that some modification should be obtained in Article II of the Anglo-Turkish Convention of the 24th October 1885, so as to extend the provisions of that Article to military operations.

Of course, no report of this kind can be deemed authentic unless confirmed by the person to whom it refers, but my informant is generally correct in his statements, and many things combine to support his present allegation.

The object of his Excellency the Ghazi is clearly to reorganize an Egyptian army in the first instance, and, with a force thus prepared, to advance himself to the Soudan and to take the measures that appear to him desirable for the pacification of the country, whether by military operations, or by negotiations, or a combination of the two methods.

In such a course of proceeding I can see much advantage for the Sultan and his Government. It would re-establish the Ottoman power not only in the Soudan, but in Egypt, to an extent which Moukhtar Pasha himself would no doubt consider desirable, but which I venture to think is not only undesirable, but dangerous, and which I should regret to see encouraged or promoted by any action of Her Majesty's Government.

To such a course I would beg leave to offer the strongest possible objection. What, I believe, we wish to see in the Soudan is not conquest, but pacification. The latter, I believe, can be achieved by the limitation of Ottoman intervention to the provisions of the Convention as they now stand. Any alteration introduced in the direction pointed out by the Ghazi would inevitably lead to warfare and conquest to an extent we cannot calculate.

The influence of the Caliph may, I think, be beneficially, if judiciously, exercised; but Turkish methods in war could lead only to bloodshed and hatred.

BRITAIN GIVES DIPLOMATIC SUPPORT TO THE UNIFICATION OF
BULGARIA

60. (*Salisbury to Morier 2 December 1885, in Cecil III, 249–50*)

The issue from the beginning to the end, under various forms,
has been whether we would or would not pledge ourselves against
any alteration of the Treaty of Berlin. We have steadily declined
to do so until some account had been taken of the desire of the
inhabitants of the Provinces concerned. The three Empires
entirely declined to take any account of the wishes of the populations, and Turkey denounced the idea as contrary to 'les idées
conservatrices' now dominant in Europe ...

I doubt very much whether any amount of Resolutions or
'sommations' or other forms of bluster will induce the Roumelians to give in. If that is so, then material force must be used.
Neither Austria nor Russia can allow the other to send troops into
Bulgaria—and if they induce the Sultan to do it, will Russian
public opinion acquiesce? Whether they do or not, we can do
nothing but stand aside if they go in for a policy of blank repression. I think Turkey is making a great mistake. An independent
national feeling might be got up in Bulgaria that, joined to that
already existing in Roumania, might make the Russian passage to
Constantinople very difficult.

61. (*Malet to Iddesleigh 21 August 1886, F.O. 343/3*)

Extract

... The sum of it is that if England shows a bold foreign policy
and makes Russia thoroughly understand that we are ready to go
to war for the sake of the integrity of the Ottoman Empire we may
count upon peace, but if we shilly-shally and let no one know what
we intend we are in a measurable distance of war.

62. (*Iddesleigh to Salisbury 31 August 1886, S.P.*)

We see what the Triple Alliance means. There is to be no fighting
between Austria and Russia. Excellent if the fighting is to be
prevented by counselling and supporting a lovely pacific policy:
but most dangerous if the only method of keeping the peace is by
treating Russia as a Juggernaut car and encouraging her to crush
all and everything in its course, so that course does not come the
way of Germany. The next thing will be the Russian occupation
of Bulgaria.

Another disagreeable feature of the business has been the attitude of Turkey. Though she would fight for Constantinople she will not say a syllable for Roumelia or at all events for Bulgaria. Perhaps she is taken with the idea that Russia should occupy the one and herself the other. This may be the solution, and a most disagreeable one it would be for us. We should soon feel the influence of a Russianized Sultan in Egypt and India.

But the great point is to influence the German powers and next to that to work on the Turk.

SALISBURY'S ANXIETY TO PRESERVE PEACE

63. (*Salisbury to Morier 19 January 1887, S.P.*)

Extract

It seems to me to be our strong interest now that Russia should not attack Austria; and therefore we must lose no opportunity of putting forward in the fairest light we can the probability that Austria will not stand alone. I do not of course want to send any direct message to Giers: I should deprecate that anything were said to show undue distrust of Russia. But you should lose no opportunity of representing the importance attached to the Austrian alliance by public opinion here . . . Of course I do not mean by the above to suggest that your tone to the Russians should be more hostile, or that you should give the impression either that we mean to encourage Austria to do so. Our interest is a peaceful issue. I am only anxious that Russia should not believe too readily that that issue is to be reached by bullying Austria. My impression is that Austria will resist and that she will not be left alone if she does. Nor will Austria want for other allies. Italy is very deeply preoccupied with the menace which any disturbance of European peace in S.E. Europe might carry with it to Italian interests on the shore of the Mediterranean and she has made overtures to us very unusual in the earnestness . . . with which they are pressed.

64. (*Salisbury to the Queen 30 January 1887, in Letters of Queen Victoria 3rd series, I, 265*)

Extract

Germany has made it more and more clear that we are to expect no help from her in resisting the pretensions of Russia. She will not even promise to rescue Austria; she will thwart Russia in nothing; her whole thoughts are devoted to the apprehended struggle with France. The effect of this attitude on our policy in the South-east of Europe is, that it makes any conflict there very much more hazardous that it was. Our own interests, in the case of a Balkan war, we can protect: we can prevent Russia acquiring any foothold on the Ægean and on the Straits. But such a conflict would *now* menace Austria also; and we can do nothing effective to save Austria. Yet it is of great importance to us that Austria should not succumb. So long, therefore, as Germany is paralysed by this terror of France, it is a matter of very great importance that no conflict should break out in the Balkan peninsula; for Austria would probably be involved in it, and would probably be overthrown.

This is *not* a reason for allowing the occupation or domination of Bulgaria by Russia: to do so would only be to bring about the same result in a more circuitous fashion. But it *is* a reason for gaining time; and for avoiding any policy which would be so obviously derogatory to the Tsar in the eyes of his subjects, that it would force him into war. He is a passionate but slow-witted man: in his cooler moments hesitating and helpless, and nervous as to the political effects of war on his own country. If he can employ himself for some months on negotiations at Constantinople, which are very unlikely to come to any practical issue, the acutest moments of the crisis which paralyses Germany will have passed by; and when Germany has resumed her freedom of action, Austria will again be safe.

THE NEGOTIATION OF THE FIRST MEDITERRANEAN AGREEMENT

65. (*Salisbury to the Queen 2 February 1887, in Letters of Queen Victoria, 3rd series, I, 268–9*)

Extract

Yesterday Count Corti came to see Lord Salisbury. He was the bearer of propositions from the Italian Government for a closer understanding between Italy and England. He left a memorandum with Lord Salisbury, of which the effect was to offer an alliance in case of war against France. There were other propositions of co-operation which were more acceptable, such as common efforts for maintaining the *status quo* in the Ægean, the Adriatic, the Black Sea, and on the African Coast. But the paper ended with a proposal that, in case either Power was at war with France, the other Power would give it naval assistance. Lord Salisbury promised to bring the matter before his colleagues; but told Count Corti, first, that England never promised material assistance in view of an uncertain war, of which the object and cause were unknown; secondly, that any promise even of diplomatic co-operation could not be directed against any single Power such as France. But that, on the other hand, the policy of Italy and Great Britain was very similar; and that, within the limit of the principles mentioned by Lord Salisbury, we should be glad to co-operate with them; especially in the maintenance of the *status quo*.

To-day the matter was discussed at length in the Cabinet; and it was resolved Lord Salisbury should draw up a reply in the above sense. This afternoon he saw Count Hatzfeldt, who brought a message from Prince Bismarck, earnestly recommending an understanding of this kind as a means of preserving peace. A similar message had been sent by Sir E. Malet in a private and secret telegram. Lord Salisbury discussed the matter at length with the German Ambassador in the same tone. He impressed upon the latter that, though the assistance of England might be confidently looked for to maintain the *status quo* in the Mediterranean, and might be very probably looked for if France were to attack Italy, and Italy found herself in any danger, it was very unlikely to be given if Italy made an aggressive war on France. Count Hatzfeldt pressed the case of a war in which Italy should be the nominal assailant, having attacked merely to anticipate a certain attack from France. In this case, Lord Salisbury did not hold out any hope of English sympathy and aid.

66. (*Salisbury to the Queen 10 February 1887, in Letters of Queen Victoria 3rd series, I, 272*)

Extract

Lord Salisbury . . . encloses—in print—two documents which have been the result of the Cabinet Council held to-day. The first is the exchange of despatches which constitute the *entente* with the Italian Government. The English despatch, which, of course, is the only one binding on this country, is so drawn as to leave entirely unfettered the discretion of your Majesty's Government, as to whether, in any paticular case, they will carry their support of Italy as far as 'material co-operation'. But short of a pledge, upon this subject, it undoubtedly carries very far the *relations plus intimes* which have been urged upon us. It is as close an alliance as the Parliamentary character of our institutions will permit. Your Majesty's advisers recommend it on the whole as necessary in order to avoid serious danger. If, in the present grouping of nations, which Prince Bismarck tells us is now taking place, England was left out in isolation, it might well happen that the adversaries, who are coming against each other on the Continent, might treat the English Empire as divisible booty, by which their differences might be adjusted; and, though England could defend herself, it would be at fearful risk and cost. The interests of Italy are so closely parallel to our own that we can combine with her safely. The despatches are only drafts; and the English one will of course not be signed till it has your Majesty's approval.

67. (*Anglo-Italian exchange of Notes 12 February 1887, Cab/37/19/13. Printed in B.D.VIII.2*)

No. 1. Count Corti to the Marquis of Salisbury.

Le Soussigné, Ambassadeur Extraordinaire et Plénipotentiaire de Sa Majesté le Roi d'Italie, a reçu de son Gouvernement l'ordre de porter à la connaissance de son Excellence le Marquis de Salisbury, Principal Secrétaire d'État de Sa Majesté Britannique pour les Affaires Étrangères, ce qui suit:

Le Gouvernement de Sa Majesté le Roi, animé du désir d'établir avec celui de Sa Majesté la Reine une entente sur diverses questions concernant leurs intérêts, est d'avis que ce but pourrait être atteint par l'adoption des bases suivantes:

1. On maintiendra, autant que possible, le *statu quo* dans la Méditerranée, ainsi que dans l'Adriatique, la Mer Égée, et la Mer Noire.

On aura, par conséquent, soin de surveiller et, au besoin, d'empêcher tout changement qui, sous la forme d'annexion, occupation, protectorat, ou d'une tout autre manière quelconque, porterait atteinte à la situation actuelle, au détriment des deux Puissances.

2. Si le maintien du *statu quo* devient impossible, on fera en sorte qu'il ne se produise une modification quelconque qu'à la suite d'un accord préalable entre les deux Puissances.

3. L'Italie est toute prête à appuyer l'œuvre de la Grande-Bretagne en Égypte.

La Grande-Bretagne, à son tour, est disposée à appuyer, en cas d'envahissements de la part d'une tierce Puissance, l'action de l'Italie sur tout autre point quelconque du littoral nord d'Afrique, et notamment dans la Tripolitaine et la Cyrénaïque.

4. En général et pour autant que les circonstances le comporteront, l'Italie et l'Angleterre se promettent appui mutuel dans la Méditerranée pour tout différend qui surgirait entre l'une d'elles et une tierce Puissance.

En exprimant la confiance que ces bases recevront l'assentiment du Gouvernement de Sa Majesté la Reine, le Soussigné saisit, &c.

No. 2. The Marquis of Salisbury to Count Corti

(Secret)

The statement of Italian policy which is contained in your Excellency's despatch of the [12 February 1887] has been received by Her Majesty's Government with great satisfaction, as it enables them to reciprocate cordially Count Robilant's friendly sentiments, and to express their own desire to co-operate heartily with the Government of Italy in matters of common interest to the two countries.

The character of that co-operation must be decided by them, when the occasion for it arises, according to the circumstances of the case. In the interest of peace, and of the independence of the territories adjacent to the Mediterranean Sea, Her Majesty's Government wish to act in the closest concert and agreement with that of Italy. Both Powers desire that the shores of the Euxine, the Ægean, and the Adriatic, and the northern coast of Africa shall remain in the same hands as now. If, owing to some calamitous event, it becomes impossible to maintain the absolute *status quo*, both Powers desire that there shall be no extension of the domination of any other Great Power over any portion of those coasts.

It will be the earnest desire of Her Majesty's Government to give their best co-operation, as hereinbefore expressed, to the Government of Italy in maintaining these cardinal principles of policy.

THE NEGOTIATIONS FOR AN EGYPTIAN CONVENTION IN 1887

68. (*Salisbury to the Queen* 10 *February* 1887, *in Letters of Queen Victoria 3rd series, I,* 273)

Extract

It has become evident that a *permanent* occupation of Egypt will not only be against our pledges, and exceedingly costly; but it also means permanent disagreement with France and Turkey, which may at any moment take an acute form. On the other hand we are pledged not to leave Egypt to the danger either of internal anarchy, or of foreign invasion. The enclosed 'suggestions' are designed to reconcile these difficulties. England undertakes to leave Egypt in five years, if at the time there is no apprehension of internal or external disturbance; but she retains the power of entering again at any time if there shall be danger of invasion, or anarchy, or of Egypt not fulfilling her engagements.

It is very probable that France will not consent to these proposals, and that the negotiations may be protracted; but they will be acceptable to Turkey, which chiefly desires to see the flag of the infidel disappear; and they will exonerate your Majesty's Government from any charge of attempting to ignore their pledges.

69. (*Salisbury to Drummond-Wolff* 23 *February* 1887, *in Cecil IV,* 41–2)

We are steering in very narrow channels and we are in constant danger of running aground on one side or the other. On the one hand, English opinion is not prepared for an evacuation of Egypt, still less for the abandonment of it. They will not be reconciled to it till they see that France is strong enough to enforce it, and that conviction they naturally cannot acquire till this suspense period is ended one way or the other. On the other hand, we must keep it diplomatically in our power to satisfy France on account of Bismarck's attitude. His policy in a humbler walk of life would be called chantage. He is perpetually telling us of the offers France is making of reconciliation on the basis of an attack upon England in Egypt, and of the sacrifices which Germany makes by refusing these proposals; sacrifices for which, he adds, England must make some return, and then he demands this and that. I heartily wish we had never gone into Egypt. Had we not done so, we could snap our fingers at all the world. But the national, or acquisitional feeling has been roused; it has tasted the fleshpots and it will not let them go . . .

However, our only safe course is to follow out our negotiations on the lines of the instruction or 'suggestions'. They are sufficiently careful of our interests to be able to produce, if at any time it should be necessary to do so; on the other hand they are reasonable enough to deprive France of the pretext for breaking off in a huff.

70. (*Salisbury to Lyons 20 July 1887, in Cecil IV, 48–9*)

Extract

We cannot leave the Khedive to take his chance of foreign attack or native riot, and the French refuse to let us exercise the necessary powers of defence, unless we do it by continuing our military occupation. I see nothing for it but to sit still and drift awhile; a little further on in the history of Europe the conditions may have changed and we may be able to get some agreement arrived at which will justify evacuation. Till then we must simply refuse to evacuate.

Our relations with France are not pleasant at present. There are five or six different places where we are at odds:

1. She has destroyed the Convention at Constantinople
2. She will allow no Press law to pass
3. She is trying to back out of the arrangement on the Somali coast
4. She still occupies the New Hebrides
5. She destroys our fishing tackle, etc.
6. She is trying to elbow us out of at least two unpronounceable places on the West Coast of Africa

Can you wonder that there is, to my eyes, a silver lining even to the great black cloud of a Franco-German war?

71. (*Salisbury to White 2 November 1887, in Cecil IV, 71*)

The Suez Canal Convention has had the effect for the moment of improving our relations with France. After the experience I got of the Chancellor's pretty ways during Wolff's negotiations, I do not wish to depend upon his good will, and therefore shall keep friends with France as far as we can do it without paying too dear for it. The threat of making us uneasy in Egypt through the action of France is the only weapon he has against us, and we are free of him in proportion as we can blunt it.

SALISBURY REJECTS RUSSIAN OVERTURES AND RELUCTANTLY EXTENDS THE MEDITERRANEAN AGREEMENTS

72a. (*Morier to Salisbury 18 August 1887, F.O. 65/1300/Tel 61*)

Extract

I had an important conversation with M. de Giers yesterday. His Ex[cellency], referring to your Lordship's speech at the Mansion House, said it had given him and the Czar sincerest satisfaction. The favourable impression produced by it had been confirmed by reports from M. de Staal, testifying to the friendly spirit towards Russia which animated H.M.G. He believed this restoration of goodwill between the two powers might be utilized with great effect to tide over the present crisis on Bulgaria . . .

. . .

His Ex[cellency] was very anxious that he should not be regarded as having made formal overtures or proposals. All he wished was a serious exchange of views between two Powers who had no real cause of antagonism and whose *rapprochement* would be a benefit to all. Least of all did he suggest an agreement apart from, or in opposition to, others. Such an understanding would almost necessarily entail a general understanding. He said there were those who had very keenly hoped that the Afghan frontier negotiations would have led to a serious rupture and who bitterly lamented its favourable issue. This was the more reason to make it a stepping stone to a better understanding all round, and this was the light in which the Emperor as well as himself regarded our late accord.

72b. (*Salisbury to Morier 19 August 1887, F.O. 65/1300/Tel. 112*)

I do not think we can safely draw closer to Russia on subject of Bulgaria. We are agreed as to policy of having a Regent but we should not agree as to choice of that Regent. At present our attitude must be negative. Italy wishes to head a movement for Prince Ferdinand: Russia is as strong the other way. Porte leans to Russia. Austria, Italy, England are pressing Porte to be quiet and we are giving same advice to Italy.

73a. (*Salisbury to Lumley 28 October 1887, S.P. Partly printed in Cecil IV, 69–70*)

This is the result of Crispi's longing for some splashy interference in Bulgarian affairs. The two Powers, Austria and Italy, have made a proposal for telling Turkey that, if she resists Russia, she will be supported, but that if she makes herself Russia's vassal she will be invaded. The language is more diplomatic but that is the drift. Germany is ostensibly no party to this project. In secret she patronizes and presses it, in public she stands aloof,—and no doubt privately expresses her horror of it at St Petersburg. England may find it necessary to adhere rather than break up the alliance. But the step in the interests of peace is an unwise one, though very useful doubtless to Bismarck for taking the strain off his eastern frontier. But for us it commits the blunder of building on the Sultan's fitful and feeble disposition. Any calculation having that foundation will certainly fail. We shall get no permanent or reliable advantage from practising on his hopes and fears, while, if the arrangement gets out, it will back up the Panslavic feeling at Moscow, which is a genuine force.

We may not be able to prevent this project going on, but we must do what we can to put the drag on. But I wish Crispi would find another Foreign Minister.

73b. (*Salisbury to Karolyi and Catalani 12 December 1887, B.D. VIII, 13*)

Extract

In view of these considerations, the Undersigned, Her Majesty's Sec[retar]y of State for F[oreign] A[ffairs], etc.: is charged by Her Majesty's Government to communicate to the Austro-Hungarian and Italian Governments their entire adhesion to the nine points recited in the identic note of the two Powers, that is to say:—

1. The maintenance of peace, to the exclusion of all policy of aggression.

2. The maintenance of the *status quo* in the East based on the Treaties, to the exclusion of all policy of compensation.

3. The maintenance of the local autonomies established by those same Treaties.

4. The independence of Turkey, as guardian of important European interests; the Caliphate, the freedom of the Straits, &c., to be independent of all foreign preponderating influence.

5. Consequently, Turkey can neither cede nor delegate her rights over Bulgaria to any other Power, nor intervene in order to establish a foreign Administration there, nor tolerate acts of coercion undertaken with this latter object, under the form either of a military occupation or of the dispatch of volunteers. Neither will Turkey, who has by the Treaties been constituted guardian of the Straits, be able to cede any portion of her sovereign rights, nor delegate her authority to any other Power in Asia Minor.

6. The desire of the three Powers to be associated with Turkey for the common defence of these principles.

7. In case of Turkey resisting any illegal enterprises such as are indicated in Article V, the three Powers will immediately come to an agreement as to the measures to be taken for causing to be respected the independence of the Ottoman Empire and the integrity of its territory as secured by previous Treaties.

8. Should the conduct of the Porte, however, in the opinion of the three Powers, assume the character of complicity with or connivance at any such illegal enterprise, the three Powers will consider themselves justified by existing Treaties in proceeding either jointly or separately to the provisional occupation by their forces, military or naval, of such points of Ottoman territory as they may agree to consider it necessary to occupy in order to secure the objects determined by previous Treaties.

9. The existence and the contents of the present Agreement between the three Powers shall not be revealed either to Turkey or to any other Powers who have not yet been informed of it without the previous consent of all and each of the three Powers aforesaid.

VI

The Partition of East Africa 1885–91

74. (*Gladstone to Granville 12 December 1884, P.R.O./30/29/144. Printed in Ramm II, 294–5*)

The Kilimanjaro papers so far as I can make out their purport, leave me, I must confess, wholly unsatisfied. I cannot see, nor have I yet conceived, an adequate reason for our being 'dans cette galère'. The tone of the Memm prepared by F.O. people or others disquiets me, and in places savours much of annexationism. As for instance when it is laid down that we are to seek 'compensation' on the East Coast of Africa for concurring in measures equal for all on the West Coast.

Either I am very blind, or you and the other Ministers concurring in the Draft dispatch must have reasons in your minds outside what are here presented.

My first sense of want of proof [of] the necessity of doing anything. My second as to the thing to be done. I remember nothing of the telegram, stated to have laid it down that we ought on no account to be forestalled by other Powers in this Kilimanjaran district. But I should have thought that the proper direction to work in, if we work at all, was to procure if possible the application on the East Coast of the principles which it is now attempted to apply on the West.

Cannot this matter stand over until we can come to understand it a little further by Conference in the Cabinet?

BISMARCK APPLIES THE EGYPTIAN LEVER IN ZANZIBAR

75. (*Malet to Iddesleigh 2 October 1886, F.O.244/415/71*)

. . . Count Bismarck spoke to me at length today by order of the Chancellor on the subject.

He said that the traditional policy of Germany and the one which was most agreeable was to be on the most friendly terms with England, that it had been a matter of deep pain and regret to Prince Bismarck to be obliged to depart from this traditional policy two years ago, in consequence of the way in which he had been treated by England in regard to the colonial policy of Germany . . .

He reverted to the subject now because he once more asked for the assistance and friendly action of H.M.'s Govt in the matter of Zanzibar. In return for that he would reject all the ouvertures which might be made to him by the new French ambassador to help France in embarrassing us in Egypt and in all questions in which our interests and those of France were in divergence, he would not only refuse to go against us but would give us such assistance as might be possible consistently with the necessities of his home position . . .

H.E. concluded by pressing on me again the great importance which Prince Bismarck attached to the question and the intimate relation which it bore to the general question of the relations between England and Germany.

BRITISH INTERESTS CLASH WITH THOSE OF GERMANY AND ITALY IN ZANZIBAR

76. (*Salisbury to Goschen 14 October 1888, in Cecil IV, 236*)

Extract

The great anxiety with respect to Zanzibar is that both Germany and Italy, if they do not get any outrageous demand gratified, are always hinting that they will bombard Zanzibar. You speak severely of Bismarck's action,—he is an angel of light compared to Crispi . . . In cynical and arrogant injustice it is impossible to surpass Crispi's policy towards Zanzibar. We have only prevented him exacting what he pleased from the Sultan, by keeping the squadron at Zanzibar and intimating pretty plainly that force would be repelled by force.

SALISBURY REJECTS A GERMAN ALLIANCE

77a. (*Herbert Bismarck to Prince Bismarck 22 March 1889, Dugdale I, 373–4*)

Extract

We discussed the probable effect of the joint naval demonstration on France and America, the relations of England and Germany towards France, and finally the possibility of an Anglo-German Alliance, open or secret. Lord Salisbury entirely agreed with me that this would be the best tonic for both countries and for European peace. He had spoken about it to Lord Hartington and his colleagues, all of whom had shared his opinion, but considered it inopportune to act upon the suggestion, since it would cause the Parliamentary majority to collapse, carrying the Ministry with it.

Lord Salisbury added: 'We live no longer, alas, in Pitt's times; the aristocracy governed then and we were able to form an active policy, which made England after the Congress of Vienna the richest and most respected Power in Europe. Now democracy is on top, and with it the personal and party system, which reduces every British Government to absolute dependence on the aura popularis. This generation can only be taught by events.'

77b. (*Hatzfeldt to Bülow April 20 1898, Holstein Papers IV, 72–3*)

Extract

Your Excellency will see at once what I mean if I tell you briefly of a conversation I had with Lord Salisbury shortly after Prince Bismarck's retirement. When I asked him in the course of a very confidential and frank discussion whether he could tell me openly what he really thought of the political suggestions which the Prince had made heretofore, the Prime Minister replied: 'I will tell you personally and quite frankly that nothing that you told me at the Prince's instructions during the past years affected my view of our policy, because I had to tell myself and recognized clearly that his whole object was to involve England in a war with France without taking part in it himself.'

NEGOTIATIONS FOR AN AFRICAN SETTLEMENT WITH GERMANY, 1890

78. (*Salisbury to the Queen 24 May 1890, Letters of Queen Victoria I, 607*)

Extract

Lord Salisbury's negotiations on the subject of the African boundary, as he telegraphed to your Majesty, are not progressing. It does not seem likely that the German Emperor will accept any terms which will be acceptable to our Companies and missionaries who are first in possession of the disputed ground; and they naturally feel very bitter at the idea that the result of their labours should be signed away in London, in order to serve the ends of British policy in Europe. It will not be practicable or desirable to come to any agreement which is not acceptable to them.

79. (*Salisbury, Memorandum for the Cabinet 2 June 1890, Cab/37/28/38*)

Extract

The English, on the contrary, rest their claims upon two grounds. In the first place, they have a claim, for which it is not very easy to discover any international foundation, that they shall have an unbroken stretch of territory from Cape Town on the south to Lado, the point at which the Nile becomes navigable, on the north; and that this stretch of territory shall only be broken by the waterway of Lake Tanganyika. Secondly, a far more tenable ground of claim consists in the fact, that on the south of Lake Tanganyika the English originally discovered, and have now for many years, through the African Lakes Company, through Mr. Stevenson and through the Scottish Missions, occupied the territory which the Germans claim. The Stevenson Road was made by a Scotchman; there are several missionary and commercial stations at the south of the Tanganyika Lake; there are (or were) two Scottish stations upon the Stevenson Road, and there are stations of the African Lakes Company on the north-west of the Nyassa Lake, all of which would become German if the German claim were admitted. To the north of Lake Tanganyika the English claim rests wholly upon the Treaties which Mr. Stanley, and possibly Mr. Jackson, have made with the King of Uganda and other natives. The weak point of such Treaties, as a ground of title, is that generally they are confronted by a parallel set of Treaties made with another European Power by the same native Potentates, or by native Potentates claiming the same country; and Mr. Stanley's and Mr. Jackson's Treaties do not seem to be exempt from this inconvenient flaw.

The question really for decision lies as to what is to be done to the north of Tanganyika and with respect to the claims of Sir William Mackinnon. That the Germans will give way on this point, and allow themselves to be shut out almost entirely from the Congo State, is, I think, most improbable. The only alternative, if Sir William Mackinnon's objections are upheld, is that no arrangement at all will be arrived at.

The Germans deprecate this result very much. They say that

there are hot-headed leaders on both sides who would certainly attempt to take by force the territory in dispute; that their enterprises would certainly lead to collision; and that if there was a defeat of one party or the other, it would produce an excitement in the public opinion and the press of the two countries which would be very prejudicial to their future friendship and co-operation. It is impossible to deny the truth of this apprehension. On the other hand, the probable result of five or ten years of such conflict would be the predominance of the English population throughout all the regions in question, for the number of English adventurers is very much larger than the German. But what political results might arise intermediately from the collisions to which this consequence would be ultimately due it is not very easy to predict. To throw up these negotiations now, and come to no result, is a step into the unknown. Its consequences may be tolerable or may be very bad.

Another evil attending any suspension or abandonment of our negotiations with Germany is, that the difficulties of a settlement with Portugal will be indefinitely increased. Germany will certainly, either openly or covertly, sustain the refractory disposition of Portugal, and the coercion of that Power may not be so simple an undertaking as it will if only the strength and the obstinacy of Portugal have to be dealt with. The question practically to which 'Aye' or 'No' must be replied is whether Sir William Mackinnon and Mr. Stanley are to be overruled or not.

80. (*Salisbury to the Queen 4 June 1890, Letters of Queen Victoria 3rd series I, 610–11*)

Lord Salisbury with his humble duty to your Majesty respectfully submits that the Cabinet yesterday was mainly engaged in discussing the question of African frontiers. After a long and patient examination of the question in all its bearings, the Cabinet came to the conclusion that it was desirable to come to an arrangement with Germany if it were possible; and that they would regard the following conditions as bases of an acceptable settlement.

1. That the Stevenson Road be taken as the frontier to the south of Lake Tanganyika. This seems indispensable, as it has been for many years occupied by British Missions and by the African Lakes Company; and the Germans have no title to it whatever, or to the territory that lies beyond it.

337

2. That in the north, on the west of Lake Victoria Nyanza, the line of one degree south latitude joining the lake to the frontier of the Congo State, which it is understood the Germans are ready to give, would be in accordance with existing rights so far as they can be laid down; but that it is desirable that the frontier should be pushed about thirty miles farther south, as Stanley's Treaties appear to extend to that point. The above arrangement would fully secure Uganda to the British Company.

3. That mutual agreements be entered into giving right of unobstructed passage and free transit of goods through each other's territory; and right of settlement and trade to be extended equally to the subjects of both Crowns, on the territory of both.

Lord Salisbury saw the Ambassador in the afternoon, and is of opinion that the above terms can be obtained, probably, with little modification. Larger demands on our part would involve breaking off negotiations, which on the whole is not expedient.

THE PROTECTION OF THE NILE

81. (*Baring to Salisbury 15 June 1889, in Cecil IV, 139*)

Extract

The argument that, if we had a right to come back, we should probably never have to execute the right is, I think, based on a fallacy. The interests, both European and native, involved in bringing us back would be stronger than those involved in getting us to stay away. Really, the more I look at it, the more does the evacuation policy appear to me to be impossible under any conditions.

82. (*Baring to Salisbury 15 March 1890, F.O.170/432/219*)

Extract

But at the same time I think it would be a great mistake to attach too much importance to it, or to suppose that general and sincere declarations of friendliness will suffice to alter the groove into which Italian African policy seems disposed to drift, and into which . . . it must almost of necessity drift. I . . . greatly doubt if the local authorities at Massowah are kept under effective control from Rome or Rome informed of all that goes on. But the Italian Government will belie all experience of all other nations if . . . they do not extend their territory in the direction where their real or presumed interests are presumed to lie . . . I have no hesitation in saying that I should prefer to see the Dervishes in possession of Kassala and Khartoum rather than that those places should be held by the Italians . . . since so long as the Dervishes hold [those places] the Egyptian Government or Her Majesty's Government . . . can choose its own time for a forward movement. But if once the Italians are in possession the case is very different.

83. (*Salisbury to Baring 31 August 1890, S.P. Printed in part in Cecil IV, 330–1*)

Extract

That we should insist upon the command of all the affluents of the Nile so far as Egypt formerly possessed them is agreed. I think you also agreed that we have no such well defined and imperative interests to safeguard on the Red Sea slope . . . There is only one point that interests me at all in that direction—namely that you should not sanction the tribal theory of dominion . . . This may prove a nuisance if it is applied to the South West corner of Abyssinia . . .

I do not think that England will lose by delay. Italy is pursuing a policy which is financially impossible . . . A good deal of exaggerated language is used in diplomatic conversation and post prandial oratory as to the value of the Italian alliance to England. It is valuable to us chiefly because it is essential to Germany: and the friendship of Germany is very important to us because she keeps Russia and France in order. In itself the Italian alliance is not very advantageous and has several drawbacks: and one of them is the habit of quarrelling with her neighbours and asking us to back them. I do not therefore put the friendship of Italy so high as some other objects of political desire. It is desirable: but it is not worth a very great price even in African square miles. We are negotiating in these African matters with somewhat greater ease now that we have agreed with Germany and France.

84. (*Salisbury to Baring 21 November 1890, S.P.*)

Surely if you are *not* ready to go to Khartoum this people were created for the purpose of keeping the bed warm for you till you can occupy it?

Suppose the authority of the Khalifah were to vanish, what would happen to the Valley of the Nile? . . . There is a meritorious nation, the object of universal sympathy, whose blessed destiny it is to profit by the trouble of others and to gain steadily by occupying teritories for which others have fought and spent and that nation would be happy to be master of the Valley of the Nile, to which as you were told at Naples the title of Egypt has lapsed.

Ever since Italy has put forward this doctrine to justify her claim to Kassala I have felt that we must reconsider our enmities and friendships so far as Egypt is concerned . . . It is evident that Italy is the most formidable enemy that Egypt has at present to fear.

If that is so the Dervishes are rendering us a service in keeping Italy out. If that be so we should think twice before we starve them out and bring their domination to a sudden close.

VII

Britain and the Franco-Russian Alliance 1888–92

British Military Weakness

85. (*Brackenbury Memorandum, Intelligence Branch War Office 22 March 1886, Cab/37/18/31*)

Army Expenditure in the Principal Countries of Europe
The following Table has been prepared at the request of the Financial Secretary, and is printed at the desire of the Adjutant-General.

The annual cost per head, all ranks, as shown in the fourth column, does not, in my opinion, convey a true idea of the relative value which the several countries named receive for the money they expend.

The average annual cost per head of Officers and men is here arrived at by dividing the estimated total military expenditure by the number of all ranks on a peace footing; Reserves, Landwehr, Landsturm, Yeomanry, and Volunteers being omitted. Troops paid on separate budgets, as our army in India, the Dutch Indian Army, and the Spanish Colonial Forces are not included.

The real test of relative expenditure is relative readiness for war, or, in other words, the number of trained and effective men, equipped in every detail, whom, with all necessary arms and stores and all auxiliary services complete, each country can put into the field immediately after the issue of an order for mobilization. For example, with an annual expenditure of 21,500,000*l.*, Germany, on mobilization, can put into the field 18 army-corps complete in every point; while Great Britain, with an expenditure of over 18,000,000*l.* has not sufficient Artillery, Engineers, Commissariat

341

and Transport Corps, Medical Staff Corps, or Ordnance Store Corps for the mobilization of two army-corps.

The returns from which the table is compiled are appended.

H. BRACKENBURY, *Major-General,*
D.Q.M.G.

Intelligence Branch, War Office,
22nd March 1886.

COMPARATIVE TABLE OF EXPENDITURE IN THE PRINCIPAL EUROPEAN ARMIES.

Country	Total Cost of Army, i.e., Military Budget	Peace Strength of Army	Annual Cost per head, all ranks
	£		£ s. d.
Great Britain	18,233,200	282,617*	54 10 4
Spain	5,254,885	93,638	56 2 4
Austro-Hungary	13,163,911	250,112	52 12 0
France	24,488,526	523,833	46 13 6
Germany	21,500,000	470,000	46 0 0
Denmark	590,000	13,000	45 0 0
Italy	10,807,237	267,550	43 18 0
Belgium	1,824,680	45,095	40 10 0
Holland	1,750,000	57,000	31 0 0
Russia	20,190,000	885,689	22 16 0
Switzerland	730,000	105,000	7 0 0

* Of these 138,000 at home (Brackenbury, 8 June 1888.)

86. (*Brackenbury Memorandum, Intelligence Branch War Office 25 January 1887, Cab/37/19/8*)

Extract

... Not for one moment do I believe that England is a modern Carthage destined to be destroyed; not for one moment do I admit that it can be said of England, as of Troy, 'fuit'. We have, on the contrary, made great progress in our defensive organization since the days of the Crimean war. But that progress is not proportionate to the progress made by other nations; and I do believe that unless our Rulers will take a business-like view of the situation, we shall suffer heavily in our first war with any great European Power, and have to buy peace at a price compared with which any expenditure upon armaments now would weigh but as a feather in the balance.

There is not a business firm that does not from time to time make a valuation of its liabilities, and see that its assets are sufficient to meet them, and nothing is easier than to make such a valuation of our liabilities. Our naval authorities are prepared to say exactly what they require in order to possess a navy capable of holding its own throughout the world. Our military authorities are prepared to say exactly what works, what guns, and what men they require for the defence of our Imperial fortresses and coaling stations abroad, of our dockyards and great commercial ports at home, the preliminaries for the defence of London, and for putting into the field a modest but complete force of all arms. Indeed, our soldiers and our sailors in responsible positions at the War Office and the Admiralty have told our Administrators what is required, but they are met by the answer that money is not forthcoming to meet the needs.

Not till our military and our naval Estimates are removed out of the arena of party conflict, not till there is a Government with the courage to tell the nation the truth, and demand the money necessary for the defence of our Imperial and commercial interests, not till there is an opposition patriotic enough to disdain to make capital out of such a demand, can we ever hope, except under pressure of a great alarm, to obtain the supplies necessary for a complete defensive scheme. When the alarm comes, money will be poured out like water, and in a few weeks, if it is not too late, there will be squandered sums, which judiciously expended in yearly instalments in peace, would have spared all alarm, and secured the national safety.

But do we make the most of the money the nation does grant? For years past the best and the cheapest army in the world has been the army of Germany, and how has that result been attained? The nation has voted a fixed sum for its army, to be paid without question for a period of seven years, and has intrusted it to its soldiers, whose reputation and whose honour depend on the army, to make the most of it. The whole responsibility, administrative, executive, and financial, is thrown upon their shoulders; and there is nothing more remarkable than the fact that, in all the recent debates in the Reichstag, not one single voice has ever hinted that a farthing of that money has been wasted. Are English officers less honest, less patriotic, or less able than Germans? In its wisdom the British nation leaves our English military officials absolutely without financial responsibility; while it never ceases to express its belief that our military administration is bad, and that there is grievous waste of the nation's money.

When war comes, unlimited power of the purse is of necessity intrusted to the Commander of the expedition, and whenever any great war comes upon us, it may safely be prophesied that the present civil administration of the army will have to give way to a military one. Were the example of other nations followed in time of peace, it is my firm belief that there would be less waste of public money, less want of preparation for war, and less occasion for such strictures as those contained in the pamphlet submitted for my observations.

THE INVASION SCARE OF 1888 AND THE ORIGIN OF THE NAVAL DEFENCE ACT

87. (*Brackenbury Memorandum 8 June 1888, Cab/37/21/15*)

Extract

... that France might land, or attempt to land, 100,000 to 150,000 men upon these shores within three weeks of our losing command of the Channel is within the mark, and is correct in every particular.

88. (*Hamilton Memorandum 19 June 1888, Cab/37/21/17*)

Extract

... the whole operation is mechanically possible if the utmost skill and knowledge be shown, and no unforeseen difficulty and no accident or miscalculation of any kind occur in an undertaking of this unexampled magnitude, but it is only possible under a combination of conditions which I will now note.

1. The sea must be perfectly calm during the whole period, and the distance between beach and transport not more than half a mile ...

2. The annihilation of our fleet in the Channel and Mediterranean is a necessary preliminary ...

3. The destruction of torpedo boats, coast defence vessels, and of every vessel in reserve at the home ports is also necessary ...

4. It is a further condition that the French fleet, inferior in strength to the fleet it had annihilated, should be in a condition of such unimpaired efficiency as to render futile all attempts of the military forces to oppose the landing.

It is only under a simultaneous combination of all these conditions that the performance as a mechanized exploit is possible.

89. (*Salisbury Memorandum in comment on above 29 June 1888, Cab/37/21/18*)

Extract

... The effect of these papers is to show that the two Departments and Count Moltke[1] agree in thinking that there are circumstances under which a French invasion may be possible, though the War Office think that the occurrence of the requisite conditions is far more within the range of probability than the Admiralty are disposed to admit. But it seems to me sufficient for the Government that they agree to think it possible. Our stake is so great that full precautions must be taken against even a distant possibility.

90. (*Salisbury Memorandum 6 November 1888, Cab/37/22/32*)

Extract

These results are not satisfactory. There are more than 10,000 men quartered within a few hours of Cherbourg, 6,000 at the port itself; 10,000 men could be conveyed from the Paris garrison by the Ouest to Havre and Dieppe, and 10,000 to Dunkirk and Boulogne by the Nord, in six or seven hours, only employing at each terminus the ten trains that are usually dispatched from it between midday and nine in the evening. (A train of thirty carriages will carry 1,000 men.) In other words, 30,000 men could be conveyed any afternoon almost without giving the railway Companies notice, by simply arresting the ordinary traffic for half a day. No mail leaves Paris after 11 in the morning, and the telegraph under proper surveillance would give no information beyond the frontier. It has been shown that the 30,000 men so conveyed would find at the ports ample tonnage to carry them across. No more

---

[1] The invasion scare originated with a long article in the Daily Telegraph of 23 May which, so its Berlin correspondent told Malet and Bismarck confirmed, was a faithful exposition of Moltke's views. Moltke thought a French invasion by surprise quite feasible.

notice would be required to get those steamers ready than could be provided by telegraphic orders sent as soon as the troops began to leave Paris. More elaborate preparations for the necessary contingent of horses and guns would have been made at Cherbourg, where they could be made in secrecy.

Military authorities do not apparently consider that the unopposed landing on an open coast of this number of men need take many hours. It would depend on the supply of boats, which the vessels from Cherbourg would have to bring. If the troops left the French coast soon after nightfall, the majority of them would be landed, say in Pevensey Bay, twelve hours later. If a Saturday night was selected for the operation, and if two or three Irish patriots were employed to cut the telegraphic wires at suitable points after 9 o'clock in the evening, a large portion of the expedition might be one day's march upon its road to London before the military authorities in that city were fully aware of what was taking place. The advance to London would presumably consist of four days' forced marches.

I have not touched on the supposed protection that might be derived from the notice given by a declaration of war, because it is notorious that a large number of wars have commenced without it. But legality might be saved by sending in a declaration of war in a sealed envelope on Saturday night before the time fixed for the landing of the expedition. It probably would not reach the hands of the Foreign Minister till some time in the middle of Sunday.

These considerations derive weight from the circumstance, that a crisis in the internal politics of France appears to be approaching; and power may fall into the hands of an adventurer. His principal difficulty will be to find any policy which will unite in his favour a majority of his countrymen; and the destruction of London would probably recommend him to them very strongly.

I do not forget that the War Office are taking precautions which, in case of need, will, I hope, be sufficient; and in any case, the enterprise must be one of extreme delicacy and hazard, which an indiscretion, or an official blunder, or a sudden change of weather may upset. Still the chances, though small, are sufficient to tempt the kind of soldier who comes to the top in a revolution; and I do not think we shall be doing our duty unless we take measures to insure that the invasion, if attempted, shall meet with a naval as well as a military resistance. For this purpose, I suggest that these four classes of precaution shall be considered:

1. That Dover Harbour should be completed.

2. That a fixed number of whatever craft is judged by the Admiralty to be best for resisting a landing should be kept in readiness at Portsmouth and Dover, able always to start at night at an hour's notice.

3. That an underground wire be laid connecting selected stations along the coast between Portsmouth and Dover with those two places; that these stations, which would no doubt be the stations of the preventive service, be so distributed that all the exposed parts of the coast shall be visible from some one of them.

4. That it be ascertained, by actual experiment, whether the reserve fleet could be mobilized in forty-eight hours. It is officially assumed that such is the case, and the assumption is supposed to be established by the feat having been performed before the manœuvres of last summer. But this was not really forty-eight hours' notice. Every one knew some time before that the manœuvres were approaching, and every one was constantly ready. What we should wish to know, and what we ought to ascertain by experience, is whether the reserve could be mobilized in forty-eight hours if the order was given at a moment when nobody was expecting it.

S.

91. (*Hamilton 10 November 1888, enclosing Hood Memorandum of July, Cab/37/22/44*)

Extract

New Ship-building Programme

The Cabinet in July last determined that Admiral Sir Arthur Hood should be requested to state the amount of force which he would require under certain eventualities. The questions and answers are inclosed; the former were drawn up after personal consultation with the Prime Minister. I impressed upon Sir Arthur Hood the necessity of moderation, and of obtaining from his colleagues a concurrence in the views he put forward.

This he has done (see attached paper), the only difference of opinion being that two of the Naval Lords wished to finish the work in four, instead of five years. The adoption of his programme will involve an increase to the ship-building expenditure of 429,000*l.* in the first year.

DISTRIBUTION OF PROPOSED EXPENDITURE ON
SHIPBUILDING

Year	New Programme	Outstanding Liabilities*	Total Expenditure
	£	£	£
1889–90	1,740,000	1,356,000	3,096,000
1890–91	2,810,000	330,000,	3,140,000
1891–92	3,330,000		3,330,000
1892–93	3,350,000		3,350,000
1893–94	3,070,000		3,070,000
1894–95	800,000	(X)	800,000
Total	15,100,000		16,786,000

* Estimated

The Requirements of the British Navy

I

What is the amount of naval force necessary in a naval war between this country without allies, and France under similar conditions, in order to protect the coasts of the United Kingdom against invasion or bombardment, and to protect the fortresses of Gibraltar and Malta, if attacked by the enemy's fleet?

It appears to me the first and most important point is to decide upon what is to be our policy in such a case.

My own views are, immediately that the relations of this country with France became strained to such an extent as to render war imminent, to dispose of our available force in home waters as follows:

1. To assemble a strong force at Gibraltar superior to that of the French at Toulon.

2. To assemble a strong force at Portland superior to that of the French at Cherbourg and Brest.

3. To assemble a small force of fast cruisers at Queenstown for the protection of our trade off the west coast of Ireland and the entrance to the Channel.

The objects which I should desire to obtain by this disposition are, to prevent the enemy's fleets from leaving Toulon, Cherbourg, and Brest, and in the event of either of the French fleets leaving these ports, to be able to pursue and bring them to action with as little delay as possible . . .

TOTAL BRITISH AND FRENCH FORCES (ARMOURED VESSELS) WHICH WOULD BE AVAILABLE *NOW* IN THE EVENT OF WAR, AND ON THE 1st APRIL, 1889, IN HOME WATERS AND MEDITERRANEAN.

| | *Now* | | | *April 1, 1889* | |
	British	*French*		*British*	*French*
Battle ships:			Battle ships:		
1st class	13	7	1st class	15	9
2nd class	10	7	2nd class	12	7
3rd class	4	3	3rd class	3	3
Armoured			Armoured		
cruizers	3	3	cruizers	10	3
Torpedo ram	1		Torpedo ram	1	
Coast-defence	3	6	Coast-defence	6	6
Armoured			Armoured		
gun-boats		2	gun-boats		2

We have, therefore, now ten more battle ships and one torpedo-ram more, and three coast defence vessels and two armoured gun-boats less, than the French for service in home waters and Mediterranean.

And on the 1st April, 1889, we shall have eleven more battle ships and one torpedo-ram and seven armoured cruizers, an equal number of coast defence vessels (although those of the French are superior), and two armoured gun-boats less than the French, for service in home waters, and the Mediterranean.

This would enable us *now* to assemble a fleet of fourteen armoured battle ships, two armoured cruizers, with the necessary number of cruizers and torpedo vessels at Gibraltar, leaving at Malta five battle ships and one torpedo-ram, and at Portland eight battle ships, one armoured cruizer, and three armoured coast defence vessels, with the necessary number of cruizers and torpedo-vessels; and at Queenstown four fast cruizers.

By the 1st April, 1889, we should be able to add two battle ships and two armoured cruizers to the Gibraltar fleet; one battle ship, five armoured cruizers, and three armoured coast defence vessels, to the Portland fleet.

This disposition would, in my opinion, render the coasts of the United Kingdom safe against invasion or bombardment, and render Gibraltar and Malta secure against attack, and provide protection for our trade at the entrance to and in the Channel.

I consider that Cherbourg could be successfully bombarded, and that it would be most desirable, as soon as possible after the declaration of war, to undertake this; and to capture and hold Goree, the most important coaling station of the French on the West Coast of Africa, and from which port, whilst in the hands of the French, cruizers would, as a head-quarters, inflict much damage upon our passing trade in the vicinity.

II

What force is required to afford (1) reasonable protection to trade routes, (2) and relief to coaling stations if attacked by a fleet?

(1.) In my opinion, the first thing in attempting to provide for the protection of our commerce is to endeavour to lock up in their ports the enemy's cruizers, which would endeavour to escape to prey upon our commerce, and to prevent from returning to their ports the fast merchant vessels which would then be armed as cruizers; in home waters the disposition of our armoured vessels which I have sketched out would, with the cruizers attached to them, have, in my opinion, a very good effect in this direction. . . .

III

What is the amount of naval force necessary in a naval war between this country without allies, and a combination of France and Russia, in which case Constantinople would have to be defended?

In the above case, with our present naval strength, the policy I should propose to adopt with regard to Russia, would be not to attempt any operations in the Baltic, but to station a small squadron off the entrance, in order to prevent the exit of Russian war-vessels and cruizers. The Russian fleet in the Baltic now completed, consists of one 1st class battle ship (turret vessel), one 3rd class battle ship, and five armoured cruizers; there are in addition a number of weak coast defence vessels, and gun-boats, not fit for service outside the Baltic.

I should propose to station at the entrance of the Baltic, if war broke out *now*, four battle ships, two battle ships from the fleet to be stationed at Gibraltar, and two from the fleet proposed for Portland, also one armoured cruizer from the Gibraltar fleet. But if war broke out, say on the 1st April, 1889, I should not reduce the strength of the Gibraltar and Portland fleets, but from the additional vessels which would then be available, station four battle ships and three armoured cruizers at the entrance to the Baltic.

With regard to the protection of Constantinople, the present Russian force in the Black Sea is now so very small that the Turkish fleet ought most certainly to be able to deal with it alone with the greatest ease; but three powerful battle ships are now building in the Black Sea. Of these, one *may* be completed by the end of this year, a second by the end of 1889, and the third by the middle of 1890. Long before that time the seven 1st class battle ships now building in this country will be completed, and we should be able, say by the end of next year, to detach three of these ships to protect Constantinople.

It must be borne in mind that in the disposition of our armoured force, both now and by the 1st April, 1889, I have included the whole of our available ships, thus there would be no reserve to meet contingencies. We have at the present time seven 1st class battle ships, and six armoured cruizers building, the whole of which will be in all probability ready by the end of 1889. The French are about to commence a 1st class battle ship and a powerful armoured cruizer. The Russians are building five powerful battle ships (three in the Black Sea and two in the Baltic) and one armoured cruizer, and I am certain that under these conditions, and looking at the vessels, both armoured and unarmoured, which will become obsolete during the next few years, it is absolutely necessary to commence next year to build more battle ships and also more fast cruizers. I have considered the question, and add to this paper a building programme, showing the number and types of vessels which I would recommend should be built during the next five years in order to place this country in a position to meet with undoubted success a combination of France and Russia in a naval war, under the existing building programmes of these countries; should they, however, continue to build more armoured vessels than those which are comprised in their present building programmes, then it would be incumbent on this country to keep pace with them.

PROPOSED BUILDING PROGRAMME TO BE SPREAD OVER FIVE YEARS, WITH THE VIEW OF PROVIDING THOROUGHLY AGAINST A COMBINATION OF FRANCE AND RUSSIA AGAINST THIS COUNTRY WITHOUT ALLIES.

Type of Vessel	*Number*
Battle ships, 1st class	8
„ 2nd class	2
Improved 'Merseys,' with speed 19½ knots	8
'Modeac,' speed 20 knots	25
'Barhams,' increased from 1,800 to 2,000 tons, with increased coal supply	4
'Sharpshooters,' with speed 21 knots	18
Total*	

* Estimate of costs deleted since superseded by that of Hamilton, 10 November.

The amount voted for Ordnance this year, to meet the requirements of ships building and ordered to be built, &c., is 1,863,500*l.* In addition, it will be necessary to provide for the armaments of the ships included in the proposed new building programme, approximately 4,000,000*l.*, to be spread over five years, but at present it is impossible to say what will be the amount by which the average annual provision for the Ordnance Votes would enable a reduction to be made in this sum.

(Signed)   A. W. A. HOOD.
A. H. HOSKINS.
W. GRAHAM.
C. F. HOTHAM.

July 1888.

THE DEVELOPMENT OF THE POLICY OF LIMITED SUPPORT FOR ITALY
IN THE MEDITERRANEAN

92. (*Salisbury to Dufferin 28 December 1888, S.P. Printed in part in Cecil IV, 105*)

Extract

The other form in which Crispi's desire for 'rem quorumque modo rem' has shown itself is much more dangerous. The armed peace is leading Italy rapidly to financial ruin. If there could be war Crispi hopes for Albania certainly, Nice probably and perhaps Tunis and Tripoli. (There is some promise of the first two Herbert Bismarck hints.) If there is to be war at all, it is to Italy's interest to have it as quickly as possible. (Both Blanc and Damiani said so.)

The consequence has been a string of quarrels with France . . . Under these circumstances our policy has altered a little—not much. At first we were very cordial with Italy—which is our normal policy. But as Crispi's character developed we came to the conclusion that it was better to give him a wide berth.

We have therefore kept out of his quarrels with France and declined to give any guarantees beyond a strong desire for the status quo in the Mediterranean. My impression is that if France attacked Italy gratuitously by sea, the English feeling would be in favour of going to her assistance, but that if a war were to arise out of one of Crispi's trumpery quarrels, England would certainly stand aloof.

93. (*Salisbury to Dering 25 July 1889, F.O. 170/416/162*)

Extract

Catalani reported that Crispi had informed Bismarck . . . that his main trust lay upon England, in accordance with the Secret Agreement of 1887; his only fear was that English help might arrive too late. Therefore he requested that a powerful British Fleet might, under the appearance of an annual Squadron of Evolution, be sent as soon as possible into the Mediterranean, in order that France might be restrained from carrying her plans into execution. Catalani was authorized to state in a most solemn manner that the King's Government will abstain from giving France the slightest pretext or provocation and that all questions between the two governments (e.g. the Tunisian Question) will for the present remain in abeyance.

I said in reply that I did not at all share Crispi's apprehensions and believed the possibility of any such design on the part of France to be very small. Some phrases in the communication caused me further to add that there were no engagements between this country and Italy pledging either to material action and that I must not be understood as making any.

However, it might be satisfactory to know that, in view of the present aspect of Mediterranean politics, Her Majesty's Government had resolved on strengthening the British Fleet in these waters after the Autumn manoeuvres.

94. (*Salisbury to Dufferin 12 August 1890, in Cecil IV, 374–5*)

. . . The Germans say they are very apprehensive about Crispi's disposition; and that unless he is assured as to the 'compensation' which is the only, but sovereign, remedy for *his* apprehensions, he will get tired of the Triple Alliance, and seek the less expensive friendship of France by coming to terms with her about Tunis and Tripoli. I do not share these fears of the German Government. I believe that Crispi discerns them, and is bluffing in consequence; and that he hopes to take advantage of this opportunity to extract from Germany, Austria and England, a written guarantee that he shall some day be the heir of Tripoli. This written guarantee I would not be a party to giving. I am quite sure that a copy of it would find its way to Constantinople and that the Sultan would see in it a confirmation of his present suspicion that among the European Powers, Russia is the one that will despoil him least. But, I should like to have your judgment as to Crispi's mental attitude. If it be what the Germans suspect, and that he is hovering on the brink of a new alliance, it might be necessary to go so far as to give him to understand *verbally*, that while we were faithful to the rights of the Sultan as guaranteed by the Treaty of Paris, we fully recognized that Italy had a special interest in the maintenance of the integrity of the Turkish Empire as regards Tripoli; and that in case any catastrophe were to overwhelm the Ottoman domination, that position of special affection and relationship would have its natural bearing upon the distribution of the inheritance . . . .

I do not like to disregard the plain anxiety of my German friends. But it is not wise to be guided too much by their advice now. Their Achitophel is gone. They are much pleasanter and easier to deal with; but one misses the extraordinary penetration of the old man.

95. (*Deym to Kálnoky 17 June 1891, S.A.W. VIII. 110/24A–C*)

Extract

... For Italy the opinion of the English press is more valuable than confirmation from the Foreign Office. It is now clear that the principle of the maintenance of the status quo in the Mediterranean upheld by Lord Salisbury is accepted not only by the Conservative Party but also by the greater part of the Liberals. Public opinion in England will not stand for a French attack upon the Italian coast and Italy can count upon British support whether or not there is any prior understanding.

I have recently spoken with Lord Salisbury about these discussions in Parliament and the press and the Prime Minister asserts that they have done him a service, since it shows that public opinion in England supports his policy.

Lord Salisbury assured me that from today no ministry in England could permit the status quo in the Mediterranean to be altered in favour of France.

There would be no change in this respect if a Liberal ministry replaced him: he could be certain that Lord Rosebery, if he were his successor, would in any event follow the same policy, which seemed to him (Lord Salisbury) to be in the interest of England.

THE DEFENCE OF CONSTANTINOPLE

96. (*Memorandum by Salisbury 4 June 1892 in comment on Joint Report of the D.M.I. and D.N.I., 18 March, Cab/37/31/10*)

A Joint Report of the Director of Military Intelligence and the Director of Naval Intelligence has just been placed in my hands by direction of the Lords of the Admiralty, who concur in it. It has reference to the possibility of a descent of Russia upon Constantinople, and upon the attitude which should be observed by this country in case of such an event.

I do not think it to be urgent, because, as far as it is possible to judge, a Russian descent is not imminent at present. They are not prepared for a general war, their fleet is not complete, their military armament is very imperfect, and their finance is in disorder.

I do not therefore advert to it as a matter requiring the immediate attention of Her Majesty's Government. But it is of the gravest possible moment, and the early attention of whoever is responsible for the conduct of public affairs cannot be withheld from it without public danger for very long.

For the upshot of this Report is, that the Foreign Office on the one side, and the defensive Departments on the other, have been proceeding on lines as far divergent as it is possible for lines of policy to diverge; and it is evident that if this difference is maintained until the moment for action arrives, nothing but the most serious disaster can be the result.

The protection of Constantinople from Russian conquest has been the turning point of the policy of this country for at least forty years, and to a certain extent for forty years before that. It has been constantly assumed, both in England and abroad, that this protection of Constantinople was the special interest of Great Britain. It is our principal, if not our only, interest in the Mediterranean Sea; for if Russia were mistress of Constantinople, and of the influence which Constantinople possesses in the Levant, the route to India through the Suez Canal would be so much exposed as not to be available except in times of the profoundest peace. I need not dwell upon the effect which the Russian possession of Constantinople would have upon the Oriental mind, and upon our position in India, which is so largely dependent on prestige. But the matter of present importance is its effect upon the Mediterranean; and I cannot see, if Constantinople were no longer defensible, that any other interest in the Mediterranean is left to defend. The value of Malta, our only possession inside that sea, would at all events be diminished to an indefinite degree.

It now appears from this Report that, in the opinion of General Chapman and Captain Bridge, it is not only not possible for us to protect Constantinople, but that any effort to do so is not permissible. Even supposing the fortifications in the Dardanelles could be silenced, even supposing the Sultan asked for our presence in the Bosphorus to defend him against a Russian attack, it would yet be, in the judgment of these two officers, a step of grave peril to employ any portion of the British Mediterranean fleet in protecting him. The peril would arise, not from any danger we might incur in meeting the Russian forces, not from the strength of any fortifications the fleet would have to pass, but from the fact that this is the extreme end of the Mediterranean and that so long as the French fleet exists at Toulon, the function of the English fleet must be to remain in such a position as to prevent the French fleet at Toulon from escaping into the Atlantic and the English Channel, where it would be a grave peril to this country. They conclude, therefore, that unless we had the concurrence of France, which is of course an absurd hypothesis, or unless we had first destroyed the French fleet at Toulon, which at all events must be a very distant contingency, it is not legitimate for us to employ our fleet at the eastern end of the Mediterranean. The presence of the French fleet therefore in the harbour of Toulon, without any declaration of hostile intention or any hostile act, has the power of entirely immobilizing, and therefore neutralizing, any force that we possess or could bring under existing circumstances into the Mediterranean.

Two very grave questions arise from this strategic declaration which it must be the task of Her Majesty's Government, before any long period has elapsed, definitively to answer.

In the first place, it is a question whether any advantage arises from keeping a fleet in the Mediterranean at all. The main object of our policy is declared to be entirely out of our reach, and it is laid down that even a movement to attain it would be full of danger. There is nothing else in the Mediterranean which is worth the maintenance of so large and costly a force. If its main duty is to protect the Atlantic and the Channel, it had better go there. If it is retained in Portsmouth Harbour it will, at least, be comparatively safe from any possible attack on the part of the fleet at Toulon, and a very considerable relief will be given to the Budget of the Chancellor of the Exchequer.

Secondly, the other consideration is that our foreign policy requires to be speedily and avowedly revised. At present, it is supposed that the fall of Constantinople will be a great defeat for England. That defeat appears to be not a matter of speculation, but of absolute certainty, according to the opinion of these two distinguished officers, because we may not stir a finger to prevent it. It would surely be wise, in the interest of our own reputation, to let it be known as quickly as possible that we do not pretend to defend Constantinople, and that the protection of it from Russian attack is not, in our eyes, worthy of the sacrifices or the risks which such an effort would involve. At present, if the two officers in question are correct in their views, our policy is a policy of false pretences. If persisted in, it will involve discomfiture to all who trust in us, and infinite discredit to ourselves.

I would merely say, in conclusion, that this momentous question is not one which either the Admiralty or the War Office can decide on their own responsibility. The Cabinet which undertakes to decide it (and the decision cannot be long delayed) must have at its command the opinion of all that England or India can furnish of naval or military strategic knowledge. We have been going on for long, evidently enormously overrating the utility of our fleet for any purpose except that of bare coast-defence at home. It is very important that the real facts, however disagreeable they may be, should be ascertained and presented in the clearest light to those who are responsible for the policy of the Empire.

S.

Foreign Office,
June 4, 1892.

Annex

Sir,   *May 20, 1892.*

With reference to your letter of the 11th instant, inclosing a joint Report drawn up by the Directors of Naval and Military Intelligence respecting the question of a possible Russian *coup de main* on Constantinople, I am commanded by my Lords Commissioners of the Admiralty to request that you will inform the Secretary of State that they have read this Report with much interest, and that they consider its reasoning and conclusions beyond dispute.

I am to add that, in the judgment of the First Lord of the Admiralty, a copy of this Report should be sent to the Prime Minister, the First Lord of the Treasury, and to the Chancellor of the Exchequer.

I am, &c.

(Signed)   EVAN MACGREGOR.

P.S.—The inclosure to your letter of the 11th instant is herewith returned, and a copy has been retained in this Office.

E. M.

1. In accordance with instructions received from the Secretary of State for War and the Lords Commissioners of the Admiralty, the Director of Military Intelligence and the Director of Naval

Intelligence met on the 18th March, 1892, and, after considering the question of a possible Russian attempt to seize Constantinople by a *coup de main*, agreed upon the following Report on the naval and military action that would be necessary in such a case.

2. There is much and convincing evidence to show that the attempt alluded to is likely to be made. The assumed *coup de main* would be most probably carried out by the dispatch of a fleet of transports conveying troops under a suitable escort of men-of-war from the Black Sea ports of Russia, and the points most likely to be selected for the disembarkation of the troops would be certain bays offering some facilities for landing to the east and west of the eastern mouth of the Bosphorus.

3. A sufficiency of transport could be collected in Russian ports for the purpose of conveying 20,000 men with their equipment; and the strength of the Black Sea fleet is now such that the expedition would be secured against interference on the part of the Turkish navy, at all events till near the very end of the voyage. Even when the voyage had been completed, it is doubtful if the Turkish navy would be able, with torpedo-boats and light craft, to molest the expedition or seriously impede its operations for the Russians would dispose of a force which ought to be ample for the purpose of warding off attacks by craft of the kind, in addition to assisting in the landing of the army.

4. The necessary preparations involved in assembling and preparing the transports and putting the troops and their equipment on board would occupy several days, probably not less than six at the least. The voyage and subsequent disembarkation would probably require four days more. Consequently, from the first commencement of active preparation till the landing had been effected fully ten days would elapse, and this estimate would, perhaps, be exceeded. In addition to this, the fact that the prevailing wind is unfavourable to disembarkation in the open bays that are likely to be used must be taken note of, as the necessity of waiting for suitable weather would, if it arose, extend the time above specified.

5. Without assigning any precise limit of time to the duration of the whole operation, it may still be affirmed that ample warning would be given to the Turks to allow of their taking precautions against the disembarkation. That it is in their power to take such precautions as would render a landing impossible is established

beyond a doubt; but the evidence before us makes it nearly certain that they will not make any endeavour to prevent it. Under these circumstances, the landing once accomplished, and the passage through the Bosphorus being secured to the Russian fleet, the fall of Constantinople is certain, and the subsequent occupation of the Dardanelles defences highly probable.

6. Supposing that there were not sufficient reasons to render such an employment of the forces undesirable, it may be accepted that the assumed *coup de main* could be prevented by the British fleet, if warned in time, were the shores of the Dardanelles occupied by a British land force of not less than 10,000 men, to give security to the fleet's communications. This latter force would require early reinforcement, and could not be furnished in time under existing arrangements. Moreover, until the neutrality of France is assured, or her fleet is paralyzed, we cannot risk the movement of troops through the Mediterranean.

7. There are certain questions of general naval strategy which are inevitably raised by proposals to employ a British fleet as above suggested, and these questions are too serious to be allowed to remain unanswered. The ships detached to prevent the assumed descent on Constantinople would not only be occupied in a remote corner of the Mediterranean; they would also be at the extreme end of a line of somewhat precarious communications. Detaching them would hand over, certainly for a time, the maritime preponderance in the western basin to the French; and, if the detached ships were long delayed in the neighbourhood of Constantinople, not only the western basin, but also the neighbouring Atlantic, and even the English Channel, might be open to a naval combination which would be a grave menace to this country.

8. We are of opinion that Great Britain, unsupported, cannot prevent the *coup de main* without endangering her general naval position; and, even if supported, that the line of communications through the Dardanelles should be made secure beyond doubt. Due regard being paid to the strategic conditions in the western basin and nearer home, there is no reason to believe that any permissible reinforcement of our Mediterranean fleet from existing resources would materially alter the situation. There is nothing new in this, for, as a matter of fact, it has always been so. A British fleet has entered the Sea of Marmora three times—once, less than a year and a-half after Trafalgar, when we had obtained an

undisputed command of the sea, including that of the whole Mediterranean; once when the British and French fleets were allied; and once when France had not recovered from the prostration due to her great contest with Germany.

9. The position may be summarized as follows: unless we are acting in concert with France, the road to Constantinople for a British force bent on a belligerent operation lies across the ruins of the French fleet.

(Signed)   E. F. CHAPMAN,
Director of Military Intelligence.
CYPRIAN A. G. BRIDGE,
Director of Naval Intelligence.

London, March 18, 1892.

VIII

Liberal Foreign Policy

ROSEBERY GIVES ASSURANCES ON THE CONTINUITY OF FOREIGN
POLICY

97a. (*Deym to Kálnoky 3 November 1892, S.A.W. VIII/112*)

Extract

The Minister of Foreign Affairs (Rosebery) told me that he had
now reached the position where he could assure Count Tornielli
that the attitude of the English Cabinet towards Italy following the
change of government would undergo no alteration, though he
was careful to add the reservation 'so long as he remained Minister
of Foreign Affairs'. In connection with this the Minister told me
that for reasons of health he had been extremely reluctant to enter
the Cabinet.

The impression that I gathered from this interview is, as your
Excellency has explained to the Delegations, that in principle
English policy towards the Eastern Question and relations with
the Triple Alliance will undergo no alteration through the change
of Cabinet, though I think it remains to be seen whether in a
concrete case we could be as certain of the support of the present
Cabinet as we could be of Lord Salisbury's.

97b. (*Memorandum by Rosebery 5 September 1892, B.D. VIII, 4*)

. . . H[is] E[xcellency] the German Ambassador and I then
diverged in conversation on the present situation of affairs which
he said did not differ very materially from what it was when I left
office. I said, however, that Lord Salisbury appeared to have
entered into closer relations with Italy than I had felt myself
justified in doing. Count Hatzfeldt said that that was true, but, as I
was aware, the note given by Lord Salisbury was of the vaguest
possible character, but that in the uneasy situation of Italy even

such a note was a satisfaction. I replied that I had not seen this communication, but that I was in a position to speak to H[is] E[xcellency] quite frankly on the subject. I thought the Italian Government would be very ill-advised if they asked me for any such communication. In the first place, its value would be very limited, for the circumstances were widely different. There was no comparison between the position of the two Ministers or of the two governments. More than that: I did not think that I could persuade my colleagues to give any such note, and therefore it would only be the expression of my individual opinion. All then I could do was to give my appreciation of the position as it struck me. But I would also say this, that in my opinion the Italian Government were as well off without the document as with it. Such a paper could only derive value, it is clear, from being the expression of the national will and the national interest. However powerful a minister might be, if his words did not represent that, they were of no account at all. My personal view was this, but it must be held to be nothing more, that in the event of France groundlessly attacking Italy, the interests of England as a Mediterranean and Indian power, would bring her naturally to the rescue of Italy, while her sympathy, as having so long and ardently co-operated in the cause of Italian freedom, would lead her in the same direction. That was my personal conviction, but beyond that I could say nothing, and in any case I could not make an authoritative communication, as from the British Cabinet, to the Italian Government. My belief was simply this, that in the eventuality that was dreaded and contemplated, the natural force of things would bring about the defensive co-operation they desired.

NAVAL EXPANSION AND FOREIGN POLICY IN 1893

98. (*Spencer Memorandum 8 December 1893, Cab/37/34/57*)

Extract

This Table[1] shows that on the 1st April, 1894, our total strength in completed battle-ships in European waters will be 56 as compared to 53 owned by the French and Russians, and that in 1st class battle-ships our relative position will be 19 and 14, while of modern cruizers we shall have 58 as against 32 French and Russian cruizers.

[1] Not printed.

Future relative Strength

Having considered the relative strength, in number of vessels, of the fleets of England, France, and Russia at the present time, we must next examine what each of these countries is doing to maintain or increase that strength.

If the same numbers of ships in each class were maintained the cost of replacing waste would be tolerably constant, an allowance being made for improvements and for the increase of size, which, up to the present, has been taking place in every new ship of a particular class.

Unfortunately, however, when we examine the number of ships which are being built by France and Russia, we find that they are not only replacing old ships by new, but are also increasing the number of their ships.

The following Table of shipbuilding in Great Britain, France, and Russia shows that, in respect of ironclads of all three classes in European waters in 1894–95 our fleet will exceed by three the combined fleets of France and Russia, in 1895–96 it will be inferior by two, and in 1896–97 by seven, or, taking 1st class battle-ships only, our present superiority of three is reduced in 1895–96 to bare equality, and in 1896–97 to a minority of two.

We cannot, however, ignore five 1st class battle-ships which France and Russia intend to lay down early in 1894. The money for commencing the three French battle-ships has been voted, and they are named. Of the two Russian vessels one has been named, and no doubt is entertained of their commencement in 1894. If these vessels are built, we shall be in a minority in 1897 of seven 1st class battle-ships.

It is further to be noted that in regard to modern cruizers, our present superiority will be greatly reduced during the same period.

THE DETERIORATION OF RELATIONS WITH THE TRIPLE ALLIANCE

99. (*Rosebery to Malet 3 January 1894, F.O. 343/3. Printed in Bayer, pp. 115–16*)

Extract

The Triple Alliance is in a somewhat parlous condition which I most truly deplore. It is mutually suspicious, which is the worst of signs.

But I do not see what we can do.

We could of course enter the Triple Alliance; or enter into a secret treaty with Italy. Neither of these is however in the range of practical politics for a British minister at this time.

In fact our only true policy is to strengthen our fleet, and that will be done.

As regards Constantinople, Currie will be instructed to act cordially with Austria. But there, too, though our interests are clear, our hands must be free: we must co-operate, but not be handcuffed to anyone.

I may send Currie through Berlin as well as through Vienna, but nothing is decided.

100. (*Deym to Kálnoky 13 June 1894, in Temperley & Penson, p. 491*)

Extract

. . . Up to the present since he has been in power, he (Rosebery) has always supported fully the policy of the Triple Alliance. The attitude of Germany in Colonial questions causes him to reflect and he asks himself whether England would not do better to alter her policy and to recover her complete freedom of action . . . it would not be possible for him to remain the friend of Germany in Europe if she shows herself hostile to England in Africa.

101. (*Rosebery to Malet 6 January 1895, F.O. 343/3. Printed in Bayer, p. 123*)

Extract

. . . as to 'la haute politique', I think Baron Holstein's remarks as reported by you, sensible enough, more especially as they confirm the view I have always held that Great Britain, if her policy be properly guided, holds the key of the situation. For about five months this year Germany appeared to ignore that fact, and so I had to send her a very plain message through Vienna. Hence, too, other developments. When Germany began to talk of being able to pursue a French policy in Africa, while maintaining the Triple Alliance in Europe, it was time to speak out, for this ignored the central keystone of the situation—through Italy, England.

You will have observed the alarm and annoyance at Vienna and also at Rome. And now we have a very different tone at Berlin, though much harm has already been done.

But what I have always believed has also now arrived—that Berlin or he who guides Berlin has been actuated by hostility to the Liberal Government in England. You, I think, were inclined to doubt this when I last saw you, but it is now openly acknowledged and Vienna (quantum mutata!) reads lectures to Berlin on concerning itself with the internal politics of other countries. Shades of Metternich! I must end.

102. (*Malet to Salisbury 7 July 1895, F.O. 343/12, Printed in Bayer, pp. 123-4*)

On your resuming the direction of Foreign Affairs I do not think that any great change has taken place in the relations between England and Germany from what they were when you left. Colonial questions continue as of yore to prevent perfect cordiality between us. The Emperor and the German Government thoroughly distrusted the late Government, though, as far as I could judge, there was no justification for their doing so. When it became apparent that the German Government was really coquetting with the Transvaal, Lord Kimberley no doubt used very strong language to Count Hatzfeldt. There is, indeed, no doubt that he threatened war. The German Foreign Office was furious but to my mind was only treated as it deserved. I, on my part, used language of a less minatory character but designed to induce them to understand that the national feeling in England was just as susceptible over Delagoa Bay as over Egypt—and I used one argument, when they dwelt on the instability of the Rosebery Government, which I could not well report to my chief. I said that it was very unwise of them in view of the approaching fall of the Government to alienate popular sympathy in England and that it might be impossible for Your Lordship when you returned to office to stem the tide of resentment which they would have raised. The thing of all others that stung them the most was an article in the 'Standard' on the isolation of Germany. The kernel of truth was extremely bitter to them. I believe it was Lord Kimberley's conviction that if he officially withdrew from the friendly understanding with Italy in regard to the Mediterranean that country would at once renounce the Triple Alliance and throw itself in desperation into the arms of France. It was, I fancy, some inkling of action of this nature being in the air that made the Emperor and his Government so profoundly distrustful of us. Things at last smoothed down and, during the winter, Dr. Kayser, the head of the Colonial Department, was fortunately ill to death's door. He has unluckily now recovered and has begun to rear his venomous little serpent head again and will assuredly sooner or later give us trouble.

I believe that the German Government is sincerely desirous of taking the opportunity of your return to Office to come to a general settlement of outstanding questions. But unless you can devise something for them to give in return it looks at present as if they counted on the 'des' without any 'do'.

ROSEBERY URGES RETENTION OF UGANDA

103. (*Rosebery Memorandum 16 September 1892, Cab/37/31/23*)

Extract

So far as I am concerned, I object strongly to the 'heads I win, tails you lose' principles of these Companies; and I would not lift a little finger to save Uganda as a valuable part of the Company's territory. Unfortunately, we cannot limit ourselves to this consideration, for Uganda has become a question of Imperial policy.

In the first place, there is the question of the Nile. At present we are the only civilized nation that has access to the Nile, and if only in view of the vital interest of the Nile to Egypt, and the peril to Egypt of any diversion of its stream, it is extremely important that we should remain so. But other nations are anxious to obtain a footing on it. The Congo State is asking for the cession of a territory which will give access to it, which we, in view of the extreme probability, to say no more, of the reversion of the Congo State to France, are unwilling to grant. France herself is making for the Nile from the west by trying to force down the boundary-line with the Congo State, so as to give her a route to the Nile, north of the Congo State, from her possessions in the French Congo. Italy on the east is pushing in the same direction. Germany would probably take advantage of our evacuation to step in. Uganda is no doubt outside her sphere of influence. But if we go, and there is a chaos of blood and destruction after our departure, the Germans, whom the Catholics have already thought of summoning, will have a right, in the name of humanity, to come and occupy this long-coveted territory, and to take up the civilizing work that we have abandoned as beyond our strength. I do not say that it is possible permanently to preserve the Nile for Great Britain and for Egypt, but I do say that if we abandon Uganda, we lose at once and by that fact the control of the Nile.

KIMBERLEY SUGGESTS CONCESSIONS IN WEST AFRICA IN RETURN FOR AN AGREEMENT ON THE NILE

104. (*Kimberley to Dufferin 14 August 1894, Cab/37/37/25*)

Extract

Her Majesty's Government are ready, as you are already aware, to enter into discussion with the French Government on the various questions (apart from that of Egypt) pending between Great Britain and France in East and West Africa.

An instruction has already been given to you with regard to the Agreement between Great Britain and Italy for the demarcation of their respective spheres of influence in Somaliland.

The other questions which remain unsettled are:

1. The claim of compensation to the French missionaries in Uganda on account of their losses during the fighting between the Protestant and Catholic sections of the Waganda.

2. The settlement of the boundary between the British and French territories in the neighbourhood of Sierra Leone.

3. The questions arising out of the collision between the British force dispatched from Sierra Leone and the French force under Lieutenant Maritz, and the collisions near the mouth of the Scarcies.

4. The delimitation between the British and French spheres to the west of the Niger.

5. The final settlement of the Say–Barruwa line under the Anglo-French Agreement of 1890; and

6. Questions relative to the proceedings of M. Mizon in the neighbourhood of that line.

Your Excellency is authorized to say that if a satisfactory arrangement is come to with regard to the British sphere in the Nile watershed, Her Majesty's Government will be prepared on all of these questions to meet the French Government in a most conciliatory spirit . . .

KIMBERLEY SUPPORTS THE GREY DECLARATION

105. (*Courcel to Hanotaux 2 April 1895, D.D.F. XI no. 429*)

Extract

Je m'apprêtais à le quitter. Il me dit alors d'un ton sérieux: 'Dites à M. Hanotaux que nous espérons qu'il sera modéré dans l'exposé qu'il fera aux Chambres françaises, car nous connaissons et apprécions son esprit conciliant. Dites-lui qu'il s'attache à nos actes plutôt qu'à nos paroles, parce que celles-ci sont toujours réparables. Quant à nos actes, nous sommes bien éloignés des entreprises que vous paraissez nous prêter. Nous n'aurons de longtemps l'intention d'attaquer le Soudan, ni d'entrer même dans les régions que vous disputez à notre sphère d'influence; nous ne projetons pas aujourd'hui d'aller au Bahr el Ghazal; les instructions dont sont munis les commandants de nos troupes qui opèrent dans l'Ounyoro leur prescrivent de circonscrire étroitement leur action et de se borner à la défense de l'Ouganda. J'ai bon espoir que les idées que nous venons d'échanger contribueront à éclairer la situation. Il y a quelque chose de vrai dans le rapprochement qu'on dit s'opérer entre la France et l'Angleterre. On nous voit agir de commun accord en Chine, en Arménie. La preuve que cela a de la portée, c'est que d'autres Puissances commencent à être jalouses. Je pourrais vous en citer une qui témoigne à ce propos beaucoup d'agitation.'

J'ai cru comprendra que ces dernières paroles s'appliquaient à l'Italie.

Vous avez vu que le soir même de mon entretien avec Lord Kimberley, Sir Edward Grey avait, en quelques brèves réponses, exposé à la Chambre des Communes un point de vue moins absolu que celui de ses premières déclarations et correspondant à ce que me disait de son côté le Secrétaire d'État. Reconnaître que la question où l'on a pris si carrément position est l'objet de discussions encore pendantes avec la France, c'est, au pied de la lettre, admettre qu'on n'a pas le droit de la trancher seul. Mais dans la pratique, je doute que cette distinction subtile fasse beaucoup impression sur l'esprit du public anglais. On a dit à celui-ci que le cours entier du Nil était sous sa loi; il ne retient pas autre chose de ces bruyants débats et, une fois son amour-propre national engagé, il ne reculera plus d'une semelle dans la défense de ce qu'il croit être son droit acquis. Un personnage en mesure de bien connaître le sentiment général de ce pays-ci me disait tout à l'heure que, si le ministère faisait mine d'abandonner le terrain qu'il a choisi, il ne resterait pas vingt-quatre heures aux affaires.

Il ne faut donc pas nous exagérer la portée pratique des atténuations qui résultent des explications de Lord Kimberley. Ce Ministre m'a montré des dispositions véritablement conciliantes dont il serait injuste de ne pas lui tenir compte; mais, à la vérité, son langage si soigneusement gardé n'a compromis en rien d'effectif la position dominante conquise à l'Angleterre par les déclarations de Sir Edward Grey. Nous pouvons faire sentir au Gouvernement de la Reine à quel point le procédé nous a blessés et peut-être nous prémunir ainsi, pour quelque temps au moins, contre l'emploi d'armes offensives de cette nature dans des discussions qui ne devraient pas cesser d'appartenir au domaine des pourparlers confidentiels et pacifiques de la diplomatie. Mais, sur les points spéciaux dont il s'est agi, il reste douteux, malgré quelques invites extrêmement discrètes de mon interlocuteur, que nous regagnions le terrain perdu.

DUFFERIN CONGRATULATES ROSEBERY ON THE SIAM SETTLEMENT

106. (*Dufferin to Rosebery 31 July 1893, Cab/37/24/42*)

To sum up the general results arrived at, Your Lordship will have the satisfaction of knowing that by your prudent conduct in not interfering between the French and the Siamese in their delimitation quarrel and by your subsequent temperate attitude, you have prevented Siam being despoiled of her two richest provinces, and have secured the consent of France to the constitution of a territorial buffer between her frontiers and our own.

THE PROBLEM IN THE PAMIRS, 1892–3

107. (*Salisbury to Morier, in Memorandum by Bertie, 24 January 1893, Cab/37/33/13*)

The adjacent Powers, China and Great Britain, both in her own right and that of Afghanistan, have a geographical, political, and strategical interest in this region, to say nothing of a natural anxiety that the iron commercial wall of the Russian Empire shall not be too far extended.

But on the narrowest view of our obligations we are bound to maintain the lawful dominions of the Ameer of Afghanistan, and we are anxious to preserve a sphere of influence outside our immediate boundaries so as to deaden the shock of contact between two colossal Empires, while it is important to prevent the contrast so disastrous in the East between Russia's constant and unresisted advance, and our passive quiescence behind our mountains.

But our policy is to some extent hampered by the fact that the line of the Oxus, adopted in 1873 before our geographical knowledge of these regions was clear or scientific, is not altogether satisfactory, and leaves besides a considerable space unmarked and undivided, while it shuts off from Afghanistan provinces claimed and occupied by the Ameer (though against our advice) for at least nine years. On the other hand, it includes in Afghanistan a large portion of the Province of Darwaz, which is claimed and, I believe, occupied by Bokhara.

Moreover, the general impression in Russia is that, under the Agreement of 1873, everything that lies beyond the Oxus belongs *ipso facto* to Russia.

For this belief is no foundation, and I need not tell your Excellency to guard against any admissions, direct or indirect, of so vast a contention; and it is scarcely necessary to say that none of Colonel Ionoff's peregrinations can be allowed to imply the vestige of a claim to the territory he has traversed.

BRITAIN ADOPTS A NEGATIVE POLICY IN THE FAR EAST

108. (*Kimberley to the Queen 23 April 1895, Letters of Queen Victoria, 3rd series II, 496–7*)

Lord Kimberley presents his humble duty to your Majesty, and has the honour to state that after the Cabinet to-day he saw M. de Staal and told him that it was impossible for your Majesty's Government to join in the proposed communication to Japan without knowing what ulterior measures would be taken in the event of the Japanese Government refusing to listen to the communication.

Lord Kimberley cannot conceal from himself that our separation from Russia in this matter must have a prejudicial effect on the understanding which had been established between the two countries. He greatly regrets this, but he is convinced that it would be a fatal mistake to deprive Japan of the fruit of her victories by compelling her to relinquish a portion of the advantages she has secured by her Treaty with China. More especially would it be contrary to sound policy to interfere with regard to the Liaotung peninsula.

This country has no special interest in that part of China, and although it would no doubt have been better if everything could have remained *in statu quo*, the events of the war have rendered this impossible.

What may [be] the ultimate result of the great changes which must follow in that part of the world cannot now be foreseen. The wisest policy will be to watch events, and it will be time enough to consider whether we should interfere, when we are convinced that British interests are really in danger.

The attitude of Germany is singular, and it is not clear why she is now so eager to join Russia in endeavouring to induce Japan to reduce her demands. It is the more surprising because it was Germany which prevented the joint representation by the Powers which your Majesty's Government proposed on the breaking out of the war. If that representation had been made, it would have probably been successful.

Lord Kimberley could not learn from M. de Staal whether measures are in contemplation by Russia to coerce Japan. With the help of the French and German squadrons the Russian fleet may be able to overcome Japanese resistance by sea, but it seems almost certain that the Japanese will refuse to yield, and Russia may yet pause before she commits herself to an armed conflict.

By land Russia is not strong in that part of the world.

IX

The Near East and Africa

THE ARMENIAN PROBLEM AND THE STRAITS

109. (*Salisbury to Currie 19, 23 August 1895, S.P.*)

I think it would hamper us seriously to bring the other Powers in. It is bad enough to have two.

. . .

I see objections to calling in the other three (or is it four) powers for these reasons.

1. It is a new policy. I accepted the Armenian policy of my predecessors not because I liked it, but for the sake of continuity. But this is a new departure and would place the responsibility wholly on me.

2. We cannot invite the assistance of the other three powers .without a sketch of the future. We should have to say that Russia wholly declines coercion: but that we cannot join in any rash disavowal. This would be to publish our disunion prematurely.

3. If we desire to take active measures it will be more difficult to do so with five Powers hanging onto our coat tails than two. No one in Europe sympathizes with our view either about Armenia or Turkey. If we were out of the way they would not stir a finger for the Armenians: but they would lose no time in dividing the Ottoman Empire.

The only counterbalancing consideration is the idea that the Sultan would pay more regard to the councils of six powers than of three. My recollection of 1876 makes me attach a very slight weight to this impression.

110. (*Goschen to Salisbury 7 December 1895, S.P.*)

Extract

I hold you to be in error in saying that the world at large—everybody *outside the Admiralty*—believes that the Straits can easily be forced. You might more correctly say that everybody who knows nothing of the defences the geography and the torpedoes of the Dardanelles is of that opinion. I know scores of naval officers quite outside the Admiralty circle, including the C-in-C who would be responsible for the operation who quite disbelieve it being an *easy* operation though of course it *can* be done. But I know the one class whom you genuinely distrust are experts, who have studied a question.

On the other hand I quite agree with you that people who have *not* studied the question, the man in the street, believes the passing of the Dardanelles to be child's play.

I quite agree that the fleet should be kept in Turkish waters. I wish you would examine the question as to a seizure of the outer forts of the Dardanelles in certain contingencies . . . *whether or not we go through the Straits* every step which might be taken as to the neck of the bottle needs consideration.

III. (*Salisbury to Currie 17 December 1895, S.P.*)

Extract

. . . the papers which represent the easier classes in this country are decidedly disposed to 'damn the Armenians'. We have got to the end of the diplomatic lane and there is a blank wall in front of us. It is proved that nothing will mend the Govt of Turkey except the application of force to the Sultan or probably nothing except his deposition. But Russia absolutely forbids these drastic methods; and now Austria forbids them also. It is curious that two psychological climates can exist side by side so utterly different as those of England and Continental Europe. I do not believe that from Archangel to Cadiz there is a soul who cares whether the Armenians are exterminated or not. Here the sympathy for them, though the area over which it extends is not very large, where the feeling exists approaches to frenzy in its intensity.

I have now got to the end of the budget of Kimberley's bequests. I wish he had never meddled with this question without first ascertaining how far France and Austria (sic) were prepared to go. I do not see how it is possible to make any effective movement further now the Sultan has given us in words all, or nearly all, we asked. But we are no forrader. Perhaps the chapter of accidents will give us another hint before long. At present we are shut up to this dilemma—we cannot mend the lot of the Armenians without quarrelling with the Sultan: and we cannot quarrel with the Sultan without quarrelling with Austria, France and Russia.

Even our old loves the Italians are pouting at us now because we will not hand over Zeila to them.

112. (*Goschen to Salisbury 7 December 1895, S.P.*)

Extract

You wrote 'In Armenia I have been told by the Cabinet practically to sit still'. That is not my impression of what the Cabinet decided (if indeed it took a decision at all). It was one particular movement namely to pass our fleet alone through the Dardanelles to which some of us were strongly opposed, but this objection did not preclude other measures nor was it equivalent in my judgment to 'sitting still'. No doubt action has become more and more difficult as Russia's policy has developed itself more openly. Still is that policy a descent on Constantinople? Surely not.

113. (*Salisbury, Report on audience with the Tsar at Balmoral 27 September 1896, Cab/37/42/35*)

Extract

I expressed the opinion, which he shared that there seemed no cause of opposition between Russia and England except this question of the Straits. I thought that the interest of England in the matter was not so large as that of others, and was purely maritime. I admitted that the theory that Turkish rule at Constantinople was a bulwark to our Indian Empire could not be maintained. But I did not see how we could abandon the allies by whom we had stood so long. The task of Russian and Austrian statesmen should be to see whether there was no contrivance by which not only compensation, but security, could be given to Austria in the case of any such change taking place on the disappearance of the Turkish Empire. I thought that if Austria, France, and Italy were (in that event) in favour of Russia having control of the Straits, England would not maintain her objection alone, but would seek for some arrangement by which it could be met.

Referring to what he said about Russian control of the Straits, I gave my opinion that it was not impossible that the claim should be admitted if made after the Turkish Empire had disappeared; because the other Powers would all have demands to satisfy, and it might be made part of a general arrangement. But I said that the idea, at which he had hinted, that this control of the Straits should be given to Russia while the Sultan was still at Constantinople, would be exceedingly unacceptable to the other Powers, and would be strongly resisted. It would not be a *situation nette*. The Sultan with his Treaty rights and his religious influence would still be there; but he would really only be a mask for Russia. He assented, and said he quite understood my objection, and would prefer the other arrangement himself. He had only proposed the course to which I objected because he wanted to emphasize what he had said before, that Russia wanted *no* addition to her territory, not the smallest; she had enough to occupy her whole energies for a century; but he wanted access to his dominions.

In discussing these future matters, I said that I was giving him my candid opinion on the questions he raised; but that I had colleagues, and Her Majesty's Government had allies, and past traditions, and therefore he must not take any expression of opinion as a pledge. To that he quite assented.

I mentioned to him at the end of our conversation that I apprehended one possible danger, against which we ought to be prepared. It is said that the next commotion in Constantinople is likely to be directed, among others, against the subjects of the Six Powers, and, still more, against the *personnel* of the Embassies. I said it would be quite impossible that, if such a thing took place, we could sit still and tolerate it. In this view he emphatically agreed. It would be necessary that we should agree upon some mode of defending ourselves. I suggested that each Power should, in that case, have the liberty of sending up not more than three ships of war. He did not contest this view; I think he partially approved of it. But he did not at all fancy the prospect, and soon afterwards closed the interview.

S.

114. (*Salisbury to Currie 23 November 1896, S.P.*)

Extract

The refusal of the Russian Government to accept our proposals as to a mutual engagement to coerce is not unexpected: but it modifies the situation to this extent—that we must not join in any demand of an important character upon the Sultan without coming to an understanding with Russia on this matter. I quite agree with the Austrian Minister for Foreign Affairs that the

Powers ought not again to expose themselves to the rebuff of a refusal and unless we are prepared to say we will insist we had better make no more demands. Such ceremonies are only methods of making time for the benefit of Russia and they make us ridiculous. As time goes on the prospect that we shall ultimately keep the Straits out of the hands of Russia becomes fainter and fainter. But we must continue to hold the old language—for though our hopes may be faint our views of policy are unaltered. The great strength of the Dardanelles and the preferences of the Sultan for the control of Russia rather than the control of England, as evidenced by his fortifying the Dardanelles and not the Bosphorous —and the fact that our sailors under the altered conditions of warfare have no stomach for a hazardous attack—all these circumstances make me feel that Russia will eventually have her way. The best we can hope for is to put off that result till *after* the catastrophe of the Turkish Empire: and the Sultan is slipping downhill so fast that I have hopes that may be done. Of course if the question of cutting up the Sultan becomes practical the sovereignty of the Straits may become both for us and for Austria a question of compensation. Of course we must say nothing of such views for the present as Austria would imagine we were going to desert her, which is certainly very far from being the case. . . .

I do not believe that the Armenian movement had any strong electoral backing at any time. Since Rosebery's speech it has become insignificant.

115. (*Salisbury to Currie 19 October 1897, S.P. Partly printed in Grenville, p. 94*)

Extract

I confess that since, some two years back, the Cabinet refused me leave to take the fleet up the Dardanelles because it was impracticable, I have regarded the Eastern Question as having little serious interest for England. We have no other way of coercing the Turk. 'Blockades' are of no use since it has been ascertained that (without a declaration of war) neutral nations need not accept them: and that America was this year very much disinclined to do so. I used to believe that the occupation of Jeddah might be a possible alternative; but the costliness of Indian troops and the extreme unhealthiness of the locality make that idea impractical.

... We have really no hold on and no interest in any of the Sultan's territories except Egypt. On the other hand our interest in Egypt is growing stronger. After the Sultan's victories it is clear that if Egypt is going to be given back at all, it must be to the Sultan and the Khedive. No one else has any legal right; the idea that the Turkish Empire is on the verge of dissolution has been dissipated; and the Concert of Europe has conclusively shown that it can never be trusted with even the slenderest portion of Executive authority. It follows that either Egypt must be given back to the Moslems—which no one except the Moslems would approve— or we must use for the purpose of maintaining peace and order there, the authority with which we have been invested by the victory of Tel-el-Kebir. This is the only policy which it seems to me is left to us by the Cabinet's decision to which I have referred —to strengthen our position on the Nile (to its source) and to withdraw as much as possible from all responsibilities at Constantinople. Of course this last can only be done gradually by reason of past engagements.

RELATIONS WITH THE TRIPLE ALLIANCE

116. (*Deym to Goluchowski 6 February 1896, S.A.W. Geheimakten XXV/463/7 A–F*)

Extract

When I saw Lord Salisbuty the day before yesterday he raised the question again himself and said that he had consulted Mr. Balfour, who enjoyed his complete confidence and who had more contact than he had himself with public opinion. He (Balfour) was convinced that in view of the great change that had taken place in public opinion in England during the last eighteen months in relation to Turkey, it would not be possible to undertake engagements since they ran the danger of not being able to keep their word when it came to the point.

Such an agreement involving the engagement to maintain the status quo in Turkey might mean a war with Russia and perhaps also at the same time with France; and judging by opinion in England to-day he would have a job to get a majority in Parliament to fight such a war. If this happened as things lay to-day it would be next to impossible in the event of a threat to Constantinople to send the English fleet to the Bosphorous to hinder the landing of troops.

That Russia sooner or later, with or without the mandate of the Powers, would occupy Armenia seemed to him quite likely. But in view of public opinion in England the Government would not be in a position to oppose such an occupation and the other Powers would not act either.

. . .

I asked Lord Salisbury if he thought that the traditional English policy in the East had been given up and whether Russia would be allowed to take Constantinople. He denied this and said that it was quite possible that in the event of this public opinion in England would change again as soon as Russia took Constantinople. He had in no way said that England would not go to war with Russia over Constantinople, only that at present he could not make engagements that would oblige England to do this.

The Prime Minister said further that he was well aware that if he made no agreement with us to cover this event England ran the danger of being without allies and he assured me that he layed the greatest value on eventually having Austria-Hungary as an ally . . . It was simply that he did not want to run the risk of leaving us in the lurch.

I asked him then how it was that only a fortnight ago he had indicated his willingness to renew the accord à trois of 1887. He answered simply: 'Je vous l'avouerai franchement. C'est que cet accord ne m'engage pas à grand chose, car il ne nous oblige pas à faire la guerre.' . . .

Lord Salisbury added that it was his greatest wish to collaborate with us since our interests did not collide anywhere and Austria-Hungary enjoyed the greatest sympathy in England. Here, Austria-Hungary was regarded as one of the few Powers upon whose friendly feeling England could count.

117. (*Salisbury to the Queen 19 February 1896, S.P.*)

Extract

Mr. Chamberlain was of the opinion that at the point where we were now our antagonism to Russia was a mistake and that we should occupy a stronger position in Europe as the friend of Russia than as the friend of the Triple Alliance. This view was not generally shared by the Cabinet but opinions were much divided. Generally it was agreed that we should never be allowed by the people of this country to go to war again on behalf of

Turkey, though we might do so in defence of the Straits to prevent them from being appropriated by Russia. The opinion was generally expressed that feeling in this country even on the Tory side was much more favourable to Russia and much more adverse to the Turks that it used to be. Lord Salisbury expressed himself strongly against any policy that would cut Austria adrift. It would reconstitute the Drei Kaiser Bundnis, a state of affairs which must be injurious to this country.

118. (*Salisbury to Lascelles 10 March 1896, S.P. Printed in G.P. XI, no. 2779*)

Extract

We certainly wish to be good friends with Germany: as we were in 1892. That is to say we wish to lean to the Triple Alliance without belonging to it. But in 1892, as now, we kept free from any engagements to go to war in any contingency whatever. That is the attitude prescribed to us on the one hand by our popular constitution, which will not acknowledge the obligations of an engagement made in former years—and on the other hand by our insular position which makes the burdensome conditions of an alliance unnecessary for our safety. Whether this attitude is reasonable or not it is the attitude we maintained from 1886–92. If the German Emperor is dissatisfied with us now why was he satisfied with us then? There is no change.

I understand that his three griefs against us are:

1. Our conduct at the close of the China-Japan war. This was under our predecessors. My knowledge of these transactions is too imperfect to enable me either to condemn or to defend the policy they pursued.

2. Our conduct about Zeila . . .

3. Our conduct in the Armenian matter—which was inconsistent with an unreserved resolve to uphold the Turkish Empire. The Emperor is old enough to remember the Bulgarian storm. I remember meeting him in England at the time. He surely must know that these philanthropic tempests are as much a recurring feature of our political climate as the 'tourmente' is in the Alps or the Typhoon in the China Seas. I came into office in the middle of one of these hurricanes. I followed, to its end, the policy to which my predecessor had pledged England but I did nothing more.

I was quite unconscious of any change from the disposition which animated us in 1892. I was therefore a little puzzled at the numerous hints which reached me of a more hostile disposition on his part. Some of his statements to Swaine had been so emphatic that I was not very much surprised at the Kruger telegram when it came. I cannot, probably I never shall be able to, explain this phase of mind: but we shall be exceeding glad to feel that the disposition mutually of the two governments is again the same as it was in 1892.

119. (*Salisbury to Currie 15 December 1896, S.P.*)

Extract

It is for the moment a question between the alliance of Austria and Russia. Russia wishes for the whole passage—though for the time she might be contented with the Upper limit of the Bosphorous. Austria would look upon the concession to Russia of this limited instalment as involving the whole concession in the end. I do not believe that Austria would acquiesce in any portion of the Straits being surrendered to Russia . . . It follows from this view that we cannot declare our advocacy of such a policy without forfeiting the alliance and provoking the distrust of Austria. She is our only real friend in Europe and her friendship has a certain positive value. She has influence with Germany: she is a cloy to Russia, so long as they are opposed. If they were to unite they could carry everything in the S.E. of Europe before them. Therefore I shrink from any action which would weaken the tie that binds England and Austria together. It must show a definite advantage sufficient to outweigh the loss of that alliance. A tentative adhesion to a policy of which, even if Russia accepted it, the future would be very doubtful, could offer no such advantage.

THE RECONQUEST OF THE SUDAN

120. (*Hicks-Beach to Salisbury 19 October 1896, P.C.C. 33*)

Extract

May I venture a suggestion about the Sudan? The present temper of Germany makes it, I suppose, pretty certain that the Court of Appeal will decide next month that the $£\frac{1}{2}$m. must be repaid to the Caisse and that besides this that when, next season, the question of a further advance arises no money will be forthcoming from that quarter . . . If we are placed in that position through the refusal of the Powers . . . why are we bound to hand over these provinces, recovered at our cost, or mainly at our cost, to Egypt? I feel sure that the House of Commons would not so much mind paying if we announced that we should hold and administer the Sudan, or any part of it, until Egypt could pay the cost of its recovery. And surely it would be a strong position to take up against French policy . . . possibly to influence them to allow a £½m. next month.

I think there will be considerable difficulty, not alone from the Opposition, in getting money from the House of Commons for any further advance to Khartoum if Egypt, deriving all the benefit, has practically nothing to pay for it.

121. *(Baring to Salisbury 22 October 1897, Cab/37/45/46)*

I have not so far written to you about Soudan affairs, as I have been hoping from mail to mail to have something definite to say. Even now I cannot speak positively about Kassala. Nevertheless, I think I should not delay any longer to let you know something of how matters stand.

In the first place, let me say that there is not the smallest question of any further advance at present. What we have to think about is to secure the territory which has been already acquired. It is abundantly clear that the reconquest of Khartoum is beyond the military and financial resources of the Egyptian Government. In moments of retrospection, I tear my hair over the hurried decision of March 1896. It has upset all my calculations, and introduced an entirely new factor into Egyptian politics. But it is of no use to worry about the past; we have to look to the present and future.

I hope to be able to telegraph to you about Kassala before this reaches you. The question is mainly military, viz., which course will most secure the safety of the present position—occupation or abandonment. My impression is, on the whole, that the balance of advantage is on the side of taking the place.

As to the financial side of the question, we shall certainly be strained, not so much by Kassala as by the fact that Kitchener's other expenses have largely increased. Still we shall not be broken. My main difficulty will be not revenue and expenditure, but ways and means, for the English advance nearly exhausts our legal powers of borrowing for Treasury purposes during the months of low revenue.

Now, as to the future, I think I should prepare you for what is evidently coming. Manifestly, the proper thing to do is to hold our present line, and nothing more. You will have a great onslaught from the soldiers on this subject. They will all tell you that we must go on—which means an English expedition. My own opinion is quite clear, that no sufficiently important English interest is involved to justify the loss of life and money which would be involved in the capture of Khartoum.

The only justification would be that the English Government has placed the Egyptians in their present position, and they are, therefore, morally bound to help. But this argument does not come into operation unless it be shown that the Egyptian army must either advance or fall back, and I am as yet not at all convinced of either necessity. Without doubt, if we are to sit down in our present position for some while—it may be for some years—the Egyptian Service will become unpopular with English officers, for the climate is fearful, but I do not believe in our not being able to get officers to serve.

What, therefore, I think we shall have to do is to sit still, strengthen our present position, and do all that is possible (and a good deal is possible) to improve our railway communication both to Cairo and Suakin.

122. (*Baring Memorandum 5 November 1897, Cab/37/45/46*)

Memorandum on the Soudan Question

(Private and Confidential)

The purely Egyptian aspect of the Soudan questions is very simple. The objections to any retreat are obvious. An unaided Egyptian advance is, for the time being at all events, out of the question. Therefore, if it be once admitted that the maintenance of the present position for any considerable length of time is either impossible or highly undesirable—as to which I am not yet convinced in one sense or the other—an English expedition becomes an unavoidable necessity, and the sooner it is undertaken, and the present financial and military tension is made to cease, the better.

But there is a good deal to be said outside the purely Egyptian view of the case.

As a matter of personal opinion, I greatly dislike the idea of an English expedition to the Soudan, either now or at any future time. I need not state at any length my reasons for holding this opinion, but I may say that my view, briefly, is: (1) That the re-occupation of the Soudan by Egypt, though not of such paramount importance as is often represented, is a considerable Egyptian interest; (2) that it is worth the while of the Egyptian Government, within reasonable limits, to make some sacrifices in order to attain that object; but (3), that so long as England, as at present, possesses merely a leasehold of Egypt, it is not worth the while of the English Government to sacrifice the valuable lives and to incur the heavy expenditure which would necessarily be involved in the reoccupation, if effected by English arms.

Whilst holding these views, I am prepared to admit that the English Government may be placed in such a position as to render an English expedition inevitable. If, for instance, it were clearly proved to me that the Egyptian army could not, without undue risk, maintain its present position, I should then be most reluctantly obliged to admit that the despatch of an English expedition was imposed on the Government by the circumstances of the situation, for it must not be forgotten that it was the sudden decision to advance to Dongola, taken in March 1896, which has brought about the present dilemma, and that as the English Government is responsible for that decision they are bound, as a matter of justice and policy, to see the Egyptian Government through its present difficulties.

Whether the Egyptian army is capable of holding its present position, and, if so, for how long it will be able to do so, are points on which I am as yet unable to express definite opinions. Before doing so I must discuss the matter fully with the Sirdar, who is expected to arrive in Cairo about a week hence. I may say, however, that even if it were proved to me that some English help were necessary, I, at present, incline to the opinion—inasmuch as the question is quite as much financial as military—that it would be preferable to afford some moderate financial assistance to the Egyptian Government, supposing adequate military security to be attainable by such methods, rather than to incur all the evils attendant on the despatch of a British expedition to Khartoum.

As regards the future, therefore, I reserve my opinion.

There remains for discussion the immediate point raised by Lord Wolseley's letter to Lord Landsowne of the 26th October, namely, whether 'we ought to push on to Khartoum this winter'.

Lord Wolseley thinks we should do so, on the ground that 'the French are now working hard to forestall us on the Upper Nile, and if they do so we may have to face serious complications with them when we attempt the job in the autumn of 1898.'

Subject to any new lights which may be thrown on the situation by the Sirdar's reports, I am unable to support Lord Wolseley's recommendation. . . .

As regards this argument, I have, in the first instance, to say that, although I should of course much prefer that the French did not establish themselves on the Upper Nile, at the same time I do not share the somewhat extreme views—as they appear to me— which are often held as to the absolute necessity of preventing them from doing so.

What is it, after all, we want in Africa? I presume that we do *not* want to acquire on behalf of ourselves or the Egyptians large tracts of useless territory which it would be difficult and costly to administer properly. What we want, as it seems to me, is to trade with Central Africa. For the purposes of trade it would certainly be preferable that no portion of the waterway of the Nile should be in the hands of an European Power. Let us, therefore, by all means do all that can be done by diplomacy, by negotiations with Menelek, who is a most important factor in the situation, and possibly by affording some reasonable aid to Egypt, whose affairs are in English hands, to prevent any such consummation. But whether it is desirable, merely in order to forestall the French on the Upper Nile, to send a large expedition to Khartoum with the possibility—for this also must not be forgotten—of being drawn by a combination of public pressure and military argument into further and more remote enterprizes appears to me to be very questionable.

It must be remembered that we can always get to Khartoum before any one else whenever we choose to send an expedition there, and that we now hold Berber, a most important commercial and strategical point. The idea of connecting the Nile and the Red Sea Coast by railway, which, whilst the Dervishes were at Berber was a mere academic question, has now come within the domain of practical politics. It will certainly have to be considered before long. Further, I do not doubt that in a future which cannot be very remote, the railway link now missing between Assouan and Wady Halfa will be supplied. Thus we may look forward to railway communication being established from the neighbourhood of Khartoum, if not from Khartoum itself, to Alexandria on the one hand, and to Suakin on the other hand. In the meanwhile, the Uganda Railway is progressing.

My contention is, therefore, that for all important commercial purposes the French are, to a great extent, already forestalled, for the trade of the regions for which there is now some competition, must in the end almost inevitably find its way either to Uganda, or else via Berber or Dongola, to Suakin or Alexandria. I should add that my belief is that the importance of the trade in question is not so great as is often supposed. . . .

Turning to the second point mentioned above, it is to be observed that the capture of Khartoum this winter affords no certain guarantee that complications with the French will be avoided. It may be admitted that those complications are likely to be more serious if the French are found in effective occupation of some part of the Upper Nile Valley than in the contrary case. But they will, under any circumstances, probably take place. Whenever we, or Egypt acting at our instigation, advance beyond Khartoum, the French will cry out; neither is it possible at present to foresee in what precise manner the difficulties which will then ensue will be capable of solution. All that can be said is that it is difficult to believe that a settlement of some kind will be impossible.

We know so little of what is really passing in Central Africa that it is difficult to discuss this branch of the subject with the same confidence as may be felt in treating other portions of the multiform Egyptian question. On the whole, however, my view is that, although some objections, which are not devoid of force, may be urged against inaction, the arguments in favour of immediate action are not nearly of sufficient strength to outweigh those on the other side. . . .

Lord Cromer to the Marquess of Salisbury.—(Received November 11)

(Private)
(Telegraphic) *Cairo, November* 11, 1897.

Sirdar arrived this morning. He seems all right in point of health. He will take leave, but not just yet.

He does not go so far as to say that the present military position is untenable, but he considers it risky, and thinks to maintain it for an indefinite period would constitute too heavy a strain on the Egyptian army.

He is in favour of an English expedition next year, but adds that if, as is not improbable, the Dervishes are obliged to retire from Metemneh by reason of the difficulty in obtaining food, the situation will be improved, and strain greatly relieved.

He thinks any immediate movement not only unnecessary but undesirable, as before there is any question of an English expedition, he considers that the railway to Berber should be finished.

Please read this in connection with my answer to your private letter of the 29th October, which is now on its way to London.

123. (*Monson to Hanotaux 10 December 1897, printed in Gooch and Temperley I, 185*)

Her Majesty's Government must not be understood to admit that any other European Power than Great Britain has any claim to occupy any part of the Valley of the Nile. The views of the British Government upon this matter were plainly stated in Parliament by Sir Edward Grey some years ago during the administration of the Earl of Rosebery, and were formally communicated to the French Government at the time. Her Majesty's present Government entirely adhere to the language that was on this occasion employed by their predecessors.

124. (*Salisbury to Monson 12 October 1898, Cab/37/48/75*)

I generally insisted on the view that the Valley of the Nile had belonged and still belonged to Egypt, and that whatever impediment or diminution that title might have suffered through the conquest and occupation of the Mahdi had been removed by the victory of the Anglo-Egyptian army on the 2nd September.

THE PORTUGUESE COLONIES

125. (*Kimberley to Malet 5 December 1894, F.O. 343/3, printed in Bayer, p. 122*)

I did not think it desirable to record in my despatch of November 19, giving an account of my conversation with Count Hatzfeldt, a rather sharp passage which you may remember I read to you from my rough notes. But it is well you should know precisely what was said, and I therefore repeat it to you confidentially.—In commenting on Count Hatzfeldt's observation that Germany could not 'permit' the Portuguese Colonies to become British territory I remarked that 'as Count Hatzfeldt has said that Germany could not permit us to take possession of the Portuguese Colonies, I must point out that if the question of the disposal of those Colonies should ever require to be considered, this country with its great sea power would be able to speak the strongest word'. 'No doubt', Count Hatzfeldt replied, 'you could easily crush Germany at sea but', here he paused evidently looking for some expression which would not be offensive, on which I said 'you could be able to do us much mischief elsewhere'. 'Exactly so', he said. I went on to observe that 'I entirely agreed and the conclusion I drew was that it was for the interest of both Powers to have no disagreement'.

Count Hatzfeldt used the word permit on the former occasion when we discussed this matter, and on this occasion he more than once used the word. His manner was perfectly friendly, but I thought it necessary to let him clearly understand that if German Power is far greater than ours by land, ours is much greater than hers by sea and that such language as 'permit' is altogether out of place.

The bullying tone which Germans habitually use towards other Powers, is, they must be made politely to understand, not suitable in communications with such a Power as England. Hatzfeldt I must add is always friendly and courteous to me personally. All this is strictly for your private eye.

126. (*Balfour Memorandum 5 September 1898, Cab/37/48/71*)
Extract

I have endeavoured in the Treaty come to with Germany about Mozambique and Angola to carry out what I understand to be the wishes of the Cabinet. Speaking generally, it secures for us the absolute exclusion of every other Power, including Germany, from what, for shortness, I may call our sphere of influence—in other words Germany resigns what she has never consented to resign before (however little title she may have had to it), a claim to regard Delagoa Bay as a port of international interest, whose fate Portugal and England could not be permitted to settle at their own sweet will. Resigning this, she also resigns all concern in Transvaal matters. That she would ever have actively supported the Transvaal is, indeed, more than doubtful; but unquestionably her supposed friendliness to the Boers encouraged them to adopt a policy towards this country which, now that they are shut out from all hope of European assistance, may perhaps be modified to our advantage.

We obtain further a complete defensive alliance with Germany against any third Power desiring to intervene in Mozambique or Angola, and Count Hatzfeldt earnestly, but somewhat vaguely, assures me that this is to be the beginning of a new era of Anglo-German co-operation in other parts of the world. I offer no estimate on the value of this prophecy.

I have taken great trouble to draw the Agreements so as to make them, if they ever become fully known, as palatable as possible to Portugal.

X

The Far East

127. (*Salisbury to O'Conor 25 January 1898, B.D. I, 8*)

Extract

Our idea was this. The two Empires of China and Turkey are so weak that in all important matters they are constantly guided by the advice of Foreign Powers. In giving this advice Russia and England are constantly opposed, neutralizing each other's efforts much more frequently than the real antagonism of their interests would justify; and this condition of things is not likely to diminish, but to increase. It is to remove or lessen this evil that we have thought that an understanding with Russia might benefit both nations.

We contemplate no infraction of existing rights. We would not admit the violation of any existing treaties, or impair the integrity of the present empires of either China or Turkey. These two conditions are vital. We aim at no partition of territory, but only a partition of preponderance. It is evident that both in respect to Turkey and China there are large portions which interest Russia much more than England and *vice versa*. Merely as an illustration, and binding myself to nothing, I would say that the portion of Turkey which drains into the Black Sea, together with the drainage valley of the Euphrates as far as Bagdad, interest Russia much more than England: whereas Turkish Africa, Arabia, and the Valley of the Euphrates below Bagdad interest England much more than Russia. A similar distinction exists in China between the Valley of the Hoango with the territory north of it and the Valley of the Yangtze.

Would it be possible to arrange that where, in regard to these territories our counsels differ, the Power least interested should give way to and assist the other? I do not disguise from myself that the difficulty would be great. Is it insuperable? I have designedly omitted to deal with large tracts in each Empire, because neither Power has shown any keen interest in them.

THE CABINET DECIDES AGAINST WAR OVER PORT ARTHUR

128. (*Balfour to the Queen 26 March 1898, Letters of Queen Victoria, 3rd series III, 238*)

Extract

The discussion was entirely confined to the policy to be pursued in the Far East; Her Majesty's Ministers held the opinion in which Mr. Balfour knows that Lord Salisbury concurs, that it was not worth while to promote a war with Russia in order to keep her out of Port Arthur: her influence at Peking depends principally on her land position; and though the possession of Port Arthur may augment it, the difference is not sufficient to justify hostilities.

It was, however, thought desirable that Great Britain should maintain her position in the Gulf of Pechili; and in the neighbourhood of Peking by closing with the Chinese offer of the reversion of Wei-hai-wai.

BALFOUR OPPOSES A FORCEFUL POLICY OVER MANCHURIAN RAILWAY CONCESSIONS

129. (*Balfour Memorandum 15 August 1898, Cab/37/47/62*)

Extract

I cannot believe that the line is of the immense benefit to Britain which Sir Claude MacDonald supposes . . . while a striking diplomatic triumph for the country would not only be very agreeable to the public, but also of enormous importance at the present moment, when we are really fighting a battle for prestige rather than for material gain, yet its utility would probably be temporary. I mean, it would not greatly affect the distant and final destinies of China or even of Manchuria!

. . . We want no more fragments of China for ourselves; we do not desire to give other people a fresh excuse for piracy. So that everything we took in order to punish a corrupt and indifferent Government would really punish ourselves.

Chamberlain advocates an agreement with Germany on the Open Door

130. (*Chamberlain Memorandum 10 September 1900, Cab/37/53/65*)

Extract

14. I am personally unable to believe in the reform of the Chinese Empire as a whole or in the permanent maintenance of its territorial integrity. Unless Russia breaks up from internal difficulties, of which there is no present sign, I believe she will ultimately secure Northern China, and that the 'Open Door' will be a mere name so far as this part of the Chinese Empire is concerned. It is certain that we are not strong enough by ourselves to prevent her from accomplishing such an annexation, and both in China and elsewhere it is our interest that Germany should throw herself across the path of Russia. An alliance between Germany and Russia, entailing as it would the co-operation of France, is the one thing we have to dread, and the clash of German and Russian interests, whether in China or Asia Minor, would be a guarantee for our safety.

I think then our policy clearly is to encourage good relations between ourselves and Germany, as well as between ourselves and Japan and the United States, and we should endeavour to make use of the present opportunity to emphasize the breach between Russia and Germany, and Russia and Japan. We should, without urging it, let it be known that we shall put no obstacle in the way of German expansion in Shantung, nor in the way of the gratification of Japan's ambition in Corea. But, in return, we should obtain written assurances recognizing our claim to predominant interest and influence in the Yang-tsze Valley. We are not likely ever to want to take possession of any territory in the interior ourselves; but we ought to try for some understanding which will keep off all others, and make it easy to maintain the 'Open Door' in at least this, the most important portion of the Chinese Empire. We should meanwhile cultivate in every way the friendship of the local Viceroys, and during the present crisis keep a larger force of troops and ships at hand in this district than any other nation.

The Far East

131. (*Lansdowne Memorandum 12 March 1901, Cab/37/56/30, printed by Grenville in B.I.H.R. 1954*)

The draft Declaration marked (C) which it is proposed to invite Germany to join with us[1] in making secretly to Japan, is intended to elicit from Germany a distinct statement of her intentions.

If she refuses to be a party to the arrangement suggested, we shall have to reconsider the situation.

(A.)
Telegram from Japanese Minister at Berlin

The German Vice-Minister for Foreign Affairs told me at an interview with him on the 6th March that the German Government discountenance any action on the part of any single Power to turn the present situation for its own use, and that therefore they entirely disapprove Russian proceedings in regard to Manchuria. He strongly denied that there is any secret understanding with Russia on Far Eastern question, and assured me that as German Government are well aware of the vital importance of Manchurian question to Japan, Germany will observe benevolent neutrality in case matters should come to a crisis. He added that this attitude of Germany will keep French fleet in check, while England will probably support Japan. I asked if he think that Russia will persist in her demands. He answered that as all Powers seem to disfavour Russian action, she will not push matters to extremity.

(B.)
Telegram from Japanese Minister for Foreign Affairs to
Baron Hayashi

You will ask Marquess of Lansdowne:

1. Has British Government been consulted by Germany on the subject of remarks of German Vice-Minister for Foreign Affairs?

2. Does his Lordship think that the remarks represent *bona fide* attitude and final intention of Germany?

3. How far may Japan rely upon the support of Great Britain in case Japan finds it necessary to approach Russia?

---

[1] (C) bears the following Minute in Salisbury's hand: Draft Decln. not to be sent, but Germany to be asked what was to be understood by 'benevolent neutrality'

(C.)
Draft Declaration

In present circumstances, the interests of England and Germany are not sufficiently involved to justify them in giving material assistance to the Chinese Government in resisting the conclusion of the Agreements. They admit, however, that the vital interests of Japan are thereby seriously jeopardized, and in reply to the inquiries of the Japanese Government as to what would be the attitude of England and Germany in the event of hostilities between Japan and Russia, they have to state that in such contingency, which they would deeply deplore, it would be their object to limit as far as possible the extent of the war, and to that end they would remain neutral, reserving, however, to themselves absolute freedom of action should the course of events require them, in their own interests, to intervene on behalf of Japan. In the event, however, of any Power joining Russia in hostilities against Japan, the British and German Governments will give naval assistance to Japan to defend herself against such attack.

132. (*Lansdowne to Lascelles*[1] *18 March 1901, B.D. II, 60–61*)

I had some conversation with Baron Eckardstein on the subject of the correspondence which has recently taken place between the German and British Governments in regard to the action which the two Powers might take should Russia and Japan go to war.

I told Baron Eckardstein that your Excellency's telegram No. 17 of the 14th instant, made it evident to us that the Japanese Minister at Berlin had misapprehended the purport of Herr von Mühlberg's statement to him, and that the German Government did not contemplate anything more than neutrality in the event supposed, and certainly not any action which would have the effect of keeping a third Power in check.

I added that Count Bülow's speech, which proclaimed the fact that in Germany's estimation the Anglo-German Agreement had no reference to Manchuria, seemed to me to emphasize what I had just said, and to put an end to any idea which might have been entertained as to the possibility of England and Germany combining for the purpose of 'keeping a ring' for Russia and Japan.

[1] Copies sent to Chamberlain, Salisbury, Devonshire, Balfour.

Baron Eckardstein said that he did not differ from me, and that, speaking for himself only, he thought that no proposal of the above kind was likely to find favour at this moment.

On the other hand, he believed that the German Government, while averse from an agreement entered into solely with reference to the present situation in China, would entertain favourably the idea of an understanding of a more durable and extended character with this country.

The kind of arrangement which he contemplated might be described as a purely defensive alliance between the two Powers, directed solely against France and Russia.

So long as Germany or England were attacked by one only of the other two Powers the Alliance would not operate, but if either Germany or England had to defend itself against both France and Russia, Germany would have to help England, or England Germany, as the case might be.

He thought England, which had scattered and vulnerable possessions all over the world, was more likely to require help than Germany.

I told Baron Eckardstein that the proximity of Russia to Germany along so extensive a frontier made the situation of Germany quite as vulnerable as ours. His project was a novel and very far-reaching one, which would require careful examination, and which obviously I could not encourage without reference to my colleagues.

I said that, assuming the two Powers to be agreeable in principle to such a transaction, I saw at first sight no small difficulty in giving effect to it. Such a contract seemed to me to entail the adoption of an identic foreign policy by both Powers in all their external relations, because every complication in which one of the two might become involved might drag the other into the quarrel. It occurred to me, moreover, that it was far from easy to distinguish between the case in which a country was acting on the defensive and the case in which it was not. The first blow might be really struck in self-defence; or, conversely, an attack might be brought on by political action of a deliberately provocative character. How were our mutual obligations to be defined so as to meet all such cases fairly?

Baron Eckardstein was careful to assure me that his suggestion was not made under instructions, but I feel no doubt that he has been desired to sound me.

133. (*Salisbury Memorandum 29 May 1901, B.D. II, 68–69*)

Extract

Anglo-German Understanding

This is a proposal for including England within the bounds of the Triple Alliance. I understand its practical effect to be:

1. If England were attacked by two Powers—say France and Russia—Germany, Austria, and Italy would come to her assistance.

2. Conversely, if either Austria, Germany, or Italy were attacked by France and Russia, or, if Italy were attacked by France and Spain, England must come to the rescue.

Even assuming that the Powers concerned were all despotic, and could promise anything they pleased, with a full confidence that they would be able to perform the promise, I think it is open to much question whether the bargain would be for our advantage. The liability of having to defend the German and Austrian frontiers against Russia is heavier than that of having to defend the British Isles against France. Even, therefore, in its most naked aspect the bargain would be a bad one for this country. Count Hatzfeldt speaks of our 'isolation as constituting a serious danger for us.' Have we ever felt that danger practically? If we had succumbed in the revolutionary war, our fall would not have been due to our isolation. We had many allies, but they would not have saved us if the French Emperor had been able to command the Channel. Except during his reign we have never even been in danger; and, therefore, it is impossible for us to judge whether the 'isolation' under which we are supposed to suffer, does or does not contain in it any elements of peril. It would hardly be wise to incur novel and most onerous obligations, in order to guard against a danger in whose existence we have no historical reason for believing.

But though the proposed arrangement, even from this point of view, does not seem to me admissible, these are not by any means the weightiest objections that can be urged against it. The fatal circumstance is that neither we nor the Germans are competent to make the suggested promises. The British Government cannot undertake to declare war, for any purpose, unless it is a purpose of which the electors of this country would approve. If the Government promised to declare war for an object which did not commend itself to public opinion, the promise would be repudiated, and the Government would be turned out. I do not see how, in common honesty, we could invite other nations to rely upon our aids in a struggle, which must be formidable and probably supreme, when we have no means whatever of knowing what may be the humour of our people in circumstances which cannot be foreseen. We might, to some extent, divest ourselves of the full responsibility of such a step, by laying our Agreement with the Triple Alliance before Parliament as soon as it is concluded. But there are very grave objections to such a course, and I do not understand it to be recommended by the German Ambassador.

The impropriety of attempting to determine by a secret contract the future conduct of a Representative Assembly upon an issue of peace or war would apply to German policy as much as to English, only that the German Parliament would probably pay more deference to the opinion of their Executive than would be done by the English Parliament. But a promise of defensive alliance with England would excite bitter murmurs in every rank of German society—if we may trust the indications of German sentiment, which we had have an opportunity of witnessing during the last two years.

134. (*Lansdowne to Lascelles 19 December 1901, Cab/37/59/141, text printed in B.D. II, 80–81*)

Extract

Having thus recapitulated the history of the above discussions, I told Count Metternich that I had waited to see whether he would mention the subject to me, as it seemed to be one to which, as soon as his position as Ambassador at this Court had been confirmed, he would be likely to refer. As, however, he had now held his appointment for some weeks, and as he had not mentioned the subject, I thought it desirable, in order that there might be no misconception, that I should approach it. I reminded his Excellency that I had not been successful in obtaining either from Count Hatzfeldt or from Baron Eckardstein anything beyond a most general indication of their views. From those indications I gathered that the proposal before us, if indeed it was still before us, was that the British Empire should join the Triple Alliance. We had considered this proposal very carefully. To my mind it certainly presented many attractive features. It was, I understood, to be a purely defensive Alliance. It would make for peace, which we desired. It would give us powerful allies, the value of whose assistance I certainly did not underrate. But we could not contemplate the possibility of entering into such a contract and withholding the knowledge of it from Parliament; and we had to consider whether, in present circumstances, it was possible for us to go to Parliament with such a proposal. His Excellency, who was so familiar with public life in this country, must be well aware of the suspicion with which any entanglement in foreign alliances was regarded by a large part of the British public. We should certainly be told that we ran the chance of involving ourselves and our great Colonies in disputes which did not concern us, and which might arise in almost any part of the world. This would be represented as a new and onerous obligation, and we should have considerable difficulty in defending ourselves for wishing to incur it. I was far from suggesting that all the arguments were on one side; but, looked at from a Parliamentary point of view, it was undoubtedly, if I might use the expression, a very stiff fence to ride at. We had to consider whether the conditions were favourable at this moment. His Majesty's Government had their hands full, owing to the South African war and for other reasons, and the temper of the two countries was not, it seemed to me, in a particularly favourable state. Germany had been suffering from a severe outbreak of Anglophobia, and I was afraid that this had provoked a corresponding feeling of irritation in this country. On the other hand, our relations with other Powers were not unfriendly, and our sudden adhesion to the German group might have unfortunate effects in other quarters. While, therefore, we certainly did not regard the German proposal with an unfriendly or indifferent eye, I did not think that for the moment we could afford to take it up.

. . .

He feared, however, that an opportunity so favourable as that which presented itself last summer might not again occur. In politics, his Excellency said, things never stood still, and his own opinion, which he expressed as one entirely personal, was that in the years which lay before us the tendency would be for Germany to move more and more towards Russia.

I replied that it would, to my mind, be most unfortunate if

there should be any estrangement between our two countries, and I trusted that he would not consider that our inability to take so serious a step as that which had been proposed to us denoted any unfriendliness towards Germany. Speaking entirely for myself, I asked him whether, assuming that we could not accept the German proposal as it stood, it might not be possible for the two countries to arrive at an understanding with regard to the policy which they might pursue in reference to particular questions or in particular parts of the world in which they were alike interested?

His Excellency unhesitatingly replied that no such minor proposal was likely to find favour with the German Government. It was a case of 'the whole or none'.

At the close of the conversation, I expressed my hope that I had made it clear to his Excellency that if for the moment we regarded the object which the German Government had had in view as unattainable, we had come to this conclusion, not because we regarded the offer with indifference, but on account of practical difficulties the importance of which I had no doubt his Excellency would fully recognize.

Note by Chamberlain:

This means that the British Government has no further intention of concluding any arrangements with Germany wh. wd prevent or impede the development of good relations with Russia and if possible with France.

NEGOTIATIONS WITH JAPAN

135. (*Selborne Memorandum 4 September 1901, Cab/37/58/87*)

Balance of Naval Power in the Far East

The recognized standard for the naval strength of Great Britain has hitherto been equality with the ships of the two next greatest naval Powers.

I have already given to the Cabinet my reasons for thinking that this standard would be beyond the strength of this country if the United States were to use all their resources to develop their naval strength, and that it is inadequate if applied to a possible war against France in alliance with Russia.

For us victory in such a war is a condition of continued

existence as an Empire. To them, defeat would bring no corresponding consequences. Accordingly it appears to me to be running too grave a risk to be content to enter upon a contest with two such Powers on terms of simple equality of strength.

In considering, however, the value to this country of some sort of naval alliance with Japan I will deal with the question from the point of view of our position in a war with France and Russia in which we started with an equality, but without any superiority, of strength in battleships.

The decisive battles in such a war would certainly be fought in European waters; but it does not follow that we should be free to concentrate the whole of our naval strength in those waters and leave the outlying parts of the Empire to await the final issue.

I am strongly in favour of concentrating our strength, as far as possible, at the spot at which the final issue will be fought out; but some risks would be too great to run even for this object.

The case of Far Eastern seas strikingly illustrates what I mean.

If the British Navy were defeated in the Mediterranean and the Channel the stress of our position would not be alleviated by any amount of superiority in the Chinese seas. If, on the other hand, it were to prove supreme in the Mediterranean and Channel, even serious disasters in Chinese seas would matter little. These considerations furnish, therefore, a sound argument for keeping our naval strength in Chinese waters as low as is compatible with the safety of the Empire. But there is a point below which it would be dangerous to go. It is true that victory in European waters would scarcely be dimmed by even serious disasters in the Far East, but its value though not obliterated would be impaired to a dangerous degree if British naval power in the Far East were crushed out of existence. We could afford to lose a certain number of merchant men, or even to see a weaker squadron of battleships blockaded for a time in Hong Kong; but we could not afford to see our Chinese trade disappear, or to see Hong Kong and Singapore fall, particularly not at a moment when a military struggle with Russia might be in progress on the confines of India.

At the present moment the naval position in the Far East is changing. Russia has increased, and is still largely adding to, the strength of what used to be her Baltic Squadron; but the whole of that squadron practically has been transferred from Cronstadt to

Vladivostock and Port Arthur. Dealing only with battleships and cruisers, the present relative naval strength in Far Eastern seas is as follows:

	France	*Russia*	*Great Britain*	*Japan*
Battle-ships	1 (2nd Class)	5 (1–2nd Class)	4	6 (1–2nd Class)
Cruisers				
1st Class Armoured	2 (old type)	6	3 (2 old type and 'Cressy')	7 (6 new)
1st Class Protected	2		4	
2nd Class	5	1	8	10
3rd Class			1	14

Russia has eleven battle-ships and rather more cruisers of various classes now building, of which three battle-ships and four cruisers (among those on the actual eve of completion) will, it is believed, be shortly added to her fleet in the Far East.

Japan has one more battle-ship nearly ready. Otherwise she has only two cruisers now building.

From these figures it will be seen that in a few months' time Great Britain will have four first-class battle-ships and sixteen cruisers in Chinese waters as against a combined French and Russian strength of seven first-class and two second-class battle-ships and twenty cruisers. It is highly improbable that France will increase her strength in those seas; her naval policy is as far as possible one of concentration in the Mediterranean and Channel, but especially in the Mediterranean.

For us the odds of nine battle-ships to four would be too great, and we should have eventually to add to our battle-ships on the China Station. The effect of this would be twofold. It would leave us with little or nothing more than a bare equality of strength in the Channel and Mediterranean, and bare equality at the heart of the Empire is a dangerous risk. It would strain our naval system greatly, and would add to our expenditure on the manning of the Navy. Every ship on the China Station must be kept in commission, and be fully manned in time of peace; for this purpose the naval reserves are never available, and special additions would have to be made to the establishment of active service ratings.

Some of the cruisers also on the China Station are badly needed elsewhere. The case would bear a different aspect were we assured of the alliance of Japan.

Great Britain and Japan together would next year be able to show eleven battle-ships against the French and Russian nine, as well as a preponderance of cruisers.

Great Britain would be under no necessity of adding to the number of battle-ships on the China Station, and at last would be in a position to contemplate the possibility of shortly establishing a small margin of superiority in reserve at home; the number of our cruisers could be reduced on that station, and increased on other stations where badly required; our Far Eastern trade and possessions would be secure.

Japan, on the other hand, would be delivered from the nightmare of seeing her rising power crushed by the combination of the French and Russian fleets.

The form which the proposed alliance or understanding might take would be somewhat of this sort: Great Britain might engage herself to come to the assistance of Japan, if in a quarrel between Japan and Russia France came to the assistance of Russia, or *vice versa*. Japan might engage herself to come to the assistance of Great Britain, if in a quarrel between Great Britain and France Russia came to the assistance of France, or *vice versa*.

Such an agreement would, I believe, add materially to the naval strength of this country all over the world, and effectively diminish the probability of a naval war with France or Russia singly or in combination.

136. (*Lansdowne Memorandum 25 October 1901, Cab/37/58/105*)

I circulate a copy of a despatch to our Chargé d'Affaires at St. Petersburgh recording a conversation between the Russian Ambassador and myself in regard to Chinese Affairs. I also circulate a copy of the Agreement believed to be in negotiation between the Russian and Chinese Governments as to Manchuria, showing the differences between the original and the revised texts. None of these versions can be accepted with entire confidence. There can, however, be no doubt that all of them contain provisions which, from our point of view, are objectionable, although the later versions are less mischievous than the old.

My conversation with the Russian Ambassador was somewhat

informal, and I do not know whether he will repeat what I said to his Government.

If my observations correctly express the feelings of the Cabinet, I think our Chargé d'Affaires at St. Petersburgh should be instructed to speak to Count Lamsdorff in the same sense.

A statement of this kind might well be made simultaneously with that which I have recommended on another paper in regard to financial assistance to Persia, the policy underlying both statements being the same, viz., that we desire to treat these matters with absolute frankness, and that we think it better to negotiate as to them directly with the Russian Government rather than with the two weak and dishonest Governments which in each case stand between us and that of Russia.

In neither case would a refusal on the part of Russia do us much harm; while in both cases our position would, I believe, be strengthened, especially with the public here, by the fact that we had made proposals of the kind.

137. (*Salisbury to Lansdowne 7 January 1902, Cab/37/60/3*)

Extract

'Japan will, in my belief, never accept a stipulation that she is not to be allowed to take without our permission measures which we might regard as provocative but which she would defend upon the ground that they were forced upon her by the conduct of Russia. If we were to tell her that should she become involved in a quarrel with Russia in such circumstances without our concurrence, the *casus foederis* would not be held by us to have arisen, she will, I am convinced, tell us that it is impossible for her to accept our terms.'

This extract is from the Minute circulated to the Cabinet by Lord Lansdowne on New Year's day. From the expressions used, I infer that it represents, not what the Japanese have actually said, but what Lord Lansdowne concludes from the language of their negotiators they would say if any such proposal were made to them.

But, if that is their last word, the prospect held out by the Agreement in that form is somewhat disquieting. It involves a pledge on our part to defend Japanese action in Corea and in all China against France and Russia, no matter what the *casus belli* may be. There is no limit: and no escape. We are pledged to war, though the conduct of our ally may have been followed in spite of our strongest remonstrances, and may be avowedly regarded by us with clear disapprobation. I feel sure that such a pledge will not be sanctioned by Parliament, and I think that in the interests of the Empire it ought not to be taken.

The suggestion that 'if Japan would be in a position to get us into scrapes by a too forward policy in Corea, we should equally be in a position to involve them by our action in the Yang-tsze Valley' does not seem to me to offer any solid comfort. If the Treaty imposes on us the liability of being committed against our will to a dangerous policy in Corea, it will be no consolation that Japan is committed against her will to a dangerous policy in the Yang-tsze. Japan offers us 'a formal declaration of non-aggressive policy;' but that will give us no security. It is a sentiment; not a stipulation.

Nor can I attach great importance to the plea of Japan that troubles are apt to break out on short notice, and that in case they should occur Japan may be compelled to adopt a line of policy without having time to consult us on the matter. The necessity for a decision so sudden that the telegraph will not be able to cope with the emergency is not a very probable contingency, and certainly does not furnish a justification for surrendering without reserve into the hands of another Power the right of deciding whether we shall or shall not stake the resources of the Empire on the issue of a mighty conflict.

We cannot rely on the goodwill, or the prudence, or the wise policy of the present Government of Japan, however conspicuous at present those qualities may be. Japan is, like ourselves, a Parliamentary country; and, like ourselves, is liable to have the policy of the Empire, on the most vital questions, reversed by the issue of a night's division. I do not think it will be wise to give to Japan the right of committing us to a war, unless the policy which Japan is pursuing has been approved by the British Government.

But, as I said, I do not gather from the papers that Japan has actually taken up the position which I apprehend. There is room for negotiation. I cannot think that Japan will definitively refuse us some discretion on the question whether the *casus belli* on which she is joining issue with France and Russia is one on which we can properly draw the sword.

S.

138. (*Lansdowne to Macdonald 7 January 1902, B.D. II, 108–9*)

Extract

During the Marquis Ito's visit to me at Bowood on the 3rd instant, I had a conversation of some length with his Excellency as to the proposed Anglo-Japanese Agreement. He told me that he had been fully informed with regard to the progress of the negotiations, and that he was in entire sympathy with the proposal, and trusted that the Agreement would be concluded.

. . .

Marquis Ito admitted that Corea and China were not treated in the same way, but thought that it would be impossible for Japan to tolerate in the case of Corea the kind of encroachments which had been tolerated, and might be tolerated again, in the case of China. It was most important that there should be no misunderstanding between Japan and Great Britain as to the definition of their respective interests, and it was much better that such points as these should be frankly faced before the conclusion of an Agreement, and that there should be no 'surprises' afterwards.

The Marquis then referred to Manchuria. Russia had, he said, obtained a strong hold upon that province. Did I think she was ever likely to relax her grip, and were we likely to go to war on this account?

I said that we had never concealed from ourselves that Russia had special interests in Manchuria, and was likely, whatever happened, to retain a predominant interest in that province, owing to her geographical position. We had to some extent admitted this by the Agreement of 1899, under which Russia had, in exchange for corresponding admissions with regard to our rights in other parts of China, obtained a preferential right to construct railways in Manchuria. . . .

. . . My impression was that Russia desired to extricate herself from military occupation of Manchuria, which was costly and inconvenient to her, but that she would arrive at an arrangement with the Chinese Government, some of the terms of which would very likely be withheld from our knowledge, under which she would retain some kind of lien upon the province. I did not, however, think it probable that the terms would be so objectionable as to force us into war with Russia. I might at any rate say that it seemed to me infinitely more probable that, if the Anglo-

Japanese Agreement were concluded, we might be dragged into war by Japan with France and Russia over Corea, than that Japan would be dragged into war by us in consequence of the Russian treatment of the Manchurian question.

The Marquis then asked me whether, assuming that the Agreement was likely to be concluded, we should see any objection to the Japanese Government entering into an amicable arrangement with Russia for the protection of Japanese interests in Corea. He explained that he meant by this an Agreement in which the policy of the Russo-Japanese Agreement of 1898 would be carried a step further, by means of an understanding which would preclude Russia from political or strategical interference in Corea.

I replied that much would depend on the character of the Agreement contemplated. It would, of course, be absolutely essential that it should be in no way inconsistent with the Agreement arrived at between Great Britain and Japan. It would obviously be improper that Japan should enter into a bargain with us affecting our common interests in the Far East, and should then enter into another bargain of a conflicting character with a third Power. If, however, the Marquis merely suggested that in the interests of peace Japan should do her best to obtain from Russia a recognition of the interests which we were ready to join her in protecting, a source of danger would be removed, and, speaking for myself, I saw no reason why His Majesty's Government should disapprove.

139. (*The Anglo-Japanese Treaty: Draft of 23 January 1902, Cab/ 37/60/17*)

(NOTE.—Alterations proposed by the Japanese Government are printed in italics. The Amendments suggested by Lord Lansdowne are printed in smaller type in parentheses.)

Draft Agreement

The Governments of Great Britain and Japan, actuated solely by a desire to maintain the *status quo* and general peace in the extreme East, being moreover specially interested in maintaining the independence and territorial integrity of the Empire of China and the Kingdom of Corea, and in securing equal opportunities in those countries for the commerce and industry of all nations, hereby agreed as follows:

Article I

Great Britain and Japan, having mutually recognized the independence of China and of Corea, declare themselves to be entirely uninfluenced by any aggressive tendencies in either country. *Having in view, however, the special interests*

(of Great Britain and Japan, of which those of Great Britain relate principally to China, while Japan, in addition to the interests which she possesses in China, is interested in a peculiar degree both politically and commercially in Corea,)

[*political as well as commercial and industrial, possessed by Japan in Corea, and the interests of Great Britain and of Japan in China*], *the British and Japanese Governments recognize that, if those interests should be threatened*

(by the aggressive action of any other Power,)

it would be admissible for each Power to take such measures as may be indispensable in order to safeguard its interests.

Article II

If either Great Britain or Japan, in the defence of their respective interests as above described, should become involved in war with another Power, the other High Contracting Party will maintain a strict neutrality, and use its efforts to prevent other Powers from joining in hostilities against its ally.

Article III

If in the above event any other Power or Powers should join in hostilities against that ally, the other High Contracting Party will come to its assistance and will conduct the war in common, and make peace in mutual agreement with it.

Article IV

The High Contracting Parties agree that neither of them will, without consulting the other, enter into separate arrangements with another Power to the prejudice of the interests above described.

Article V

Whenever, in the opinion of either Great Britain or Japan, the above-mentioned interests are in jeopardy, the two Governments will communicate with one another fully and frankly.

Article VI

The present Agreement shall come into effect immediately after the date of its signature, and remain in force for five years from that date.

In case neither of the High Contracting Parties should have notified twelve months before the expiration of the said five years the intention of terminating it, it shall remain binding until the expiration of one year from the day on which either of the High Contracting Parties shall have denounced it. But, if when the date fixed for its expiration arrives, either ally is actually engaged in war, the alliance shall, *ipso facto*, continue until peace is concluded.

In faith whereof the Undersigned, duly authorized by their repective Governments, have signed this Agreement.

Draft notes to be exchanged between the two Governments:
'Sir,

'In reference to the Agreement concluded by us to-day on behalf of our respective Governments, I have the honour to inform you that the $\frac{British}{Japanese}$ Government recognizes that the naval forces of $\frac{Great\ Britain}{Japan}$ should, so far as possible, act in concert with those of $\frac{Japan}{Great\ Britain}$ in time of peace, and agrees that mutual facilities shall be given for the docking and coaling of vessels of war of one country in the ports of the other, as well as other advantages conducing to the welfare and efficacy of the respective navies of the two Powers.

'At the present moment Japan and Great Britain are each of them maintaining in the extreme East a naval force superior in strength to that of any third Power. $\dfrac{\text{Great Britain}}{\text{Japan}}$ has no intention of relaxing her efforts to maintain, so far as may be possible, available for concentration in the waters of the extreme East, a naval force superior to that of any third Power.'

NOTE.—The final draft of 30 January approximates closely to Lansdowne's amendments. For this and the successive drafts since October 1901 see B.D.II. 115–21.

140. (*Salisbury to Balfour 9 November 1905, B.P. Add. Mss. 48758*)

Lansdowne's speech on Tuesday was a most important one. He declared in effect that we had abandoned the policy of isolation, not only in Asia but also in Europe: that we must do as other Powers do, who are distributed in groups: that the Japanese treaty and the French agreement have carried this change of policy into effect: and he almost treated these two instruments, though no doubt different in form, as substantially similar.

All this is, of course, largely true, but I should be inclined to take some exception to the last. Circumstances no doubt have driven us in respect to France further than we intended. There can be no doubt that originally French policy was wholly different from the Japanese. The latter, on the face of it, though defensive only, was essentially military. The former had its sanction and was intended to have its sanction in diplomatic measures alone.

In truth the French agreement was in its inception not a departure from our previous foreign policy, but strictly in accordance with it. For the last twenty years we have been engaged with different Powers,· notably with Germany and with France, in adjusting conflicting claims, and in bargaining so as to get rid of causes of friction and if I spoke about our agreement with France, I should treat it rather as a development of past policy than as a new departure.

INDEX

Index

413

Index

414